THE POLICE POWER

THE POLICE
POWER

PATRIARCHY
AND THE FOUNDATIONS
OF AMERICAN GOVERNMENT

MARKUS DIRK DUBBER

COLUMBIA UNIVERSITY PRESS

New York

Columbia University Press
Publishers Since 1893
New York, Chichester, West Sussex
Copyright © 2005 Columbia University Press
All rights Reserved

Library of Congress Cataloging-in-Publication Data
Dubber, Markus Dirk
  The police power : patriarchy and the foundations of American government / Markus
Dirk Dubber.
    p. cm.
  Includes bibliographical references and index.
  ISBN : 0–231–13206–9 (cloth : alk. paper)
  Police power—United States—History.
  I. Title
  KF4695 .D82   2005
  342.73/0418 22   2004043140

Columbia University Press books are printed on permanent and durable acid-free paper
Printed in the United States of America

c 10 9 8 7 6 5 4 3 2 1

To Sara

Contents

Acknowledgments

Many friends and colleagues have helped me write this book, by listening, providing encouragement, giving advice, or by reading and commenting on all or parts of the manuscript, including Guyora Binder, Susanna Blumenthal, Jonathan Bush, Hanoch Dagan, Lindsay Farmer, Samuel Gross, Klaus Günther, Daniel Halberstam, Don Herzog, Tatjana Hörnle, Klaus Lüderssen, Elizabeth Mensch, Wolfgang Naucke, Cornelius Nestler, Cornelius Prittwitz, Karl Shoemaker, Michael Stolleis, Robert Weisberg, and James Whitman, along with participants in workshops at SUNY Buffalo, the University of Frankfurt, the University of Iowa, the University of Munich, the University of Michigan, the University of Toronto, and the University of Wisconsin. Thomas Green, Robert Steinfeld, Mariana Valverde, and Peter Westen were particularly generous with their time and advice, though I am sure that not even their exemplary efforts could save me from committing errors, for which I am happy to take the blame.

I am also grateful to the Alexander-von-Humboldt Foundation and to Nils Olsen, my dean at SUNY Buffalo, for generously supporting my research on this book. As always, Bernd Schünemann was the perfect host at the Institute for Legal Philosophy at the University of Munich.

It is only fair and proper that I dedicate this book to my wife, Sara. Without her aid and comfort over many years and in many places this project would not have seen the light of day. Finally, thanks to Clara, Dora, Maura, and Sophie for reminding me that being silly is almost always a good thing.

Markus Dirk Dubber
June 2004

Introduction

"The power to govern men and things"[1]

Among the powers of government none is greater than the power to police, and none less circumscribed. For centuries, it has been a commonplace of American legal and political discourse that the police power "is, and must be from its very nature, incapable of any very exact definition or limitation."[2] Upon the police power, "the most essential, the most insistent, and always one of the least limitable of the powers of government,"[3] hinges nothing less than "the security of social order, the life and health of the citizen, the comfort of an existence in a thickly populated community, the enjoyment of private and social life, and the beneficial use of property."[4] As such "[i]t extends to the protection of the lives, limbs, health, comfort, and quiet of all persons, and the protection of all property," and underlies a vast expanse of legislation and regulation at all levels of governance, from the national government through the states and down to the smallest municipalities.[5]

This book explores the origins of this most expansive, and most amorphous, of governmental powers with a particular focus on its most awesome manifestation, the law of crime and punishment.[6] The results of this genealogical investigation then are used to set the framework for a critical analysis of the police power in general, and the criminal law in particular.

The concept of police entered American political and legal discourse in the late eighteenth century. Many of the early state constitutions contained references to "the internal police" of a state.[7] A decade later, at the federal constitutional convention, James Wilson insisted on the preservation of state governments "in full vigor," for the sake not only of "the freedom of the people," but also "their internal good police."[8] In 1779 Thomas Jefferson established a chair of "law and police" as one of eight professorships at the College of William & Mary, in the course of replacing several of the original charter professorships, including one of divinity.[9]

But where did Jefferson, Wilson, and their fellow Founding Fathers get the idea of police? And what did they mean by it? As so often in the historiography of American law, the best place to start is Blackstone's *Commentaries on the Laws of England*, which "rank second only to the Bible as a literary and intellectual influence on the history of American institutions."[10] In the fourth, and last, volume of the *Commentaries*, published in 1769, Blackstone set out a definition of police that would shape American legal discourse for centuries to come:

> By the public police and oeconomy I mean the due regulation and domestic order of the kingdom: whereby the individuals of the state, like members of a well-governed family, are bound to conform their general behaviour to the rules of propriety, good neighbourhood, and good manners: and to be decent, industrious, and inoffensive in their respective stations.[11]

Until well into the twentieth century, American legislators, courts, and commentators would consult Blackstone when it came time to turn their attention to the police power. Legislators used Blackstone's police categories to structure their new codes;[12] courts invoked Blackstone to police the scope of the police power, as well as to create police offenses of their own (which they called "common law misdemeanors");[13] and commentators built their more or less comprehensive analyses of the police power in action on Blackstone's definition of their subject.[14]

Accordingly, we will devote considerable attention to Blackstone's treatment of police in the *Commentaries*. Blackstone, however, is only the beginning of an inquiry into the roots of the police power. For however influential Blackstone proved to be in the New World, he could not, and did not, make any claim to originality. (In fact, it is doubtful that his influence would have been quite as broad had he been more original than conveniently familiar.) At any rate, Blackstone's view of police in particular was radically unoriginal. It reflected a long tradition of governance that can be traced back to the very roots of Western political thought, or so I argue in this book. To make sense of the power to police we therefore must widen our genealogical focus and reach back to the notion of household governance, as first developed in early Greek writings on economics, understood in its original, literal, sense, as the art of "the government of the house for the common good of the whole family."[15]

We will trace this mode of patriarchal governance through Roman law, which granted the *paterfamilias* plenary power over the *familia*, and medieval law, which recognized a similar discretionary authority of every householder over his household, the *mund*, with the eventual expansion of the king's *mund*, or royal peace, to cover each constituent of the state considered as "members of a well-governed family."[16]

As a well-entrenched, and truly *basic*, mode of governmentality,[17] one would expect to find manifestations of policing before Blackstone, including in colonial America. In fact, Americans were policing long before they imported the concept of policing from overseas in the late eighteenth century, combining long-standing governmental techniques from English law, such as the regulation of vagrants and the punishment of petit treason, with innovations and adaptations of their own, including the comprehensive warning-out system in New England, the internal disciplining of church members, and most significantly the management of slaves in plantation households. Americans of the revolutionary generation thus may well have embraced the concept of police because it named, and apparently systematized, a wide array of governmental practices with which they were intimately familiar.

It's clear that Blackstone did not originate the idea of state government as household management. Nor, it turns out, did he come up with the idea of naming it *police*. By the eighteenth century, the term had been around on the continent for at least four centuries, and even had blossomed into "police science," a full-fledged academic discipline, complete with treatises, university faculties, and training academies. On Blackstone's side of the Channel, the Scots had been thinking and writing about police for decades. Adam Smith, for one, began delivering his famous *Lectures on Justice, Police, Revenue and Arms*, which he eventually developed into the *Wealth of Nations*, at Glasgow in the 1750s, well before Blackstone sat down to write his *Commentaries*.[18]

It is of course possible, perhaps even likely, that at least some of the Americans who began speaking of police and the police power in the late eighteenth century did not get the concept from Blackstone, but from any of the representatives of this much more developed, and older, literature on police. Contributors to this body of work included, after all, not only Smith, but also such influential thinkers as Rousseau, Beccaria, Bentham, and even Vattel.

To understand the American concept of the police power, as well as Blackstone's own view of police, we will have to take a close look at the continental tradition that culminated in the science of police. The police of the police scientists, like the police in Blackstone's "offenses against the police and oeconomy," will turn out to rest on a conception of state government as household governance, with the one difference that this conception was worked out into a science of political economy, i.e., an enormously detailed, comprehensive, and complex system of social—"economic"—control, assembled for the benefit of the enlightened prince.[19]

More power than science, American police thrived in the new republic as the revolutionaries-turned-governors proceeded to order their new realm. A healthy police power was needed "to provide for the 'execution of the laws that is necessary for the preservation of justice, peace, and internal tranquility.' "[20] Following the violent removal of the old government, the new one had to remind its subjects of their duty of obedience. By 1789, Benjamin Franklin warned that "our present danger seems to be *defect of obedience* in the subjects."[21]

And so the new rulers put their police power "to govern men and things"[22] to work. Legislatures passed statute upon statute, regulation upon regulation, and ordinance upon ordinance, policing everything from "apprentices and servants," "bastards," "beggars and disorderly persons," and "dogs," to "the exportation of flaxweed," "gaming," "idiots and lunatics," and "stray cattle and sheep."[23] Courts, too, looked after the public police, by supplementing the legislature's policing efforts with "common law misdemeanors," which captured any threat to the public welfare that might have slipped through the legislature's regulatory net. Needless to say, the remaining branch of government, the executive, assumed important policing functions as well, so much so that it institutionalized a growing part of itself under that very name, as "police departments" and "police officers" appeared in city after city, and eventually throughout the land.

Occasional attempts to limit it notwithstanding, the police power continued to expand virtually unchecked until, by the 1930s, it had become all but synonymous with immunity from constitutional review. The now famous 1905 case of *Lochner v. New York*,[24] in which the Supreme Court struck down a purported exercise of the police power, was branded, and vilified, as an antidemocratic act of judicial despotism. The police power has played its role as "an idiom of apologetics which belongs to the vocabulary of constitutional law" admirably ever since.[25]

While the U.S. Supreme Court has largely abandoned serious scrutiny of the police power as such, state courts have been more willing to subject state actions justified as police actions to critical analysis, including the use of the criminal law. Sodomy statutes, for example, have been struck down by state courts as illegitimate exercises of the police power—in this case to protect the "moral police" of the state citizenry—under state constitutional law, while the federal supreme court not only upheld them, but upheld them without acknowledging their origin in the power to police.[26]

There is some indication, therefore, that the paradox of the patriarchal police power, as the apparently most problematic and yet factually least scrutinized power of government, might be solved by subjecting the police power to the critical analysis it deserves. The question of how the power to police, and the criminal law with it, can survive in a modern democratic state is as important as it is difficult. But more than two centuries after the creation of the new republic on the basis of the idea of equality, it is high time that American law face the question of the legality, and legitimacy, of the police power and its most patriarchal manifestation, the criminal law.

The remainder of this book will proceed as follows. Part I begins, in chapter 1, by tracking the genealogy of the notion of household governance, from the original Athenian distinction between politics (self-government by equals) and economics (other-government by superiors), through the concept of *mund*, or peace, in medieval law, to the eventual expansion of the king's peace across the entire realm, by means of the establishment of the royal common law. In chapter 2, we shift our attention to the great putative systematizer of the common law, Blackstone, whose patriarchal concept of police was to find such resonance among those eager to transform the new republic into a well-ordered society. Chapter 3 discusses the science of police, which preceded Blackstone's musings about the king as the "*paterfamilias* of the nation"[27] and developed a notion of police as state household governance both more sophisticated and less parochial than Blackstone's.

Part II then documents the growth of American police power into a broad and multi-faceted mode of governance beyond principled scrutiny. Particular attention will be devoted to those features of American police power that continued to bear witness to its patriarchal origins, including its defining undefinability (exposing its radically discretionary nature), the ahumanity of its objects (encompassing "men and things" as constituents of the household), the strict hierarchy of governors and governed (echoing the categorical distinction between householder and household), and, most important, its basic alegitimacy (reflecting the ancient insight of Greek economics that household governance was measured by efficiency, not justice).

In part III, we turn to possible limitations upon the police power, from within and from without, that can be extracted even from the generally toothless scrutiny of state actions in the purported exercise of the police power. Besides internal constraints, such as the prudence and fitness of the policer-householder, we consider external principles such as Mill's harm principle, the right to privacy, and "substantive due process," famously associated with the infamous *Lochner* case.

The conclusion suggests that, after all is said and done, the origins of American police power may not only illuminate the nature and extent of its essential problem, but also hold the key to its solution. The revolutionaries-turned-rulers of the new republic, after all, were revolutionaries first, and rulers second. While they might have enthusiastically thrown themselves into policing, they did so in the name of erecting a novel system of government under law. While they did not succeed in answering the question of how police is possible in an egalitarian political community based on the idea of self-government, and eventually became engrossed by the business of governance, they felt the question's significance—and difficulty—more acutely than anyone since. Recovering this historical sense of urgency may well be the first step toward a critical analysis of the police power today.

THE POLICE POWER

PART I

From Household Governance to Political Economy

1

Police as *Patria Potestas*

To basic modes of state governance can be traced throughout the history of Western political thought and practice. Autonomy, or self-government, is the basic norm of modern state governance through *law*. Thomas Paine was right: in America the law is king, as it is in every other modern democratic state; but it's not everything.[1] There is another mode of governance, police. While the state may govern its constituents through law, it also manages them through police. In contrast to law, police is defined by heteronomy, or other-government, of the people by the state. And so Thomas Jefferson was right as well when, eager to enlist institutions of higher learning in the formidable task of governing his newly independent state of Virginia, he established not the first American professorship of law, as is commonly supposed, but a chair in "law and police."[2]

These two modes of governance, law and police, reflect two ways of conceptualizing the state. From the perspective of law, the state is the institutional manifestation of a political community of free and equal persons. The function of the law state is to manifest and protect the autonomy of its constituents in all of its aspects, private and public. From the perspective of police, the state is the institutional manifestation of a household. The police state, as *paterfamilias*, seeks to maximize the welfare of his—or rather its—household.

Politics and Economics in Athens and Rome

Government, and politics, has always meant both resolving conflicts among equals, and managing inferiors, with modes of governance appropriate to each. And so autonomy and economy, justice and police, can be found to underlie political institutions as far back as the beginnings of Western civilization, in the Greek city-states. As Hannah Arendt has argued,

> [t]o be political, to live in a *polis*, meant that everything was decided through words and persuasion and not through force and violence. In Greek self-understanding, to force people by violence, to command rather than persuade, were prepolitical ways to deal with people characteristic of life outside the *polis*, of home and family life, where the household head ruled with uncontested, despotic powers, or of life in the barbarian empires of Asia, whose despotism was frequently likened to the organization of the household.[3]

Autonomy occupied a central place in Greek political thought, in two senses. First, autonomy was a communal attribute. One political community was autonomous insofar as it was free from oppression by another; autonomy in this sense meant the absence of heteronomy. This communal sense of autonomy—or sovereignty—still plays an important role in international politics. Complaints by one state about another state's interference in its internal affairs are as familiar as they are legitimate.

But autonomy had intracommunal significance as well. One political community could be externally autonomous from another in the above sense without being internally autonomous. To be internally autonomous, a political community had to be democratic.[4] Through participation in political affairs, the constituents of the community governed themselves. They were not governed by another community—or rather its governors; neither were they governed by other members of their own community.

In this sense, autonomy is both a communal and an individual attribute. A political community is autonomous to the extent that its constituents govern themselves, i.e., are autonomous. The distinction between government and individuals disappears along with the distinction between the governors and the governed, or the subjects and objects of government. At any rate, we will be concerned with autonomy primarily as an individual attribute, leaving autonomy as a communal attribute, or sovereignty, to discussions of international politics.

Because autonomy as sovereignty is compatible with internal heteronomy, it must be sharply distinguished from individual autonomy.[5] A dictatorship can make claims to sovereignty, and therefore to noninterference from the outside, just as well as a democracy.

The tension between sovereignty and autonomy was already very much evident in *internal* Greek politics. The participant in political life, the subject-object of Athenian self-government, was the head of the household.[6] But while this head of the household enjoyed political autonomy, the other members of his household lived in utter heteronomy, and more precisely, in utter heteronomy under the autocratic rule of the very man who claimed autonomy for himself in the political realm.

What's more, it was the very heteronomy of mere *members* of the household that qualified their head as autonomous.[7] Throughout most of the history of democratic government only propertied heads of household were qualified to participate in political life.[8] All others were considered insufficiently autonomous to lend legitimacy to the government through their participation. This lack of autonomy derived either from their inability or failure to exercise their capacity for autonomy, as in the case of the poor and children, or the complete lack of the capacity itself, as in the case of slaves, livestock, plants, and inanimate objects.[9]

We've noted that in the intercommunal realm, sovereignty was compatible with intracommunal autonomy as well as heteronomy. Within a democracy, sovereignty didn't merely permit heteronomy; it required it. Greek political thought recognized two separate, but mutually dependent, spheres of governance. In the public sphere of the city-state, governance was self-government for and by autonomous constituents. In the private sphere of the family, however, governance was economy for the household by its head.

Much of Greek political thought was devoted to exploring the connections, as well as the distinctions, between the modes of governance in these two realms.[10] According to Aristotle, in his *Politics*, "the state is made up of households."[11] Each household, in turn, was under the management of its chief. The head was entitled, and obligated, to maximize the welfare of his household. To this end, every member of the household was at his disposal. The entire household, in other words, consisted of instruments the skillful operation of which made up the art of household management.

Moreover, as Aristotle emphasizes, these "instruments are of various sorts; some are living, others lifeless."[12] The power of the head extends over the household in its entirety, over things and persons and animals and plants alike. Household management is *resource* management, not person governance. For this reason, as Aristotle explains in the *Nicomachean Ethics*, matters of household governance lie beyond the realm of justice: "there can be no injustice in the unqualified sense, towards things that are one's own, but a man's chattel, and his child until it reaches a certain age and sets up for itself, are as it were part of himself" so that "justice can no more truly be manifested towards a wife than towards children and chattels."[13]

Political government and household management should not be confused. Here is Aristotle's way of drawing the distinction between these two modes of governance: "[T]here is one rule exercised over subjects who are by nature free, another over subjects who are by nature slaves. The rule of a household is a monarchy, for every house is under one head: whereas constitutional rule is a government of freemen and equals."[14] In other words, political government, and only political government, is autonomy: "in most constitutional states the citizens rule and are ruled by turns, for the idea of a constitutional state implies that the natures of the citizens are equal, and do not differ at all."[15]

One finds very much the same arrangement in Roman and medieval law. Roman law in particular paid much attention to defining the obligations and rights of the *paterfamilias*. The Roman *paterfamilias*, like his Greek analogue, was in charge of the welfare of his household, or *familia*.[16] To discharge his obligation he was equipped with extensive powers to discipline those constituents of his household who—or which—interfered with his management.[17]

Roman society closely resembled the two-level system familiar from Greek politics. "We must imagine," explains James Strachan-Davidson, "a number of households, each united under its own *paterfamilias*. Inside the household the father is the sole judge. The relations of the household and its members to other households resemble . . . international concerns rather than transactions between individuals."[18]

Over his *familia*, the *paterfamilias* enjoyed unlimited authority in practice, and virtually unlimited authority in theory. Since the power to discipline arose from his duty to maximize the welfare of the household—and its members—the head was not authorized to discipline for any other reason. In particular, he was prohibited from disciplining out of what common law courts would, much later, call "malice," as we'll see in greater detail below.[19] A household head who maliciously harmed members of the household forfeited his title; as no longer worthy of his position of responsibility, he also was no longer worthy of protection from the state for measures necessary to discharge that responsibility.

This limitation on the father's disciplinary power was particularly important in the case of inferior members of the household who had the capacity for autonomy, and therefore for participation in the political life of the state. A father who maliciously stunted the development of his children, in particular, therefore harmed not only them, but the state as well:

For, inasmuch as every family is a part of a state, and these relationships are the parts of a family, and the virtue of the part must have regard to the virtue of the whole, women and children must be trained by education with an eye to the constitution, if the virtues of either of them are supposed to make any difference in the virtues of the state. And they must make a difference: for the children grow up to be citizens, and half the free persons in a state are women.[20]

The relationship between the household head and his slaves differed from those between him and his wife, and between him and his children. As one of the master's possessions, "an instrument of action," the slave was literally to be mastered: "the slave has no deliberative faculty at all; the woman has, but it is without authority, and the child has, but it is immature."[21]

Now in Greek writings on economics—the science of household management—one finds slight variations on the question of what constitutes the household. Xenophon, in his *Oikonomikos*, "probably the oldest and certainly the most influential discourse on 'economics,' " limited the household to "the material possessions of the household head."[22] Aristotle, by contrast, included within the household not only inanimate possessions, but persons and relatives as well, "all those persons subject to the authority of its chief."[23]

Apparently this ambiguity persisted in Roman economic thought. According to Herlihy,

[i]n classical Latin, the word *familia* carries equivalent meanings. It designates everything and everybody under the authority (*patria potestas*) of the household head. *Familia* in classical usage is often synonymous with patrimony. . . . *Familia* could also mean persons only, specifically those persons subject to the authority of the *paterfamilias*, the household chief, usually the father. . . . Thus, the jurist Ulpian, in the second century A.D., defines "family" as those persons who by nature (that is, natural offspring) or by law (wife, adopted children, slaves) are subject to the *patria potestas*. This definition still recognizes no distinction between the primary descent group and servants and slaves. But it does retain a crucial distinction between the father and the family, the ruler and the ruled, even though by Ulpian's day the *patria potestas* had considerably weakened. . . .

[T]he classical understanding of the word *familia* excluded from its membership its chief, the *paterfamilias*. He was not subject to his own authority, as Ulpian requires. Nor was he his own offspring.[24]

It thus appears that the concept of the household progressed from a set of inanimate objects, the "material possessions" of the household, to a sphere of authority that included animate and inanimate objects alike. Some writers, especially early on, thought of the household as encompassing only inanimate objects, while others limited the household to persons, and others yet thought of it as including both. But no matter which definition of household these early economists preferred, it was clear that there was nothing incompatible between the project of economics, of household management, and the nonhuman status of its object. The project of familial governance was one and the same, no matter what the exact contours of the family might be. Economics was a matter of the household head taking proper measures to maximize the welfare of his household, regardless of what or whom the household encompassed.

The ambiguity of the concept of household is noteworthy itself. While different writers might hold different views about the extent of the household, the precise definition of its contours was not very important. The best definition of the household probably always was "whatever and whoever is under the authority of the household head." This of course is a tautological definition. But economics was a question of power, and power is as consistent with tautology as it is with ambiguity. The *paterfamilias* was in charge of maximizing the welfare of whatever and whoever was his. What wasn't his, he couldn't control. And what he couldn't control, he couldn't benefit.

Finally, note the clear separation between household and its head, and more generally of the governed and the governor, of *oikos* and *oikonomos*, of *domus* and *dominus*. No matter what or who constituted the household, it was clear that the head did not. And, we might add, even if the head could be seen as belonging to the household, that didn't mean that he was any less the ruler and the others the ruled. Economics is a heteronomous affair.

We will encounter these three characteristics of household governance, the ahuman nature of its object, the indefiniteness of its scope, and the qualitative distinction between its subject and its object, again and again as we trace the evolution from patriarchal power to state power.

The Medieval Household

The two interdependent paradigms of autonomous and heteronomous governance survived into the Middle Ages. Like the Roman and the Greek polity before it so too the "Germanic *Sippe* . . . was made up of separate households,"[25] each in turn governed by a householder. Here too we find, on the one hand, the system of conflict resolution among equal autonomous heads of household—the realm of autonomy—and on the other the realm of internal, or domestic, management according to the art (and later the science) of household government, or economy—the realm of heteronomy. These two paradigms of governance shared the same subject (the householder), but differed both in their object as well as in the relation between subject and object.

In political life, the subject and object coincided: i.e., their relation was one of identity. That's what *autonomy* means: government of the self by the self. In domestic life, by contrast, the subject of governance was still the adult male householder, the same individual who governed himself in the political realm. But the object of government was now the household, and everyone and everything that constituted it. That's what *economy* means: government of the household (*oikos*, Latin *domus*).[26] Here the relation between subject and object of governance was no longer that of identity, but of difference. It was, in other words, an instance of heteronomy, of government of one thing or being by another.

Much has been written, and for centuries, about the old Germanic system of participatory government. In the nineteenth century Germanists, in Germany as well as in England, marveled at lay participation in adjudication, and at the direct democracy of the *thing*, as the purest manifestation of an ideal of autonomous government long before the expansion of political communities appeared to call for such complicating and compromising prudential devices as representation and the separation of powers.

Enthusiasm for the ancient Saxons also ran strong among the Founding Fathers. Jefferson in particular was eager to replicate their "government truly republican," "that happy system of our ancestors, the wisest and most perfect ever yet devised by the wit of man, as it stood before the 8th century."[27]

It went without saying that self-government was limited to the heads of household. The regular meetings to discuss matters of common concern, whether they were legislative or adjudicative or executive, were attended by the chiefs. While these chiefs represented their households, it would be a mistake to say that they represented the *members* of their households as well. They stood for the household insofar as they and their household were merged; they were one and the same. Their interest was the household's, and vice versa.

Now the political, rather than domestic, relation among chiefs was not limited to the disposal of matters of common concern. The political relation also manifested itself in the resolution of conflicts among them. Take the composition system, for instance, which nicely captures the interplay between intertribal relations among chiefs and the chief's intratribal relations to his household. When a member of the household of one chief harmed a member of the household of another, the former had two options. He could either deliver the offending member (the noxal surrender of Roman law) or pay *wergild*.

The chief was liable for any damage caused by any member of his household.[28] It did not matter who or what caused it. Just as every member, animate or not, was subject to the chief's authority, so the offending chief had to compensate the offended chief for harm caused by his relatives, his slaves, his animals, or any inanimate objects in his possession. Swords, and also trees, were common offenders. For purposes of liability—as well as representation at the *thing*—the household with all its members was merely an extension of the householder.[29] In medieval English law, "in defining the master's liability for wrongful acts done by his dependants, the same principles as regards authorization and ratification seem to be applied whether the dependants be free servants or serfs," Pollock and Maitland discovered.[30] "It is rather for the acts of members, free or bond, of his household *(manupastus, mainpast)* that a man can be held liable than for the acts of his serfs."[31]

If the chief did not turn over the offending member, he would become liable; he would have to pay *wergild*. The *wergild* varied by the nature of the offender and the nature of the victim. The offender had to be surrendered within a specified period of time. And even a timely surrender would require the payment of *wergild* if the householder did not sufficiently disassociate himself from the offender. For example, he was liable if he used an axe that had caused the harm, perhaps by falling on the unsuspecting victim, or fed an offending dog or slave.[32] This affirmative and speedy disassociation was necessary to sever the essential connection, in fact the identity, between chief and every member of his household.

Contrary to frequent historiographical practice, we will pay close attention to this relation between the householder and the household, rather than to that among the householders themselves. The proto-democracy of the Anglo-Saxon freemen (and of Athenian householders) assembled in the open field tends to get all the attention. This is understandable. But for the vast majority of people, and for the facts of everyday governance, intra-household relations were far more important. Household governance was not a once-in-a-while affair. Instead it defined daily life. It was the reality of governing and being governed. To study the composition system rather than paternal discipline thus is a bit like studying criminal trials instead of plea bargaining today; the records (and transcripts) are a lot better, but it's not even half the picture.[33] Or as Julius Goebel pointed out some time ago, it would be a similar mistake to neglect the institutions of English manorial justice, no matter how attractive a field of study the common law of the royal courts might be, if it turns out in fact that the Englishmen who came to the

New World had virtually no contact with royal justice, but were very much familiar with the manorial justice dispensed in *courts leet* and *baron*.[34]

The internal governance of the household by its head deserves more attention not merely because it's significant from the point of view of social history. For our purposes, it's of particular interest because it established a mode of governance traces of which can be found even today.

The *Mund*

The relation between Germanic householder and household resembled that between the Roman *pater* and his *familia*: "The authority which the father exercised over all his dependents—wife, children, and slaves—was called *munt*, or *munduburdium* in Frankish law."[35] The father's *mund*, however, "was analogous to the Roman *manus*, but was not as absolute and permanent," insofar as mature sons were no longer subject to their father's *mund*. Instead, they became *sui juris*, which also meant that the father was no longer liable for harm they caused.

The idea of *mund* will play a central role in the history of English law. Holmes famously attempted to trace the law of "agency," and the rule of respondeat superior in particular, to the relation between master and slave.[36] As Pollock and Maitland pointed out, the general concept of *mund* might be a more promising source.[37] They also suggest the common law of husband and wife is best understood not in terms of any notion of a "unity of person," but in light of "the guardianship, the *mund*, the profitable guardianship, which the husband has over the wife and over her property."[38]

For our purposes, two aspects of the concept of *mund* are of particular interest. First, the householder enjoys *external* authority to protect his household, his *mund*, against outside threats. And second, he has *internal* authority to discipline recalcitrant members of his household. In the end, both of these powers derive from the same idea, the *mund*, or more abstractly the maximization of the welfare of the household, which—among many other things—demanded its protection against interference from within and without.[39]

The householder's authority to extinguish external threats to his household was unquestioned, and originally unlimited.[40] It derived from his status as householder, regardless of the nature or size of the household. "The sheriff has his peace, the lord of a soken has his peace; nay, every householder has his peace; you break his peace if you fight in his house, and, besides all the other payments that you must make to atone for your deed of violence, you must make a payment to him for the breach of his *mund*."[41] Echoing Pollock and Maitland, Paul Vinogradoff highlighted the "germ existing in every Teutonic household," the power of the ruler of such a household over the inmates of it, both free and unfree. Even a ceorl, that is a common free man, was master in his own house and could claim compensation for the breach of his fence or an infraction of the peace of his home. In the case of the King and other great men the fenced court became a burgh, virtually a fortress. Every ruler of a household, whether small or great, had to keep his sons, slaves and clients in order and was answerable for their misdeeds. On the other hand he was their patron, offered them protection, had to stand by them in case of oppression from outsiders and claimed compensation for any wrong inflicted on them.[42]

The householder's protection of his household and everything and everyone within it against external threats assumed various forms. Take, for instance, the peace that attached to religious institutions, or rather to their head. That religious institutions represented households in the traditional sense was generally acknowledged. So in 1014, we find "the venerable man Burchard, bishop of the holy church of Worms," complaining about "the frequent injuries and unjust laws imposed upon the *familia* of his church."[43]

Religious orders, and their monasteries, provided a particularly well organized example of a household.[44] Since these religious households were also unusually transparent and well documented, they deserve a closer look, if we are to get a better sense of medieval household governance. Consider, for instance, the Rule of Augustine, from about the year 400. The Rule lays out the details of household governance in considerable detail. This is how it instructs the abbot on the art of proper disciplinary action:

> But whenever the good of discipline requires you to speak harshly in correcting your subjects, then, even if you think you have been unduly harsh in your language, you are not required to ask forgiveness lest, by practicing too great humility toward those who should be your subjects, the authority to rule is undermined. But you should ask forgiveness from the Lord of all who knows with what deep affection you love even those whom you might happen to correct with undue severity.[45]

Under the heading "Governance and Obedience," the Rule then defines the basic duty of familial obedience, as well as the means for its enforcement:

1. The superior should be obeyed as a father with the respect due him so as not to offend God in his person. . . .
2. But it shall pertain chiefly to the superior to see that these precepts are all observed and, if any point has been neglected, to take care that the transgression is not carelessly overlooked but is punished and corrected. . . .

3. . . . He must show himself as an example of good works toward all. *Let him admonish the unruly, cheer the fainthearted, support the weak, and be patient toward all* (1 Thes. 5:14). Let him uphold discipline while instilling fear.[46]

Pollock and Maitland in particular stressed the analogy between the relation of monk and abbot, and of villein and lord, though they remark on the distinction between the villein's oath of fealty and the monk's vow of obedience, which they interpret as "not very unlike a submission to slavery."[47] The precise difference between villeinage and slavery is difficult to pin down, not least because—as Pollock and Maitland explain in compelling detail—whatever difference existed in theory gradually disappeared in fact in the course of the great social leveling that occurred not only as a result of the Norman Conquest, but already had begun earlier, and was to continue in future centuries.

What's more the distinctions between slave, servant, villein, and monk paled in comparison to the fundamental distinction between householder and household. The institution of the household made for internal leveling vis-à-vis the *paterfamilias* long before social upheavals resulted in the general leveling that eventually reduced even the householder to household status vis-à-vis the *pater patriae*, the king.[48]

From the perspective of household governance, in other words, the distinctions among different household members are largely irrelevant. As Pollock and Maitland put it, whatever may distinguish the relation between a monk and his abbot and that between a villein and his lord, or even that between wife and husband, they are all alike in that "[t]hey all may be offshoots of one radical idea, that of the Germanic *mund*, a word which we feebly render by *guardianship* or *protection*."[49]

Religious institutions also had their *mund*. This meant that the bishop was responsible for the appearance of his clerks in lay courts. If he failed to produce them, he was treated as personally liable. "For this purpose the clerks are treated as forming part of his *familia*—as being within his *mund*."[50]

In general, it appears that the heads of religious institutions did everything they could to protect members of their *familia* from the arms of lay justice. The primary disciplinary mechanism was internal; discipline was a matter between the abbot and his monk, or the bishop and his clerk. Apparently a bishop could choose among a fairly extensive disciplinary palette, which included corporal punishment and confinement: "The chief limit to his power was set by the elementary rule that the church would never pronounce a judgment of blood. He could degrade the clerk from his orders and, as an additional punishment, relegate him to a monastery or keep him in prison for life. A whipping might be inflicted, and Becket, it seems, had recourse even to the branding iron."[51]

Now it was one thing for an abbot to protect one of his monks. It was quite another for him to protect others. The church's *mund* covered not only members of the household, but also the house itself. As in any other house, carrying weapons in church broke the church's peace, and so did any act of violence committed by an outsider within it. To the considerable frustration of lay authorities, this gave rise to a widespread practice in which fugitives from lay courts would find refuge in church buildings, including the church itself, as well as adjoining buildings and even the house of a bishop or a priest.[52]

At any rate, the householder's power to quench external threats to his peace, or *mund*, manifested itself most dramatically when peacebreakers were caught redhanded.[53] Under Anglo-Saxon law, the householder was authorized to kill a thief caught in the act.[54] This authority extended to thieves caught at nighttime.[55] (This is the origin of the distinction between daytime and nighttime burglary that can still be found in many American jurisdictions.[56]) As late as the thirteenth century, royal charters typically granted local lords jurisdiction over cases of *infangenethef*,[57] i.e., over thieves "caught within" the lord's territory, as opposed to *utfangenethef*, which would authorize the lord to hang the thief even if he was "caught without." "Handhaving" (*hand-haebbende*) thieves were disposed of in a summary procedure, and hanged.[58] This power over nonmembers of the household was distinct from, and granted in addition to, the internal jurisdiction over members, captured by the common formula of "*cum saca et soca et toll et theam.*"[59]

Heinrich Brunner in particular stressed the historical significance of the summary disposal of handhaving thieves.[60] Brunner saw in this very procedure nothing less than the roots of criminal law. According to Brunner, the punishment in these cases of interference with the householder's *mund* merely manifested the outlaw status the offender had assigned himself through his act. Through his act, the offender rendered himself peaceless, i.e., beyond the protection of any *mund*. Once peaceless, the offender was entirely at the mercy of others, and in particular of the man whose peace he violated. Since the offender was peaceless, anyone could inflict whatever harm he wished without interfering with another's peace. This utter peacelessness justified the summary disposal procedure as well as the indignity of the punishment inflicted.

Before we move on to consider the offshoots from outlawry as the original penalty (*Abspaltungen der Friedlosigkeit*), as described by Brunner, let's note some of the features of outlawry itself. To begin with, outlawry is self-inflicted. Its punishment merely recognizes a state of affairs created by the outlaw, through his act.[61] Second, outlawry is a status as much as it is a punishment. The outlaw is outlawed because he already has revealed himself as, or transformed himself into, an outlaw. Third, outlawry is exclusion. Although outlawry does not by itself exclude the offender—since he already has excluded himself—it cements his status as an outsider. The outlaw is the ultimate outsider. He belongs nowhere and to no one. Outlaws were not merely lawless, but lordless as well. And any lordless man, anyone "of whom no right can be had," poses a continuous threat. In Anglo-Saxon law the lordless man is thus considered "a suspicious if not dangerous person; if he has not a lord who will answer for him, his kindred must find him one; if they fail in this, he may be dealt with (to use the nearest modern terms) as a rogue and vagabond."[62] The outlaw is not merely lordless, but permanently so.

Having laid out the process and substance of outlawry, Brunner went on to argue that subsequent punishments, and eventually the criminal law, simply differentiated the original, and ultimate, penalty of outlawry for the rightless thief caught in the act of violating the householder's *mund* into its various components. Pollock and Maitland agreed that so-called afflictive or physical punishments (as opposed to fines or *wergild*, for instance), "have their root in outlawry" and are but "mitigations of that comprehensive penalty" as "[t]he outlaw forfeits all, life and limb, lands and goods."[63]

To understand the process of differentiation of the *ur*penalty (and -status) of outlawry, one needs to consider another important development: the expansion of the king's peace. The king, as householder, had his own *mund*. And as any householder, the king had the power to protect his *mund*, and everyone and everything within it, against external attacks. The history of crime, in Brunner's view, is the history of violations of the king's *mund*, and the history of punishment that of the king's power of imposing outlawry as a sanction for such violations.

The expansion of royal power, now, is simply the expansion of the royal household and its *mund*, the royal peace.[64] Pollock and Maitland, once again, capture this evolution with characteristic succinctness:

> Breach of the king's peace was an act of personal disobedience, and a much graver matter than an ordinary breach of public order; it made the wrongdoer the king's enemy. The notion of the king's peace appears to have had two distinct origins. There were, first, the special sanctity of the king's house, which may be regarded as differing only in degree from that which Germanic usage attached everywhere to the homestead of a free man; and, secondly, the special protection of the king's attendants and servants, and other persons who he thought fit to place on the same footing.[65]

This "extension of the king's peace" continued until "it becomes, after the Norman Conquest, the normal and general safeguard of public order."[66] But its eventually enormous expanse should not obscure its origin in the idea of the householder's *mund*. At bottom and in essence, "[t]he kingly power is a mode of *dominium*; the ownership of a chattel, the lordship, the tenancy, of lands, these also are modes of *dominium*."[67] The analogy between kingly and baronly power is pervasive, and not limited to the power to dispose of hand-having thieves:

> [The king] has hardly a power for which an analogy can not be found else-where. If he holds a court of his tenants in chief, his barons will do the like; if he asks an aid from them, they will ask an aid from their knights; if he tallages his demesne land, they can exercise a similar right. It is with diffi-culty that they are restrained from declaring war. If he prosecutes crimi-nals, this is because his peace has been broken, and other lords are often proceeding against offenders who have done them "shame and damage" by breaking their peace.[68]

The extension of the king's household to encompass the entire realm also manifested itself in the traditional institutions of English government. In fact, "all medieval governmental departments began as a division of the household, including chancery, exchequer, the chamber, the wardrobe, and the royal courts of law."[69]

Now the expansion of the king's authority as householder of the realm also implied a transformation of every resident of the realm into a member of his household. While built on the model of the *mund* shared by all household-ers as such, no matter how big or small, the king's peace therefore eventually spelled the demise of that very power throughout the land. While the lords retained local power over their tenants, eventually that power could no longer be derived directly from their status as householder. Instead, their au-thority came to be granted to them by the king via royal charter, which con-ceded them whatever rights the king, as the ultimate householder, saw fit to surrender, or more precisely, to delegate (even the power to dispose of hand-having thieves, mentioned earlier).

At least that's how the king's lawyers saw the matter. That local lords con-tinued to cling to the original *fons et origo* of their power over their house-hold goes without saying. And in reality, if not in theory, they did manage to run their possessions in very much the same way as they did before royal charters. Certainly from the point of view of their tenants, it made little dif-ference in the regular course of things whether their lord's power stemmed from his householder status or from royal delegation.[70]

While the expansion of kingly power, and the concurrent reduction of lordly power, had begun among the Anglo-Saxons, the fundamental distinction between king, as householder, and everyone else, as household, was illustrated most dramatically by the Laws of William the Conqueror. William let it be known that his peace encompassed the entire realm, comprising English and Normans alike. Then to symbolize the expansion of his household to all of England, he required that every free man swear him an oath of fealty: "We decree also that every freeman shall affirm by oath and compact that he will be loyal to king William both within and without England, that he will preserve with him his lands and honor with all fidelity and defend him against his enemies."[71] And so they did: "there came to him all the land-sitting men who were worth aught from over all England, whosoever men they were, and they bowed themselves to him, and became this man's men."[72]

Whatever distinctions might exist among the member of the kingly household, before the king everyone was equal, equal in their inferiority as constituents of the king's *familia*. This is, after all, one of the features of the familial model of governance. There always existed differences of status within the household, which included not only the wife and children, male and female, but also servants, animals, and various "material possessions." And these differences in status were reflected in different relations between the head and the various household members, inanimate and animate, as Aristotle had pointed out. A good householder didn't manage his wife the way he did his son, his slave, or his mule. But these differences paled in comparison to the one defining distinction, that between every constituent of the household and the householder.

Needless to say, from the perspective of the royal householder the distinction between (free) villeins and (unfree) serfs also mattered little. After all, if the distinction between lord and tenant meant nothing, there was no need to differentiate carefully among the tenants themselves. Here too, and even more clearly, the Norman Conquest merely crystallized a development that already had occurred in previous centuries. William in 1085 sent out his officials to take stock of the resources of his fairly new realm, the results of which became known as the Domesday Book. Now the point of the Domesday Book was not to collect interesting bits of information about local English habits for William's entertainment. The point, as Maitland reminds us, instead was to raise money. And from a central fiscal perspective differences among potential sources of revenue were irrelevant: "We may strongly suspect that the king's commissioners were not much interested in the line that separates the *villani* from the *servi*, since the lord was as directly answerable for the geld of any lands that were in the occupation of his villeins as he was for the geld of these plots that were tilled for him by his slaves."[73]

Taxation levels everything, and everyone. And so does the generation of statistics. As Foucault recently emphasized, the transformation of individuals into "population," the characteristics of which can be captured in statistical data is a significant moment in the history of governance, a point we'll have a chance to explore in greater detail later on.[74] It makes the central government of an entire realm possible, partly by reducing its multifarious objects to a set of manipulable variables.

The King's Peace

With the expansion of the king's *mund* to the entire realm, it becomes difficult to separate internal discipline from defense of the household against external attack. Within the king's household, the kingdom, every attack is internal. External attacks are now limited to attacks on the kingdom itself. And in fact, the disposal of external and internal threats to the kingdom become conceptualized as distinct aspects of the royal authority. Several centuries later, John Locke would distinguish between two powers, the executive and the federative. He notes, however, that "though they be really distinct in themselves, yet one comprehending the execution of the municipal laws of the society within itself upon all that are parts of it, the other the management of the security and interest of the public without with all those that it may receive benefit or damage from, yet they are always almost united," namely in the person of the king.[75]

Within the household, and therefore also within the royal household, relations were governed by the feudal nexus. In exchange for loyalty and obedience, the tenant received the lord's protection. This relationship was founded on an oath of allegiance and fealty, the very oath that William decreed "every freeman" swear to him, that Locke still recognized six centuries later,[76] and Blackstone another century after him.[77] The oath of fealty in turn was but one instance of a general ceremony that could be found throughout medieval Europe. Here is Vinogradoff's general account of how the bond between chief and household member is forged:

> The relation is generally initiated by two acts: firstly, the submission of the follower to his chief as symbolised by the former stretching out his folded hands which the latter receives in his own; secondly, an oath of fidelity by which the follower promised to support his lord and to be true and faithful to him in every respect. The corresponding duties of the lord were to afford protection to his followers and to keep them well.[78]

The Laws of Alfred, Guthrum, and Edward the Elder, from the tenth century, provided the following formula (complete with a place holder for the name of the lord):

Thus shall a man swear fealty oaths.

By the Lord, before whom this relic is holy, I will be to ____ faithful and true, and love all that he loves, and shun all that he shuns, according to God's law, and according to the world's principles, and never, by will nor by force, by word nor by work, do ought of what is loathful to him; on condition that he keep me as I am willing to deserve, and all that fulfil that our agreement was, when I to him submitted and chose his will.[79]

Along with his duties of protecting members of his household and maintaining their well-being, and in fact *in order* to discharge these very duties, the householder enjoyed widespread authority to enforce submission and fidelity in return. Breach of the bond of fealty constituted a *felonia*, viewed both as the most serious and as the root of all offenses. In theory at least, it appears that the lord could be guilty of *felonia* as well. But the villein's remedy, again in theory, was to be freed of his obligation of fealty to the lord or, if the lord had falsely evicted him, to be permitted to reassume that very obligation—as opposed to being disposed of as an outlaw, or not, in the lord's discretion.[80]

The imbalance in consequences of offenses against the bond between lord and man is perhaps best illustrated by the radically unequal punishment for the most serious violation, homicide: "To kill one's lord is compared to blasphemy against the Holy Ghost; it is a crime punished by a death cruel enough to seem a fit beginning for the torments of hell. If, on the other hand, the lord slays his man who has done no wrong, the offence can be paid for with money."[81]

The consequences of the villein's violation of his fealty were dramatic. Any act of recalcitrance or disloyalty might be perceived as felony and trigger the discipline of his lord: "a man can hardly go against any one at his lord's command without being guilty of the distinctively feudal crime, without being guilty of 'felony.' "[82] The word felony apparently is of French origin, where it was limited to breaches of the feudal nexus between lord and his man. It did not encompass other offenses, such as homicide or theft. Originally, it appears to have had this narrow meaning in England as well. In the *Leges Henrici*, for example, it still appears as but one crime among many.[83]

But, as Pollock and Maitland report, "[a] little later it seems to cover every crime of any considerable gravity, and seems to have no reference whatever to the feudal bond, save in one respect, namely, that the felon's land escheats to his lord." In fact, they continue, "a charge of *felonia* has become an indispensable part of every charge of every crime that is to be punished by death or mutilation." Eventually, "[a]ll the hatred and contempt which are behind the word *felon* are enlisted against the criminal, murderer, robber, thief, without reference to any breach of the bond of homage and fealty."[84]

Pollock and Maitland find the transference of felony from the feudal context to serious offenses "obscure."[85] One may suspect, however, that the expansion of the concept of *felonia* accompanied the expansion of the king's *mund* to cover the entire realm. As Pollock and Maitland remarked, "[b]reach of the king's peace was an act of personal disobedience, and a much graver matter than an ordinary breach of public order; it made the wrongdoer the king's enemy."[86] And once the king's peace encompasses the entire kingdom, every serious offense amounted to a breach of the offender's duty of fealty to the king. Every breach of the king's peace therefore constituted not only a felony, but a felony of the most serious kind, namely a felony against the ultimate householder, the king.

The felon thus emerged as the quintessential outlaw. He was entirely at the mercy of the king: "Some of the gravest offenses, especially against the king and his peace, are said to be *bótleás*, '*bootless*'; that is, the offender is not entitled to redeem himself at all, and is at the king's mercy."[87] He was, as the old sources put it, "in misericordia, in potestate regis, ducis, en merci du roi, du seigneur."[88] The king had the power to exterminate him, as a peaceless and lordless man, or to mitigate his punishment by imposing an offshoot of outlawry, in Brunner's sense.[89]

These lesser punishments could take several forms. William the Conqueror, for instance, along with spreading his peace all throughout England and requiring English freemen to swear him fealty, replaced capital punishment with mutilation: "I also forbid that anyone shall be slain or hanged for any fault, but let his eyes be put out and let him be castrated."[90] Rather than signaling weakness, this discretionary mitigation reflected William's plenary power. He could manipulate penalties as he pleased because he held the power of the ultimate punishment. It's no accident that the "mitigated" punishment he chose was one traditionally associated with slaves.[91]

The lord's, and therefore the king-as-lord's, arbitrary power to reduce the ultimate punishment of outlawry manifested itself most starkly in the system of amercements, or fines. As Brunner explains, amercements originally were paid to receive the king's *misericordia*, i.e., quite literally his mercy.[92] By the late thirteenth century, a complex system of amercements, operating at various levels, was in place:

> Thousands of amercements are being inflicted by courts of all kinds. The process is this:—So soon as the offender's guilt is proved, the court declares that he is in mercy (*in misericordia*). If it be a royal court, he is in the king's, if it be a county court, he is in the sheriff's, if it be a seignorial court,

he is in the lord's mercy. Thereupon, at least in the local courts, the of-fender 'waged' an amercement, that is to say, he found gage or pledge for the payment of whatever sum might be set upon him when he should have been amerced. For as yet he had not been amerced (*amerciatus*). At the end of the session some good and lawful men, the peers of the offender (two were to be enough) were sworn to "affeer" the amercements. They set upon each offender some fixed sum of money that he was to pay; this sum is his amercement (*amerciamentum*).[93]

It's important to recognize that the entire system of amercements was based on the concept of the king-as-lord's arbitrary power to exterminate the outlaw. In the end, the offender is at the king's mercy not only for tradition-ally *bootless* crimes, but also for all breaches of the king's *mund*. The thirteenth-century system of amercements thus was but a simplified and cen-tralized version of the old Anglo-Saxon system of *bót* and *wíte*. Under both systems, the offender could "buy back the peace that he had broken."[94] Tra-ditionally, he would have to pay *wíte* to the victim and *bót* to the king. But with the expansion of the king's *mund*, the presumptive victim was always the king. It therefore made sense that the dual system of *wíte* and *bót* be stream-lined into a single system of *bót*, or royal misericordia, which was then dis-seminated as amercements throughout the various layers of the state-as-royal-household, with the sheriff's, and even the lord's, authority to amerce offenses flowing from the king's central authority to mitigate the ultimate punishment of outlawry.

Outlawry thus was the beginning and the end of the practice of disposing of threats to the king's *mund*. It was the beginning because all lesser penal-ties derived, or in Brunner's phrase, split off from it. It was the end because it remained as the ultimate punishment for anyone who could not, for what-ever reason, buy back the king's peace. And those unlucky enough to be in this position faced severe penalties indeed: "We read of death inflicted by hanging, beheading, burning, drowning, stoning, precipitation from rocks; we read of loss of ears, nose, upper-lip, hands and feet; we read of castration and flogging and sale into slavery," while as Pollock and Maitland remind us, "the most gruesome and disgraceful of these torments were reserved for slaves."[95]

Treason and Felony

Since the lord's disciplinary authority derived from the oath of fealty, and the obligation of submission and loyalty it established, it's no surprise that the most serious offense consisted in the most blatant violation of that duty:

killing one's lord, or treason. Treason struck at the very foundation of the fealty relationship, and therefore of power in the medieval household, and therefore in the medieval state. Its centrality manifested itself in two ways. The offense was very broadly cast, and its punishment was extremely severe.

To appreciate the severity of the crime of treason, however, it's not enough to focus on the feudal nexus between the lord and his man. One must go back further to the original conception of the relation between the householder and his household. The householder was not merely responsible for the welfare of his household. Household and householder were, in the end, identical, and their interests were one and the same. The household, after all, was nothing but an instrument in the hands of the householder who wielded it according to "the art of managing the household," the science of "economics."[96]

The lord thus was not simply the head of his household, but was actually its very essence. Or in the words of Coke, the king "est caput et salus reipublicae, et a capite bona valetudo transit in omnes."[97] For a member of the household to kill its head therefore was twice reprehensible: as a breach of his duty of submission and loyalty and as a destruction of the well-being of the entire household.

Given the two-pronged attack implicit in treason, every effort was made to prevent it, rather than punish it after the fact. Punishing treason, in fact, was impossible. For once the head of the household was dead, the well-being of the community had been destroyed. What's more, the community itself ceased to exist. It had to be reconstituted. Preventing treason, however, meant extinguishing it at its root. The threat of treason had to be eliminated, for one could not afford to await its realization.

Treason thus became the original inchoate offense. In the language of the Treason Act of 1351, to commit treason was not to kill the king, but to "compass or imagine the death of our lord the King":

> Whereas divers Opinions have been before this Time [what case should be adjudged Treason, and what not;] the King, at the Request of the Lords and of the Commons, hath made a Declaration in the Manner as hereafter followeth, that is to say; When a Man doth compass or imagine the Death of our Lord the King, or of our Lady his [Wife] or of their eldest Son and Heir; or if a Man do violate the King's [Wife] or the King's eldest Daughter unmarried, or the Wife [of] the King's eldest Son and Heir; or if a Man do levy War against our Lord the King in his Realm, or be adherent to the King's Enemies in his Realm, giving to them Aid and Comfort in the Realm, or elsewhere, and thereof be [proveably] attainted of open Deed by [People] of their Condition: And if a Man counterfeit the King's Great or Privy Seal, or his Money; and if a Man bring false Money into this Realm,

counterfeit to the Money of England, as the Money called Lushburgh, or other, like to the said Money of England, knowing the Money to be false, to merchandise or make Payment in Deceit of our said Lord the King and of his People; and if a Man slea the Chancellor, Treasurer, or the King's Justices of the one Bench or the other, Justices in Eyre, or Justices of Assise, and all other Justices assigned to hear and determine, being in their Places, doing their Offices: And it is to be understood, that in the Cases above rehearsed, [it] ought to be judged Treason which extends to our Lord the King, and his Royal Majesty: And of such Treason the Forfeiture of the Escheats pertaineth to our Sovereign Lord, as well of the Lands and Tenements holden of other, as of himself: And moreover there is another manner of Treason, that is to say, when a Servant slayeth his Master, or a Wife her Husband, or when a Man secular or Religious slayeth his Prelate, to whom he oweth Faith and Obedience; and [such Manner of Treason giveth Forfeiture of Escheats] to every Lord of his own Fee. . . . [98]

Note that treason was not defined as killing the king *or* compassing or imagining his death. There was no point in prohibiting killing the king. Treason was not *also* an inchoate offense, treason was *only* an inchoate offense. In modern doctrinal terms, it wasn't as though attempted treason was punished along with its consummation, but treason itself was an attempt.

And yet treason did not constitute, strictly speaking, an attempt. An actual attempt to kill "our lord the King" was not required. Not even *preparing* to kill him was necessary to commit treason, to use the distinction between (nonpunishable) preparation and (punishable) attempt familiar from modern criminal law. In fact, no act of any kind was necessary. Merely compassing or imagining the king's death was enough.

But that was not all. It's easy to forget that treason covered far more than killing the king (or compassing or imagining his death). As the Treason Act makes clear, it also was treason to compass or imagine the death of "our lady his [wife] or of their eldest son and heir." Only when it came to royal officials was compassing or imagining no longer enough. Actual homicide was required. But this too was treason ("if a man slea a chancellor, treasurer, or the King's justices of the one bench of other, justices in eyre, or justices of assise, and all other justices assigned to hear and determine, being in their places, doing their offices").

Treason wasn't limited to homicide, either, as it also included rape ("if a man do violate the King's [wife] or the King's eldest daughter unmarried, or the wife [of] the King's eldest son and heir"). Nor was it limited to offenses against persons. Much of the Treason Act is devoted to all manner of counterfeiting ("if a man counterfeit the King's great or privy seal, or his money;

and if a man bring false money into this realm, counterfeit to the money of England, as the money called lushburgh, like to the said money of England, knowing the money to be false, to merchandise or make payment in deceit of our said lord the King and of his people").

The Act also listed the one offense that contemporary criminal law continues to recognize as treason, namely "levy[ing] war against our lord the King in his realm, or be adherent to the King's enemies in his realm, giving to them aid and comfort in the realm, or elsewhere." Very much the same definition of treason would appear in the U.S. Constitution some four hundred years later.[99] (The Constitution also authorizes the federal government to punish counterfeiting, but does not call it treason.[100] Treason is explicitly limited to "levying war against [the United States], or in adhering to their enemies, giving them aid and comfort."[101])

But treason was not only broadly defined. Several other doctrines further widened its sweep and expanded the protection of the king against assaults on him and his. So the distinction between principals and accomplices was disregarded in treason cases, meaning that accomplices were punished as harshly as principals.[102] Such niceties of doctrinal differentiation were entirely misplaced when it came to preventing and extinguishing threats to the king. The insanity defense didn't apply to treason for the same reason.[103]

Now, despite the breadth of the definition of treason in the Treason Act of 1351, it's worth noting that the mere fact of definition—no matter how broad—constitutes a limitation on the king's arbitrary punitive power. Perfectly discretionary power permits no definition. The *ur*offense, *felonia*, of which treason was but the most egregious example, originally was thought neither to require nor to permit definition. Not even a complete list of the various possible violations of the duties of fealty was thought possible, or necessary for that matter.[104] Felony was whatever violated the fealty oath. The definition of felony was its very undefinability.

The Treason Act therefore also can be seen as an attempt on the part of the lords to delineate, if not constrain, the authority of the king. That the king took the opportunity to set into statutory stone the full extent of his authority and clearly to demarcate that authority from the inferior one of the lords, is another matter. Note the preamble of the Treason Act, which explains the—at that time highly unusual—practice of defining crimes in statutory form as the king's response to a request for clarification by Parliament, "of the lords and of the commons": "[W]hereas divers opinions have been before this [what case should be adjudged treason, and what not;] the King, at the request of the lords and of the commons, hath made a declaration in the manner as hereafter followeth. . . . "

Getting the king to clarify the limits of treason would have been in the lords' interest for one reason in particular. Treason benefited the king, felony the lord: "while the felon's land escheated to his lord, the traitor's land was forfeited to the king."[105] This distinction between treason and felony dates back beyond the Norman Conquest. Already in Anglo-Saxon law, upon conviction of felony, and "after the king has exercised the very ancient right of wasting the criminal's land for year and day, the tenement returns to its lord."[106]

Kings apparently had developed a tendency to give ever-expanding interpretation to the naturally fluid concept of treason. And any expansion of treason came at the expense of felony, and therefore of the lords whose offending tenants were now viewed as traitors rather than felons. This expansion of treason occurred largely with the help of the doctrine of constructive treason. Constructive treason turned any attack on a royal official into an act of treason, no matter where it occurred. The more, and the more often, royal officials traveled the realm, the greater became their exposure to attack, and therefore the king's opportunity to take the spoils of their suffering.

If it was a limitation of the concept of treason that the lords were hoping for when they asked Edward III to explain treason to them, they can't have been all too satisfied with the result. In hindsight, getting the king to put some, any, limit on his arbitrary punitive power (which included, up to that point, the power to define, or rather *not* to define, what sort of behavior, or "compassing," might call forth its exercise) must have seemed somewhat of a Pyrrhic victory.

For not only did King Edward specifically include constructive treason (though in the restricted form of homicidal attacks on royal officials), but perhaps more significant, he for the first time clearly delineated kingly (or high) treason from lordly (or petty) treason. After dealing with assaults, real or "imagined," on himself, his wife, his son, his daughter-in-law, on all and sundry officials, and with forgeries of various kinds, as well as with giving aid and comfort to the enemy, each and every one of which resulting in "the forfeiture of the escheats . . . to our sovereign lord, as well of the lands and tenements holden of other, as of himself," only after circumscribing *real* treason, that is, does Edward get around to mentioning "another manner of treason" namely that petty treason which occurs "when a servant slayeth his master, or a wife her husband, or when a man secular or religious slayeth his prelate, to whom he oweth faith and obedience," resulting in "forfeiture of escheats to every lord of his own fee."

What had been a single feudal offense committed by a member of the household against his householder has been divided into two classes, one grand (or high), the other petit (petty). From then on, treason committed against a lord remained treason, but was merely petty. Treason against a lord not only was petty, but it was also more narrowly defined. In contrast to high treason, petty treason included only an actual homicide. Compassing and imagining did not petty treason make. Petty treason also covered only one victim, the householder himself. As we just saw, high treason protected, in addition to the king-householder, his wife, his son, his daughter-in-law, and a whole gamut of officials. Petty treason required homicide. High treason applied also to rape. Petty treason encompassed only offenses against a person. High treason included counterfeiting of various sorts, i.e., violations of the king's seal and his currency.[107] In the end, Edward located petty treason against a lord somewhere below constructive high treason committed indirectly against the king through the killing of one of his evergrowing army of officials.

It's not clear how much of this is new, and how much of it merely declared the common law as it had developed up to that time. It appears that at least some of the statutory distinctions between high and petty treason were not made before Edward's statutory clarification.[108] That doesn't much matter for our purposes, however. Either way, the Treason Act reinforced the common core of a general offense of treason, while differentiating between two versions of it.

In English law, both varieties of treason persisted until well into the nineteenth century. So did its essence, the nexus of fealty between lord and man, as Blackstone's discussion of treason, from 1769, illustrates:

> Treason, *proditio*, in it's [sic] very name, which is borrowed from the French, imports a betraying, treachery, or breach of faith. It therefore happens only between allies . . . : for treason is indeed a general appellation, made use of by the law, to denote not only offences against the king and government, but also that accumulation of guilt which arises whenever a superior reposes a confidence in a subject or inferior, between whom and himself there subsists a natural, a civil, or even a spiritual relation; and the inferior so abuses that confidence, so forgets the obligations of duty, subjection, and allegiance, as to destroy the life of any such superior or lord. This is looked upon as proceeding from the same principle of treachery in private life, as would have urged him who harbours it to have conspired in public against his liege lord and sovereign: and therefore for a wife to kill her lord or husband, a servant his lord or master, and an ecclesiastic his lord or ordinary; these, being breaches of the lower allegiance, of private and domestic faith, are denominated *petit* treason. But when disloyalty so rears it's [sic] crest, as to attack even majesty itself, it is called by way of eminent distinction *high* treason, *alta proditio*; being equivalent to the *crimen laesae majestatis* of the Romans.[109]

England did not abandon the distinction between petty treason and murder until 1828.[110] In the colonial United States, petty treason played a crucial
role in the attempt to maintain social discipline. The crime began to disappear only after the revolution, in the late eighteenth century. New York, for
instance, did away with petty treason only in 1787.[111] Nonetheless, as a sign
of petty treason's continued vitality as a concept if not as a statutory crime,
the revised N.Y. Penal Code of 1881 found it necessary explicitly to abolish
petit treason, once again, almost a century later.[112]

Apart from the disposal of his property, it went without saying that the
traitor was to suffer the harshest possible penalty. The punishment for treason was always something special, reflecting the special status of the offense.
When, under the influence of Christianity, early English law experimented
with rendering all offenses amenable by fine, treason against one's lord remained bootless.[113] By the thirteenth century, when other serious crimes
were punished by hanging, the law still provided that the petty traitor "shall
be drawn as well as hanged and a woman shall be burnt, while, at least in the
worst cases, high treason demands a cumulation of deaths."[114] It was felt that
"hanging was too good a death for one who killed his lord": "[h]e should per-
ish in torments of which hell-fire will seem a relief." The penalty for regicide was further aggravated to "drawing, hanging, disembowelling, burning,
beheading, quartering."[115]

And not much changed in the next half millennium, according to this remarkable passage from Blackstone detailing the gruesome, cumulative, punishments reserved for the high traitor, which takes from medieval law not
only the nature of the punishments but even the king's arbitrary power of
amercement, to a point:

> The punishment of high treason in general is very solemn and terrible.
> 1. that the offender be drawn to the gallows, and not be carried or walk;
> though usually a sledge or hurdle is allowed, to preserve the offender from
> the extreme torment of being dragged on the ground or pavement. 2. That
> he be hanged by the neck, and then cut down alive. 3. That his entrails be
> taken out, and burned, while he is yet alive. 4. That his head be cut off.
> 5. That his body be divided into four parts. 6. That his head and quarters
> be at the king's disposal.
>
> The king may, and often doth, discharge all the punishment, except be-
> heading, especially where any of noble blood are attainted. For, beheading
> being part of the judgment, that may be executed, though all the rest be
> omitted by the king's command.[116]

At around the same time, and across the Channel, the regicide Damiens was executed according to a complex plan that closely resembled Blackstone's list of torments, as described in the famous opening paragraph of Foucault's *Discipline and Punish*:

> On 2 March 1757 Damiens the regicide was condemned to make the *amende honorable* before the main door of the Church of Paris, where he was to be "taken and conveyed in a cart, wearing nothing but a shirt, holding a torch of burning wax weighing two pounds"; then, "in the said cart, to the Place de Grève, where, on a scaffold that will be erected there, the flesh will be torn from his breasts, arms, thighs, and calves with red-hot pincers, his right hand, holding the knife with which he committed the said parricide, burnt with sulphur, and, on those places where the flesh will be torn away, poured molten lead, boiling oil, burning resin, wax and sulphur melted together and then his body drawn quartered by four horses and his limbs and body consumed by fire, reduced to ashes and his ashes thrown to the winds."[117]

These examples could easily be multiplied by references to the laws and practices of other European countries. More interesting for our purposes, however, is the remarkable career of treason, and petty treason in particular, in the colonial United States, long before the Founding Fathers found themselves on the wrong side of the law of "constructive" treason and, eventually, "real" treason as well.[118]

Petit Treason

Long, or really not that long, before the traitor/revolutionaries who came to be known as the Founding Fathers came "Salvadore, an Indian, and Scipio, a negro" from Virginia, whose complaint was not taxation without representation but, presumably, the conditions of their enslavement. In 1710, Salvadore and Scipio were convicted of high treason for their part in plotting a slave insurrection. Compare their execution with that described by Foucault:

> 'It is Ordered that Salvatore be executed . . . and that his body be disposed of as follows viz. his head to be delivered to the Sherif of James City County and by him sett up at the City of Williamsburgh. Two of his quarters likewise delivered to the second Sherif of James City one whereof he is to cause to be sett up at the great guns in James City and the other to deliver to the Sherif of New Kent County to be sett up in the most publick

place of the said County, and the other two quarters to be disposed of and sett up as the Justices of the County of Surry shall think fitt to direct.'

Scipio was to be executed in Gloucester County, and his head and quarters were to be exhibited in various parts of Gloucester, Lancaster, and King and Queen counties.[119]

The application of the English concept of treason to the colonies was straightforward. The colonies were dominions under the king's prerogative, without representation in Parliament, and therefore without even the opportunity for giving (never mind denying) consent to royal measures of government.[120] The model of household governance thus applied with particular force to the colonies, even though the enormous distances often interfered with the enforcement of the king-householder's exercise of his patriarchal power. The king's peace very much and very directly extended to the colonies, making any disturbance of order there a personal affront against the authority of the king, and therefore high (as well as petty) treason.

In the colonies, petit treason was used to enforce plantation discipline when internal managerial measures by the master had failed. It thus was one, and the most extreme, way in which the courts supplemented the maintenance of discipline in the micro household. Faced with an obvious breakdown of internal household discipline, the courts simply did what the master could not do.[121] If the master survived, they whipped the disobedient household members, *in loco parentis*, so to speak. If he did not, or his very existence was threatened, they extinguished the offender. Here are several illustrations of the former method of supplemental household discipline, from early Maryland:

> When David Stevens admitted that he "scandalously" abused Richard Preston, his master, the members of the provincial court ordered the sheriff to give him ten lashes on his bare back. Even more severe was the punishment administered to another servant named Owen Morgan who was employed by William Hopkins, and who complained to the provincial court that when he was giving Morgan some "correction," the latter struck him with a club and threatened him "with many uncivil and opprobrious words, with cursing, swearing, blaspheming, etc." For such actions Morgan was given thirty lashes.[122]

In another case, also from colonial Maryland, four servants were sentenced to thirty lashes for "complain[ing] to the provincial court that their master did not allow them 'sufficient provisions for the enablement to our work.'"[123] In this case, however, the judges exercised the householder's traditional discretion to mitigate punishments in his mercy, because the proper relation between servant and master had been reestablished, in a ceremony reminiscent of the medieval fealty oath:

> Kneeling before the judges of the provincial court, they begged their master, Mr. Preston, and the court to forgive them "for their former misdemeanors" and promised obedience in the future. In view of this humble attitude, the members of the court declared that they would suspend the sentence of the whipping for the present, but at the same time warned the four servants that they must be on their good behavior towards their master "ever hereafter."

Ideally of course the master himself would maintain discipline within his household, without the need to have recourse to the courts. But that was not always possible. The killing of master by slave—petit treason—constituted the most egregious violation of plantation discipline, and required governmental intervention precisely because the original organ of discipline, the master, was no more. Petit treason, following the English model of constructive *high* treason, also applied to killings of the master's wife and agents, in particular of overseers. Arthur Scott reports from colonial Virginia that "[d]uring the eighteenth century all the recorded cases of petit treason involved slaves."[124]

The punishment for petit treason bore a certain resemblance to that for high treason. In 1733 two Virginia slaves, named Champion and Valentine, stood convicted of petit treason for the murder of an overseer and were dismembered, like Salvatore and Scipio before them. Then it was "ordered that the heads & quarters of Champion & Valentine be set up in severall parts of this County."[125] Four years later, in the case of a slave convicted of killing his master, it was "Ordered by the Court that the Sheriff cut off his head and put it on a Pole near the Courthouse to deter others from doing the Like."[126]

The practice of "qualified" execution for petit treason was not limited to Virginia. Raphael Semmes mentions a petit treason case from colonial Maryland, once again involving a slave, although this time the victim was the mistress of the house. Upon conviction after a bench trial, "the governor immediately passed sentence of death using the following words: You, Jacob, shall be drawn to the gallows at St. Mary's and there hanged by the neck till you are dead."[127]

Plantation Discipline

Petit treason was by definition invoked only in extraordinary cases of the total collapse of order in the household of the plantation. It is in the nature of treason, after all, that its prevention is everything, its punishment nothing. Ordinarily, all threats to the authority of the householder-master were disposed of by the head of the household himself. Here he enjoyed a discretion as wide as that of the medieval chief, the Roman *paterfamilias*, or the Greek *oikonomos*-householder.

Corporal punishment was the preferred means of discipline used by plantation masters, as it had been for heads of household since time immemorial. In medieval England, the lord could "beat or imprison his serf," although Pollock and Maitland are quick to point out that "of such doings we do not hear very much,"[128] which of course doesn't mean that it didn't happen very much.[129] We've already seen that the bishop was likewise authorized to whip or imprison members of his *familia*.[130] And in colonial Virginia, as on American plantations everywhere, "[t]he power of masters to whip their slaves was in practice almost unlimited."[131]

Of the two measures of domestic discipline, whipping and confinement, whipping tended to be the sanction of choice, and so it remained on the colonial plantation. Not only did it inflict the required punishment with a minimum investment of time and effort, it had the additional benefit of not necessarily incapacitating its object for extended periods of time. That was of course not the case for a particularly cruel whipping, which could kill or maim its victim. Excessive whippings of this type were, therefore, irrational from the perspective of the householder as wealth maximizer. For that reason, the loss of life or limb, and later on any permanent injuries, suffered by an object of domestic discipline were considered as evidence of an ulterior motive, usually called "malice," on the part of the household head, or its designate, such as an overseer or another relative, often the lady of the house, his wife.

But before we consider the limitations on the master's power of discipline, let's take a closer look at its substance. The father, as head of household, retained the right to "chastise" his wife and children through the nineteenth century.[132] Even today, heads of household still enjoy considerable authority to discipline inferior members of their small community. The prevalence and ferocity of domestic violence attests to the widespread assumption of the *fact*, and the exercise of that authority, even if it is no longer sanctioned by law. Modern law on parental discipline, in fact, limits—rather than eliminates—the authority, by restricting its object (from all household members to children only) as well as its severity. The Model Penal Code, for example, still authorizes parents to discipline their children if "the force used is not designed to cause or known to create a substantial risk of causing death, serious bodily harm, disfigurement, extreme pain or mental distress or gross degradation."[133] This right of parental (no longer paternal) discipline is remarkable not only for its extensive scope. More distressing, the list of impermissible purposes (though not *effects*!) can be read as a reflection of the actual practice of parental use of force against children. The reference to "gross degradation" in particular captures the essence of household discipline through the ages.

Corporal punishment, and once again whipping in particular, was considered indispensable for enforcing discipline in settings of domestic governance beyond the family itself. Take the military, for example. The hierarchical organization of the military unit resembled that of the traditional family. Head and member were bound together in a similar nexus of mutual obligation, one to obey, and the other to provide for his welfare. And like in the family, the military superior turned to whipping to enforce his authority. Roman soldiers were beaten with a stick (the *fustis*) for leaving the ranks. Disobedience or mutiny was punished with death. Deserters were in effect outlawed: they "forfeit all their privileges, and may be crucified or thrown to the beasts."[134]

Military discipline highlights several essential characteristics of householder power, characteristics that otherwise can be obscured by the benevolent presumptions generally attached to the exercise of that power. These features have been nicely captured by Max Radin:

> The one obvious military offense is, of course, disobedience of orders, but the essence of military discipline is that any act which seems to threaten the authority of the commander or the safety of the [unit], is punishable at once, and that no complete list of such acts can be made up in advance. . . . The determination that the act is an offense and, that it needs immediate suppression is necessarily discretionary and must remain so.[135]

In the American military whipping was the original punishment for disobedience.[136] An 1816 case involving a homicide on an American navy ship illustrates that this practice was alive and well at the time. In that case, Justice Story emphatically rejected defense counsel's suggestion that "a power of unlimited and arbitrary discretion resides in the officers of the ship to compel obedience of all commands, at all times, and under all circumstances, even by taking away life."[137] Story expressed astonishment at such a notion: "I confess that it never occurred to me until this trial that any person in this country ever dreamed of the existence of such an arbitrary power. This is emphatically a government of laws, and not of men."[138]

But clearly Story protests too much. The 1800 federal law he cites in support of his rejection of the superior's arbitrary authority to discipline with corporal punishment actually establishes the opposite.[139] That law provides "that no commanding officer shall, of his own authority, inflict a punishment on any private, beyond twelve lashes." Far from eliminating the officer's unlimited discretion to whip his inferior to enforce obedience, this law merely restricted the scope of that discretion to sanctions of a certain, and still considerable, quantity. Moreover, even Story conceded that naval officers retained "the right, in case of necessity, to enforce obedience to orders and a performance of duties by the punishment of death." And wholly apart from its legal limits, defense counsel's argument strongly suggests that the superior's authority to use corporal punishment was widespread and generally recognized in fact.

Corporal punishment in the navy rests on a particularly solid historical footing. It combines two long established systems of domestic governance, the ship and the military. The naval officer thus could draw on two sources of disciplinary authority, the captain and the military commander. And both sources in turn derive from the authority of the head of the household. That's why, when Bishop, the great nineteenth-century commentator on American criminal law, sought to illustrate the scope of *parental* authority, he used the case of a "master seaman" chastising a "seaman."[140]

Whipping also was a common disciplinary measure in prisons, once prisons began to be used more broadly than they had been in medieval law, and as *correctional* institutions, rather than as holding pens or as a means to encourage prompt payment of pecuniary penalties.[141] In this respect, it mattered little whether the prison was thought—and designed—to resemble a family (with the warden as father), a military unit (with the warden as commander), a factory (with the warden as employer), or a plantation (with the inmate as "slave of the state"[142]), or all at the same time.[143] Either way, the "keeper" or "warden" enjoyed wide disciplinary discretion, with its heavy reliance on corporal punishment, characteristic of household governance.[144] Already in seventeenth-century Maryland, prisoners who refused to work for their keep could be whipped by the prison keeper.[145]

Some two hundred years later, whipping still was recognized "as a legitimate power in keepers of prisons and wardens of penitentiaries to administer corporal punishment to refractory prisoners."[146] Writing in 1886, Christopher Tiedeman reported that "[t]his power is exercised generally throughout the country," though he adds, interestingly, that "it is hard to say, to what extent with the direct sanction of law."[147] This is a rare acknowledgment of the fact that, wholly aside from official legal doctrine, householders assumed—and to this day continue to assume—a certain disciplinary authority as part of their status, and their concomitant obligation to maintain the welfare of their household. Law can attempt to place general limits on that authority, but it can never eliminate it.[148]

The analogy between the household and the prison, and between household discipline and prison discipline, becomes clear if we see the prison as a supplementary household that picks up where the traditional household leaves off.[149] As such, prisons appear as an initially rather modest, and eventually terribly ambitious, attempt by the governing authority to discharge the responsibility that came with transforming the entire state into a single household under central control, by the king and later by the state. Now that the very purpose of prison was to correct, where else might one correct the recalcitrant but in a *house* of correction? And what was more natural than to use the same correctional tools that had always been available to the master of the house?

But whipping was not confined to the prison any more than the prison was the only means of public discipline. Corporal punishment naturally appeared wherever the state asserted itself as the macro household, and its head as the macro householder. In the household of the state, after all, not only prison inmates were in need of correction. They formed a small, and at the beginning rather insignificant, portion of the mass household which the state had taken upon itself to discipline.

The prison was only the most extreme and always limited form of state household discipline. In the prison, the state treated the recalcitrant not merely as members of the state's macro household. It went so far as to construct a replica of a micro household. Its discipline didn't just supplement, or sublimate, that of the micro householder, it sought to mimic it, and in that sense replace it.

Outside the traditional micro household, whipping was used for the same purpose, and carried the same meaning, as within it. Corporal punishment, and whipping in particular, thanks to its use over centuries as a means to enforce household discipline by the head upon inferior members of the household, human or not, acquired tremendous symbolic significance. Its effectiveness, and popularity, as a tool of discipline thus derived not only from the physical pain it inflicted on its object, but also from the clear communication of the inflictor's superior status vis-à-vis its object.

Corporal punishment marked its object as inferior, and in particular as inferior *to its subject*. It was perceived as humiliating, demeaning, degrading.[150] As the Texas Supreme Court put it somewhat theatrically in 1851, "among all nations of civilized man, from the earliest ages, the infliction of stripes has been considered more degrading than death itself."[151] And degradation was, literally, the point of disciplining disobedient inferiors. They had assumed a station not befitting them by resisting the authority of their superior. The corporal punishment was designed to reduce them to their proper status. More precisely, as Howard Garfinkel has remarked, the point of the "degradation ceremony" was ultimately *not* to degrade, but to unmask. The ceremony merely revealed the proper status of its object, rather than reducing it from a higher to a lower status.[152]

Corporal punishments traditionally were reserved for lower status offenders, the unfree, the "mean," and slaves. In Republican Rome, for instance, "mean persons are sent to the mines or crucified, persons of rank (*honestiores*) forfeit half their goods and are banished for life."[153] And "the most obvious mark of the difference between the common herd and the decurions is the liability to beating with the stick *(fustis)*."[154]

In colonial Maryland, corporal punishment in the state household still was limited to those of inferior status. Although whippings were used freely to enforce the authority of the colonial authority, "no corporal punishment could be inflicted upon a gentleman."[155] Likewise, in early Virginia, the law of punishments explicitly distinguished between the free and the unfree, reserving fines for the former and corporal punishment for the latter: "in all cases where a freeman is punishable by fine a servant shall receive corporal punishment, viz., for every 500 lbs. of tobacco, 20 lashes . . . unless their master or other acquaintance will redeem them."[156]

Virginia law in this case simply made explicit what the English *wergild* system had implied. The *wergild* system put a price on every offense, with the assumption that anyone who could not pay it would be subject to afflictive punishments, often at the hands of the victim. This meant, in effect, that the poor would suffer punishment of life and limb, unless they could find a lord to "redeem them."

As Pollock and Maitland make clear, the system of *bót* and *wíte* was "[f]rom the very first . . . an aristocratic system." Already on the face of it, it distinguished between the "dearly born" and the cheaply born. The freeman's *wergild* was greater than that of the unfree, and the nobler freeman's greater than the lesser's: "If any one be slain, let him be paid for according to his birth."[157] A man's worth also determined the worth of his word: "A twelve-hynde man's oath stands for six ceorls' oaths: because, if a man should avenge a twelve-hynde man, he will be fully avenged on six ceorls, and his wer-gild will be six ceorls' wer-gilds."[158] A twelve-hynde man commanded a *wergild* of 1,200 shillings, a six-hynde-man 600, a two-hynde-man, or ceorl, 200.

Moreover, the composition regime demanded "so much money that few were likely to pay it."[159] In effect, if not also on its face, the composition system was a system for propertied householders. The propertyless faced not fines, but afflictive penalties, outlawry, and enslavement to their victim.

Eventually, however, the *wergild* system disappeared, "with marvelous suddenness,"[160] and so did its apparent, if hypocritical, avoidance of punishments of life and limb. Afflictive punishments, once reserved for inferior household members, were expanded to all members of the macro household.[161] The index of *bót* and *wíte* was replaced with threats of afflictive punishments against life and limb, while discretionary amercements still permitted the king to mitigate punishments in his mercy.[162] Other crimes remained subject to money penalties, which were now also discretionary, however, rather than predetermined. The distinction between freeman and man disappeared from the laws, much as the distinction between villein—the lowest grade of freeman—and serf had largely lost its meaning. In Maitland's words, "[t]he gallows is a great leveller,"[163] though no greater than the Domesday Book, and the transformation of individual households and individual men, free or not, into fiscal data.

Micro and Macro Households

The great leveling raised up the serf, but depressed the villein. By the eleventh century, evidence of the villein householder had become difficult to find. Independent poor householders, the lowest of the freemen, were integrated into larger feudal estates.[164] Householders thus were transformed into members of a household, another's household. This development is difficult to explain, although we can assume—with Maitland—that it was attributable in large part to the growth of super-familial power after the Norman Conquest. Beginning with William, all property derives from the king. "Every holder of land, except the king, holds it of [de] some lord."[165] And the lord to whom the king assigned his rights over property, and those residing on it, became the householder who over time managed to bring other householders within his realm, eventually "transmuting a village full of free landholders into a manor full of villeins."[166]

Integration into another's household, however, also meant the obligation of fealty to the householder and, more to the point, exposure to the householder's disciplinary authority to enforce that obligation. To what extent the lord's relation to nominally free members of his household differed from that to the nominally unfree is difficult to determine. It's likely that these relations, and therefore the distinctions among them, themselves differed from manor to manor, from lord to lord, as well as over space and time. From the perspective of fiscal obligations, as we noted above, free villein and unfree slave were indistinguishable.[167] The same holds for the lord's vicarious liability for acts of his villeins and serfs. He is liable "for the acts of members, free or bond, of his household *(manupastus, mainpast)*."[168]

The integration of free villeins into the lord's household meant that one householder assumed householding power over another. This change occurred both at the micro and at the macro level of governance. At the micro level, the once free householding villein had to be integrated into the lord's household. At the macro level, the lord himself had to find a place in the super-household, the *über*family, of the king.

The regulation of micro households, and their heads, within a macro household raises at least three distinct questions. First, there is the general question of what type of disciplinary action, if any, the macro householder could take against a micro householder. Second, there is the question of what limits the macro householder might place upon the micro householder's authority within his own household. Third, a mechanism for the resolution of disputes among micro householders *inter pares* must be devised.

We will focus on the former two questions, as they alone pertain to the macro householder's police authority over the members of his household, the focus of our study. The problem of dispute resolution among micro householders is political, rather than merely economic, in the Aristotelian sense. The resolution of conflicts among micro householders, as autonomous—or at least potentially autonomous—parties, does not primarily concern household discipline. It pertains to the relation among two parties who are free and equal in the relevant, political, sense of the time, namely as house- and *mund*-holders. Here the challenge for the superior householder is to put in place—or rather to facilitate the evolution of—an institution that reflects the autonomous, or potentially autonomous, status of the parties. The point of this process is not to enforce obedience, but to do justice, and to be seen as doing justice, though still against the background of the remaining, fundamental, distinction between the macro householder and everyone, and everything, else, at least until the enlightenment and its literally revolutionary notion of full personal equality and political, as well as moral, autonomy.[169]

This is surely a powerful, and familiar, ideal. But it is one that belongs to the realm of law, rather than that of police. It's the much explored realm of the jury of one's peers (as that notion came to be understood, rather than as it came to be, namely as a royal inquisitorial tool), and of the common law (once again, as that notion came to be understood, i.e., *not* as a species of *royal law*, but as the embodiment of basic personal rights).[170] Our focus, at least for the moment, is on the realm of police, not on that of law. While the rhetoric of Anglo-American criminal law has tended to treat the problem of punishment as a problem of justice, and in that sense a legal issue, the current study explores the extent to which the power to punish remains *in fact*, if not in theory, rooted in the notion of police.

Now as to the question of what sorts—or qualities, as opposed to quantities—of punishment could be inflicted on householders-in-a-household, it is significant that certain punishments had become associated with the internal discipline of inferior household members. The use of these punishments therefore would threaten the distinction between the micro householder and other members of the macro household, who (or which) were not considered autonomous.

The most demeaning punishment always had been corporal punishment, and whipping in particular. As a general rule, the distinction between corporal and other nonafflictive punishments—like exile, forfeiture, or fine—tracked the distinction between householder and household. Put another way, corporal punishment in the macro household of the realm was reserved for those who were subject to private corporal punishment in the micro household. This meant that the householder generally was free from corporal punishment, though not necessarily from punishment altogether. In general, those who inflicted whippings could not receive them.

Whipping, in other words, was particularly appropriate to signify, and reestablish, the meanness of its object. Now meanness came in two senses. On the one hand, meanness meant simply inferior status, as in the "mean persons" of Republican Rome.[171] On the other, meanness, or baseness, came to refer to a particular character trait. Stripped of all "merely" social, and descriptive, sense meanness carried a strong normative meaning.

The quintessence of meanness was the mean person's violation of the obligation of submission and loyalty to the lord, felony. In this sense, only the socially mean (the villein) could be normatively mean. And conversely, being identified as a felon meant being likened to a villein. According to Pollock and Maitland, who follow Coke on this point, the etymology of felony illustrates its connection to meanness: " 'of the many conjectures proposed, the most probable is that *fellonem* is a derivative of the Latin *fell-*, *fel*, gall, the original sense being one who is full of bitterness or venom.' " They continue, *felon* "is as bad a word as you can give to man or thing, and it will stand equally well for many kinds of badness, for ferocity, cowardice, craft."[172]

At any rate, we have already seen how whipping was used against the socially inferior. It was soon applied to anyone, villein or free, whose offense "betray[ed] a meanness of disposition" (rather than merely of position) as well.[173] Prominent among the behavior that provided evidence of the requisite meanness was petit larceny. Petit larceny was punished by disgraceful afflictive penalties, including whipping, loss of ear, and sometimes by pillory, wholly out of proportion to the damage caused (it was after all, not *grand* larceny).[174] Petit larceny combined social with moral meanness: its "pettiness" revealed the offender as a socially inferior person, who would have to stoop so low as to steal items of little value, and larceny itself had long been thought particularly good evidence of moral meanness, particularly as compared with robbery.[175] "[T]heft is far more dishonourable than robbery," with one being the clandestine version of the other.[176] And we've already seen that few offenders suffered a worse, and faster, fate than the thief caught in flagranti delicto. As late as 1869, New Mexico still punished a horse thief by "not less than thirty lashes, well laid on his bare back, nor more than sixty, at the discretion of the court."[177]

Despite the persistent connection between normative and social meanness, and even the origin of the one in the other, the very existence of a notion of normative meanness carried within itself the possibility of extending meanness beyond the lower social classes. And in fact the concept of felony came to be attached to certain acts betraying a particular moral depravity, captured by the notion of *mens rea*, which could be found among members of various social strata. Anyone committing a murder "with malice aforethought" or, more specifically, with stealth or by ambush,[178] exposed himself as a felon, be he free or unfree, lord or villein. Of course, as a matter of fact, the label of felon still came to mark the poor almost exclusively. But at least as a matter of theory, the label was no longer restricted to them. Meanness of character was no privilege of the socially mean.

It should be noted, however, that this expansion of the concept of felony— and its associated concepts of *mens rea* and malice—across social distinctions does not imply the abandonment of the notion of the state as the macro household under the king's authority. Instead, it reflects the leveling of status distinctions—at least in this sense, and in theory, if not in practice— among all members of the king's household.[179] A felony still remained *felonia*, the violation of the nexus between "our lord the king" and all his men, high or low, rich or poor. To reveal oneself as a felon meant, first, to reveal oneself as the inferior in the feudal nexus between lord and man, and, second, to have violated one's duties of submission and loyalty as a mere man vis-à-vis one's lord. It meant to be socially as well as normatively mean.

The most dramatic illustration of this inferior status of the micro householder within the macro household was the use of corporal punishments, and of whipping in particular, against him. Never does the micro householder's meanness reveal itself more clearly than in the case of treason. In fact, (high) treason can be seen as the quintessential felony against the supreme householder, committed by anyone, free or unfree, within his household of the realm. Already in Rome, when it comes to directly challenging the authority of the head of the macro household, everyone is but a member of the household. In Roman law, treason, *majestas*, "levels all distinctions." While *honestiores* were generally exempt from torture, not so if they stood accused of treason. And *majestas* already encompasses forgery, as treason would in English law centuries later.[180]

When micro householders within the macro household exposed themselves as mean, particularly by violating their obligation of fealty to the macro householder, they thus exposed themselves to punishments appropriate to their mean station. But meanness not only qualified a householder as the object of corporal punishment; it also disqualified him as a *subject* of this demeaning penalty.

Limitations on the micro householder's internal disciplinary authority within his household applied to all householders and quasi-householders within the family of the realm, from the father, and those acting in his stead (in loco parentis), such as the teacher and the master, to the military officer and the prison keeper.[181] The most general limitation came in the form of what might be called a requirement of worthiness, or fitness. The householder worthy of his title enjoyed virtually unlimited discretion in his use of disciplinary measures; the unfit, however, were stripped of their authority. Here the notion of "malice" is, once again, central. The householder who acts out of malice has revealed himself to be merely mean. As a mean person, however, he is unworthy of the elevated position of householder, unworthy of respect, and unworthy of disciplinary authority. As a mean person he deserved to be disciplined, rather than to discipline.

The father, as economist, is charged with maximizing the welfare of his family. To discharge this obligation, he is equipped with disciplinary authority. That disciplinary authority is presumed to be exercised with an eye toward the well-being of the familial community, including that of its particular object.[182] In fact, the father is not only entitled, but obligated, to correct his child. The child has a right, loosely speaking, to be disciplined: "Parental discipline, rightly understood, is to assist the strivings and aspirations of the child's better nature. And the child, needing this assistance, is therefore entitled to it."[183]

In disciplining his child, for instance, the father is presumed to be "prompted by true parental love," to act in "good faith" and "without malice." But that presumption is not irrebuttable. Evidence to the contrary can come, not in the form of testimony from the presumptively incompetent object of discipline, but in the form of objective manifestations of malice: the physical impact of discipline. In medieval English law, the householder's disciplinary authority, even that of the lord over his serf or of the bishop over his clerk, stopped short of depriving his inferior of "life or limb," or "slaying or maiming" him.[184] The same limitation on the father's authority over inferior members of his household, including wife, children, and servants, can still be found in American law centuries later:

> But where the batter was so great and excessive to put life and limb in peril, or where permanent injury to the person was inflicted, or where it was

prompted by a malicious and wrongful spirit, and not within reasonable bounds, the courts interposed to punish, for as was said in one case, "there is no relation which can shield a party who is guilty of malicious outrage or dangerous violence committed or threatened."[185]

And we can find it also in the quasi-households of the military unit (the "host") and the prison. As to constraints on the disciplinary authority of military officers, an American case from 1887 remarked that

> a public officer, invested with certain discretionary powers, never has been, and never should be, made answerable for any injury, when acting within the scope of his authority, and not inflicted by malice, corruption, or cruelty. . . . The officer, being intrusted with a discretion for public purposes, is not to be punished for the exercise of it, unless it is first proved against him, either that he exercised the power confided to him in cases without his jurisdiction, or in a manner not confided to him, as, with malice, cruelty, or wilful oppression, or, in the words of Lord Mansfield, that he exercised it as if "*the heart is wrong*."[186]

Most recently, the U.S. Supreme Court clarified that prison disciplinary measures do not implicate the constitutional prohibition against cruel and unusual punishments unless they reflect "malice and sadism,"[187] thus effectively immunizing prison officials against liability in all other cases.[188]

Once exposed as mean, and therefore unfit to serve as head of his household, the discipliner could turn into the disciplined. A particularly stark illustration of this fall from grace is provided by a Maryland law from 1882. This law, entitled "An Act to inflict corporal punishment upon persons found guilty of wife-beating," did just that: it provided for the beating, and more particularly the whipping, of wife-beaters.[189] It thus subjected the head of a household to the demeaning punishment reserved for inferior members of the household and, as the Maryland Supreme Court remarked, for "negroes and slaves" in particular. The infliction of demeaning punishment on the husband for "brutally" beating his wife was fitting because the householder had revealed himself to be a mean person, despite his elevated position within the micro household. Subjecting him to corporal punishment in the macro household of the state thus merely confirmed his meanness.

And, once revealed, the imposter householder's meanness stripped him of the privilege that once protected him from the ordinary punishment for any breach of the macro householder's *mund*. For that *mund*, he was reminded, extended to every member of the king's household, even those under the delegated authority of the local lord, or family head. Here the local householder appears as an analogue to the slave overseer who exercises disciplinary authority only upon delegation from the master. And this was in fact how disciplinary power was dispersed throughout the realm, although local lords continued to hold on to the notion that they exercised that power over their tenants as an original householder's right, rather than by royal charter.

This limitation of the micro householder's authority over his household dramatically reflected the micro householder's integration into the king's macro household. The lords were reduced to the status of overseers who enjoyed disciplinary authority over their charges only within the limits set by the macro householder. An excessively violent lord was subject to the macro householder's discipline as a bad overseer, or administrator. A fourteenth-century text explains that "the king now had a kind of 'fee sutyl en noun de seigneurie' in each man, so that *the lord became a sort of mesne between the king and the serf whom he ought to treat 'pur lui enprower e ne nie dampner.'* "[190] The remedy for the loss of life or limb thus was, naturally, an appeal in the royal courts, in the nature of a complaint by the king's man that the lord had exceeded his disciplinary authority over him.[191] Excessive discipline violated the peace of the king's macro household, to which both discipliner and disciplined belonged. An appeal against a lord in the royal courts thus served as a, presumably painful, reminder of his equality with the villein vis-à-vis their common master.

Enforcing the king's ultimate authority against the facts of local power proved particularly difficult in the American colonies. Occasionally, the king reminded the colonial authorities of the basis of their might in the royal prerogative, and of their status as mere overseers within the royal household. Slaves were within the royal *mund*, and so were their administrators.[192] For instance, Arthur Scott cites a missive to the Virginia colony, in which the king expresses his displeasure about the failure to prosecute masters who had killed their slaves: "at the time, the Slave is the Master's Property he is likewise the King's Subject, and that the King may lawfully bring to Tryal all Persons here, without exception, who shall be suspected to have destroyed the Life of his Subject."[193]

The king's interest in preserving the lives of all of his royal subjects—no matter what inferior householder might claim the victim as his subject as well—also accounts for the presumptive punishability of any homicide, no matter how "excusable" or "justifiable."[194] Taking the life of a member of the king's macro household affected the king's householder authority in two ways. It deprived the king of a resource, an object of household governance.[195] What's more, it assumed a power—in fact, the most awesome power—reserved for the supreme *paterfamilias*, the power of life and death. If anyone had the authority to take the life (or limb) of a member of the household, it was the king (whether or not he enjoyed that power courtesy of yet another, and yet more powerful, householder, God). Faced with the fact of death, the very least the king could do to exercise his prerogative over life and death, the *ius vitae necisque* of the Roman *paterfamilias*, after the fact so to speak, was to apply it to the person who had assumed it, the offender. Whether he pardoned him or disciplined him, in one way or another, through physical pain or monetary fine, was entirely within his discretion. (English criminal law still struggled to legalize this discretion in the late nineteenth century.[196]) Under this view of homicide as a particularly serious interference with the king-householder's economic authority, it's no surprise that intentional killings, as *intentional acts of disobedience*, would be liable to trigger a harsher disciplinary response than nonintentional ones. Nonintentional killings, and excusable killings, drained the household resources just as intentional ones, but they did not manifest contempt.[197]

In theory, masters were liable for the malicious homicide of their slaves. In practice, however, they could kill their slaves with impunity. Scott reports that "in all doubtful cases the master received the benefit of the doubt." Masters simply were not prosecuted for killing their slaves.[198] Moreover, as a matter of law and not merely of practice, "[a]s early as 1669 the [Virginia] Assembly specifically provided that if a slave resisted lawful correction, 'and by the extremity of the correction should chance to die,' his death should not be accounted felony, 'since it cannot be presumed that prepensed malice (which alone makes murther ffelony) should induce any man to destroy his owne estate.' "[199] This law was reaffirmed in 1705, and again in 1723, when the Virginia Assembly categorically declared that murdering one's slave constituted manslaughter, never murder, and that "[i]n such a case there was to be no penalty at all."[200]

Scott's research once again makes an important point about the householder's disciplinary authority. Its legal limitation is one thing, its reality is another. Too difficult is it to pierce the domestic veil, and too entrenched the notion of the householder's discretionary disciplinary authority over his household.

In fact, the power to protect the family's welfare against threats from the inside, through discipline, as well as from the outside traditionally has been considered a necessary corollary of household governance, and of governance in general. And that power is of necessity arbitrary because it enables the head of the household to preserve its welfare by any means necessary. Surrendering this power means surrendering the power of governance. Every householder, much as every individual, has the right of self-preservation; and that right extends to the household just as the householder's self extends to the household. As we saw from our discussion of treason, the householder's welfare is the household's, and vice versa. Without this identity of interests, the householder ceases to be a householder. That's why internal discipline for the sake of the householder as a private person, rather than as keeper of the household, is beyond the pale.[201]

These fundamental characteristics of the householder's power manifest themselves in various contexts. First, the essential connection between the very notion of household government and the power of household self-preservation means that the power cannot be taken away without dismantling the institution for whose governance it is required. This means, as we've seen, that the father's power of discipline cannot be eliminated without eliminating the institution of the family. Public norms can limit this power, but they cannot eliminate it.

More generally, the integration of smaller communities of governance, considered as a household, into a larger one will raise the question of the retention of the householder's power of self-preservation. This, as we'll see, emerged as one of the central struggles of the early American Republic, and continues to shape the discourse of federalism today. This is the question of the "police power," and more specifically of the retention of that power by the states. Without the power to police, it was universally agreed, the states could not continue as separate institutions of governance: to surrender the police power, literally, was to surrender the right, and the power, of self-preservation.

Second, the householder's power was essentially arbitrary, as well as broad. This meant that it was not susceptible to prior definition. Its limits were defined in terms of the person wielding it. The householder's purpose is all-decisive. The end of preserving the community against internal and external threats justifies the means. Conversely, means are improper only to the extent that they reveal an improper end. More intrusive review of the relation between means and end is inappropriate. The householder enjoys a presumption of propriety. That presumption can be overcome only (if at all) by contrary evidence of means utterly inconsistent with his proper purpose.

If we once again consider the analogy to American law, the police power of a state is not only vital for its survival as a subject of governance; as we'll see, it is also undefined, and indeed indefinable. As a general rule, to identify an act of state governance as an exercise of the "police power" has meant to insulate it from serious constitutional scrutiny.[202]

Third, a householder who was unfit for his position of disciplinary authority exposed himself to disciplinary action from without and to disobedience from within. By acting upon his self-interest, rather than the interest of the household, he has revealed himself to be a mere member of that household, rather than its head, driven by private rather than public, personal rather than communal, interest. Incapable of demanding obedience, he is at best capable of giving it. By failing to police himself, he has shown himself unworthy of policing others.[203]

So far we have focused on the external consequences of this failure in office, the most dramatic illustration of which was the whipping of "brutal" wife beaters. Throughout the history of political theory, however, the *internal* consequences of unfitness have attracted far more attention. In feudal terms, the lord's pursuit of his self-interest at the expense of the interest of his household could amount to a felony, i.e., to a breach of the bond between lord and man. Theoretically, at least, we can surmise that the lord's violation of his obligation to care for his tenants released them from their duty of submission and loyalty to him. The feudal nexus of fealty had been broken.

Locke's *Second Treatise*, published in 1690, merely extends this conclusion from the lord's micro household to the macro household of the realm. While he insists that the power of lawmaking can be derived only from the consent of the governed, he does make room for the feudal bond in "some commonwealths," like England, "where the legislative is not always in being, and the executive is vested in a single person who has also a share in the legislative." In these political communities, "oaths of allegiance and fealty are taken to him," that "allegiance being nothing but an obedience according to law, which, when he violates, he has no right to obedience." That feudal bond is broken when he acts not by the "public will" manifested in law, but "by his own private will." In that case "*he degrades himself*, and is but a single private person without power and without will."[204] In that case, the Pennsylvania Constitution from 1776 concluded, "all allegiance and fealty to the said king and his successors, are dissolved and at an end, and all power and authority derived from him ceased. . . . "[205]

"[A] king," in other words, "may unking himself."[206] And to illustrate how the king can demean himself, Locke invokes the authority of none other than James I, whom he quotes at length:

> King James, in his speech to the Parliament, 1603, tells them thus: "I will ever prefer the weal of the public and of the whole commonwealth, in making of good laws and constitutions, to any particular and private ends of mine, thinking ever the wealth and weal of the commonwealth to be my greatest weal and worldly felicity—a point wherein a lawful king doth directly differ from a tyrant; for I do acknowledge that the special and greatest point of difference that is between a rightful king and an usurping tyrant is this—that whereas the proud and ambitious tyrant doth think his kingdom and people are only ordained for satisfaction of his desires and unreasonable appetites, the righteous and just king doth, by the contrary,

acknowledge himself to be ordained for the procuring of the wealth and property of his people."[207]

James frequently referred to the mutual bond connecting the king to his household, the realm. Already in 1598, he had declared that

> [b]y the law of nature the King becomes a naturall Father to all his Lieges at his Coronation. And as the father of his fatherly duty is bound to care for the nourishing, education and vertuous government of his children: even so is the King bound to care for all his subjects. . . . As the kindly father ought to foresee all inconvenients and dangers that may arise towards his children, and though with the hazard of his own person, presse to prevent the same: So ought the King toward his people. As the Fathers wrath & correction upon any of his children, that offendeth, ought to be by a fatherly chastizment seasoned with pity, as long as there is any hope of amendment in them: So ought the King towards any of his Lieges that offends in that measure. . . . As to the other branch of this mutuall, and reciprock band, is the duty and alleagance, that the Lieges owe to their King.[208]

At first sight, Locke's reliance on James I might be surprising; in fact, it surprised Pollock.[209] Locke certainly would not have agreed with James's derivation of his paternal power from God. Locke, after all, wanted to replace this attempt at divine legitimation of royal power with a theory of consent.

That doesn't mean, however, that Locke entirely rejected the familial model of governance.[210] Rather than abandoning it, and with it the king's authority as the father of the realm, Locke sought to put it in its place. The supreme power, he explained, was the power to make law. And this power could derive only from the consent of the governed. But the execution of law thus made and the protection of society against external threats, i.e., the maintenance of internal and external order, was an entirely different matter. These two powers, which Locke called executive and federative, respectively were analogous to the internal and external aspects of the householder authority to maximize the welfare of his family.[211]

2

Blackstone's Police

We are interested here not so much in Locke's distinction between the legislative and executive powers of government, on which Locke and political theory generally focus, but in the more fundamental distinction that underlies and motivates it, namely that between law and police. Of these two modes of governance, only law is based on consent. Clearly the attempt to separate the realm of legislation from the realm of execution is what's new about Locke's theory. But drawing a line between legislation and other governmental powers, and then declaring the supremacy of legislation (i.e., lawmaking), is significant precisely because it permits Locke to carve out a space for his theory of legitimacy based on consent.

That is not to say that Locke disregards the actual business of governing, which in his view is execution, not legislation. (After all, the executive never sleeps, while the legislative only meets occasionally.) And in this realm of administration, or housekeeping, the model of household governance survives intact, undisturbed by political theory and its elaborate apparatus for scrutinizing the legitimacy of state action. After Locke, governing through law must be legitimate—and for him, that meant consensual. Governing through police, by contrast, came to be held to a lower standard, of minimum competence; it must be not so irrational as to draw the householder's fitness into question.

The management of the societal household, in fact, becomes the subject of an altogether new discipline, the science of police (as opposed to political science). Thus freed of concerns about legitimacy, the science of police can concentrate itself entirely on the management of the household, on maximizing the wealth of the commonwealth. Here the state, and in Locke's time that meant the king, enjoys the same discretion that householders have enjoyed since time immemorial.

When Rousseau, some sixty years later, briefly turns his attention to the new subject of police, in his *Discourse on Political Economy*, he clearly sets out the line separating political philosophy from political economy, or law from police:

> I must here ask my readers to distinguish also between *public economy*, which is my subject and which I call *government*, and the supreme authority, which I call *Sovereignty*; a distinction which consists in the fact that the latter has the right of legislation, and in certain cases binds the body of the nation itself, while the former has only the right of execution, and is binding only on individuals.[1]

The similarity between Rousseau's distinction and Locke's is startling. Both view their task as differentiating between state and familial governance. And both end up drawing the same distinction. Rather than reject the familial model, they restrict it to the state, considered as a family. If anything, Rousseau is even clearer on this point than is Locke. The state remains a family, even to Rousseau, except that in "the great family" of the state, "all the members . . . are naturally equal."[2] This natural equality, however, only means that all should have an equal part in the *making* of laws. The inferiority of the citizen vis-à-vis the executive, acting under these laws, remains. The only difference, once again, between Rousseau, and Locke, on one side, and King James and Robert Filmer, on the other, is that this inferiority is not a command of the "law of nature." It is instead self-imposed insofar as the citizen binds himself through laws, which in turn authorize, and constrain, the executive who looks after the public economy, i.e., after the police of the state. From the point of view of governance and history, public economy is but an extension of private economy; they both seek to maximize the welfare of their household. As Rousseau explains:

> The word Economy, or Œconomy, is derived from *oikos, a house*, and *nomos, law*, and meant originally only the wise and legitimate government of the house for the common good of the whole family. The meaning of the term was then extended to the government of that great family, the State.[3]

This concept of police, as the governance of the state *as a household*, also plays a central role in Blackstone's *Commentaries on the Laws of England*, published shortly after Rousseau's *Discourse*. And from here it spread throughout

American law, from treatises on the police power to statutes to court opinions declaring common law misdemeanors to the police power jurisprudence in state and federal courts.

The concept of police as household management first, and appropriately, appears in Blackstone's discussion of the royal prerogative, in volume 1, published only ten years after Rousseau's *Discourse*, in 1765. The king's prerogative to regulate domestic commerce, and "public marts" in particular, "as may be most convenient for the neighborhood," derives from his power as macro householder. This regulation "forms a part of oeconomics, or domestic polity; which, considering the kingdom as a large family, and the king as the master of it, he clearly has a right to dispose and order as he pleases."[4]

Blackstone elaborated on the king's power to police in volume 4, published four years later, which contains his treatment of criminal law. There Blackstone explains that the king, as the "father" of his people,[5] and *"pater-familias* of the nation,"[6] was charged with

> the public police and oeconomy [, i.e.,] the due regulation and domestic order of the kingdom: whereby the individuals of the state, like members of a well-governed family, are bound to conform their general behaviour to the rules of propriety, good neighbourhood, and good manners: and to be decent, industrious, and inoffensive in their respective stations.[7]

This definition of police is of no mere theoretical interest. It appears at the outset of the section on offenses "against the public *police* and *oeconomy*." Blackstone clarifies that no comprehensive list of these offenses is possible. "This head of offences must therefore be very miscellaneous, as it comprises all such crimes as especially affect public society, and not comprehended under any of the four preceding species," i.e., offenses against public justice, the public peace, public trade, and the public health.

Given the influence Blackstone's notion of police was to have in American law, down to the chapter headings of nineteenth-century statutory revisions,[8] it's worth taking a closer look at the sort of offenses he categorized as violations of police. In this way, we may get a better sense of the concept itself.

As we read Blackstone, it's important to keep in mind the pedigree of his view of the king as parens patriae. Otherwise we might mistake it for the apologia of a royal sycophant, as a sort of proto-positivist enamored with law as royal command. Blackstone merely follows a long tradition of political and legal thought that viewed the king as the head of the macro household of the state. To appreciate just how straight the line from the feudal nexus of the household to Blackstone is, consider this passage on the relationship between king and subject, taken from volume 1 of the *Commentaries*: "Allegiance is the tie, or *ligamen*, which binds the subject to the king, in return for that protection which the king affords the subject."[9]

At the origin, and the heart, of this tradition lay the powerful notion of the householder's *mund*, which as we've seen can be traced back to Germanic law, and farther yet to the power of the Roman and eventually the Greek householder.[10] It's no surprise that Blackstone himself speaks of the king as the "*paterfamilias*" of his country. The source of royal power, in this tradition, is the *mund* attached to the household of the king. The story of the expansion of royal power is the story of the expansion of that *mund*, in the form of the king's peace, which eventually encompassed the entire realm, and all of society.

Eventually and gradually, the institutional significance of the original household gave way to that of the new and expanding macro household. With the shift of the center of institutional gravity came a shift in the center of disciplinary authority. The family as a model of central governance replaced the network of individual families. As the entire state transforms itself into a single family, Rousseau's "great family of the state,"[11] the *ur*family, becomes one social group among others within the *über*family of the entire realm, under the authority of the *über*father, the king.

This transformation, the beginnings of which we saw in the expansion of the king's *mund* and the leveling of all men before his superior authority, occurred not only gradually, but also in stops and starts. Yet occur it did, and certainly by the time of Blackstone, but very likely earlier, the king is firmly entrenched as the father of his people, equipped with wide disciplinary authority over the members of his household, all in the name of the household's welfare. The core family continues to play an important role, but only to the extent it fits into the larger governmental scheme of the *über*father. So the king-father may assign certain tasks of control to the family, and to its head, much as he might assign them to his officials in the field.[12] In the large scheme of things, the family head occupies a role roughly analogous to a royal official, as opposed to a member of the royal family, a fact that already was reflected in the similar treatment of lords and royal officials in the Treason Act of 1351.

Vagrants and Other Disorderly Persons

A particularly dramatic sign of the king-father's adoption of tasks originally performed by the non-royal householder came with the breakup of feudal estates in the fourteenth century, which resulted in considerable social disorder, further aggravated by the devastating effects of the Black Death. The Statute of Labourers, enacted shortly before the Treason Act, marked a comprehensive attempt to discipline the macro household of the realm.[13] That central ordering effort still made heavy use of the local institutions of disciplinary power, namely the households. Able-bodied men were prohibited from refusing offers of work, which also meant integration into the structure of a local household, under the direction of a householder.

The Statute of Labourers would become only the first in a long line of increasingly complex, and punitive, efforts to control the members of the *über*-household, particularly those who were not under the authority of the network of ordinary households dispersed throughout the country. The concept of vagrancy was born.

The control of vagrants and various and sundry "disorderly persons" became one of the central preoccupations of the macro household. In fact, of the nine offenses on Blackstone's list of police offenses, three dealt with various forms of vagrancy. This made sense. A vagrant, after all, was someone who had fallen outside the scope of traditional government in the micro household. He therefore was the perfect candidate for early governance at the macro level.

Beginning in the first half of the sixteenth century with Henry VIII's Act relating to Vagabonds of 1536,[14] the English macro householder began to pay serious attention to the problem of idle unattached persons roaming the countryside. Later in the century, during the reign of Elizabeth I, we find a statute providing for the execution of "idle soldiers and mariners wandering about the realm."[15] Another imposes the same punishment on any one of those "outlandish persons calling themselves Egyptians," "a strange kind of commonwealth . . . of wandering impostors and jugglers," as well as on "any person . . . which hath been seen or found in the fellowship of such Egyptians . . . [and who] shall remain in the same for one month."[16]

These two offenses were felonies, which by that time meant they were punishable by death, the days of *bót* and *wíte* having long since passed. And they still appeared on Blackstone's list of police offenses in 1769, two centuries later.

The next milestone in the control of vagrancy came in 1597, with another Elizabethan statute. This statute proved popular in the American colonies as well, thus illustrating the appearance of macro policing in the New World long before the wholesale adoption of Blackstone's notion of police in the late eighteenth and nineteenth centuries. Here is Arthur Scott's account of the state of vagrancy law in Virginia circa 1750:

> In 1672 the Assembly found it necessary to order that the English laws against vagrants should be strictly enforced. The chief of these laws was the 39 Eliz., chapter 4 (1597), which permitted the erection of houses of correc-

tion in any county, and directed that rogues and vagabonds were to be whipped by order of a justice, constable, or tithingman, and sent to their own parishes, there to be put in the house of correction until employment was found for them, or until they were banished. The law of 1 James I, chapter 7 (1604), provided that incorrigible and dangerous rogues might by order of the justices be branded with the letter R. . . . The English statute 17 Geo. II, chapter 5, repealed the earlier laws on vagrancy, and went on to provide for the punishment of idle and disorderly persons, vagabonds, and incorrigible rogues. It was from this statute that the Assembly copied extensively in 1748. . . . The law defined vagabonds, and provided that they were to be taken by warrant before a justice, who might order them whipped from constable to constable like runaways, until they reached the parish in which their families last resided. At that point the local justices were to take a bond that the delinquents would find work. Failing this, the next County Court might bind such persons to work for a year.[17]

Notice here the combination of two aspects of traditional household governance. First, there is the use of whipping—the traditional disciplinary tool against inferior household members—by state officials, reflecting the central authority's assumption of certain comprehensive order maintenance tasks. But second, the use of central householding power still serves merely to return the lordless to an established household. By now, however, the household no longer is the traditional familial community, but consists of a quasi-family, the "house of correction," where a warden performs the disciplining for a network of traditional households grouped into a new political entity, the county.

This strategy of social control did not differ substantially from the traditional practice of forcing all men to attach themselves to a lord, or face outlawry as "lordless" men instead. The Laws of King Æthelstan, for example, had this to say "of lordless men": "And we have ordained: respecting those lordless men of whom no law can be got, that the kindred be commanded that they domicile him to folk-right, and find him a lord in the folk-mote; and if they then will not or cannot produce him at the term, then be he thenceforth a 'flyma' [outlaw], and let him slay him for a thief who can come at him: and whoever after that shall harbour him, let him pay for him according to his 'wer,' or by it clear himself."[18]

The macro householder here is using his paternal authority indirectly. Rather than assume the correction of the disorderly personally, he assigns that task to the existing micro households. The family has been instrumentalized, and integrated into the state's comprehensive system of social control. With the erection of houses of correction, the state begins to take more direct responsibility for maintaining order within the realm. Its general strategy, however, still relies on the distribution of responsibility to the proper local authority, as evidenced by the requirement that vagrants be returned to "their own parishes."

Other colonies, particularly those in which the central police authority was less well developed, did not concern themselves much with the problem of assignment. Someone who did not belong to a resident household had two options: join one or be banished.

First came the attempt to identify the unattached. So a Massachusetts law from 1668 required towns "to take a list of the names of those young persons within the bounds of your Town, and all adjacent Farms though out of all Town bounds, who do live from under Family Government, viz. do not serve their Parents or Masters, as Children, Apprentices, hired Servants, or Journey men ought to do, and usually did in our Native Country, being subject to their commands and discipline."[19]

Then came the order to integrate, or to leave. As Robert Steinfeld reports, the Plymouth Colony followed suit the next year by passing a law regarding single persons: "Whereas great Inconvenience hath arisen by single persons in this Collonie being for themselves and not betakeing themselves to live in well Governed families It is enacted by the Court that henceforth noe single persons be suffered to live of himselfe."[20]

So much for those already living in a community. Newcomers faced the same choice between integration or banishment. They could either produce a household that assumed responsibility for their well-being, and discipline, or they were "warned out."[21] No one cared where they might go, the presumption being that they might "returne to the place from whence [they] came."

Offenses Against "the Public Police and Oeconomy"

Vagrancy, or rather idleness, figured prominently on Blackstone's list of police offenses. Under the newest vagrancy statute, 17 Geo. II, chapter 5, which we've already encountered, the severity of discipline increased as the amenability to correctional treatment decreased. "Idle and disorderly persons" were punished by one month's imprisonment, "rogues and vagabonds" by whipping and imprisonment of up to six months, "incorrigible rogues" by whipping and imprisonment of up to two years. While the least serious type of vagrant retained the title of a "person" with the incidental qualities of being "idle and disorderly," the more serious types were defined exclusively by their deviant status: they are "rogues and vagabonds," rather than persons. Any hope for a reclassification as a person was lost in the case of the most aggravated type of vagrant, the "incorrigible rogue."

All of these vagrants posed a threat to the public police simply by their existence. They were, in Blackstone's words, "offenders against the good order, and blemishes in the government, of any kingdom."[22] As blemishes, they had to be removed. Removed they could be through reeducation or, if they are inherently and unalterably deviant, through incapacitation.

These vagrancy laws, however, were only the tip of a police iceberg. Even before their categorization (and correction) as deviant, suspicious persons were subject to control under an altogether different set of preventive measures, sureties for keeping the peace or for good behavior "intended merely for prevention, without any crime actually committed by the party, but arising only from a probable suspicion, that some crime is intended or likely to happen."[23] Any justice of the peace could demand such a guarantee on his own discretion or at the request of any person upon "due cause."[24] If the bound person violated the conditions of his bond (to keep the peace or to show good behavior), he forfeited to the king the amount posted.[25]

The recognizance for good behavior "towards the king and his people" applied to "all them that be not of good fame." Just who fell in this category was up to the individual magistrate. There appears to have been a substantial overlap between members of this group and those convicted of police offenses. Here is Blackstone's attempt to illustrate the scope of the limitless concept:

> Under the general words of this expression, that be not of good fame, it is holden that a man may be bound to his good behaviour for causes of scandal, contra bonos mores, as well as contra pacem; as, for haunting bawdy houses with women of bad fame; or of keeping such women in his own house; or for words tending to scandalize the government; or in abuse of the officers of justice, especially in the execution of their office. Thus also a justice may bind over all night-walkers; eaves-droppers; such as keep suspicious company, or are reported to be pilferers or robbers; such as sleep in the day, and wake on the night; common drunkards; whoremasters; the putative father of bastards; cheats; idle vagabonds; and other persons, whose misbehaviour may reasonably bring them within the general words of the statute.[26]

Threats to the public police, then, were subject to a three-step disposal regime. First came the surety bond, designed to avert the manifestation of the threat by tying it to conditional financial loss. Next, for police threats so substantial as not to be amenable to such inducements for self-correction, came the forced correction through fines, whipping, infamous punishments, or imprisonment. And finally, for the incorrigible rogues beyond all hope of reintegration, there was the prospect of incapacitation through prolonged and repeated imprisonment.

So far, we have dealt with the three vagrancy-type offenses on Blackstone's list of police offenses. In addition to the vagrancy laws themselves, we mentioned the sixteenth-century laws against "soldiers and mariners wandering about the realm" and against "outlandish persons" and their fellows. Six of the nine police offenses still remain.

Two of these were felonies, and therefore punishable by death. The offense of "clandestine marriages" protects the integrity of the family by policing its origin in the marriage ceremony, as well as the authority of the (Anglican) state church, which holds the monopoly on performing this foundational ceremony. In particular, it prohibits "solemnizing" marriages outside certain churches ("except by licence from the archbishop"), marriages without publishing "banns" (absent a "licence obtained from a proper authority"), and various forgeries and false entries in the marriage register. The first two are punished by fine ("pecuniary forfeiture"), the third by death.

Note the brutal punishment of official forgeries. The attempt to assume official authority, to elevate oneself from an object to the subject of power, threatens the very order upon which the hierarchical edifice of the quasi-familial commonwealth is built. The king, after all, also was "the head and supreme governor of the national church."[27] This phenomenon is not new. Recall that counterfeiting originally was punished as a form of treason.[28]

Bigamy is the other capital police offense. It so disrupts the "public oeconomy and decency of a well ordered state" that it too is felony (but with benefit of clergy, meaning that it will not be punished by death absent an earlier conviction of a clergiable felony). Though he stresses the seriousness of the offense, Blackstone struggles to justify it. He associates it darkly with habits of "eastern nations," which are contrasted with the "rational civil establishment" of the English commonwealth.[29]

Bigamy threatens the foundation of the familial model central to the notion of police in at least three ways. First, it disrupts the orderly functioning of individual families, not only by creating uncertainties about the place of the additional wife (or husband) within the familial hierarchy, but also by complicating questions of legitimacy and eventually of inheritance. Second, because the family was the model for the structure and operation of society in general, any challenge to the structure and operation of individual families threatened disruptions on a societal scale.

Third, the existence of alternative familial communities posed a threat to the orderliness of society simply because they were alternative. Bigamous or polygamous families hinted at a foreign origin and were associated with foreigners, and as alien institutions represented potential threats the depths of which could not be fathomed and therefore warranted extreme caution. As the persecution of "outlandish persons calling themselves Egyptians," the punishment of bigamy thus appears to reflect the general xenophobia that pervaded early modern society even more so than in does today.[30]

Among the non-capital police offenses listed by Blackstone, common nuisances occupy the first spot. These "inconvenient or troublesome offenses, as annoy the whole community in general" include

(1) various acts or omissions (such as "annoyances in highways, bridges, and public rivers, by rendering the same inconvenient or dangerous to pass," "the keeping of hogs in any city or market town," lotteries, and "the making and selling of fireworks and squibs, or throwing them about in any street"),

(2) various persons ("[e]aves-droppers, or such as listen under walls or windows, or the eaves of a house, to hearken after discourse" and the "common scold, communis rixatrix, (for our law-latin confines it to the feminine gender)"), and

(3) various inanimate objects, most particularly buildings ("disorderly inns or ale-houses, bawdy-houses, gaming-houses, stage-plays unlicensed, booths and stages for rope-dancers, mountebanks, and the like" and cottages "being harbours for thieves and other idle and dissolute persons").

Without going into these offenses in any great detail, it's worth noting that this list displays the sort of impatience with principle and specificity that characterizes household governance and, as we will see in greater detail below, the police power and its exercise in the macro household of the state. The point of police is the suppression of threats to the public police. It's governed by considerations of efficiency, not formal justice. In this light, the vagueness of a concept such as "nuisance" is not a problem, but an asset. Unconstrained by notice concerns, state officials—not only courts, but executive officials as well—could mold it as they saw fit to deal with "annoyances" to the public at large.

Already a quick glance at the mishmash of offenses on Blackstone's list makes it clear that, in the face of a threat to the communal police, familiar niceties of criminal law doctrine, such as the distinction between omissions and commissions, were of no significance. The general unwillingness to extend criminal liability to omissions was not to stand in the way of the public welfare. The traditional "act requirement," which limited criminal liability to behavior rather than status or thought, similarly lost all purchase when it came to policing gypsies, eaves-droppers, or common scolds. Another great bulwark of Anglo-American criminal law, the "mens rea requirement," which frowned upon punishing nonintentional conduct, fared no better.

Likewise, when the public police was at stake, vicarious criminal liability was no longer objectionable. In the end, it mattered not whether the annoyance was a person (such as a communis rixatrix) or a thing (such as a building). As a nuisance, it required removal.

The status-focus of police offenses comes through loud and clear in the remaining four categories of police offenses Blackstone identifies. People at the bottom of the hierarchy were policed whenever they fell out of line. In fact, they were caught in a bind. If they didn't fulfill their obligation to contribute to the familial community's well-being by performing the menial tasks appropriate to their status, they were policed as idle persons. On the other hand, if they did work hard and through their industry gained the means to acquire the external trimmings of someone higher up in the hierarchy, they ran afoul of another set of police offenses, sumptuary laws against "*luxury*, and extravagant expenses in dress, diet, and the like,"[31] number 7 on Blackstone's list.[32]

"Gaming" statutes too concerned themselves with status and station.[33] Their central concern—apart from some gentle reminders to gentlemen about the dangers of compulsive gambling—was to eliminate the threat any sort of amusement posed to the public police, by "promot[ing] public idleness, theft, and debauchery among those of a lower class." Based on this inchoate idleness theory, gaming statutes were designed "to restrain this pernicious vice, among the inferior sort of people." So we find a statute from the time of Henry VIII. "prohibit[ing] to all but gentlemen the games of tennis, tables, cards, dice, bowls, and other unlawful diversions there specified, unless in the time of christmas."[34] People of "the inferior sort" were not to gamble because it kept them from contributing to the public welfare through their labor both directly, as they could make more productive use of their time, and indirectly, by plunging them into the abyss of a debauched lifestyle. Plus, since gaming was acceptable for gentlemen, but not for others, playing tennis by itself amounted to trying to pass for a gentleman, a violation of the familial order akin to the excessive dress or diet policed by the sumptuary laws, or by the prohibitions against counterfeiting or fraudulent marriages.[35]

The final item on Blackstone's list of police offenses are the game laws, which concern the "destroying such beasts and fowls, as are ranked under the denomination of game." According to Blackstone, "it is an offence which the sportsmen of England seem to think of the highest importance; and a matter, perhaps, the only one, of general and national concern."[36] It is also an offense that is entirely about the oppression of "low and indigent persons," in particular—and once again—those who act (or simply are) out of place, either by claiming for themselves a right reserved for those of higher status (the "sportsmen of England") or by—once again—doing something, in this case hunting, that "takes them away from their proper employments and callings; which is an offence against the public police and oeconomy of the commonwealth."

The game laws, however, are noteworthy because they too illustrate the use of police offenses to maintain the lines separating various levels within the (macro) familial hierarchy, and therefore familial order. They also show that not all of these lines are created equal. The one line that counts above all, and the one whose strict maintenance is vital to the maintenance of the community, is that between the head of the household (here, the king) and everyone else. In the end, "the inferior sort of people" includes also "the sportsmen of England" who delight in whipping their respective inferiors into place.

At bottom, game laws are pure obedience offenses. Game is royal property and it is within the king's pleasure whether or not to grant someone a license to kill it. So, while game laws on their face govern the relationship between license holders and others, they themselves are based on the fundamental distinction between the king and all other members of his communal family. Without a license, anyone who kills game is guilty of trespass, i.e., of "encroaching on the royal prerogative." But this fact is often forgotten for all the attention is focused on those "indigent persons," who are guilty not only of an offense against the king, but more immediately against their local lord. These supplemental offenses, as Blackstone himself noted, are "so severely punished, and those punishments so implacably inflicted, that the offence against the king is seldom thought of, provided the miserable delinquent can make his peace with the lord of the manor."[37] According to Blackstone, then, the problem with game laws is not their existence, but their enforcement, and interpretation. They are enforced by local patriarchs, whereas they ought to be seen as manifestations of the power of the royal patriarch. They protect the peace of the king, not that of the local lord, no matter what the latter might think (and have "the miserable delinquent" believe).

In sum, Blackstone regards the power of police as deriving from the king's obligation to maximize the welfare of his household, the realm. The king's police regulates the public oeconomy of the state, as the father's discipline does the private oeconomy of the family.[38] As the father, as *paterfamilias*, is entitled to enforce his authority through disciplinary measures, so is the king as *pater patriae*.[39] Any violation of the order of the family, and any challenge to his authority, may be punished by the head of the petty, or of the grand, commonwealth. No more precise definition of offenses against the police of the family or of the realm can be given than of the notion of police itself. Any correction inflicted for such an offense, however, occurs for the benefit of its object *as a member of the household*, and therefore ultimately for the benefit of both the micro and the macro household and its respective heads.[40]

Police in Colonial America

Blackstone's discussion of police offenses in volume four of the *Commentaries* exerted tremendous influence on American legislators, judges, and commentators. Blackstone's general influence on American law, and on the thought of the revolutionary generation, was of course monumental, and would remain so for decades, even centuries, from the most general issues of political theory to the most specific issues of legal doctrine.[41] And his discussion of police was no exception. When it came time for state legislators to order the internal police of their state, they turned to Blackstone for drafting advice. Ernst Freund, the last great American police commentator, noted in 1904, in the introduction to his monumental treatise on the police power: "The influence of Blackstone's arrangement is noticeable in the legislation of those states which have made police one of the principal divisions of their statutory revisions." Freund continues: "The term police appears first as a division of legislation in the Revised Statutes of New York in 1829, Massachusetts adopted it in the Revision of 1836, it is now also found in Delaware, Iowa, New Hampshire, Ohio, Rhode Island, Washington, and Wisconsin."[42]

Blackstone's influence can also be seen among the commentators on the police power, including Freund himself. As a matter of course, every major treatise on the police power quoted, in its introduction, Blackstone's definition of police from his discussion of police offenses in volume four of the *Commentaries*.[43]

Judges, too, frequently invoked Blackstone's concept of police, often quoting his definition at length, and so did counsel. Few general discussions of the police power were complete without reciting Blackstone's demarcation of the king-father's responsibility for maintaining "the public police and oeconomy" of his kingdom-family. So in an 1843 case before the Illinois Supreme Court we find counsel for the appellant, convicted of "secreting" a slave from Missouri, invoking Blackstone's definition in support of the—unsuccessful—claim that Illinois's fugitive slave law was not a police regulation, and therefore not immune from federal constitutional scrutiny.[44] To cite another example, the quote also appears, some forty years later, at the heart of a much cited Pennsylvania Supreme Court opinion on the courts' authority to punish nonstatutory, "common law," crimes.[45] Courts continued to rely on Blackstone's definition until well into the 1970s.[46]

But simply to trace Blackstone's influence on American law would not be enough. It would fail to capture the full scope of the police concept in American political and legal thought and practice. It would also create the false impression that the notion of police had played no role in American governance before the enthusiastic reception of Blackstone's work.

Different colonies were governed according to different models of the household. In Maryland and South Carolina, for example, the framework for government derived from its proprietary origin as a commercial enterprise.[47] Its government was a matter of managing property, or of running a corporation. Governed by charters the king granted to private proprietors, the colony was administered to maximize profit. Governing Virginia also was an economic affair, but for a different reason and in a different sense. It spent several of its early years under military government, which presumably influenced the way its colonial administrators conceived of their task.[48]

Whether they ran a commercial or a military enterprise, colonial officials were keen on protecting their authority. And they did not hesitate to correct any of their charges who did not display the proper respect and obedience, usually with the traditional measures of household discipline, particularly whipping.[49]

The model of governance in the Northeastern colonies was different. Nonetheless here too the idea of household governance manifested itself, though not primarily in the form of a corporate enterprise, or a military camp, but as a religious community. In Massachusetts and Pennsylvania, for example, religious communities, no matter of what denomination and or size, were run and viewed as larger scale families under the authority of ministers or elders.[50] Congregations were large families, and families little churches.[51] In the words of Edmund Morgan, "[t]he essence of the social order lay . . . in the superiority of husband over wife, parents over children, and master over servants in the family, ministers and elders over congregation in the church, rulers over subjects in the state."[52]

The church constituted not only an expanded familial community, but itself formed part of a larger family, which reached beyond the local pastor to the king and eventually to God, the Father. "Authority," under this view of the social world, "should descend, that is, be derived from a superior to an inferior, from God to fathers and kings, and from kings and fathers to sons and servants."[53] Every political community thus found its place within the universal family of the Christian Church, under the limitless, even incomprehensible, authority of God.

Here too, all were equal, but only in their inferiority to a superior being.[54] Whatever authority any human enjoyed over another, he enjoyed at the discretion and by delegation of God. This meant that the power of every head of a political household was limited, and subject to divine revocation. It also meant that every threat to the authority of any person of authority in any political community also was a threat to the authority of God. As such, it shook the foundation of the entire social order and could not be tolerated.

In addition to the quasi-households of the military, the corporation, and the church, there was another model of governance that must have influenced the way the colonists approached the task of governance in the New World. This household was the English manor, the models' model, so to speak. The significance of this influence may have varied, depending on where in England the colonists originated. Those who came from sparsely populated rural areas may well have lived without meaningful contact with manorial government. Yet even the fairly independent farmer would be familiar with household governance, simply because he would have to govern a household of his own. At any rate it would seem that, to the extent they were integrated into any system of government in the home country, that system was the manor, run by the lord and subject to manorial jurisdiction. Just what manorial government looked like is a fairly difficult, and contested, question. Suffice it to say that manorial government functioned as another model of household governance that guided the early colonists' ideas about how to govern.[55]

The most clear-cut illustration of police power before the invention of American "police power," however, is provided by the governance of slaves in the American colonies. We've already mentioned the efforts of plantation owners, supplemented if necessary by the public discipline meted out by officials in colonial Virginia, to govern slaves as members of their household. Now as Jonathan Bush has brilliantly shown, the law of slavery was in fact "an extensive set of police measures" at both the level of the private household of the plantation and of the public household of the colony.[56] On the plantation, the internal police was maintained according to guidelines of good household government, or domestic economy, "described in plantation manuals and rule-books, and enforced with whipping and other punishments, including death."[57]

The internal police of the colony in turn relied on slave codes that resembled Blackstone's treatment of police offenses in that they too lacked conceptual structure and were content to accumulate, without any claims to comprehensiveness, lists of illustrative offenses. As an example, Bush cites the Virginia Slave Code of 1705, which listed, "under four dozen more or less random titles, the activities that slaves and indentured servants cannot do, must do, or cannot do with whites, the things that whites cannot do for slaves, and that blacks cannot do even if free."[58]

Neither the private, nor the public, version of these compilations of police measures was addressed to those who would suffer from their violation. The slaves were the objects of police, but they were not the audience of police measures. The plantation manuals and slave codes were just that, manuals designed to guide the administration of the private or public household. They were handbooks of good housekeeping, in the tradition of Greek economics.

But Bush makes another, more general and more important, point. He remarks that these guidebooks were examples of "boundary law": the slave codes "defined and patrolled the public boundaries between free and slave and between non-white and white."[59] And the plantation manuals performed the same function, in the private context of the micro household.

Policing the boundary between black and white, however, was only one, early, strategy for the maintenance of the distinction between householder and household. Crossing the line between black and white was an inchoate offense against the all-important line between governor and governed. Any black man who failed to show the proper respect for any white man mounted an inchoate challenge against the authority of the white householder over his household.[60]

So by the time Blackstone published his catalogue of offenses against "the public police and oeconomy" in 1769, American governance could look back on an extensive tradition of policing in fact, if not in name. What's more, colonial officials employed some of the very laws that Blackstone would later list as exercises of the king's power to police. As we saw, Blackstone's police offense par excellence, vagrancy, was a colonial police offense long before anyone thought of it as such. None of this is a surprise, of course, since Blackstone merely classified statutes that were around at the time, and many of which dated back centuries. And these very statutes applied to the American colonies just as they did to the English home country.

A contemporary American reader of the *Commentaries* thus wouldn't have been surprised by any of the policing offenses on Blackstone's list. Perhaps he might have added a few policing tools that were genuine American innovations, in particular the slave codes, but in general the list would have looked familiar indeed.

3 | Continental Police Science

The one thing that might have given our American reader pause is Blackstone's categorization of patriarchal governance as "police." By the late 1760s, the concept of police had been around for four hundred years, and had become a mainstay of continental political and legal thought and practice for at least a century. Particularly in France and then in Germany, an entire "science of police" had been created, and since the fifteenth century police laws, regulations, and ordinances, as well as police courts, and eventually police officials and officers, had appeared all over continental states and cities. In Scotland too, the first "Commissioners of Police" had been appointed by Queen Anne in 1714.[1] These "six noblemen and four gentlemen" were in charge of the "general internal administration of the country."[2]

The Scottish Enlightenment also had taken an interest in the concept, as illustrated by Adam Smith's *Lectures on Justice, Police, Revenue and Arms*, delivered at Glasgow in the 1750s and early 1760s.[3] Smith differentiated between "political regulations" founded "upon the principle of *justice*" and upon that of "*expediency*," the latter being "calculated to increase the riches, the power, and the prosperity of a State."[4] Jurisprudence, according to Smith, involves both right and prudence, justice and police:

Jurisprudence is the theory of the general principles of law and government.

The four great objects of law are Justice, Police, Revenue, and Arms.

The object of Justice is the security from injury, and it is the foundation of civil government.

63

The objects of Police are the cheapness of commodities, public security, and cleanliness.[5]

Smith was mainly interested in one particular aspect of police, the "cheapness of commodities," or "the opulence of a state." The other two aspects of police, cleanliness and public security, he mentioned only briefly, finding them "too minute for a lecture of this kind."[6] His concern with the opulence of a state eventually produced the *Wealth of Nations*.[7]

Unlike Blackstone, Smith presented an account of the origins of the concept of police. This account is worth a closer look, for several reasons. It gives us a fairly good sense of common notions of police at the time, for Smith presents this part of his lectures as conventional summary, in sharp contrast to his expansive and detailed explorations of what we might call political economy in the narrow sense. In particular, Smith here repeats the conventional wisdom that "police" is of French origin,[8] a fact that made little difference to thinkers like Smith (or Bentham, or Blackstone), but may explain why, in England, the word police "was still viewed with disfavour after 1760."[9] Moreover, it captures some of the familiar features of police, including its means (prevention and intimidation), its ends (public security, public peace, and intercourse), and its objects (disturbances and villains). Finally, it highlights the conceptual connection between public security and neatness, between keeping the streets safe and clean:

> Police, the word, has been borrowed by the English immediately from the French, tho it is originally derived from the Greek *politeia* signifying policy, politicks, or the regulation of a government in generall. It is now however generally confind to the regulation of the inferior parts of it. It comprehends in generall three things: the attention paid by the public to the cleanlyness of the roads, streets, etc; 2d, security; and thirdly, cheapness or plenty, which is the constant source of it. When Mr. Lamonion was constituted Intendant of Paris he was told by the officers that the king required three things of him, that he was to provide for the neteté, surete, and bon marché in the city. . . . The *neteté* of a country regards the regulations made in order to preserv(e) cleanlyness of the roads, streets, etc. and prevent the bad effects of corrupting and putrifying substances. . . . The security of the people is the object of the second branch of police, that is, the preventing all crimes and disturbances which may interrupt the intercourse or destroy the peace of the society by any violent attacks. In generall the best means of bringing about this desirable end is the rigorous, severe, and exemplary execution of laws properly formd for the prevention of crimes and establishing the peace of the state.—Other

methods are sometimes more directly taken for this purpose—more immediately striking at the injurious persons. Of this there is a great deal in the French towns. Every one has a march possé or town guard who patrole in the streets and by that means intimidate villains from attempting any crimes and make the escape of a murder(er) or robber more difficult, and also give their assistance at the extinguishing of fires or other hazardous accidents.[10]

According to Smith, then, jurisprudence—or "juris prudence"[11]—falls into two parts, each of which governed by its own set of three principles. The more familiar cry for "égalité, liberté, fraternité" in law confronts, in Smith's account, the kingly instruction of "neteté, sureté, and bon marché" in police.

England was, apparently, a different story. The Oxford English Dictionary quotes an article from 1763, which explains that "from an aversion to the French . . . and something under the name of *police* being already established in Scotland, English prejudice will not soon be reconciled with it."[12] In 1756, another magazine writer had commented that "[w]e are accused by the French . . . of having no word in our language, which answers to their word *police*, which therefore we have been obliged to adopt, not having, as they say, the thing."[13]

Blackstone himself doesn't use the term police until the last volume of his *Commentaries*, published in 1769. In the first volume, published in 1765, he still speaks in terms of the king's right, as "master" of the kingdom considered as a "large family," to regulate "oeconomics, or domestic polity . . . as he pleases."[14] Only four years later, Blackstone explains that the king is responsible for "the public police and oeconomy" of the state."[15]

Now, to the extent Americans thought of Blackstone's police when they thought of police, they adopted a concept that was, as we've seen, steeped in the long tradition of household management. Blackstone's definition makes sense only if we see it in the context of his general theory of the royal prerogative, which is nothing but a modernization and radicalization of the age-old power of the householder over his household. Blackstone of course is remarkably explicit about this foundation in "economics." After all, he again and again refers to the king as the father of the kingdom, the pater patriae, and even the *paterfamilias*.

Following a long royalist tradition, Blackstone is careful to point out that, despite the common roots of the power of all householders, large and small, the king's *mund* nonetheless surpassed that of ordinary lords. So, for example, he explains that the king is owed allegiance and fealty, whereas the "inferior lord" is owed only the latter: "With us in England, it [is] becoming a settled principle of tenure, that *all* lands in the kingdom are holden of the king as their sovereign and lord paramount, no oath but that of fealty could ever be taken to inferior lords, and the oath of allegiance was necessarily confined to the person of the king alone."[16]

In fact, the very concept of police can be seen as a similar attempt to differentiate between the king's householder power and that of other householders. The task of governing the macro household of the state and the micro household of the family is essentially the same. The two households differ in size, not in quality. The one after all developed through an extension of the other. Yet, once the king has extended his household to cover the entire realm, and thereby to encompass all the other households, the next step is to stress the uniqueness of his householding task, and therefore of his position. And so that task receives a new name: police. Police is *public* police and by definition concerns itself with the welfare of the people, the nation, the community, in distinction from the father's traditional task of looking out for his family.

Yet police, at the same time, remains that concept in the discourse of governance which most vividly recalls the familial origins of state power. Even Blackstone, otherwise so concerned to emphasize the king-householder's special status, derives the concept of police from the authority of the *paterfamilias* over his kingdom, considered as a family. The king's prerogative may mark him off from members of his household, including the "inferior lords," but a householder he remains nonetheless. Even the "lord paramount" remains a lord.

Still, it's noteworthy that in accepting Blackstone's concept of police, the Americans enthusiastically embraced a mode of governance that was intimately connected to the royal prerogative, precisely the kind of arbitrary rule based on the strict separation between governor and governed that they found so intolerable in other contexts. It's one thing to adopt a notion of police; it's another to adopt a notion of royal police. Yet adopt it the Americans did, presumably on the ground that police was not necessarily royal police, and that police was a mode of governance common to all government as such. Possibly the idea of police could be cleansed of its monarchical elements, perhaps by resurrecting the traditional notion of police as patriarchal household governance, which arose long before the English monarchy and what Americans saw as its oppressive potentialities and tendencies.

There were after all other sources of the concept of police that Americans might have adapted, or adopted. Blackstone certainly didn't invent the concept. We've already noted that the concept of police can be traced back to the fourteenth century. Its origins are hazy, though pretty much everyone agrees that they are French.[17]

The Science of the Police State

Unfortunately, these non-Blackstonian sources presented Americans with a concept of police no less monarchical, and oppressive. If anything, the police of the continental tradition was even more closely associated with princely power, and plenary princely power at that.[18] Police, after all, was the paradigmatic mode of governance in the absolutist monarchies of continental Europe. The science of police was the art of regulating the police state.

The Americans of the time clearly paid much attention to Cesare Beccaria's *Crimes and Punishments*, as did everyone else interested in matters of criminal law, including Blackstone.[19] If they also came across Beccaria's lesser known work in the area of "public economy," they might have noticed that Beccaria held the uncontroversial view that police was an "object" of public economy and that it comprehended such matters as "the sciences, education, good order, security and public tranquility."[20] They also would have learned that Beccaria approached the subject of public economy from a distinctly familial perspective. To him, public and private economy were different, yet intimately connected: "the study of public oeconomy must necessarily enlarge and elevate the views of private oeconomy, by suggesting the means of uniting our own interest with that of the publick." From the point of view of public economy, we "no longer look upon ourselves as solitary parts of society, but as the children of the public, of the laws, and of the sovereign."[21]

Beccaria's fleeting comments on police and public economy are neither fertile nor original. It's unlikely that they would have done much to inspire American minds of the revolutionary era. At any rate, our earlier discussion of Rousseau's far more widely read sophisticated essay on political economy shows that Rousseau said what Beccaria said, and said it better, even if he doesn't use the term "police."[22]

We know that Emmerich de Vattel's *Law of Nations* was widely read in America by the early nineteenth century. Whether he was quite as popular during the formative period of the police concept in American discourse during the 1770s and 1780s isn't so clear. Although his treatise first appeared in 1759, its first American edition didn't appear until 1805.[23] His importance in treatments of the question of police appears to have grown as that question increasingly transformed itself into one regarding the proper relations between the federal government and the states, which resisted all attempts to interfere with their "internal police."[24] Vattel's primary interest, after all, was international law, not domestic law.

For that reason, anyone turning to Vattel would have found his comments on police, the domestic matter par excellence, rather sketchy, as well as rather republican. Still, there too the reader would have encountered the now familiar view that "the sovereign . . . ought in every thing to appear as the father of his people."[25] Vattel's definition of police is not particularly helpful. He simply remarks that "[t]he internal police consists in the attention of the prince and magistrates to preserve every thing in order."[26] Wisdom is the mark of good policing, for "[b]y a wise police, the sovereign accustoms the people to order and obedience, and preserves peace, tranquility, and concord among the citizens."[27] Vattel's scattered comments on police read like fragments from an old guidebook on good princely government.

American writings on police occasionally refer to Bentham's treatments of the subject. So Cooley quotes Bentham's definition of police in his influential *Treatise on Constitutional Limitations*.[28] In Bentham's case we can be fairly certain that any influence came after the first appearance of the concept in American political thought.

Unlike Beccaria, Rousseau, and Vattel, however, Bentham had a lot to say about police. Like them, what he said was not original, nor was it meant to be. Still, it's worth a look, not only because of its influence on later American police discourse, but also for Bentham's characteristic attention to analytic distinctions. Plus, it captures many of the features of police worked out by continental police theory over the previous two centuries or so. This is no surprise, given that Bentham during his long stay in Paris must have become familiar with the long tradition of French police science.

Bentham's discussion of police begins with his distinction among three types of "mischief," or harm. Harm, according to Bentham, can "come either from external adversaries, from internal adversaries, or from calamities."[29] Police is one of the means for averting mischief originating from *internal* adversaries. Justice is the other. Police is preventive, justice remedial:

> As to mischief from internal adversaries, the expedients employed for averting it may be distinguished into such as may be applied *before* the discovery of any mischievous design in particular, and such as can not be employed but in consequence of the discovery of some such design: the former of these are commonly referred to a branch which may be styled the *preventive* branch of the *police*; the latter to that of justice.[30]

In another context, Bentham elaborates on the distinction, and further differentiates between the different types of sanctions employed by police and justice, precautions and punishments:

> It is difficult to draw the line which separates these two branches of administration. Their functions have the same object—that of maintaining the internal peace of the state. Justice regards in particular offences already

committed; her power does not display itself till after the discovery of some act hostile to the security of the citizens. Police applies itself to the prevention both of offences and calamities; its expedients are, not punishments, but precautions; it foresees evils, and provides against wants.[31]

This distinction between preventive police and remedial justice had been a mainstay of police theory for centuries.[32] As we will see, it played an important part in early American writings on police as well.

Writing in 1781, Bentham also reconfirms that police at that time had only recently entered the English language, from Greece via France, with a possible assist from Germany: "As to the word *police*, though of Greek extraction, it seems to be of French growth: it is from France, at least, that it has been imported into Great Britain, where it still retains its foreign garb: in Germany, if it did not originate there, it has at least been naturalized."[33]

Whatever the origin of police, Bentham, like so many before and after him, notes the impossibility of defining it. In his words, "the idea belonging to it seems to be too multifarious to be susceptible to any single definition."[34] Given Bentham's insistence on precision, which generated the excruciatingly detailed taxonomies scattered throughout his work, this is an extraordinary admission. If Bentham can't define it, one might think, then no one can. And yet Bentham doesn't reject the concept as useless, as one might expect. Famously, he was not so kind to other concepts of uncertain scope, such as the idea of natural rights.[35]

Bentham's discussion of police, however, not only illustrates the difficulty of defining this amorphous concept but also suggests an explanation for the difficulty. Bentham can't keep police and justice apart because to him they are, in the end, one and the same thing. Both are means for the enforcement of paternal, and quasi-paternal, authority. What the power of chastisement is to one, the power to punish and to police is to the other. What are threats to the well-being of the family to one are "*diseases* of the body politic"[36] to the other:

> The magistrate and the father, or he who stands in the father's place, cannot maintain their authority, the one in the state, and the other in the family, unless they are armed with coercive means against disobedience. The evil which they inflict is called punishment or chastisement. The whole object of these acts is the good of the great or little society which they govern.[37]

In basing the power of police on the father's authority, and responsibility, to maintain discipline among his societies petit and grand, Bentham could look back on several centuries of continental police control over public households of various shapes and sizes. Charles VI began delegating the power of police ("la policité" and "trébonne police") to French cities in the late fourteenth century.[38] In Germany, similar assignments of imperial privileges to the cities date back at least to the mid-fifteenth century. After the first such delegation to the city of Nuremberg in 1464, the bishop of Würzburg finds it necessary in 1490 to pass sumptuary laws dealing with the dress of "common" women.[39]

In the late fifteenth century, the emperor also began to issue imperial police regulations of his own. The earliest one of these, from 1495, sought to maintain "order and police" in the Holy Roman Empire of German Nation by the control of blasphemy, drunkenness and luxurious dress.[40] Some years later, in the first imperial police ordinance (1530), that list of police offenses was expanded to include the following titles, in roughly that order:[41]

- Of blasphemy and oaths
- Of drunkenness
- Of disorderly and Christian dress
- Of excessive expenses for weddings, baptisms, and funerals
- Of day laborers, workers, and messengers
- Of expensive eating in inns
- Of civil contracts
- Of Jews and their usury
- Of the sale of wool cloth
- Of the sale of ginger
- Of measures and weights
- Of servants
- Of carrying weapons on horse and on foot
- Of beggars and idle persons
- Of gypsies
- Of jesters
- Of flute players
- Of vagrants and singers
- Of sons of craftsmen and apprentices

These central police ordinances were meant as supplements to the local enforcement of police by the inferior superiors within the empire. For instance, the second imperial police ordinance, from 1548, instructed all superiors (Obrigkeit) "to establish and maintain among their inferiors (Untertanen) good and honorable order and to punish the disobedient."[42] Moreover, the father of every house (*Hausvater*) was instructed to ensure that his servants and children refrain from blasphemy and drunkenness.[43]

So far the list of continental police offenses looks a lot like Blackstone's lackluster compendium from 1769, both in form and in substance. Eventually, however, the science of police sought to bring order into the princely pursuit of order within his realm, down to the level of the individual father householder.

Policing Populations

The science of police, which blossomed particularly in France and in Germany, became the science of administering a "population" with the aim of maximizing its welfare. Much as William the Conqueror had done in the preparation of his Domesday Book, the entire realm was transformed into a bundle of resources, which it was upon the macro householder to administer. Beginning in earnest in the seventeenth century, everyone and everything within the macro household was leveled into a statistic.[44]

There were human resources, and natural resources. The mode of the resource made no difference to the science of police; all resources were to be utilized by the householder so as to maximize the welfare of the state-household. Just as the difference between resources was one of quantity, or perhaps of functionality, so was the difference between the micro household of Aristotelian economics and the macro household of the regent. As a German police scientist put it in 1745, police consists of "the good order and constitution of a state's *persons and things*."[45] Already in 1567, an early French writer on police defined government as "the right disposition of things, arranged so as to lead to a convenient end."[46] Michel Foucault captures an important point about police, in contrast to law, when he remarks that "with government," and with police in particular, "it is a question not of imposing law on men, but of disposing things: that is to say, of employing tactics rather than laws, and even of using laws themselves as tactics—to arrange things in such a way that, through a certain number of means, such and such ends may be achieved."[47]

Police deals with any threat to the macro household's welfare. The nature of the threat is irrelevant. Human threats are policed like nonhuman ones, animate like inanimate ones. Recall that Bentham mentioned "calamities" as one group of police objects. The other two, internal and external adversaries, are personal.

From the perspective of police what matters is managing something, or someone, by someone. The policer is always a person; the policed needn't be. In fact, we might go farther and say that, *insofar as he is an object of police*, he is not a person. For policing disposes, in Foucault's term, rather than influences, persuades, or convinces or even commands. Police controls, rather than governs.[48]

When the police concerned itself with persons in particular, these persons always appeared as the ruler's inferiors (*Untertanen*). As inferiors, and therefore as incapable of providing for themselves, they were entitled to the ruler's protection and provision. Police, one could read in a German encyclopedia in 1748, was an "institution so that the subjects may have good nourishment and convenience."[49] And again, in 1808, a Prussian ordinance declared that "[a]s provincial police agencies the local governments are charged with the commonweal of our loyal subjects, both in a negative as well as in a positive sense."[50]

But even in the statistical world of population management according to the principles of police science, police always remained rooted in private householding. The king-householder's subjects were not merely inferior, but inferior to him as the head of the household to which they belonged. We've already seen that Rousseau highlights this connection between private and public economy in his *Discourse on Political Economy*, written at the height of police science, in 1755. Commenting on the French literature, Foucault recognizes that the central problem of the police scientists was "to introduce economy—that is to say, the correct manner of managing individuals, goods and wealth within the family . . . and of making the family prosper—how to introduce this meticulous attention of the father towards his family into the management of the state."[51] And, invoking Rousseau's essay, he continues:

> To govern a state will therefore mean to apply economy, to set up an economy at the level of the entire state, which means exercising towards its inhabitants, and the wealth and behaviour of each and all, a form of surveillance and control as attentive as that of the head of a family over his household and his goods.[52]

In the era of police science, police applied to everyone and everything and everywhere. To serve its comprehensive purpose, police was an enormously flexible, and broad, concept. Police was an end, the means to that end, and the institution enforcing the means. In other words, police was the goal that the police achieved by means of police.

Flexibility also meant essential vagueness. A good police required discretion in the policer. He needed to be able to do whatever needed to be done. There could be guidelines, but no firm principles. And the concept of police had to be broad enough to leave room for the sort of on-the-spot judgment that was required in unpredictable situations. Many writers on police attempted a definition of their subject matter. Even more critiqued existing definitions.[53] In the end, not even police science managed to produce a definition of police that was flexible and comprehensive enough without being meaninglessly broad. What remained were, as in the sixteenth century, more or less illustrative lists of various objects of police: agriculture, hunting, fishing, coalmines, crafts, arts,[54] but also construction, fire, health, and the poor,[55] and, eventually, mountains, dikes, forests, commerce, and markets as well.[56]

Anything and anyone could be policed. And anyone—though *not* anything—could do the policing. The king policed the realm. The provincial official policed the province. The family householder policed the family household. And the individual policed itself. A German source from 1770 speaks of "internal policing of humans and states." The well policed person is said to be "polite," considerate, even beautiful.[57]

Police always also meant coercion. Without the power to coerce, no householder could be expected to discharge his duty as protector of his household. And to coerce didn't just mean to enforce obedience. Obedience was necessary to guarantee the smooth operation of household management. Interference on the part of members of the household, as idleness or general recalcitrance or direct contempt, was a nuisance. It was difficult enough to manage the household without having to contend with malfunctioning tools. As Bentham put it, the power to coerce was crucial since "no one would choose to be a magistrate or a father, if he were not secure in the exercise of his own power."[58]

But police didn't only mean coercion. After all, most of police had nothing do with persons. Resources are not coerced; they are manipulated, drawn upon, maximized. But even when police dealt directly with persons, it need not coerce them. Since their welfare, as members of the household, was its end, police could rely on the cooperation of its personal objects. Violence thus was necessary only to correct persons for their own good. Discipline only served to force persons to fare well, literally.

Occasionally of course it might be necessary even to destroy a particular threat to the community's well-being. A resource, human or not, that had lost all, even potential, utility for the project of maximizing the household's welfare might have to be discarded, provided the destruction did not consume more resources than it preserved. In that case, it could not be said that the policing would benefit its immediate object, but the point was not to benefit individual items, but to benefit them as members of the household. And if their benefit was the household's loss, then they were beyond the scope of police.

In continental police science, police also wasn't only about prevention of harm to the community. A householder who concerned himself only with preventing harm, i.e., loss to his family's welfare, would not be doing his job. Ideally to maximize the family's welfare meant to increase it, and not merely not to decrease it.

The police in police science, in other words, was affirmative as well as restrictive, positive as well as negative. Recall that the Prussian ordinance from 1808, which we've already encountered, instructed local governments, as police agencies, to look after "the commonweal of our loyal subjects, both in a negative as well as in a positive sense."[59] It went on to remind the local governments that their effectiveness "in executing the power of police must extend not only to the prevention of dangers and disadvantages and to the maintenance of the current state of affairs, but also to the expansion and advancement of the common welfare."[60] In particular, this meant that "they therefore are entitled and obligated not merely to prevent, and to remove, anything that can bring danger or disadvantage to the state and its citizens, i.e., to take the necessary measures to maintain public tranquility, security, and order, but also to ensure that the commonweal is advanced and increased and that every state citizen have the opportunity to develop his abilities and powers in moral as well as in physical regard and to apply them within legal bounds in the manner most suitable to him."[61] For that reason, the local governments were also charged with overseeing "the edification of the people, public education, and cultural programs."[62]

This program for the establishment of a well policed population, in the sense discussed above, should not be confused with a program for the establishment of a self-governing citizenry. Recall that this was still a Prussian ordinance issued by the government of a highly autocratic and centralized monarchy to local governmental entities which enjoyed their power of government in general, and of police in particular, through delegation from the Prussian king. It is an internal administrative decree from a superior administrative agency to an inferior one. It is not addressed to the population whose police it calls upon the inferior bureaucratic agency to maximize. In particular, the point of educating "our loyal subjects" was to maximize their welfare as members of the Prussian state, not to maximize their welfare for their sake, and certainly not to transform them into self-governing individuals whose creation would destroy the very state that brought it about.

To what extent the policing of subjects in fact contributed to the collapse of the Prussian state is of course another question. The point is merely that the last thing this Prussian ordinance regarding police in the positive sense was designed to achieve was the collapse of the Prussian state whose welfare it calls upon Prussian bureaucrats to maximize.

Prevention, which Bentham took to be the essence of police, thus was only one side of the police concept in continental police science. Prevention of "mischief" could only be one aspect of policing the household because police was the household's welfare, and not merely its freedom from threats external or internal.

Police and Crime

Still, the distinction between prevention and remedy did play a crucial role in the attempt to distinguish police offenses from criminal offenses. The need to differentiate between the two arose as police offenses began to multiply along with novel procedures and institutions to enforce them, leading to predictable jurisdictional conflicts with traditional courts. Prussia, for example, developed a system of police offenses that included police orders issued by police agencies, enforced by police officers, adjudicated by police judges, and punished by police sanctions served in police prisons.[63] Police sanctions ran from fines to fourteen days' imprisonment per offense (dubbed "transgression"), and three months per sentence.

Here we have Prussian police integrating the three powers, or branches, of government—defining, imposing, and inflicting, or legislating, adjudicating, and executing. In a system of police, the distinctions among various modes of power are difficult to maintain. The father of the household always had been legislator, judge, and executioner all wrapped in one. He made the rules, decided when they had been violated, and inflicted disciplinary measures, if and when appropriate. The separation of powers is designed to place checks on government. Police authority is exercised without checks, other than the ultimate end of the community's welfare. From the perspective of police, a division of power retards the execution of the superior's measures designed to maximize community welfare.

By their nature, police offenses wouldn't fit easily into the new criminal codes that began to appear throughout continental Europe. Bavaria, which had produced what is generally considered to be the first "modern" German criminal code in 1813, tried to collect its police offenses in a separate "police criminal code." Here are a few samples from the 1822 draft:

- failing to sweep the sidewalk every Saturday
- unauthorized placing of a flower pot
- attaching a weather vane without a lightning rod
- skating on thin ice
- begging
- untimely chimney sweeping
- failing to supply one's dog with a city tag
- keeping a pigsty that faces the street
- establishing a chemical laboratory in one's kitchen
- unauthorized river bathing
- disposing waste onto the street
- obstructing a narrow street with a cart

- carrying a stick in a crowd
- ringing church bells during a rainstorm
- operating a coach at excessive speed
- horseback riding by a child
- interrupting another's concert through excessive noise
- drinking alcohol in a bar after 11 P.M.
- failing to have one's child inoculated by age three
- failing to make a timely appearance at the water pump in case of fire
- failing to keep one's fire bucket in proper repair
- failing to heed a request to abstain from exciting animals
- engaging in an act that may endanger a pregnant woman or her fetus
- failing to assist runaway children until official action has been taken
- disseminating principles, opinions, or dispositions dangerous to the state
- disseminating principles, opinions, or dispositions that are directed against the foundations of morality and religion or otherwise tend to discredit morals or religion
- publicly making statements gravely insulting the admiration of the Highest Being[64]

Police offenses of this ilk were said to differ from "real" crimes in that they merely threatened protected interests, instead of violating them.[65] Punishing the former thus served to *prevent* harm, whereas punishing the latter constituted *remedial* punishment.

Other attempts to separate police crimes from true crimes drew on the *communal*, rather than the preventive aspect, of police. So Paul Johann Anselm Feuerbach argued that police offenses interfered with a public interest, whereas only crimes constituted a violation of a private right of a person.[66] For purposes of police, after all, the individual is significant only as a member of the household.

Feuerbach (the drafter of the Bavarian Criminal Code of 1813) also argued that penalties for police offenses are "nothing but disobedience penalties,"[67] thus highlighting the *hierarchical* aspect of the police concept. This idea was later developed by the influential positivist criminal law scholar Karl Binding, who argued that the difference between police offenses and real crimes lay in the fact that police offenses were "pure disobedience offenses."[68] They were punishable only because they violated a state command. Real crimes too were disobedience offenses, in that they also manifested disobedience. But they were not purely disobedience offenses, because they also threatened or violated a protected interest.

None of these attempts to differentiate between police offenses and crimi-

nal offenses proved successful, though all of them invoked familiar characteristics of the concept of police. Doesn't the punishment of traditional crimes
serve a preventive purpose as well? Isn't every crime also a violation of a public interest? How can we tell—and why should it matter—whether an offense
is only, or also, an act of disobedience? Even if we could draw these distinctions, what would follow for the different—or not-so-different—institutional
treatment of police offenses and "true" crimes? As we'll see shortly,
nineteenth-century American courts struggled with similar questions—and
reached similarly unsatisfactory answers—when they faced police offenses of
their own.

PART II

American Police Power

4

Policing the New Republic

I t's not entirely clear, of course, exactly whom and what the American political and legal thinkers and doers who first spoke of a power to police read and when they read it. It's also unclear, therefore, to what extent these Americans were directly influenced by any, or all, of the various facets of the concept of police in early modern Europe or in the police science of the seventeenth and eighteenth centuries, or if, perhaps, they got their police entirely from Blackstone's *Commentaries*, the source of so much institutional inspiration in the new republic.

Luckily, however, we learned it doesn't much matter whether the Founding Fathers picked up the police concept from Blackstone or Beccaria or Bentham, or Adam Smith or any of the other eighteenth-century police scientists. It doesn't matter because the core idea of police was the same on both sides of the Channel, for the simple reason that its roots reached back far beyond the divide between continental and English politics and law, to the very origins of Western political thought and practice. Already the Greeks had differentiated between politics, the self-government of householders by householders, and the other-government of households by their householders. Police marked the point of convergence between politics and economics, when one mode of governance merged into the other, and created the oxymoronic science of political economy. The police power was born when the governmentality of the private (micro) household was expanded, and transferred, onto that of the public (macro) household. Equipped with the power to police, the sovereign ruled "the individuals of the state, like members of a well-governed family," in Blackstone's words,[1] or "of that great family, the State," in Rousseau's.[2]

It's no surprise that the Founding Fathers took easily to this theory of government as patriarchy, and of politics as economics, as they had been practicing it for quite some time. In their corporations, their camps, their towns, their churches, their families, and on their plantations, they had been doing police long before they had a name for it, that modern, enlightened, scientific concept of police.

The problem, of course, was that this mode of governance stood in deep tension with the principle upon which the American Republic was built, and that gave legitimacy to it, *self-government*. It was one thing for the Kings of England and of Prussia to think of themselves as policing their respective realms, as a more or less benevolent father might his family. It was quite another for the governors of a democratic republic built upon the equality of all, governors and governed alike, to adopt this patriarchal posture.

But adopt it they did, as they applied themselves to the task of policing the new state with a vengeance, developing a distinctly American version of police along the way, turning *police science* into *police power*. Recognized as the very foundation of government, and even as synonymous with government itself, American police power remained true to the common core of all varieties of police, from France to Germany to Scotland to England: its foundation in the householder's governance of the household. All of the components of American police power can be traced back to that model. Its undefinability derives from the father's virtually unlimited discretion not merely to discipline, but to do what was required for the welfare of the household. The ahumanity of its object derives from the essential sameness of all components of the household, animate and inanimate, as tools in the householder's hands. That essential sameness, however, also implies the essential difference between the householder and his household, and therefore the hierarchical aspect of American police power, along with its fundamental amorality. The power to police seeks efficiency, not legitimacy. Patriarchy's concern for the welfare of the household is the police power's concern for the welfare of the state, a concern that expresses itself positively and negatively, in the correction of inferior members of the state household as well as in its protection against threats.[3]

As we've already noted, the Americans, when they revealed the sources of their view of police, were quite explicit about its patriarchal essence. The one definition of police they quoted again and again was, after all, Blackstone's and Blackstone could not have been clearer on this point. It bears repeating that he viewed the police power as that power which the king, as "*pater-familias* of the nation,"[4] possessed vis-à-vis his kingdom, as *familia*.

This persistent reliance on Blackstone is truly remarkable. For what relevance could a theory that rooted state power in the king's obligations toward, and authority over, his kingdom retain in a republic? Wasn't the American revolution all about independence, independence also from the king's arbitrary prerogative, which he exercised over his American subjects like a householder over his household? In short, wasn't the revolution meant precisely to rid the Americans of the patriarchal police power of the King of England?

Ending the king's police power, it turns out, did not mean ending police power altogether. Nor did it mean depriving oneself of that power. We have already seen that policing in fact if not by name already had shaped American government since long before the revolution, and it continued to do so long thereafter. Americans had no objections to the notion of one person policing another, or rather a community of others. American society was deeply hierarchical, organized into households of various sizes and types. The kingdom-household under the authority of the king-father was only one of these households, and in many ways the least significant in everyday life. The English king, with "his" law, was very far away. Government occurred at the local level, in the family, the church, the town, perhaps the colony, and of course the plantation.

Americans didn't appreciate being policed, but they had no qualms about policing. The revolution thus can be seen as the removal of a higher layer of household governance. Americans extracted themselves from the kingdom-household so that they could go about policing their respective households without interference from the macro householder, the king.[5] After the revolution, for example, now-state officials no longer would have to deal with royal missives reminding them that slave owners should be held to account for killing their slaves, because slaves were members not only of a plantation household, and the then-colonial household, but also of the grand household of the king. These decrees had been annoying during the colonial era because they interfered with the proper policing of the then-colony, while they reminded the officials of their inferior status vis-à-vis the royal paterfamilias. Under the loose supervision of the king-father, Americans had been free to enslave, in Jonathan Bush's phrase. After the revolution they were truly free to police.

They were free because they were free from someone else's police power. They were also free because they were free to police others. Their autonomy consisted in not being under heteronomy *and* in exercising heteronomy over others. This is the model of republican government familiar from Greek politics, which the American revolutionaries studied with great interest. The new American state was to be a republic, but a republic of householders. It was the householders who were to participate in government, indirectly and directly, by voting and being voted for, and resolving disputes among themselves. But the business of government did not end there. Government also meant, as it always had, policing others. And so everyone, and everything, else incapable of self-government was to be policed by those who were so capable.

It's not clear exactly what the drafters of the early state constitutions meant when they spoke of "governing and regulating the internal police" of the state. Judging by what governing and regulating American state legislatures actually did under the heading of "internal police of the state" when they got around to revising their statutes in the early republic, the objects of their police included, among other things (and people), taverns, brothels, bawdy houses, lost goods, and gunpowder, paupers, vagrants, disorderly persons, prostitutes, drunkards, tipplers, gamesters, the unemployed, jugglers, common showmen, as well as illegitimate children, and stray animals.[6]

Suffrage limitations didn't just discriminate against the propertyless, women, slaves, children, animals, and inanimate objects.[7] They eliminated those who were under the police of *another* person, or—in the case of those who were denied the status of personhood, including slaves, children, animals, and inanimate objects—under the police of *some* person. In the householder's republic, the household had no right to govern, only to be governed, or rather policed.

A fully matured capacity for self-government was required for participation in the self-government of the political community. That capacity was thought to be lacking in those who were mere objects of another's police, whether their householder was the family patriarch, as in the case of wives, children, servants, animals, and other household property, or the state as macro householder, in the case of those receiving public poor relief. Even if the capacity for autonomy wasn't lacking entirely under these conditions, its actual exercise was surely thought to be impossible. Even if objects of police could be free in the abstract, they were not, and could not be, free in fact.

As "persons of indigent fortunes, or such as are under the immediate dominion of others," objects of police were "suspected to have no will of their own," and therefore incapable of exercising whatever capacity for self-government they might possess.[8] That "suspicion" in fact manifested itself as an irrebuttable presumption in the form of categorical property qualifications, which persisted in some states until the 1930s.[9]

Now given that there remained so many objects of police, animate and inanimate, even after the revolution and the ejection of the royal householder and his overseers, there was never any question *whether* there was to be continued policing in the new republic but merely *who* was to do the policing. So obvious was the continued need for police that Americans never managed, or bothered, to develop an indigenous account of the nature of police. In fact, early American treatments of police devoted themselves largely to the task of explaining, and repeating, the very obviousness of police. Take for example the concluding passage of Judge Redfield's opinion in *Thorpe v. Rutland & Burlington Railroad* Company,[10] an 1854 case from Vermont that came to be cited as one of the classic discussions of the police power:

> One in any degree familiar with this subject would never question the right depending upon invincible necessity, in order to the maintenance of any show of administrative authority among the class of persons with which the city police have to do. To such men any doubt of the right to subject persons and property to such regulations as the public security and health may require, regardless of merely private convenience, looks like mere badinage. They can scarcely regard the objector as altogether serious. And generally, these doubts in regard to the extent of governmental authority come from those who have had small experience.[11]

The answer to the question of who would get to do the policing in the new republic was just as obvious: we. "We" originally meant "the people," in the sense of the collection of householders entitled to participate in government. So some of the early state constitutions feature declarations such as this one, taken from the Pennsylvania Constitution of 1776: "the people of this State have the sole, exclusive and inherent right of governing and regulating the internal police of the same." Here the householder-citizens of Pennsylvania are defiantly throwing off the police power once held over them by their erstwhile macro householder, the king.

But the people of Pennsylvania not only announced that they no longer would be policed by the King of England. They also made clear that the departure of the ultimate policer didn't mean the departure of police. That the power of police was intimately connected to the king's prerogative didn't cause much of a problem, and certainly no more of a problem than the transfer of any other aspect of the royal prerogative, i.e., the authority enjoyed by the king as father of the kingdom family. Now that the king was gone, his prerogative was simply transferred onto the new sovereign: "the people of this State." In the context of police, Thomas Paine's famous answer to the question "where . . . is the King of America?", that "in America THE LAW IS KING,"[12] meant that the prerogative police power of one man, the king, now belonged to a group of men, the people, who had assumed the power to police.

Once the people of the various states had freed themselves from the king's policing of their police, they were understandably wary of subjecting themselves to the police power of another master. To many the creation of an

American nation meant being reintegrated within a larger household under another superior householder. And it is in the context of the debates about the federal constitution that one finds the most extended discussions of the obviousness of police power. So we learn that the power to police is an inherent attribute of all government, or least of any free government, where "free" here meant free from a superior police power.

This point about the inevitability of policing in any government was so universally conceded that it helped forge the very consensus upon which the American federalist system of government was built. By leaving "the people of this State" the "sole, exclusive and inherent right of . . . regulating the internal police of the same," the United States preserved the States' status as independent households, or units of police. They, in other words, remained free to police. But they gave up that other aspect of government, namely that of "governing" in the narrow sense. Government *by law* now became a matter not only of the states, but also of the national government. The state-householders could still police their household, but they were now subject to the *laws* of the nation. Those laws, however, were not to be measures of police, issued by a higher power. They were to be laws made with their participation, as always had been appropriate for a government of autonomous householders.

In fact, American constitutional discourse went one step farther. It left the states' power of "internal police" untouched, while it denied the federal government any police power of its own. In other words, it retained the household status of the states by denying the household status of the union.

This arrangement was self-contradictory; nonetheless, it has remained in place to this day. The problem with the compromise upon which the union was built was that it insisted that the power to police was inherent in the very concept of government, while at the same time ostensibly erecting a government without that very power. But this inconsistency has not interfered with the rhetorical usefulness of the police concept over the past two hundred years. The clear assignment of police power to the states, and only to the states, dramatically simplified constitutional analysis. If it was police, it was the states' business.

As a matter of political fact, if not of rhetoric, the inconsistency did manage to resolve itself. As Ernst Freund remarked in 1904, after only the first century of federal legislation, it had become "impossible to deny that the federal government exercises a considerable police power of its own."[13] Despite all the rhetoric about the policeless federal government, already the Federalist Papers claimed a federal police power, even if not in so many words. So Hamilton spoke of the need of government to hand out "a penalty or punishment for disobedience,"[14] and in particular "the disorderly conduct of refractory or seditious individuals."[15] Here a "vigorous"[16] government was needed to dispose of those "seditions and insurrections . . . that are, unhappily, maladies as inseparable from the body politic as tumors and eruptions from the natural body."[17]

And this became the general modus operandi of the federal government: use your police power, but call it anything but that. One of the most obvious, and extreme, uses of the federal police power took the form of federal control over Native Americans and their "Indian affairs," under the auspices of that most police scientific institutions of princely government, a "Bureau." This clear and prolonged exercise of comprehensive householder authority over a household composed of inferior objects who could have no say in their government, this textbook example of police, was in fact carried out mostly under the commerce clause, which authorized the national government not to regulate the "police" of the nation, but instead to regulate "commerce" among the micro households (i.e., the states) within the nation, as well as between the nation and other macro households (i.e., other nations).[18]

The commerce clause early on emerged as the favorite cover for the exercise of federal police power. The most recent example is the creation of a comprehensive federal code of drug criminal law, all under the guise of preventing interference with interstate commerce.[19] In fact, almost the entire edifice of federal criminal law, which has reached proportions that would have surprised even a police realist like Freund, derives from the commerce clause. Only recently has the U.S. Supreme Court begun to review the federal government's use of the commerce clause to generate police measures. In *United States v. Lopez*,[20] the Court even went so far as to strike down a federal criminal statute ostensibly based on the federal commerce power. On what ground? Because to uphold the statute would "bid fair to convert congressional authority under the Commerce Clause to a general police power of the sort retained by the States."[21] In other words, the fiction of exclusive *state* police power is alive and well, even after *Lopez*.

Having secured "the sole, exclusive and inherent right of governing and regulating the internal police of the same" twice over, once against the king and then against the union, "the people" of the states turned their attention to the task at hand. With the revolutionary work complete, the time had come to govern. As Benjamin Rush gushed in the summer of 1787: "the same enthusiasm *now* pervades all classes in favor of *government* that actuated us in favor of *liberty* in the years 1774 and 1775, with this difference, that we are more *united* in the former than we were in the latter pursuit."[22]

And to govern also, and especially, meant to police. For there was much policing to be done. As Benjamin Franklin cautioned in 1789: "We have been guarding against an evil that old States are most liable to, *excess of power* in the rulers, but our present danger seems to be *defect of obedience* in the subjects."[23] Others warned that "[t]he principal fault seems to be, a want of energy in the administration of government." What was needed was "an increase of magisterial power in order to provide for the 'execution of the laws that is necessary for the preservation of justice, peace, and internal tranquility.' "[24]

It was high time that order be restored in the American state household. Household members had to be put—back—in their proper place, lest they mistake themselves for householders capable of government. There were plenty of people in need of policing. The recently liberated householders saw post-revolutionary America teeming with men *"whose fathers they would have disdained to have sat with the dogs of their flocks*, raised to immense wealth, or at least the appearance of a haughty, supercilious and luxurious spendthrift."[25]

The comprehensive pursuit of police permeated every branch, and every level, of government. We've already heard about the police commissioners and peace officers who began to appear in American cities in the 1770s and 80s. And these agents were not long confined to executing the statutes on Blackstone's list of police offenses.

Soon the legislative bodies of the states began issuing their very own police regulations, from the state on down to cities, towns, and villages. As an illustration, the New York state legislature passed police regulations in these areas between 1781 and 1801. The list is compiled by William Novak:[26]

- lotteries
- hawkers and peddlers
- the firing of guns
- usury
- frauds
- the buying and selling of offices
- beggars and disorderly persons
- rents and leases
- firing woods
- the destruction of deer
- stray cattle and sheep
- mines
- ferries
- apprentices and servants
- bastards
- idiots and lunatics
- counsellors, attorneys and solicitors
- travel, labor, or play on Sunday
- cursing and swearing

- drunkenness
- the exportation of flaxseed
- gaming
- the inspection of lumber
- dogs
- the culling of staves and heading
- debtors and creditors
- the quarantining of ships
- sales by public auction
- stock jobbing
- fisheries
- the inspection of flour and meal
- the practice of physic and surgery
- the packing and inspection of beef and pork
- sole leather
- strong liquors, inns, and taverns
- pot and pearl ashes
- poor relief
- highways
- quit rents

There it is again, the typical hodgepodge of activities and objects, animate and inanimate, we've come to associate with police legislation.[27] And as Novak has shown with example after example, American state legislatures, directly or by delegation to smaller entities within the state, continued producing police measures of this sort throughout the nineteenth century.[28] By the 1820s and 1830s, when the state legislatures began taking stock of their regulatory output, and consolidating and "revising" it in the process, they began grouping these measures under their proper title, police, often using Blackstone's police categories.[29]

Returning from the constitutional convention to Virginia as governor, Thomas Jefferson too was eager to begin the process of reform, and to get down to the business of running a state, including providing for its internal police. His reform plans, and particularly his comprehensive educational program, reflected the positive aspect of police, which sought to increase the community's welfare, and not merely to maintain it. Jefferson set out to train capable ("wise and honest") policymakers and administrators, for "it is generally true that the people will be happiest whose laws are best, and are best administered, and that laws will be wisely formed, and honestly administered, in proportion as those who form and administer them are wise and honest."[30] To that end, he proposed establishing elementary schools for all children, reforming the College of William & Mary, and setting up a library.[31]

For our purposes most interesting is his transformation of the College of William & Mary from an institution of the Anglican Church into a training ground for the new state's future policymakers and administrators. By the time Jefferson established the chair of law and police, the education of state officials in the science of police already had had a long tradition in the increasingly bureaucratized European monarchies. In the German states, for example, the study of police began in training academies for state officials, the so-called *Kameralbeamten*, or bureau-crats (literally chamber or office deputies—offic-ials). These administrative officials were schooled in cameral science, the science of the chamber (*Kameralwissenschaft*), which included the administration of any policies the king or his delegates had seen fit to decree so as to provide for the police of his subjects.

These training academies were dedicated to disseminating the raison d'état throughout the respective state bureaucracies, and thereby to render the management of the state household more efficient. This required proper maintenance of statistics about the objects of state government, the population, and competent enforcement of royal and superior administrative decrees. Eventually, these training academies were integrated into the state universities. In 1727, William I of Prussia set up two chairs in cameral science, in Halle and Frankfurt/Oder. Soon chairs in other cities and states followed: Rinteln (1730), Leipzig (1742), Vienna (1752), Göttingen (1755), Prague (1763), Freiburg/Breisgau, Innsbruck, Klagenfurt (1768), and Ingolstadt (1780).[32] Even after becoming part of the university curriculum, courses in cameral science (or "economic police and cameral science"[33]) remained practice oriented. They encompassed a broad spectrum of topics, ranging from general economic policy to administrative science to accounting and statistics.[34]

Jefferson's reference to "police," "politics," "commerce," and "oeconomical law," in the appendix to his bill to amend the constitution of the College William & Mary,[35] of course comes nowhere near the sophistication of the systematic curriculum in the continental departments of police science. Americans, after all, had neither a police science, nor powerful state bureaucracies devoted to the raison d'état as manifested in the decrees of an enlightened monarch.

And yet the challenge of police that Jefferson—and his American contemporaries—faced was very much the same.[36] Since its earliest manifestation as the householder's management of his household, police meant the maximization of resources. To this end, it helped if one had a clear picture of what these resources were at a given point in time, and how they changed over time, in response to certain managerial choices. It also helped if these choices were put into operation quickly and completely, which required an obedient household as well as—if necessary—a loyal and competent staff of administrators, or overseers.

This is an important point. The American revolutionaries were right, and so were the defenders of states' rights: police is an essential component of *any* government. A look at the continental roots of the police concept reveals, however, that *any* government also includes highly centralized European states under the absolute authority of the members of a hereditary monarchy. It is no accident that the notion originated and found its most complete exposition and manifestation in France and Prussia, and that in the English tradition it was closely associated with the prerogative of the king as the father of his people. Given its derivation from the power of the paterfamilias over his household, police is easily compatible with hierarchical, and in particular patriarchal, regimes that at the same time maintain a strict division between ruler and ruled, and abstract away distinctions among the ruled, which make up the household as a set of management tools distinguished (only) by functionality.

The categorical distinction between ruler and ruled, on the one hand, and the categorical denial of any significant distinctions among the ruled, on the other, became difficult to maintain in America after the revolution. That revolution, after all, had stressed again and again the fundamental identity of all persons as such, and had founded the power to govern on a compact among all persons, rather than between the ruler and the ruled.

At the same time, however, deep social divisions remained in American society, revolutionary proclamations, and declarations, notwithstanding. The concept of police was only one way of capturing these divisions and finding room for them in the government of the newly independent American states. Everyone agreed, after all, that the power to police was an inherent right of any government. And this much is true, depending on what police meant. If the power to police meant the power to regulate matters of common interest to all members of a political community, then surely a power to police was not merely necessary to government, but one of its primary functions. Also, if the power to police meant the power to enforce the law against unjustified violations, then no objections to its legitimacy could be raised.

The challenge was to bring the legitimate functions of police in line with a system of government that could not bear the distinction between policer and policed. The problem of government was no longer merely to put in place the most efficient system of police. Instead, police had to be rendered compatible with the one legitimating principle that remained after the American revolution, the principle of self-government, or autonomy. The challenge of police thus was central to the more general project of erecting a system of government based on the autonomy of all persons as such, rather than on the autonomy of some persons as a factor of their heteronomy over others, i.e., of transforming America from a democracy of householders into a democracy of persons.

Jefferson saw this challenge, and took steps toward meeting it. His educational program, after all, called not only for the proper training of state police officials, by attracting the best and the brightest among the state's subjects, "those persons, whom nature hath endowed with genius and virtue, . . . without regard to wealth, birth or other accidental condition or circumstance."[37] While continental monarchs had long ago noticed the inefficiency of a non-meritocratic bureaucracy, the distinctive, and distinctively American, aspect of Jefferson's educational plan lay in his call for "[e]lementary schools for all children generally, rich and poor." Now this provision of course can be seen as simply a prerequisite for the establishment of a merit-based system of administration. But it served another purpose as well: as a protection against, rather than facilitation of, oppressive police. As Jefferson explained in the introduction to his education bill, entitled "A Bill for the More General Diffusion of Knowledge":

> it appeareth that however certain forms of government are better calculated than others to protect individuals in the free exercise of their natural rights, and are at the same time themselves better guarded against degeneracy, yet experience hath shewn, that even under the best forms, those entrusted with power have, in time, and by slow operations, perverted it into tyranny; and it is believed that the most effectual means of preventing this would be, to illuminate, as far as practicable, the minds of the people at large, and more especially to give them knowledge of those facts, which history exhibiteth, that, possessed thereby of the experience of other ages and countries, they may be enabled to know ambition under all its shapes, and prompt to exert their natural powers to defeat its purposes.[38]

In other words, American education was to be used not only to produce competent police officials but also to transform mere objects of police into self-governing persons who, just like Jefferson and his fellow householder citizens, would not tolerate the police of another under conditions of "tyranny," that is, the denial of their fundamental right to self-government as persons.

The European monarchies also had recognized the need for public education. But they continued to perceive it as a matter of police, rather than of self-government. Already the future James I, in 1598, remarked upon the king-father's duty to educate his children: "as the father of his fatherly duty is bound to care for the nourishing, education and vertuous government of his children: even so is the King bound to care for all his subjects."[39] In 1656, a German police treatise, entitled "The German Prince State," classified education alongside other police objects such as the church, public economy, public order, peace, welfare, and morals.[40] By the end of the seventeenth century, the school system in Germany was thought of as a police "institution" *(Anstalt).*[41] And as late as 1808, a Prussian police ordinance called on local police organs to look after the police of its "loyal subjects" by overseeing public education.[42] In fact, education was simply another word for police, as correction was a synonym for a police sanction. The goal of education was to produce "polite" objects of police who appreciated their place among the household.[43] The aim was self-police, not self-government.

By contrast, Jefferson's plan can be seen as an attempt to develop the capacity for self-government among children, who were only temporarily condemned to the status of an object of police. The idea was not to produce objects of police, but to prevent them. For in Jefferson's view only a body of autonomous citizens would provide a permanent guarantee against the tyranny of police.

Police in American Courts of Law

Wholly apart from the various specific parallels, and differences, between American and continental police, one basic distinction remained. This was the role of the judiciary in the state system of police. The American judiciary very quickly assumed an important role in the police regime, in practice as well as in theory. American courts, while helping to exercise the police power, in their applicatory function as inferior state officials, did more than anyone else to define and justify it.

Courts contributed to the police regime in two general ways. First, they took it upon themselves to protect the police even in the absence of legislative prohibitions, thereby continuing an English tradition, although one unknown in continental Europe. Judicial police employed two general police offenses, the common law misdemeanor and the public nuisance.

Second, American courts did what their European—and their English—colleagues had done for centuries. They applied the police measures generated by the legislature. Eventually special courts emerged, particularly in large cities, to dispose of police cases. This new summary disposal system managed by statutory courts occasionally came into tension with the traditional system of common law courts.

But, even in applying others' police measures, American courts did more than merely apply. They went on to *test* them as well, through judicial constitutional review. The quintessentially American contribution of the new nation's courts resulted from their opportunity, and their duty, to investigate, and act upon, the tension between police and law, rather than merely to observe it. The judiciary in England or on the continent enjoyed no such power.

And so it is in judicial opinions, specifically in judicial opinions on the constitutional limits of the power to police, that we find the most extensive, and certainly the most influential, treatments of the nature and sources of the police power. And it's in this context, as a question of constitutional law, that the police power has received most attention in American legal and political discourse, to this day.

One of the effects of this judicial focus has been to approach the subject of police as a mode of governance backwards, from the perspective of its limits, and of its constitutional limits in particular. The vast expanse of the police power thus remained uncharted, as only those aspects of its exercise that touched upon constitutional principles attracted attention. Even the authors of the two leading nineteenth-century treatises on the police power, Thomas Cooley (a Michigan state judge) and Christopher Tiedeman, took a judicial perspective. Unconstrained by the constitutional issue raised in the case before them and thus free to take a more comprehensive view of the matter, Cooley and Tiedeman nonetheless felt compelled to write treatises on the "*Constitutional Limitations* Which Rest Upon the Legislative Power" and "the *Limitations* of Police Power," respectively.[44] Even the last, and most systematic, treatise on police, published by Ernst Freund in 1904, concerned itself with the police power as a matter not only of "Public Policy," but of "Constitutional Rights" as well.[45]

This focus on the limits of a species of state of power, rather than on the power itself, can create the mistaken impression that the power is both carefully circumscribed, and limited in scope. As any look at the actual coverage of these three treatises, not to mention the tables of contents of various nineteenth-century police codes and ordinances, makes clear, however, this impression would have been mistaken. After all, the essence of the police power was widely thought to consist in its comprehensiveness, even its undefinability. As Freund's treatise in particular illustrated, within the very wide boundaries of constitutional limitations, whatever they might be, there remained a body of state action enormous in scope as well as in variety.[46]

The assumption of the judicial perspective as a *constitutional* perspective obscures another reality of the American police system. Not only was there more to the police system than its constitutional limitations, there was also more to the courts' role in that system than their enforcement of these limitations. They not only applied existing police measures, but also took it upon themselves to create new measures to preserve the police as they saw fit. And it is to this, often overlooked, role of the American courts that we turn first.

Making Judicial Police

Long before American courts began waxing eloquent about the legislature's police power, and its constitutional limits, they exercised a police power of their very own, as their English predecessors had done before them. Among Blackstone's list of police offenses, several were not of statutory (and therefore legislative) but common law, (and therefore judicial) origin. English judges thus had been engaged in judicial policing for centuries, if only in fact if not in name, and American judges were eager to continue the tradition.

Nuisance was the original common law police offense.[47] Blackstone's definition of nuisance makes the police core of nuisance explicit: "*Common nusances* are a species of offences against the public order and oeconomical regimen of the state; being either the doing of a thing to the annoyance of all the king's subjects, or the neglecting to do a thing which the common good requires."[48] American courts operated with the same police-centered concept of nuisance. The connection between police and nuisance survived even after American legislatures began taking away courts' authority to punish common law crimes of their own making. So the New York Criminal Code of 1909 still defined nuisance, in relevant part, as:

> a crime against the order and economy of the state, . . . in unlawfully doing an act, or omitting to perform a duty, which act or omission:
>
> 1. Annoys, injures or endangers the comfort, repose, health or safety of any considerable number of persons; or
>
> 2. offends public decency; or. . . .
>
> 4. in any way renders a considerable number of persons insecure in life or the use of property.[49]

Nuisance was a police offense in more ways than one. To begin with, it was a crime against "the order and economy of the state," which was just another way of saying that it was a crime against the police of the state. But it also bore several other distinctive features of police offenses. Note, for example, the inclusion of commissions and omissions. It did not matter whether a threat to the police of the state emanated from doing an act, or not doing it.

In fact, it was the failure to do something, to "perform a duty" that was the essence of a police offense. That duty, however, was the duty of orderly behavior, of acting according to one's proper place in the community-family. Any violation of this duty amounted to a challenge to the authority of the householder, who bore the responsibility of maintaining order. In this sense, the duty of orderliness was merely one instance of the more general duty of obedience that members of the household owed the householder.

But the distinction between omissions and commissions, of considerable importance in Anglo-American criminal law, was irrelevant for another reason. In the face of a challenge to the public order, doctrinal distinctions, and constraints, had a tendency of melting away. When the very survival of the community, as a community, was at stake, it made sense to err on the side of safety. When in doubt, the reach of police was expanded, rather than contracted. In this context, vague offense definitions (like annoying the "repose" of any "considerable number of persons") were acceptable, even necessary. One simply couldn't afford to await the actual infliction of an injury. It was enough that the police of the state was "endangered."

The nature of the threat to police was irrelevant, if the threat existed in fact. So nuisances included acts and omissions, and also persons as well as inanimate objects, like buildings or ox carts. As we've seen, Blackstone's illustrative catalogue of nuisances included, in order, inanimate objects ("annoyances in *highways, bridges,* and public *rivers*"), an act, or rather a status ("keeping of hogs in any city or market town"), a mixture of acts and inanimate objects ("disorderly *inns or ale-houses, bawdy-houses, gaming-houses, stage-plays* unlicensed, booths and stages for *rope-dancers, mountebanks,* and the like"), an institution ("lotteries"), inanimate objects ("*[c]ottages . . .* being harbours for thieves and other idle and dissolute persons"), another act ("the making and selling of *fireworks* and *squibs,* or throwing them about in any street, is, on account of the danger that may ensure to any thatched or timber buildings"), a type of person ("*[e]aves-droppers,* or such as listen under walls or windows, or the eaves of a house, to hearken after discourse"), and another a type of person ("*common scold, communis rixatrix*").

Since nuisance police didn't discriminate between animate and inanimate threats, never mind between persons and non-persons, it made sense that it would pay no heed to another bedrock principle of Anglo-American criminal law, the act requirement. *Being* a nuisance was a state of being, a status. The eavesdropper was a nuisance because he *was* an eavesdropper. The offense was not eavesdropping, but being someone who eavesdrops. Similarly, a common scold was just that, "a public nuisance to her neighbourhood," in Blackstone's words. Here Blackstone doesn't even specify a particular behavior, as in the case of the eavesdropper, that constitutes the nuisance. Just being a common scold was annoying, and therefore specific, enough.

Nuisances, once identified, were "abated."[50] In the case of inanimate objects, and animals, that meant they were destroyed:

> Where the condition of a thing is such that it is imminently dangerous to the safety, or offensive to the morals, of the community, and is incapable of being put to any lawful use by the owner, it may be treated as a nuisance *per se.* Actual physical destruction is in such cases not only legitimate, but sometimes the only legitimate course to be pursued. Rotten or decayed food or meat, infected bedding or clothing, mad dogs, animals affected with contagious diseases, obscene publications, counterfeit coin, and imminently dangerous structures, are the most conspicuous instances of nuisances *per se.*[51]

In the case of personal nuisances, the abatement took different forms. Eavesdroppers were punished by a fine. They also had to find sureties for good behavior, one of the preliminary policing strategies we've already encountered in our discussion of the English system of policing vagrants and disorderly persons.[52]

A particularly demeaning disciplinary measure was inflicted on a woman found to be a common scold. According to Blackstone, the *communis rixatrix* faced being placed in "a certain engine of correction called the trebucket, castigatory, or *cucking* stool, which in the Saxon language signifies the scolding stool; though now it is frequently corrupted into *ducking* stool, because the residue of the judgment is, that, when she is so placed therein, she shall be plunged in the water for her punishment."[53]

In America, prosecutions of common scolds occurred both before and after the revolution. Arthur Scott reports from colonial Virginia that women received the "ducking stool" for "highly abusive and slanderous language."[54] Later on, common scolds apparently were disciplined in much the same way as eavesdroppers, namely by fine and securities for good behavior, with imprisonment as the alternative in case of a failure, or inability, to pay either.[55] (As late as 1929, a Pennsylvania court affirmed the continued vitality of the police offense of being a common scold, though it must be said that few courts took their duty to protect the police more seriously than did the Pennsylvania courts, as we will see shortly.[56])

In all its comprehensiveness, the law of common, or public, nuisances did face one limitation. To be "criminal," and therefore subject to public police discipline, annoyances had to be common, or public. Mere private nuisances weren't enough.[57] These constituted a tort, and therefore were a matter of private law. They did not disturb the police of the state, and therefore left the authority of the sovereign charged with maintaining that police undisturbed.

This limitation proved too constraining for many American courts. They turned to another broad policing tool, the common law misdemeanor, to reach cases beyond the scope of public nuisance.[58] Eventually, the doctrine of the common law misdemeanor emerged as a general authorization for the exercise of a comprehensive police power by the judiciary.

Judicial exercises of the police power, beyond the police offense of nuisance, initially remained implicit. In 1815, for example, the Supreme Court of Pennsylvania upheld a common law indictment for "exhibiting an indecent picture to divers persons for money," a clear offense against the moral police of the state, if not in so many words. There was no statute criminalizing the conduct in question. But there was no need for such a statute, for the court concluded that, under the common law, "[w]hat tended to corrupt society was held to be a breach of the peace and punishable by indictment." What's more "[t]he courts are the guardians of the public morals, and therefore have jurisdiction in such cases."[59]

In fact, as early as 1664, an English court had declared itself " 'custos morum' of all the king's subjects,"[60] in an opinion that is widely cited as creating the common law offense of grossly scandalous behavior. In that case, Sir Charles Sedley had appeared naked on a balcony in Covent Garden, and may also have thrown bottles down into the crowd. Yet in 1708, an English court still denied that it could punish publishing an obscene book as libel: "There is no law to punish [obscene writings], I wish there were, but we cannot make law."[61] The judiciary, however, managed to untie its hands some twenty years later, in 1727, when it was decided that the offense of obscene libel existed after all.[62] By 1809, six years before the Pennsylvania decision just mentioned, a bathing Englishman was convicted of a common law misdemeanor for dressing and undressing on the beach, on the ground that "the necessary tendency of his conduct was to outrage decency, and to corrupt the public morals."[63]

Now indecency is a classic police offense; it's an attack on the moral police of the state, by "*tend[ing]* to corrupt society."[64] (And the indecent materials were clearly subject to abatement as nuisances per se.) But American courts were not content to find common law misdemeanors only in public offenses of this sort. After all these might very well have been handled by public nuisance doctrine. Instead they began to find common law misdemeanors in acts that appeared, upon first inspection, to inflict merely private harm, and therefore fell outside the realm of traditional criminal nuisance.

In this attempt to reach conduct that couldn't be classified as a nuisance, despite the notorious vagueness of the nuisance concept itself, the courts eventually settled on the concept of police. This made some sense. Nuisances were, after all, merely a particular type of police offense, as Blackstone had explained. The larger point was not the abatement of annoyances, but

the protection of the "public police and oeconomy." Blackstone's police offenses, including nuisance, were mere illustrative instances of this more
comprehensive project. All the courts needed to do was fill in the remaining
blanks.

The challenge was to connect the conduct, or the person, in question with
the police of the community. Here the moral aspect of police proved particularly useful. For police was thought to encompass all components of a
community's well-being, including its "moral health."[65] While Blackstone
preferred not to justify even such offenses as gambling, indecency, or prostitution as threats to the moral well-being of the state, American courts (and
legislators) had no similar qualms. They appeared to relish their self-
imposed responsibilities as the "guardians of the public morals."[66] Police offenses like gambling, which Blackstone had tried to connect to public police,
however meekly, by stressing their tendency "to promote public idleness,
theft, and debauchery among those of a lower class," were simply classified
as threats to the public's moral police.[67]

The protection of public morality as a distinct aspect of the welfare of the
state facilitated comprehensive and intrusive police campaigns against intox-
icating substances, like liquor and drugs, the consumption of which was
thought to be injurious to public morals.[68] But even here the public nature
of the threat to be eliminated derived at least in part from the frequency of
its occurrence. Drinking threatened the public morals because too many
people already did it, and more and more would do it, or so the police argument went.

There was, however, another element to the protection of public morals,
and to the temperance movement in particular. The problem with drinking
wasn't just that it tended to corrupt society and therefore ultimately to bring
about its collapse. Drinking also was immoral in and of itself. It offended the
moral sense of "the people." From this point of view, the threat of drinking
to the public morals of the community actually wasn't a threat at all. It constituted an offense—rather than a mere threat—to the moral sense of the
community, or rather a particular segment thereof. It offended the public's
sense of morality rather than threatening the public morals.

And it's this second, not always explicit, aspect of moral policing that the
courts took as the foundation of their judicial police power through the use
of common law misdemeanors. Certain types of conduct, and certain types
of people, didn't simply pose a threat to the public's moral police. They were
actually directly offensive to the public morality, as interpreted by the judiciary. Protecting the moral health of the people meant identifying and eliminating immorality, wherever and however it reared its ugly head.

Under this view of common law misdemeanors as offenses against public morals, i.e., against the public's moral police, the courts now could reframe private nuisances as police offenses. "[W]hatever amounts to a public wrong may be made the subject of an indictment," the Pennsylvania Supreme Court explained in the 1788 case of *Respublica v. Teischer*, upholding a conviction of "maliciously, wilfully, and wickedly killing a Horse."[69] And as the state's attorney general argued successfully in that case, a public wrong included "every act of a public evil example, and against good morals."[70]

In this broad interpretation, the common law misdemeanor functioned as a sort of fall back charge whenever the public nuisance, the judiciary's traditional common law police offense, didn't stick. As another example, take the case of *Commonwealth v. Wing*, from 1829. Mr. Wing had been indicted for "maliciously discharging a gun, whereby a woman, named M.A. Gifford, was thrown into convulsions and cramps." The problem was that Mr. Wing, who was out goose hunting, knew that Ms. Gifford "was subject to such convulsions and cramps upon the firing of a gun," and that "at the time when the offense was committed, he was warned and requested not to fire."[71] After explaining that this conduct constituted at best a private nuisance, since it affected only a single person rather than the public at large, the Massachusetts Supreme Judicial Court nonetheless upheld the indictment. For even if Mr. Wing's conduct didn't amount to a public nuisance, it nonetheless was indictable as a common law misdemeanor, as a "want and deliberate act of mischief."

Seven years later, a New Hampshire case provided another illustration of the usefulness of the common law misdemeanor as an all-purpose moral police offense. In *State v. Buckman*, the defendant had been convicted of "knowingly and maliciously" poisoning the Wilson family's water well with "the carcase of an animal."[72] Once again, the court explained that public nuisance wasn't available because, although "said Wilson and his wife and family became greatly injured in health thereby," there had been no threat to the public at large. And once again, the court had recourse to the common law misdemeanor, citing "strongly analogous" offenses such as "the selling of unwholesome provisions, or the mixture of poisonous ingredients in food or drink, designed for any individual, are indictable offenses at common law." Note that the analogy between the poisoning of the Wilson family well and these other offenses does not lie in their common dangerousness to the broader public. In that case, Buckman would have committed a public nuisance. Instead these offenses, in the court's view, all constituted acts "of a public evil example, and against good morals." They are punishable as offenses against public morals, not as offenses against public health.

The clearest and most influential statement of the police foundation of common law (i.e., judicially created) crimes came in 1881, in the case of

Commonwealth v. McHale.[73] McHale and others had been indicted for conspiracy to commit election fraud, in particular "to procure a false, fraudulent and untrue count and return of the votes" cast by "divers tricks and devices, and other illegal and corrupt means." This conduct, the justices of the Pennsylvania Supreme Court felt, could not go unpunished. Unfortunately, however, they were not "able to find any . . . Act of Assembly which will sustain these indictments." In fact, they were forced to concede "that if the question depends upon the fact whether a precise definition of this offence can be found in the text books, or perhaps in the adjudged English cases, the law is with the defendants."

But the absence of statutory prohibition, or precedent, was not dispositive, it turned out. For there still remained the courts' power to police, by means of the common law misdemeanor. A common law misdemeanor, however, is nothing but an offense against the police of the state, as the court explained in a remarkable, and much quoted, passage:

What is a common-law offence?

The highest authority upon this point is Blackstone. In chap. 13, of vol. 4, of Sharswood's edition, it is thus defined: "The last species of offences which especially affect the Commonwealth are those against the public police or economy. By the public police and economy I mean the due regulation and domestic order of the kingdom, whereby the individuals of the state, like members of a well-governed family, are bound to conform their general behavior to the rules of propriety, good neighborhood and good manners, and to be decent, industrious and inoffensive in their respective stations. This head of offences must therefore be very miscellaneous, as it *comprises all such crimes as especially affect public society*, and are not comprehended under any of the four preceding series. These amount some of them to felony, and others to misdemeanors only."[74]

The common law crime and the police offense were one and the same thing. And so the following definition of the common law crime was derived:

We are of opinion that all such crimes as especially affect public society are indictable at common law. The test is not whether precedents can be found in the books, but whether they injuriously affect the public police and economy.[75]

This definition remained the guiding principle of common criminal lawmaking in the busiest common criminal lawmaking state, Pennsylvania, until the abandonment of common criminal lawmaking there with the new Pennsylvania Crimes Code of 1972.[76] Perhaps the best known application of the *McHale* principle came in the 1964 case of *Commonwealth v. Keller*, a staple of American criminal law casebooks, though it is rarely thought of as a police power case.[77] Violet Keller had hidden away two newborns, to whom she had given birth secretly and who may or may not have been born alive, in boxes, one in the basement, the other in a bathroom closet. She was convicted of two counts of a common law misdemeanor, dubbed "indecent disposition of a dead body." There was no relevant criminal statute, nor was there, in the words of the court, "precedent in this Commonwealth that is on all fours with the facts in this case." "Indeed," the court acknowledged, "there is no case at all dealing with the indecent or immoral disposition of a dead body."

Nonetheless, the court affirmed the conviction under the rule in *McHale*, quoting once again Blackstone's definition of the power to police. "The *McHale* doctrine," the judge explained, "has been held to be applicable to any conduct which is inherently offensive to the public peace, decency, morals, and economy." And "indecent disposition of a dead body" certainly fit that bill, or so the court thought. An English court had reached the same conclusion, some two hundred years earlier, in a case of "grave-snatching" for purposes of anatomical dissection, which was held to constitute an indecent act "*contra bones* [sic] *mores.*"[78]

Notice that these common law offenses were of an entirely private nature. Unlike a public nuisance, or even an offense against the moral well-being of a group of persons, Ms. Keller's "indecent disposition of a dead body" wasn't committed in public, nor did it—or was it intended to—offend the public. On the contrary, the point of the "indecent disposition" was to hide, not to publicize. In some cases, "indecent disposition of a dead body," in particular through burning rather than burying, may offend the public, or a considerable segment thereof, and therefore constitute a nuisance, as James Fitzgerald Stephen pointed out in an 1884 case.[79] The private, and in Ms. Keller's case the secret, disposal of a dead body, however, offends nothing other than the moral sensibilities of the judge.[80]

Although Pennsylvania courts may have been particularly enthusiastic in their protection of the public morals, the connection between common law crimes and police wasn't limited to that state. With the *McHale* rule, Pennsylvania judges simply made that connection most explicit. Even some of the jurisdictions that did away with judicial criminal lawmaking *codified* the common law misdemeanor, and thereby American judicial police. The New York Penal Law of 1909, for example, punished as a misdemeanor "any act which seriously injures the person or property of another, or which *seriously disturbs or endangers the public peace or health, or which openly outrages public decency*, for which no other punishment is expressly prescribed."[81]

In other jurisdictions, courts preferred to speak of morality alone, without making clear that good morals was an aspect of the overall police, or communal well-being, of the state. As the Maine Supreme Court explained in 1939, the courts were obliged to "give expression to the changing customs and sentiments of the people," and moral sentiments in particular.[82]

Still, even if courts didn't always identify—or perhaps even recognize— the police roots of the common law misdemeanor, it's important to keep these roots in mind. American, and before them English, courts began exercising a judicial police power with the powerful control tool of public nuisance in all its myriad permutations. When that seemingly all encompassing concept was still not quite flexible enough, the courts turned to the common law misdemeanor. Nuisances and common law misdemeanors, in the end, made for a dynamic duo of judicial police power.

But even with their full police arsenal of nuisance and common law misdemeanor, the courts' police power still could not match that of the legislature, and by delegation, of the executive. Courts could expand the definitions of offenses to reach ever wider circles of conduct, and of people, but they could not legislate. Their institutional role limited judges to the resolution of particular cases or controversies before them. This meant that they could not take proactive measures. They were always reacting to particular offenses that already had taken place. They could do nothing to prevent them. They could only deal with their occurrences.

That doesn't mean that nuisances and common law misdemeanors required the actual infliction of harm. The Wilsons may have gotten sick from drinking water out of their poisoned well. Ms. Gifford may have suffered from convulsions at the sound of the gun. Likewise Blackstone's cart stuck on the bridge may actually have interfered with the flow of traffic. But the essence of a common law misdemeanor, as well as that of a nuisance, was not the infliction of harm, but the *threat* of harm. Common law misdemeanors needed to be punished because they *tended* to corrupt public morals. For nuisances it was enough to "endanger the comfort, repose, health or safety" of the public.[83]

Nuisances, in other words, were also about prevention. And still, even if they did not require the infliction of harm, they nonetheless required the creation of danger. To establish a nuisance, the prosecutor needed to prove that the particular person, thing, or act in question in fact posed a threat to the police of the community.

And the same was true of common law misdemeanors. Commission of a misdemeanor required at least that one "seriously disturb[ed] or endanger[ed] the public peace or health." And even offenses against the moral police needed to be, well, in fact offensive, they needed to "openly outrage public decency."[84] Offenses *contra bonos mores* needed actually to be *contra bonos mores*.

The legislature, by contrast, could provide the public police with an additional layer of protection. It could set up rules designed to prevent nuisances, or common law misdemeanors. In other words, it could make police offenses out of threats of threats of harm, or dangers of dangers to the police. The courts didn't have to wait until actual harm was done. With nuisances and common law misdemeanors they could go after threats of harm. Legislatures didn't even have to wait that long. They could prevent the threat itself. They could, in other words, nip any police threat in the bud; they could "stifl[e] the fountains of evil."[85] But the legislature's police measures weren't self-enforcing: they needed the courts to apply, interpret, and affirm them. This is the other, indirect, side of American judicial police, which we will discuss next.

Enforcing and Defining Legislative Police

The distinction between legislative exercises of the police power and the common law of nuisance lay at the heart of the opinion which became the most cited discussion of the police power in American jurisprudence. Chief Justice Shaw's opinion in *Commonwealth v. Alger* illustrates two important ways in which the courts, indirectly, contributed to the police of the state.[86] Most immediate, *Alger* was an ordinary case of a court enforcing a legislative police measure. The legislature could pass preventive police measures, but it depended on the judiciary to punish their violation. *Alger* was about a classic police regulation, the 1837 "act to preserve the harbor of Boston, and to prevent encroachments therein."[87] In this act, the Massachusetts legislature decreed that "no wharf, pier or building, or incumbrance of any kind" was to extend into the harbor water beyond a certain line. Any structure offending this provision was to "be removed and abated as a public nuisance." Moreover, any person offending it was to "be punished by a fine not less than one thousand dollars, nor more than five thousand dollars." Cyrus Alger had done just that, and was convicted by a jury, after the judge had instructed it "that on the evidence introduced, if believed, the government were entitled to a verdict."

But *Alger* did more than illustrate judicial enforcement of the myriad of legislative police measures, against inanimate and animate objects. On appeal, it also provided the court with an opportunity to explore the nature of the police power in general. The most influential American discussions of the police power appeared in judicial opinions written by state judges, not in treatises or other commentary, and certainly not in legislative debates or even the statutes they preceded. And *Alger* was the most influential of the lot.

Given *Alger's* importance in the American police power canon, it produces remarkably little in the way of theory. About the origins of the power, Shaw makes three suggestions: the royal prerogative, the Massachusetts constitution, and "the nature of well ordered civil society." Of these three, only the third attracted attention. And so the paragraph asserting the origin of the police power in "the nature of well ordered civil society," without explaining what such a society consisted of, was reproduced time and time again, not only in other judicial opinions, but in the treatises as well.[88]

We too will spend some time examining this oft-cited passage. But first it's worth taking a look at the two ignored hints about the origin of the police power. They will be familiar to us. Shaw suggests that the power to police derives from the king's prerogative. As we know already, all land in England was held at the mercy of ("de") some lord, and eventually the lord of lords, the king. As the ultimate landholder, the king had the power to regulate its use, just as he had the power to regulate its possession. This regulatory power, however, was the power of the householder. As such, it was to be exercised with an eye toward discharging the householder's responsibility to maximize the welfare of the household.

The power to regulate property in the public interest thus was but one aspect of the general power to regulate the entire royal household, encompassing animate and inanimate objects alike. In America, the colonial governments exercised that police power, as an aspect of the royal prerogative, on behalf of the king. From there it passed onto the various states, because "when relinquished by the parent country" it had to "vest somewhere; and, as between the several states and the United States, whatever may have been the doubts on the subject, it is settled that it vested in the several states, in their sovereign capacity, respectively, and was not transferred to the United States by the adoption of the constitution intended to form a more perfect union."[89]

The second source of the police power Shaw considers is the state constitution. According to article IV of the Massachusetts constitution, "full power and authority are hereby given and granted to the [legislature], from time to time, to make, ordain, and establish, all manner of wholesome and reasonable orders, laws, statutes, and ordinances, directions and instructions, either with penalties or without; so as the same be not repugnant or contrary to this constitution, as they shall judge to be for the good and welfare of this commonwealth, and for the government and ordering thereof, and of the subjects of the same."[90] Quoting this passage almost in its entirety, Shaw declares that it defines "the police power vested in the legislature." It's the only time the term "police power" appears in the opinion.

Now sources one and two aren't mutually exclusive. One might say, although Shaw doesn't, that article IV merely constitutionalized the fact that

the police power had been transferred onto the legislature of the newly independent state, along with every other aspect of what was once the royal
prerogative. Moreover, the quoted passage could be read as clarifying the
governmental branch onto which this power was to be conferred, the legislature. At the very least, there is nothing about the formulation of the police
power in the Massachusetts constitution that is inconsistent with the derivation of the power from the king's prerogative.

In fact, the references to the two sources of the police power are best read
together, and in sequence. Shaw does not draw a sharp line between the royal
prerogative and the constitution. Instead, he stresses their connection. The
constitution doesn't constitute a new sort of police as the self-government of
the constituents, in sharp contrast with the authoritarian police power of autocratic Britain. It merely announces the transfer of that patriarchal power
from the king to its new holder, the state (not the federal) legislature. To ignore this fact is to ignore those parts of Shaw's opinion which are devoted to
tracing the police power of the Massachusetts legislature to the royal prerogative.

The police power, as Shaw stresses again and again, is rooted in the *jus publicum*, which is distinguished from the *jus privatum*, the "right of property in
the soil, which the king may grant, and which may be held by a subject, and
the grant of which will confer on the grantee such privileges and benefits, as
can be enjoyed therein, subject to the *jus publicum*."[91] To say that the right of
property is subject to the police power is simply a modern way of saying that
the *jus privatum* is subject to the *jus publicum*. The *jus publicum*, however, is
nothing other than "the royal prerogative," or "royal right," which is "vested
in the king, as the head and sovereign representative of the nation."[92]

Ernst Freund, in his great police power treatise, quotes a passage from
1606 which nicely captures both the distinction between *jus privatum* and *jus
publicum* and the connection between the latter and the notion of police
(here referred to as "policy and government"):

> The king's power is double, ordinary and absolute, and they have several
> laws and ends. That of the ordinary is for the profit of particular subjects,
> for the execution of civil justice, the determining of *meum*; and this is ex-
> ercised by equity and justice in ordinary courts, and by the civilians is nom-
> inated *jus privatum*, and with us common law; and these laws cannot be
> changed without parliament; and although that their form and course may
> be changed and interrupted, yet they can never be changed in substance.
> The absolute power of the king is not that which is converted or executed
> to private use, to the benefit of any particular person, but is only that which
> is applied to the general benefit of the people, and is *salus populi*; as the peo-

ple is the body, and the king the head; and this power is not guided by the rules which direct only at the common law, and is most properly named policy and government, and as the constitution of this body varieth with the time, so varieth this absolute law, according to the wisdom of the king, for the common good; and these being general rules, and true as they are, all things done within those rules are lawful.[93]

As Freund points out, this passage not only differentiates between "justice (maintenance of private right) and police (promotion of the public welfare)," but also suggests that the distinction between the two "nearly coincided with the division of judicial or legislative and executive power."[94] This meant that the laws of *jus privatum* required the *consent* of parliament, whereas the exercise of the *jus publicum* did not. The king's power to maximize the *salus populi*, the object of his *jus publicum* or royal prerogative, was "absolute." Its contours are flexible, and vary over time, "according to the wisdom of the king," who stands to his people as a head stands to its body. The king, after all, is in the words of a 1637 case, the "head and supreme protector of the kingdom," in other words the, "*pater-familias*, which by the Law of OEconomick is, not only to keep peace at home, but to protect his wife and children, and whole family from abroad."[95]

The rough parallel between police and the executive, on the one hand, and between justice and legislative and judicial power, on the other, still held, even after the transfer of the police power to American state legislatures. To see this continuity, however, it helps to differentiate among the powers and branches of government. Police is an executive matter, as opposed to a legislative or judicial one, to the extent that it deals with the ordering of the state family so as to maximize its welfare. Lawmaking and law-applying— *legis*lation (the setting of law) and ad*ju*dication, or *juris*diction (the announcing of law)—require consent and participation by their object. In fact, in modern law they require the identity of subject and object, of the person making and applying the law and the person about whom the law is made and against whom it is applied. There is no similar requirement in police.

Police is done by whoever is charged with protecting the welfare of the state family, no matter what branch of government he or she may belong to. As we've just seen, American judges were not content to leave policing to the legislature. Courts policed just as the legislatures did. The differentiation of legislative and judicial functions is, after all, a fairly recent development. It's no accident that the article of the Massachusetts constitution Shaw quotes (without saying so) assigned the power of police to the "general *court*,"[96] the name of the Massachusetts legislature to this day.

Now, to say that Shaw attempts to connect the police power of the Massachusetts legislature to the prerogative *jus publicum* of the English king is not to say that he succeeds in this attempt. Throughout the opinion, Shaw vacillates between discussions of the *jus publicum* over the particular type of property at issue in *Alger* (namely the land between high and low tide) and over property in general. Detailed doctrinal examinations of the specific public—and royal—restrictions on the former give way to sweeping pronouncements about general restrictions on the latter. Moreover, the line from the king's prerogative through the colonial charter, the Declaration of Independence, and the Peace Treaty, and ending with the commonwealth of Massachusetts, but not the United States, is anything but neat and straight. It's certainly no more direct than any other attempts to trace American state powers to their English roots, especially if these roots turned out to fall within the royal prerogative rather than, say, the English Parliament.[97] While the precise nature of the connection between the state legislature's police power and the royal patriarchal prerogative remained obscure, its existence was a commonplace at the time:

> [W]hen this country achieved its independence, the prerogatives of the crown devolved upon the people of the states. And this power still remains with them, except so far as they have delegated a portion of it to the federal government. The sovereign will is made known to us by legislative enactment. The state, as a sovereign, is the parens patriae.[98]

But none of this mattered very much for the future history of American police power. The possible historical or constitutional origins of the police power, hinted at rather than fully developed by Shaw, attracted little attention. Instead it was Shaw's claim that such a power grew out of "the nature of well ordered civil society" that struck a cord with his nineteenth-century audience, and was to have a lasting effect on American police thought. The relevant passage is worth a careful reading because it touches on many of the issues that would preoccupy American police power discourse for some time to come:

> We think it is a settled principle, growing out of the nature of well ordered civil society, that every holder of property, however absolute and unqualified may be his title, holds it under the implied liability that his use of it may be so regulated, that it shall not be injurious to the equal enjoyment of others having an equal right to the enjoyment of their property, nor injurious to the rights of the community. All property in this commonwealth, as well that in the interior as that bordering on tide waters, is derived directly or indirectly from the government, and held subject to those

general regulations, which are necessary to the common good and general welfare. Rights of property, like all other social and conventional rights, are subject to such reasonable limitations in their enjoyment, as shall prevent them from being injurious, and to such reasonable restraints and regulations established by law, as the legislature, under the governing and controlling power vested in them by the constitution, may think necessary and expedient.

This is very different from the right of eminent domain, the right of a government to take and appropriate private property to public use, whenever the public exigency requires it; which can be done only on condition of providing a reasonable compensation therefor. The power we allude to is rather the police power, the power vested in the legislature by the constitution, to make, ordain and establish all manner of wholesome and reasonable laws, statutes and ordinances, either with penalties or without, not repugnant to the constitution, as they shall judge to be for the good and welfare of the commonwealth, and of the subjects of the same.

It is much easier to perceive and realize the existence and sources of this power, than to mark its boundaries, or prescribe limits to its exercise. There are many cases in which such a power is exercised by all well ordered governments, and where its fitness is so obvious, that all well regulated minds will regard it as reasonable. Such are the laws to prohibit the use of warehouses for the storage of gunpowder near habitations or highways; to restrain the height to which wooden buildings may be erected in populous neighborhoods, and require them to be covered with slate or other incombustible material; to prohibit buildings from being used for hospitals for contagious diseases, or for the carrying on of noxious or offensive trades; to prohibit the raising of a dam, and causing stagnant water to spread over meadows, near inhabited villages, thereby raising noxious exhalations, injurious to health and dangerous to life.[99]

Here, then, is Shaw's account of the police power, which soon emerged as the most influential American (that is, non-Blackstonian) one. An indigenous American theory of the police power this is not. In fact it is startlingly doctrinaire, especially if compared to the careful, if circuitous, argument from royal prerogative. Without argument, or citation, Shaw simply declares it to be a "settled principle" that all property is held subject to the state's police power. As Judge Redfield would do in the Vermont case of *Thorpe*, published two years later,[100] Shaw portrays the "fitness" of the police power enjoyed by "all well ordered governments" as too obvious to require elaboration, at least for "well regulated minds," which presumably are as well policed as is their government. Instead of citing precedent, or developing a rationale, Shaw assembles a list of what he considers illustrative exercises of the police power. What justifies these exercises he doesn't say.

There is no discussion of the king's—or the legislature's, the judiciary's, the state's, the commonwealth's—quasi-paternal obligation to provide for the welfare of his public family, as there was in Blackstone. There is likewise no discussion of police as a mode of local self-governance.[101] And, needless to say, there is no attempt to derive police from some theory of "the state," charged with maximizing the happiness of its subjects. There is no theory at all.

The obviousness of police in Shaw's discussion hints at a tautology. The power to police, Shaw explains, grows out of the nature of "well ordered society." That's another way of saying that a well ordered society wouldn't be well ordered without the people in charge of running it being empowered to order it. Good order implies the power to order in the first place, presumably because the state of nature is chaos. If that's so, then of course the power to police is of the essence in any well ordered society.

This tautology, however, begs the question. If the power to police is implied by the very concept of a well ordered society, we must then ask ourselves what makes a society well ordered—and a mind well regulated, for that matter. This would require a political theory, however, and this Shaw doesn't seem to have, or at least doesn't feel compelled to lay out.

Instead of a theory, Shaw produces a motto: use of one's property "may be so regulated, that it shall not be injurious to the equal enjoyment of others having an equal right to the enjoyment of their property, nor injurious to the rights of the community." He doesn't explain where this fundamental, or at least broad, principle comes from. Once again, there are no citations, and no arguments, presumably because it is so obviously true. Here Shaw appears to be invoking the familiar principle of *sic utere tuo ut alienum non laedas* (use what's yours so that you don't harm another). This time honored rule at least would account for the first clause of Shaw's motto, dealing with one person's interference with the rights of another.

But there is more to the motto than that, for Shaw doesn't limit the state's power to police to interpersonal matters. *Sic utere* is concerned with the rights of "another" (alienum). Shaw's principle, by contrast, deals with the "rights of the community" as well. But this, the second clause, of Shaw's motto also can be seen as reflecting another "lawlatin" principle, one that deals not with individual rights, but with the welfare of the community, namely that *salus populi suprema lex est* (the people's welfare is the supreme law).

Now once Shaw's rule is parsed in this way, several problems emerge that Shaw might have addressed. To begin with, the two principles are incompatible. The first is a principle of justice, the second a rule of police, if I may use Freund's (and Bentham's) distinction here. Put in terms of the distinction between *jus privatum* and *jus publicum*, which Shaw also invokes, *sic utere* governs the former, and *salus populi* the latter. *Sic utere* protects the rights of persons, and to that end places restrictions on the rights of other persons. *Salus populi* limits the rights of persons, not for the sake of protecting those of other persons, but for the sake of the *salus populi*, the people's welfare, i.e., the police. To quote again from Chief Baron Fleming's argument in Bates' Case from 1606, the "absolute power of the king is not that which is converted or executed to private use, to the benefit of any particular person, but is only that which is applied to the general benefit of the people, and is *salus populi*."[102]

Sic utere isn't a maxim of police. It's the application of the fundamental principle of law to a particular legal right, the right to property. The fundamental principle is familiar since at least Justinian's Institutes, which in its opening chapters present the three precepts of law ("iuris praecepta"): *honeste vivere, alterum non laedere, suum cuique tribuere* (live honorably, don't harm others, give everyone his due).[103] Leibniz erected his moral philosophy on these three principles.[104] Kant also recognized them as principles of right, but identified the second one as the basic maxim of law (lex iuridica), or of external duty: "neminem laede," harm no one.[105] The basic idea here is that law concerns itself with, and only with, the harm one person inflicts upon another. The realm of law is limited to persons as both offenders and as victims. A person who suffers harm from something other than another person is not the law's concern. The same goes for a person who inflicts harm on something other than another person. The paradigmatic subject and the object of law, in other words, is the person. None of this has anything to do with the public welfare, the *salus populi*. Strictly speaking, law concerns itself neither with anyone's *salus*, nor with the *salus* of the *populus*. It concerns itself only with the rights of persons.

The principle of *sic utere tuo ut alienum non laedas* applies the general principle of "alienum non laedere" to the particular case of one person's harming another through the use of his or her property ("utere tuo"). It makes clear that the law forbids one to harm another, even if the harm is inflicted in the course of exercising a right, such as the right to use one's property as one sees fit. That's not to say, of course, that one is never justified in harming another under any circumstances. It merely says that the exercise of one's right to property is not, by itself, a sufficient justification for doing so.

At any rate, *sic utere* is directed at persons, and only at persons. It is framed in terms of rights—rights that are exercised and rights that are violated. It does not apply to things. And it's designed to protect persons, and only persons. It does not protect the state, the people, or some other community. In these senses, it is a maxim of law, rather than a rule of police—or if you will, a categorical, rather than a hypothetical, imperative.

Salus populi, by contrast, is directed at any and all threats to the welfare not of a particular person, but the people. It speaks not in terms of rights, but in terms of *salus*, i.e., of well-being or health. It may of course affect rights, in cases where it is applied to threats emanating from a person, i.e., a rights bearer. In those cases, it restricts rights of one person without protecting the rights of another. It instead protects, in Shaw's somewhat misleading phrase, "the rights of the community." In some cases, the threat to be eliminated is human, as in the case of vagrants or immigrants or paupers. In others, the threat has no human element whatsoever, as in the case of wild animals, natural disasters, or abandoned property.

In others yet, persons are only indirectly affected, often through a relationship of ownership, possession, or use, to the dangerous object. This was the case in *Alger*. The threat to be eliminated, or the nuisance to be abated, was the wharf. Alger's rights were affected because the wharf was his. The same goes for most of the other objects of police power regulation Shaw listed in his opinion, such as gunpowder warehouses, wooden buildings, hospitals. (In the other examples, the object of police is the particular individual, who becomes a threat through an activity, such as carrying on a "noxious" trade or raising a dam.)

Given the irrelevance of the nature of a threat to public police, however, as long as it is, or at least might become, a threat, the distinction between the dangerous object and its owner (or possessor, or user) is irrelevant as well. Note in *Alger*, for instance, that the challenged regulation applied both to the wharf and its builder. The wharf was to be abated as a public nuisance. But that was not all. Alger, too, was to be punished for having erected it.

Now the *salus populi* maxim needn't be interpreted as establishing the superiority of communal rights over individual rights. Much depends on one's understanding of what constitutes "salus" and whose "salus" is at stake. So even Kant could endorse the maxim, or rather a variation of it, "salus reipublicae suprema lex est." Note first that Kant speaks of the well-being of the republic, rather than of the public, or the people, or even the commonwealth. This distinction is crucial because to him the community is not a uniform mass whose welfare needs maximizing. Instead, he regards it as a republic of self-governing persons. And the welfare, or salus, of this republic of self-governing persons consists specifically in the manifestation of their freedom, i.e., their capacity for self-government. To Kant, the salus of the state as a republic is the autonomy of its constituents, which it achieves by "organizing, forming, and maintaining itself in accordance with the laws of freedom." It represents not "merely the individual well-being and happiness of the citizens of the state; for—as Rousseau asserts—this end may perhaps be more agreeably and more desirably attained in the state of nature, or even under a despotic government. But the welfare of the state, as its own highest good, signifies that condition in which the greatest harmony is attained between its constitution and the principles of right. . . . "[106] In this interpretation, *salus populi*—or rather *reipublicae*—*suprema lex est*, is no longer misleading, nor is it a maxim of police. Instead, it captures the moral foundation of law: self-government, or autonomy.

Another way of capturing the distinction between *sic utere* and *salus populi* is by analogy to that between private and public nuisance. The analogy isn't perfect because the police power in the name of *salus populi* is far broader than the power to abate nuisances. Both protect "the public" (or, in the case of some versions of public nuisance, "a considerable number of persons"[107]), and both abate threats without awaiting harm. But nuisances, as we noted above, still require the actual presence of a threat. Police offenses in the name of *salus populi* eliminate anything, and anyone, that, and who, fits the definition of a police rule designed to eliminate threats, regardless whether that something, or someone, poses a threat or not.

The reason for this expansion of state power to the elimination of threats of threats is the cardinal importance of the target of the threat, and the beneficiary of this extra protection, the *salus populi*. Since the welfare of the entire community is at stake, rather than merely the rights of an individual person, early intervention becomes essential. Here, the welfare of the people is conceptualized as distinct from the welfare, and the rights, of any particular person or group of persons, and as obviously superior to it.

The necessarily preventive character of police lies at the heart of *Alger*. As we know by now, Shaw wasn't the only one, nor even the first, to highlight this feature of police. So did Bentham, for example, and the continental police scientists. In fact, *Alger* wasn't the first time Shaw had worked out the distinctively preventive nature of police. *Alger* in many ways applies conclusions Shaw had reached several years before, in the case of *Commonwealth v. Tewksbury*.[108] This case involved a police action against a person, rather than an object, who through an activity, rather than through a particular characteristic, had shown himself to be a threat to the public police. William Tewksbury had been fined under a statute for removing sand and gravel from his beach. Like *Alger*, this was not a common law nuisance case, private or public. There was no allegation that Tewksbury had made himself, or created, a nuisance. I have nothing to add to Leonard Levy's perceptive discussion of the central issue in the case:

> Could the legislature interfere with his use of his own property *before* he became amenable to the provisions of the common law? Shaw explained that the common law did not adequately protect the public. What might

be dangerous under one set of circumstances might in another be harmless, but the safety, health, and comfort of the community could not be left to the restraint of a nuisance already committed. It was, therefore, competent for the legislature, said Shaw, "to interpose, and by positive enactment to prohibit a use of property which would be injurious to the public, under particular circumstances." In other words, by showing that the general welfare might require the anticipation and prevention of prospective wrongs, Shaw established for the police power a broader base than the conventional restraints of the common law normally permitted.[109]

Alger starkly highlighted the distinction between police and nuisance. For in *Alger* it was settled that the wharf in fact did not constitute a threat, never mind a harm, to the public. It therefore could not have been abated under public nuisance law. It could only be abated as a violation of a statute passed *with the aim of* preventing threats to the public, no matter whether a particular object constituted such a threat or not.

The preventive, even anticipatory, aspect of police cannot be understood unless one views it within the context of the concept of police as a whole. Police was a matter of life and death, not merely of this or that individual, but of the community as a whole. When the survival of the community household was a stake, the macro householder could not afford to take chances. In Levy's words, "the safety, health, and comfort of the community could not be left to the restraint of a nuisance already committed." Police regulations had to paint with a broad brush, if they were to do their job, protecting the community against all threats. Given the gravity of the task of police, the occasional false positive, as Alger's wharf for instance, could not stand in the way of the elimination of threats.

Prevention, i.e., early state interference, reflects the foundation of police in the unquestionable right of self-preservation under conditions of necessity.[110] This is not a general right of preservation enjoyed by all persons as such. It's the right of the householder to do whatever he deems prudent and necessary to protect his household, and everyone and everything within it, against threats from within and without. Note that this right of self-preservation is also essentially individual; it's the right of the householder to defend himself, where his self encompasses his household as well, rather than vice versa. At bottom, police is therefore, paradoxically, not a matter of social, or communal, or societal, self-defense at all. It's not a matter of simply weighing the interests of the community against the interests of the individual; it's a matter of the *householder* determining the most appropriate means to the end of maximizing, or at least maintaining, the welfare of *his* household. From the perspective of police, the interests of "the community" are of crucial significance, but that significance is only instrumental with respect to the householder's truly fundamental interest in his self-preservation.

Many American writers have stressed the connection between the police power and the right of self-preservation. In fact, if there is an indigenous American contribution to the theory of police, it may be the emphatic, even enthusiastic, endorsement of this relationship. This tendency to equate policing with self-preservation also helps explain why so many Americans found the power of police so obviously legitimate. Who, after all, would deny anyone the power to defend him- or herself, or even itself, as we shall see?

Among the many discussions of the police power's foundation in the right of self-preservation, one deserves our special attention. For it nicely captures not only the urgency of survival driving the police power, but also the essential apersonality and ahumanity of police as a mode of governance. I mean Judge Redfield's exploration of the nature and origin of the police power in *Spalding v. Preston*, a Vermont case decided in 1848, after *Tewksbury* and before *Alger*.[111] Other than Shaw, Redfield was probably the most cited state judge on the definition of the police power. But it's not the *Spalding* opinion that made his name, but *Thorpe*, which we have already had occasion to quote. Much as *Alger* presupposes *Tewksbury*, however, *Thorpe* presupposed *Spalding*. While the *Thorpe* case involved an issue of greater moment, namely the state's power to regulate the railroads under the police power, it's in *Spalding*, a factually trivial case, where Redfield takes time to explore the contours of the police power.

Spalding is noteworthy not only because of Redfield's attempt to ground the police power, rather than merely to assert the obviousness of its existence. It also illustrates the breadth of the power. American discussions often treat the police power mostly, if not merely, as a regulation of property, and by implication as a limitation upon the right of property.[112] As we'll see, the police power today survives in federal constitutional jurisprudence mainly as a point of contrast to the power of eminent domain, unless it's invoked to delineate the scope of state sovereignty in the face of federal legislation, particularly in purported exercise of the commerce clause. But, as *Spalding* makes clear, and Shaw's much cited opinion in *Alger* does not, the power of police is far wider than the power to regulate objects that happen to be in someone's possession. The power instead is the comprehensive power of a state to maintain its good police by any means necessary, including the elimination of threats internal and external, human and nonhuman, animate and inanimate. It is the mode of governance which "rests upon necessity and the right of self-protection."[113]

Spalding was about a tort suit (in trover, to be exact) brought against a sheriff "for eleven hundred pieces of German silver, of the precise size and thickness of Mexican dollars, and made in that form for the purpose of being stamped and milled into counterfeit coin of that description." Now it turned out that the state statute which authorized sheriffs and other officers to seize counterfeit money and tools listed only "bank bills" and "stamps, dies, plates, blocks, and presses," but made no reference to counterfeit coins or the implements for making them. For that reason, the court had to turn to nonstatutory authority to justify the seizure and to throw out the suit. And this nonstatutory authority Redfield found in the power of police:

> [T]he [sheriff's] authority must rest merely upon general grounds of preventive justice, aside of any statute whatever upon the subject. All governments, upon the most obvious principles of necessity, exercise more or less of preventive force, in regard to all subjects coming under their cognizance and control. This is in analogy to the conduct of individuals, and, indeed, of all animal existence. Many of the instincts of animals exhibit their most astonishing developments in fleeing from the elements, from disease, and from death, at its most distant sound, long before the minutest symptom appears to rational natures. This is the great secret of personal enterprise and success. So, too, in the history of civil governments prevention is more important, and far more available than cure. All sanitary cordons and preventive regulations, every thing in regard to the police of our cities and large towns, indeed prohibitions of lotteries, gambling houses, brothels and disorderly taverns, whether done by general statutes, or mere police regulations, all come under the right of preventing more serious injuries by stifling the fountains of evil.[114]

What mattered was stifling the fountains of evil. Their nature, apart from their dangerousness, mattered not. The police power authorized the elimination of all threats, be it through the destruction of buildings, the incapacitation of mad dogs or men (mad or not), and through the seizure of counterfeit coin poised to infiltrate the currency:

> Society, in all these cases and many others, has the right to anticipate, in order that it may prevent, the injury, which is thus threatened. If it were not so, men, in a social state, would be far more powerless, for purposes of defence, than in a natural state. All will admit the right to restrain a mad man, or a mad animal, from committing injury. And is the rational man, or the senseless material, which threatens crime or irreparable injury, less subject to control, than the maniac, or his torch?[115]

In sum, police prevents. It must prevent because the survival of the community is at stake. The object of the threat is any group. It may be a group of persons; it may be one of animals. The source, or subject, of the threat is any fountain of evil. It may be personal, but it need not. It might be an animal, or an inanimate object. The goal of police is stifling these fountains, eliminating these threats. The object of police, the policed, is any threat, which is apersonal in the sense described. The subject of police, the policer, is the leader of the group, the individual charged with its welfare. In human society, police can take many forms. An exercise of the police power may come in the shape of a general statute, or it may appear as a police regulation. Form here is secondary to substance, the need to do whatever it takes to protect the community.

Police thus is a matter of group survival. The exercise of police power is a necessity, as any threat to the community is an emergency. In Shaw's words, the legislature was authorized, even obligated, to supplement ordinary nuisance law with the police regulation in question in the name of "maintaining and protecting the acknowledged public right." It was "this consideration, (the expediency and necessity of defining and securing the rights of the public,) which creates the exigency," and therefore justifies exercising the police power.[116]

By portraying the power of police as a matter of instinct, Redfield dramatically highlights its inevitability, its obviousness. "All governments, upon the most obvious principles of necessity, exercise more or less of preventive force, in regard to all subjects coming under their cognizance and control." Again and again, the police power is said to "rest upon necessity and the right of self-protection."[117]

The paradigmatic case of an exigency triggering the exercise of the police power was the burning of a house to prevent the spread of fire. In such a case, the state was authorized to summarily destroy buildings without compensating the owner. In the words of Judge Cooley, "Here the individual is in no degree in fault, but his interest must yield to that 'necessity' which 'knows no law,' "[118] but, we might add, does know police.

Now there are two ways of reading these exercises of police power in cases of necessity. If we interpret them as manifestations of the natural instinct of self-preservation, they appear as analogous to what the criminal law calls necessity as an excuse. Just as we expect a person to act on his self-protective instinct by pushing another off the plank they share adrift in the ocean, even if the other is entirely without fault, so we expect the householder to eliminate any threats to his household.[119] Under this reading, the exercise of the police power in an emergency is beyond the realm of law, and its constraints. Hence the absence of a requirement to pay the owner of the destroyed property just compensation (technically, because the destruction was an exercise of the police power, rather than the takings power).[120] Necessity as self-preservation makes no claims to justice.

Then again, perhaps the exercise of police power here is closer to necessity as a justification. (Incidentally, the razing of the house cannot have constituted the justification of self-defense, rather than self-preservation. That would require fault on the part of its owner, just as self-defense in criminal law requires fault on the part of the assailant.) In that case, the claim would have to be that the destruction of the house was not a matter of instinctive self-preservation, but of right. The result would be the same; on balance the rights of the individual owner would give way to the interests of the community, or the rights of its other constituents. If that were so, however, one would expect the owner to be compensated for his or her sacrifice later on.

In the second case, one would also expect the courts to engage in a careful analysis of the necessity for the state action, including the need for interference, the proportionality of means and ends, and the likelihood of success, in the event of an unsuccessful intervention. Yet such a judicial scrutiny never materialized.[121]

In general, the fire wall cases were of rhetorical significance. They put the exercise of the police power in the best possible light. Here was a real threat to the survival of the community, or at least its architectural manifestation, a threat so grave that it amounted to an emergency. Robust and decisive action was necessary to prevent permanent harm to the public. There was no time for legal niceties, such as a prolonged process of adjudication. The time had come to save the state, or at least the city.

The vast majority of police power actions, however, had none of the exigency of putting out a fire. The whole point of the police was, after all, the prevention of threats, not their frantic limitation. Police regulations sought to prevent fires, rather than extinguish them. So they called for fire proof buildings, minimum distances between buildings, and so on. The idea was to prevent the exigency. And so the possibility of an exigency became the justification for police power actions, rather than the exigency itself.

No court seriously held the legislature to an exigency standard. As Shaw explained in *Alger*, the need to enhance the preventive potential of the common law of nuisance by itself was enough to create the "exigency" required for exercise of the police power. The existence of anything, or anyone, that "tend[s] to injurious consequences"[122] to the public was the exigency the state needed to police.

In the pursuit of stifling the fountains of evil, the policer enjoyed wide latitude. The policer, in Shaw's case the Massachusetts general court, judged the need for police intervention, the exigency of the situation. Once the exigency was found to exist—and it always existed since the welfare of the community was too important to leave unprotected even for an instant—the power of police was to be exercised as its holder "may think necessary and expedient" and as it "shall judge to be for the good and welfare of the commonwealth, and of the subjects of the same," to quote once again from Shaw's opinion in *Alger*.

The necessary discretion in the diagnosis and elimination of threats to the police also prevented an overly restrictive definition of the police power. As Shaw recognized, "[i]t is much easier to perceive and realize the existence and sources of this power, than to mark its boundaries, or prescribe limits to its exercise." Chief Justice Taney made much the same point a few years earlier, in the *License Cases*, when he pointed out that "[i]n all matters of government, and especially of police, a wide discretion is necessary. It is not susceptible of an exact limitation, but must be exercised under the changing exigencies of society."[123]

5

Definition by Exclusion

The police power's defining characteristic became its very undefinability. Virtually every definition of the police power was accompanied by the remark that it cannot be, and has not been, defined. Recall that even Bentham, who rarely shied away from analytic challenges, threw up his hands when faced with the concept of police, which we found "too multifarious to be susceptible to any single definition."[1] We've also seen that the very idea of common law misdemeanors as fall-back police offenses was to punish offenses that had not previously been defined. For that purpose, the notion of police had to remain sufficiently unspecified to equip policers, in this case judges, to eliminate threats to the public police on the spot. And even police offenses that were identified as such ex ante, such as nuisance and vagrancy, displayed sufficient flexibility so as not to constrain the policers' ability to do whatever was necessary to maintain the public welfare.

By the early 1900s, after more than a century of discussions of the police power in American court opinions and treatises, nothing had changed. As Freund noted in his 1904 police treatise, "[t]he term police power, while in constant use and indispensable in the vocabulary of American constitutional law, has remained without authoritative or generally accepted definition."[2] Instead, "the general tendency is to identify it with the whole of internal government and sovereignty, and to regard it as an undefined mass of legislation."[3]

And this is still where things stand today. American Jurisprudence (Second) puts it simply, "the police power is *by its nature* incapable of any satisfactory or exact definition or limitation."[4]

Since the police power is, and must be, impossible to define, courts and commentators turn to the next best alternative, talk about what it isn't rather than what it is. The two most important powers the police power isn't are, first, the power of eminent domain and, second, the power to regulate commerce. These distinctions eventually achieve constitutional significance. For it turns out that the police power "knows no law," so that the classification of a particular state action as an exercise of the police power amounts to a finding of constitutionality. Or more precisely, that classification removes state action from the realm of constitutional law, and from general considerations of justice, altogether.

Shaw's opinion in *Alger* provides an early illustration of a definition, and rhetorical use, of police power as that-which-is-not-the-power-of-eminent-domain. *Alger* is a case of policing property, i.e., "senseless material," in Judge Redfield's phrase. For a case illustrating the other use of police power—as that-which-is-not-the-federal-commerce-power—in the judicial review of a police regulation directed at human, rather than inanimate, threats, we'll turn to the famous U.S. Supreme Court decision in *New York v. Miln*,[5] decided a decade earlier. In the realm of people police, rather than thing police, we will encounter another distinction, between policing and punishing, or between police measures and criminal law. This distinction will generally track that between police and nuisance law, namely roughly that between prevention and remedy. As we'll see, however, it's a difficult distinction to draw, never mind to maintain, considering that the criminal law itself is said to derive from the police power of the state.

Thing Police: Not Taking

The power of eminent domain was not the only contrast Shaw invoked to sketch the contours of the police power in *Alger*. We've already seen that exercises of the police power differed from traditional nuisance law in that police regulations could anticipate potential threats, rather than eliminating them after they had appeared, or perhaps had even resulted in actual harm to the public. The distinction between the power of eminent domain and the power of police likewise arises from the nature of police as self-preservation through anticipatory prevention. In the case of takings under the power of eminent domain, the state appropriates property for public use. The police power, by contrast, doesn't take property, nor does it take it for public use. Instead the police power regulates, or "restrain[s]," the "noxious" (i.e., dangerous) use of property. Since the state doesn't take the property, and the private owner retains ownership in it, it also can't use it in any way, even for public purposes. Alger's wharf was torn down, thus limiting his use of his harbor property. And it was torn down under a regulation passed to protect the public harbor. The state of Massachusetts had no intention of putting Alger's property to some other use, say, to broaden a waterway or to build a bridge.

Over the next century and a half, the Supreme Court would develop this distinction between police power regulation and eminent domain taking into a complex set of linedrawing rules. This isn't the place to rehearse the details of this jurisprudence, which has exasperated a long line of commentators. It will suffice to focus on some features of its taxonomy that are worth noting for our purposes.

The first thing to note about the project of differentiating between takings and police regulations is that it is conceived as a problem of property law, or rather the constitutional limitations upon the state's interference with the right of property. To retain a sense of the police power in general, it's important to keep this limitation in mind. The power to police is far broader than the power to regulate things that happen to be someone's property. Even within the realm of things, it extends also to things that don't belong to anyone in particular. Moreover, still within the same realm, it reaches all types of property, "real" and "personal"; it extends to land as well as to trees, rivers, buildings, liquor, and guns. And, from the perspective of police rather than constitutional law, what's significant about these things is *not* that they are property but that they pose a threat to the police of the state. The wharf in *Alger* was policed because it might have been dangerous (though it actually wasn't); that the wharf was Alger's (or anyone's for that matter) made no difference to its policeability, but was merely an incidental complicating factor.

In a system of law that plumbs the depths of the police power primarily in the context of property regulation it is all too easily forgotten that the power of police captures everything and everyone within the dominion of the policer, including both inanimate and animate objects. The power of the proto-policer, the Roman householder, extended over "everything and everybody" in his *familia*, and so does the power of the macro-householder in the modern state. In Anglo-Saxon law, the householder was held liable for any damage caused by members of his household, including "his slaves, his beasts, or—for even this we must add—the inanimate things that belonged to him."[6] As Freund points out, a precautionary police measure "operates on persons, things or conditions no matter whether in every individual case the precaution is necessary or not."[7] What Chief Justice Taney said of the police power in the License Cases, still holds today: the police power is "the power of sovereignty, the power to govern men and things within the limits of its dominion."[8]

This is a crucial point of distinction between police and law, though it's one that tends to be overlooked in discussions of that very distinction. Police applies to all threats as threats, no matter who or what they might be. Law, by contrast, applies only to persons. There is nothing, and no one, that, and who, cannot be policed, unless of course it cannot be policed for some other reason, i.e., unless it falls outside the limits of a state's dominion. The forces of nature are a case in point. The state can attempt to minimize the effects of the weather by taking certain precautions, such as building dams, requiring the construction of tornado-proof buildings, or prohibiting the development of certain areas altogether. But it cannot prevent these harmful effects by eliminating the cause. Storms cannot be abated, only controlled. Nature as the fountain of evil cannot be stifled.

But the limits to the state's police power result from limits to its power, not from limits to its police. What, as a matter of fact, comes within the state's power, also comes within its power to police.

Within the realm of thing police, the distinction between police power and the power of eminent domain illustrates the immunizing function of the police power, which results from the absence of nonfactual limits upon its exercise. In this area, the classification of a particular state interference with private property always has been the end of the constitutional inquiry. The only question of interest was whether the state had to pay the property owner just compensation, as required by the Fifth Amendment for takings in the exercise of the power of eminent domain. Once classified as policing, rather than taking, the state action underwent no further scrutiny. So potent was the police power rationale that it was inappropriate to second-guess the legislature's determination that an exigency required the exercise of the police power, nor its choice of means to advance its end of safeguarding the public police.

The association between policing and immunity from constitutional oversight, at least in this area of the law, became so close that when Justice Holmes in 1922 wanted to subject a particular police regulation of property to constitutional scrutiny, in *Pennsylvania Coal Co. v. Mahon*,[9] he reclassified it as a taking. This reclassification had the opposite, and presumably desired, effect: the state action in question automatically emerged as *unconstitutional* since the central question in this type of case always was the state's failure to pay just compensation. The classification as a taking thus didn't by itself spell constitutional trouble. In practice, however, it did just that, given that no compensation had in fact been paid, in violation of the Fifth Amendment. Once again, the classification as a taking settled the question. No further inquiry into the *justification* of the taking, rather than its fact, was undertaken.[10]

Brandeis's dissenting complaints about Holmes's abandonment of the traditional distinction between policing and taking, familiar at least since Shaw's opinion in *Alger*, proved futile. He was right to protest that "a restriction to protect the public health, safety, or morals from dangers threatened," that is, a regulation of property to safeguard the public police, "is not a taking." As Shaw had explained, police regulation didn't appropriate property for some "public use," but merely limited their use in the interest of public police. A police measure involves "merely the prohibition of a noxious use." "The property so restricted," however, "remains in the possession of its owner."[11]

So far so good. Brandeis, however, didn't stop there. He went on to point out that the mere classification of a state regulation of private property as an exercise of the police power didn't shield it from constitutional scrutiny, for that regulation must not only be designed to advance the public end of protecting the public police, but it must also be an "appropriate means to the public end."[12] This, however, was precisely the problem. As Holmes had indicated seventeen years earlier in his dissent in *Lochner v. New York*, and Shaw in his police power opinions generally, the police power of the state was in fact, and even in theory, unlimited.[13] Brandeis, in other words, had made a category mistake. He had misinterpreted police as a species of law. Driven by the continuing exigency of safeguarding the welfare of the community, police "knows no law." The question of "just" compensation therefore is completely alien to the realm of police. For police isn't concerned with justice, or with rights, interference with which would call for "compensation." As Bentham had recognized, police is about preventing threats, rather than remedying harm.

People Police: Not Punishment

So much for thing police and takings, and for our discussion of *Commonwealth v. Alger*[14] and its progeny. Although technically also a case about thing police, *Spalding v. Preston*[15] took a wider view. Instead of limiting his discussion to the policing of counterfeit coins, Judge Redfield in that case stressed the comprehensive scope of preventive police, which sought to stifle any fountain of evil, including human ones. The power of police was the power to eliminate any and all threats, by any means necessary, regardless of whether they be man, animal, or "senseless material," "the maniac, or his torch."[16] As Chief Justice Taney put it at just about the same time in the *License Cases*, which technically dealt with a dangerous thing, liquor, the police power "is a power essential to self-preservation, and exists, necessarily, in every organized community. It is, indeed, the law of nature, and is possessed by man in his individual capacity. He may resist that which does him harm, *whether he be assailed by an assassin, or approached by poison.*"[17]

People police, the policing of human threats, can look back on a long tradition in Anglo-American law. Police measures that looked very much like sixteenth-century English vagrancy statutes, if they weren't identical to them, did not run into serious constitutional trouble in the United States until the 1970s. At that time, their vagueness was said to interfere with "due process" by not providing persons with sufficient notice of what constituted vagrancy and giving police officers too much discretion in deciding what did. Today, vagrancy has been replaced, or at least supplemented, by a far more sophisticated policing device, possession offenses, which has yet to raise similar constitutional concerns.[18]

Compared to the policing of things, and in particular things in someone's possession, the policing of people has attracted little scrutiny in the courts or among commentators. Property owners repeatedly and persistently forced the courts to consider the constitutionality of police regulations of their property. As a result, courts developed a jurisprudence of the police power, even if it often amounted to little more than the sort of ex post classification exercise of takings jurisprudence. Commentators proposed further distinctions among types of property. Christopher Tiedeman, for example, suggested that the police power over *real* property was far more extensive than that over *personal* property, on the ground that the state can claim to be the ultimate owner of only the former type.[19]

No similarly detailed attention was lavished on the policing of people. Vagrancy was but one aspect of a comprehensive system of people police. Protecting the public police was always understood to require the policing of "dangerous classes."[20] In Tiedeman's system of police, for example, the police of the "dangerous classes" fell into two categories, "Police Control of CRIMINAL Classes" and "Police Control of DANGEROUS Classes, Other Than by Criminal Prosecution."[21] The entirety of criminal law fell under the first heading. According to Tiedeman, criminal punishment was but one exercise of the police power. It had nothing to do with justice, and everything with prevention:

> The human infliction of punishment is an exercise of the police power, and there is no better settled rule than that the police power of a State must be confined to those remedies and regulations which the safety, or at least the welfare, of the public demands. We punish crimes, not because the criminals deserve punishment, but in order to prevent the further commission of the crime by the same persons and by others by creating the fear of punishment, as the consequence of the wrongful act.[22]

Like Redfield before him, Tiedeman recognized that a police based system of criminal law could not distinguish among different types of threat.

Redfield had pointed to the need to eliminate the threat posed by the "mad man" and the "rational man," and so did Tiedeman:

> The confinement of a violent lunatic is as defensible as the punishment of a criminal. The reason for both police regulations is the same, viz.: to insure the safety of the public. . . . If, therefore, the protection of the public be the real object of the legal punishment of crimes, it would be as lawful to punish an insane person for his wrongful acts as one in the full possession of his mental faculties.[23]

The "criminal classes" were the proper objects of policing because they, through their criminal act, had become rightless. They had revealed themselves not to be persons, so to speak. They had forfeited their personhood: "The commission of crime, in the discretion of the government, subjects all rights of the criminal to the possibility of forfeiture. Life, liberty, political rights, statutory rights, relative rights, all or any of them may be forfeited by the State, in punishment of a crime."[24]

Though Tiedeman was right that his contemporaries were not quite ready to punish the insane—he lamented that "the moral aspect of punishment has too strong a hold upon the public"[25]—his more general observation that the power to make criminal law sprang from the power to police was neither idiosyncratic for his time, nor limited to it. For an earlier, though less well-developed, statement of the same position, we can once again turn to Chief Justice Taney's response to the question he posed himself in the *License Cases*, "What are the police powers of the state?" His answer: "the powers of government inherent in every sovereignty to the extent of its dominions. And whether a state passes a quarantine law, or *a law to punish offenses*, or to establish courts of justice, or requiring certain instruments to be recorded, or to regulate commerce within its own limits, in every case it exercises the same power. . . . "[26]

By the early decades of the twentieth century, the view of criminal-law-as-police had blossomed into a full-fledged theory. So, in 1927, Roscoe Pound explained that the criminal law was not, or at least should not be, about punishing at all, but instead about the "securing of social interests regarded directly as such, that is, disassociated from any immediate individual interests with which they may be identified."[27] Not punishment, but "interference to prevent disobedience," was the aim of criminal law.[28]

Pound clearly saw the patriarchal origins of the power to punish and police. As he explained, "the authority of the State to punish is derived," at least in part, "from the authority of the head of a patriarchal household."[29] Another "point of origin" of the power to punish and police lay in the quasi-familial "magisterial discipline." "[T]he Roman magistrate," Pound went on, "had *imperium*, i.e., power to command the citizen to the end of preserving order in time of peace and discipline in time of war."[30]

As Pound saw it, the traditional view of criminal law as remedial, and the system of punishment associated with it, was to give way to a "machinery of detection, conviction, and penal treatment."[31] The criminal law "should be reserved for the direct and immediate maintaining of the general security and the general morals," and transformed into an "effective agency of social control" dedicated to "preventive justice."[32] In fact, Pound concluded hopefully that "there is no reason to doubt that the development of preventive justice is destined to be as epoch-making for the science of law as the development of preventive medicine has been for medical science."[33]

One of the reasons why the connection between police and criminal law has remained obscure is that courts, or commentators, in general find little reason to explore the origin of the state's power to make criminal law. The source of the state's power to punish attracts judicial attention, if at all, only when a particular exercise of that power is challenged on constitutional grounds. A large chunk of criminal law never is; no one has yet questioned, in a court of law, the state's right to criminalize intentional homicide. (This doesn't explain, of course, the failure by others, in particular commentators, to ask that question. When scholars tackle this issue, they tend to speak, abstractly, in terms of theories of punishment, rather than of theories of state power.[34])

The connection between criminal law and the police power is straightforward. The police power is the power to maintain the police of the state, which is nothing less than the general well-being, or welfare, of the state considered as a family. That well-being, the *salus populi*, has different aspects, physical, economic, and moral.[35] And the criminal law is simply one way in which the state protects the physical well-being of the community, the "security of the people."[36]

This role of the criminal law in the service of the *physical* aspect of *salus populi* has been too uncontroversial to deserve mention, never mind argument. Courts have been less willing to assume the state's right to use criminal law to protect another aspect of the *salus populi*, its *moral* police. (Recall the English courts' initial qualms about policing obscenity.) Still, even when it comes to morals offenses, it is generally assumed that there is but one power from which moral criminal law can, and does, spring, the police power. There is also a broad consensus that there is nothing illegitimate about the state using the criminal law to protect its moral police. The problem, if there is one, is not with the notion of moral criminal law in general, but with some of its instances.

No court striking down a sodomy statute, for instance, has doubted the state's authority, under its police power, to invoke the criminal law to protect all aspects of the public police, including its moral well-being.[37] As we will see a little later on, courts instead tend to conclude that private consensual sodomy did not in fact pose a threat to the public's moral police.[38]

Police and Criminal Law

Two possible views regarding the connection between police and criminal law can be distinguished. In one view, *all* criminal law is an exercise of the police power. Every criminal prohibition, be it against theft or against public intoxication, is designed to protect the public police. Different crimes differ only in the particular aspect of the public police they're protecting. So assault laws protect the physical police, and pornography laws protect the moral police. This appears to be the view held by Tiedeman and Pound— though Tiedeman was remarkably uncomfortable with using the criminal law to police morality.[39]

In another view, only *some* criminal laws constitute exercises of the police power. Others instead derive from the state's obligation to do justice. So, a murder statute would be a criminal law of justice, and a public intoxication statute a criminal law of police. This appears to have been the view of another important American police commentator, Ernst Freund, who differentiated between "the power to define and punish crimes" and the police power.[40] While there was "no brief or comprehensive word to designate" the former power, there was one for the latter because it had been "conspicuously the subject of constitutional contention or discussion."[41]

Freund's distinction between criminal law and police must be seen in the context of his more general distinction between justice and police. To him justice was a matter of "[t]he maintenance of right and the redress of wrong."[42] The realm of justice, criminal and civil, was the common law, or the *jus privatum*. Police, by contrast, was concerned not with justice, but with the "prevention and anticipation of wrong" through the exercise of the state's "compulsory powers." The "essence of the police power" was the use of state control for the public welfare, i.e., "the improvement of social and economic conditions affecting the community at large and collectively."[43] The realm of police, or "internal policy," was the prerogative, or the *jus publicum*. In the words of Montesquieu, quoted by Freund, "[i]n the exercise of police, it is rather the magistrate who punishes than the law; in the judgment of crimes, it is rather the law which punishes than the magistrate."[44] In sum, police restraint is "not a matter of justice, but of policy."[45]

Freund's distinction between police and criminal law, however, faced one obvious problem. On their face, police measures tend to look very much like criminal statutes. Their violation "constitutes technically a crime."[46] Cyrus Alger not only saw his wharf pulled down, but he also was convicted of a misdemeanor and sentenced to a fine. Several of the police offenses on Blackstone's influential list were felonies, and therefore punishable by death; all of them were at least misdemeanors.

Freund attempts to resolve this difficulty by distinguishing between "real" crime, the subject of criminal law, and "technical" crime, the subject of "police regulation":

> There is however a difference between police legislation and criminal legislation which is popularly well understood and which is not without legal and constitutional significance. The peculiar province of the criminal law is the punishment of acts intrinsically vicious, evil, and condemned by social sentiment; the province of the police is the enforcement of merely conventional restraints, so that in the absence of positive legislative action, there would be no possible offense. The difference here referred to roughly corresponds to that between misdemeanors and felonies or infamous crimes, or perhaps still more to that between mala prohibita and mala in se.[47]

These substantive differences, however, are of no consequence for procedural purposes. Since police offenses are crimes, "technically" speaking, "police legislation is criminal legislation, especially in the matter of protection against self-incrimination, the guaranty of a jury trial, and the prohibition of ex post facto laws."[48] The ex post facto prohibition, however, doesn't apply to the police measure itself, but only to the punishment for its violation. That's so because the police measure, such as a licensing requirement for liquor, isn't itself a criminal statute. For that reason, there isn't a problem with passing a retrospective law denying a liquor license to "ex-convicts," for instance.

Recall that Shaw had justified police measures on the basis of their *prospective* orientation. According to Shaw in *Alger* police regulations benefited not only the public, but also the individual. They provided more extensive protection to the public police. At the same time, they provided the individual with notice. They allowed people to determine ahead of time the legality of a particular action, such as building a wharf, instead of having to take their chances in the courts, only to learn that they had acted illegally, perhaps by erecting a public nuisance. Freund here makes clear, to the contrary, that there is nothing unconstitutional about a retrospective police regulation, provided it does not itself constitute a penalty. So there is nothing improper about retrospectively providing that no wharves may be built beyond a certain line, nor presumably about abating any building beyond that line as a public nuisance.

Even though courts rarely, if ever, considered the issue at this level of generality, it appears that, at least implicitly, some judges shared Freund's, rather than Tiedeman's, view of the relationship between police and criminal law. Perhaps because they clung to the "moral aspect of punishment" just as much as "the public" did,[49] courts retained a distinction between punishment and police, between redress and prevention. But where that distinction was to be drawn was anything from clear.

And the distinction was of considerable significance. Note that Freund had followed the familiar trend of relegating police to an aconstitutional realm. He did announce, in general, that the "police power like other powers of government may be subjected to limitations both from the point of view of its purposes and from the point of view of its means and methods."[50] But then, when push came to shove, important constitutional limitations applied to exercises of the police power only insofar as they were "technically a crime." These constitutional limitations included, in addition to the ones Freund mentioned (self-incrimination, jury trial, ex post facto), the prohibition against cruel and unusual punishment, double jeopardy, and the right to counsel.

The Trouble with Vagrancy

The traditional police offense of vagrancy illustrated the difficulties associated with Freund's insistence on the substantive distinction between police offenses and crimes, while allowing for their formal, "technical," identity. The problem with vagrancy was that it ran afoul of several principles of substantive and procedural criminal law. It punished status and omission in the teeth of the act requirement. It punished without regard to fault in violation of the mens rea requirement. Procedurally, it was applied in summary proceedings in a police court before a statutory magistrate—a police judge—without a jury, without a record, and in general defiance of the rules of the common law.

Vagrancy was a central tool of people police, of eliminating human threats. Under the heading of "Police control of vagrants," Tiedeman provides a typical criminogenic diagnosis of "the vagrant":

> The vagrant has been very appropriately described as the chrysalis of every species of criminal. A wanderer through the land, without home ties, idle, and without apparent means of support, what but criminality is to be ex-

pected from such a person? If vagrancy could be successfully combatted, if every one was engaged in some lawful calling, the infractions of the law would be reduced to a surprisingly small number; and it is not to be wondered at that an effort is so generally to suppress vagrancy.[51]

At the turn of the last century, the Ohio Supreme Court was particular emphatic about the dangerousness of vagrants. In 1900, it upheld a conviction under the state's "tramp law," which the court described as employing "the old method of describing a vagrant, and vagrancy, time out of mind, has been deemed a condition calling for special statutory provisions, *i.e.*, such as may tend to suppress the mischief and protect society."[52] There could be no doubt about the constitutionality of this sort of police measure, for it rests "upon the economic truth that industry is necessary for the preservation of society, and that he who, being able to work, and not able otherwise to support himself, deliberately plans to exist by the labor of others, is an *enemy to society* and to the commonwealth."[53]

In the cities, public officials like "overseers of the poor" or "police judges" took on the task of enforcing the vagrancy laws by committing vagrants to public institutions such as workhouses, poorhouses, almshouses, houses of refuge, penitentiaries, or prisons. The vast majority of these cases never saw the light of an ordinary court room. Every once in a while, however, habeas corpus proceedings brought by inmates did reach a reviewing judge. The constitutionality of the underlying statutes was never doubted. Nonetheless, judges on occasion did feel the need to comment on their legitimacy. In reviewing the legality of a committal, the judges also described the summary proceedings that gave rise to it. The tone of exasperation in these accounts, one suspects, results as much from the difficulty of reviewing the legality of a committal without sufficient information about what happened when and how, as it does from the traditional common law courts' desire to distance themselves from the lower status statutory courts filled with mere magistrates, rather than real judges.

At any rate, many of these opinions attempt to draw a line between police regulations and criminal statutes. One finds the now familiar distinction between prevention and punishment. Police regulations are said to benefit their objects, as all paternal, and quasi-paternal, discipline. The irrelevance of fault is also said to be typical of police offenses—the threat alone is sufficient. The strategy is the same throughout. If an attempt is made to justify vagrancy laws, and the procedures for their enforcement, it is based on their classification as a police matter, rather than as a matter of criminal law.

A Maine vagrancy statute from 1821 provided "'that any two or more of the overseers in any town . . . are hereby authorised, empowered, and directed to commit to such house [work-house] by writing under the hands of the said overseers, to be employed and governed, according to the rules and orders of the house,' &c. 'all persons able of body to work and not having estate or means otherwise to maintain themselves, who refuse or neglect so to do; live a dissolute vagrant life, and exercise no ordinary calling or lawful business, sufficient to gain an honest livelihood.'"[54] In the 1834 case of *In re Nott*, the Maine Supreme Judicial Court upheld the commitment under this statute of a vagrant woman to the Portland "work-house," by "two of the Overseers of the Poor" of that city. These police officials had directed the "master" of the work-house "to receive her into said house, and there employ and govern her, according to the rules and orders of the same, until she should be discharged by order of law."[55] The court explained that, although the overseers had no *criminal* jurisdiction, the woman had no reason to object because the police measure was enforced for her benefit. In fact, "[w]hen enlightened conscience shall do its office, and sober reason has its proper influence, she will regard the interposition as parental; as calculated to save instead of punishing."[56] Moreover, the overseers, as public officials, had every right to protect the police of the public by eliminating her as a threat. In this light, her commitment "may be viewed as a police regulation, to preserve the community from contamination," analogous to the quarantining of any "victim of contagious sickness, to whom no fault can be imputed."[57]

In the metropolis of New York, the police of vagrants was handled by special police judges in police courts. An 1847 case, *People v. Phillips*, describes the summary vagrancy process before a New York City police magistrate:

> Our Revised Statute (vol. i. p. 633) declares that if a magistrate be satisfied, by the confession of the offender, or by competent testimony, that the accused is a vagrant within the description of the statute, he shall make up and sign a record of conviction thereof, which shall be filed in the office of the clerk of the county, and shall by warrant under his hand, commit such vagrant, etc. . . .
>
> And the mode of proceeding is not by a formal trial by a jury, but is by a summary conviction. . . .
>
> The power thus exercised is not in conformity to, but is in derogation of, the common law, is derived solely from the statutes, and all the proceedings under the authority so created must be strictly conformable to the special law, in each, from which all their force is derived.[58]

Apparently the problem with these summary vagrancy procedures wasn't so much that they were summary, but that even they weren't followed. The passage quoted above stems from a lengthy opinion outlining the proper procedures to be applied in such cases. As the circuit judge explains at the outset of his opinion, "I have been so frequently called upon to discharge from the penitentiary, prisoners committed on summary convictions for vagrancy, on the ground of some alleged defect or irregularity in the proceedings of the sitting magistrate, that I have deemed it advisable, on this occasion, to give the subject a full examination, in the hope that the matter, being thoroughly understood, the correction for the evil may once for all be applied."[59]

The 1860 case of *In re Forbes*, perhaps the best known of the vagrancy cases of the time, also arose in New York City, which appears to have had a very active and comprehensive vagrancy police system.[60] Catharine Forbes was convicted of "being a vagrant in this, that she is a common prostitute and idle person" by a "Mr. Quackenbush, one of the police-justices of this city." On habeas corpus—the only remedy available in these cases, besides certiorari, since appeals were not permitted[61]—the court granted relief on the ground that being "a common prostitute and idle person" didn't constitute vagrancy, without a further showing that Ms. Forbes was in fact "without any lawful employment whereby to maintain herself."

The court reached this conclusion on the basis of a close reading of the two vagrancy statutes under which Ms. Forbes could have been convicted, one statewide and the other citywide, both of which listed the absence of lawful employment as one element of the offense of vagrancy:

> By certain statutes all persons coming within a certain description defined and declared by the statutes, are declared to be vagrants, and provision is made for their trial, conviction, and imprisonment. We have two such statutes. By the Revised Statutes (2 *Rev. Stat.*, 879, 5 ed.), all idle persons, who, not having any visible means to maintain themselves, live without employment; all persons wandering about and lodging in taverns, groceries, or beer-houses, outhouses, market-places, sheds, or barns, or in the open air, and not giving a good account of themselves; all persons wandering abroad and begging, or who go about from door to door, or place themselves in the streets, highways, or other public places to beg or receive alms, shall be deemed vagrants. Common prostitutes as such are not named in this statute, and although they may be, and are, perhaps, most likely to be, or to become vagrants within the description of the statute, yet it is plain if a common prostitute is lawfully convicted of being a vagrant under this statute, she must be so convicted, not merely on her confession, but on competent testimony that she is a common prostitute or an idle person, or that she is both a common prostitute and an idle person. This statute does not declare common prostitutes as a class or by name to be va-

grants, nor does it declare all idle persons to be vagrants, but only such idle persons as live without employment, and yet have no means to maintain themselves. By an act passed January 23, 1833 (*Laws of* 1833, 9, ch. 11), which from its title and provisions would appear to be confined in its operations to the city of New York. "All common prostitutes who have no lawful employment whereby to maintain themselves," are declared vagrants.[62]

What's remarkable about this opinion is the care with which the court parsed the language of the vagrancy statutes in question. The very flexibility and breadth of vagrancy statutes, their vagueness, had always been considered essential to their police function. As Freund recognized, "the comprehensive definition of the offense affords the means of dealing with the criminal elements of the population and keeping them temporarily under restraint in cases of emergency."[63] Undoubtedly, the police justices of New York were surprised to find this general sweep offense subjected to such intense linguistic scrutiny. Surely, they were used to cutting corners substantively and procedurally as they processed characters like Ms. Forbes. Note that the judge in *Forbes* complained of the fact that no record of the conviction could be found, and that in all probability none had ever been filed "in the clerk's office of the Court of Sessions, as required by the act of 1833, and the act of April 10, 1835, amending it."[64]

It is unlikely that the decision in *Forbes* made much of a dent in the case management in New York's police courts. After all, as the failure to file the conviction illustrates, the stern warnings about attention to procedural details issued in *Phillips* a decade or so before apparently had gone unheeded as well.

In a sense, the judge in *Forbes* treated the vagrancy statutes as criminal statutes. As a criminal statute "penal in its character," vagrancy was to be strictly construed.[65] And strict construction in *Forbes* meant not ignoring an element of the offense, namely the absence of lawful employment. Whereas common law judges were free to define offenses, a statutorily created magistrate applying a statute had only one job, applying the statute exactly as written. His authority rested on the statute, and on the statute alone. "The magistrate in acting under the act, had no right to disregard one word of that description."[66]

At the same time, however, the judge insisted that vagrancy was not a criminal offense. It was a police measure. And only as such could it be legitimated. No criminal statute, it is implied, could similarly ignore basic principles of substantive and procedural law. The principle of strict construction in this light emerges less as a feature of the interpretation of criminal statutes than as a general note of caution directed at the police magistrate, or for that matter at any police official, not to abuse his essentially limitless discretion in identifying and eliminating human threats in the form of vagrants:

The object of this act is not to punish common prostitutes as a sin or moral evil, or to reform the individual, but to protect the public against the crimes, poverty, distress, or public burdens, which experience has shown common prostitution causes or leads to.

These statutes—declaring a certain class or description of persons vagrants, and authorizing their conviction and punishment as such; as well as certain statutes declaring a certain class or description of persons to be disorderly persons, and authorizing their arrest as such—are in fact rather of the nature of public regulations to prevent crime and public charges and burdens, than of the nature of ordinary criminal laws prohibiting and punishing an act or acts as a crime or crimes.

If the condition of a person brings him within the description of either of the statutes declaring what persons shall be esteemed vagrants, he may be convicted and imprisoned, whether such condition is his misfortune or his fault. His individual liberty must yield to the public necessity or public good; but nothing but public necessity or the public good can justify these statutes, and the summary conviction without a jury in derogation of the common law authorized by them. They are constitutional, but should be construed strictly, and executed carefully in favor of the liberty of the citizen. Their description of persons who shall be deemed vagrants, is necessarily vague and uncertain, giving to the magistrate in their execution an almost unchecked opportunity for arbitrary oppression or careless cruelty. The main object or purpose of the statutes should be kept constantly in view, and the magistrate should be careful and see, before convicting, that the person charged with being a vagrant is shown either by his or her confession, or by competent testimony, to come exactly within the description of one of the statutes (see opinion of Edmonds, Circuit Judge, in The People *a.* Phillips, 1 *Park. Cr.*, 95, &c.).[67]

Here too, then, we find the tacit acknowledgment that police lies beyond the limits of principles of justice, substantive or procedural. The power of the police magistrate, who according to Montesquieu does the punishing instead of the law, is constrained at best by general guidelines. Guidelines, rather than legal codes and principles, are the medium of police. That was so in the days of Aristotelian household economy, as well as in the slavery South, with its guidebooks for better plantation management. In the end, everything turns on the good faith of the policer. And all the law, and its courts, can do is implore the policer to use that discretion wisely, so that "[t]he main object or purpose of the statutes . . . be kept constantly in view," unless of course, in extreme cases, the policer proves himself to have a "malignant heart" and thus unworthy of his authority, and is degraded.[68]

Forbes and its predecessor, *Phillips*, focused on the discrepancies between the summary vagrancy disposal procedure and the procedural principles of criminal law, and common criminal law in particular. But this focus on procedure shouldn't obscure that vagrancy deviated from traditional principles of *substantive* criminal law as well. We've already noted the irrelevance of fault, which the judge in *Forbes* once again made explicit. More technically speaking, there was never a *mens rea* requirement in vagrancy. While courts often found *mens rea* requirements that did not appear on the face of a statute, they found no such requirement in vagrancy statutes. What mattered for vagrancy was the fact that someone was a vagrant, period, not whether he or she was a vagrant intentionally, or recklessly, or in some other culpable way. Culpability didn't matter.

Vagrancy, however, lacked not only a *mens rea*. More important, it lacked an *actus reus*. The offense consisted of being a vagrant, i.e., a status, rather than an act, not becoming a vagrant, or acting like a vagrant. Thus, people were not "convicted" of vagrancy, as they might be of, say, robbery, they were "deemed" and "declared" a vagrant instead.

As a police offense, it was only proper that vagrancy would criminalize a status. The point of police, after all, was not to punish wrongdoing, and thereby to redress wrong. Instead, it sought to identify and eliminate threats. The relevant status of the vagrant was that of a human threat. Vagrancy was the "chrysalis of every species of criminal." To incapacitate the vagrant therefore meant to stifle a human fountain of evil.

Courts, and commentators, occasionally found it necessary to at least note, presumably with some embarrassment, the tension between vagrancy and the act requirement. None of them, however, thought that this conflict amounted to a constitutional defect. In 1881, the Ohio Supreme Court, in fact, made it clear that even the slightest embarrassment was misplaced, as it rested on an altogether erroneous view of the act requirement. In upholding a conviction of "being a known thief," the court declared, in *Morgan v. Nolte*, that "[i]t is a mistake to suppose that offenses must be confined to specific acts of commission or omission."[69] In support, the court could point to a long tradition of status based police offenses, many of which we've already encountered, including being a common scold, being a common barrator, being a vagrant, being a rogue, and being a disorderly person.[70] As the court remarked, "[i]n such cases the offense does not consist of particular acts, but in the mode of life, the habits and practices of the accused in respect to the character or traits which it is the object of the statute creating the offense to suppress."[71]

Police offenses without *mens rea* or *actus reus*, in sum, didn't run afoul of the traditional common law requirements of *mens rea* and *actus reus* because these requirements had never applied to them in the first place. While "real" criminal law concerned itself with acts and intentions, adding up to wrongs, police offenses could serve their purpose of threat elimination unencumbered by legal technicalities.

Freund, for one, found this position unacceptable. Yet he too maintained the distinction between police and criminal law, on the one hand, and the association between principles and criminal law, on the other. The judges in *Nolte*, but also in *Forbes, Phillips*, and *Nott*, had justified vagrancy as a police measure, which by its nature was not subject to the principles of substantive and procedural criminal law. Freund, by contrast, suggested that vagrancy could be justified insofar, and only insofar, as it was treated as a criminal statute. Contrary to the views expressed in cases like *Nolte* and *Nott*, he argued that "the sound doctrine is undoubtedly that vagrancy and criminal idleness do not constitute in the eye of the law a social status to be dealt with by police control, but criminal acts to be punished by the criminal courts."[72] In other words, by reclassifying vagrancy as "technically a crime," and only in this way, could it be brought within the reach of the principles of substantive and procedural criminal law. Freund's response to the claim that vagrancy was merely a police offense and therefore beyond principle was not that police offenses were not immunized from legitimacy scrutiny, but that vagrancy was, at least in form, a species of criminal law. (Recall that Holmes employed a similar mode of argument in *Mahon*, where he found it necessary to reclassify police regulation as a taking to bring it within the realm of justice, and constitutional scrutiny, presumably because he too believed that police measures belonged to a different realm, that of policy, to use Freund's distinction once more.)

To summarize, then, vagrancy is beyond constitutional doubt. That's so because it is a police offense, and as an exercise of the police power it isn't subject to the principles, constitutional and otherwise, that govern the criminal law. On the other view of criminal law as *in its entirety* based on the police power, apparently held by Tiedeman and Pound, among others, the insulation of the police power from inquiries into the legitimacy of its exercises would have an even greater effect: it would remove all of criminal law, real or not, from principled scrutiny.

The Supreme Court didn't address the constitutionality of vagrancy laws until 1972, in *Papachristou v. Jacksonville*, when it struck down a city vagrancy ordinance that closely resembled the old English vagrancy laws and the nineteenth-century statutes that underlay the cases we discussed above.[73] It's noteworthy, however, that the Court did not rely on any of the inconsistencies between vagrancy laws and the principles of substantive and procedural criminal law that gave—some—nineteenth-century judges and commentators pause, and that required the invocation of a distinction between police offenses and criminal laws. The court instead constructed a vagueness rationale. The statute was too vague to notify potential vagrants of what did and didn't constitute vagrancy, and to provide police officers on the beat with meaningful guidance on the same issue. The decision nowhere even mentioned the police power, or explored the possible sources of the state's authority to control, and punish, vagrants. As a result, it did nothing to dispel the notion that exercises of the police power are beyond constitutional scrutiny.

6

Police Power and Commerce Power

That vagrancy laws are an exercise of the police power was clear to the Supreme Court more than a century before *Papachristou v. Jacksonville*.[1] In fact, the Court's leading case dealing with vagrancy—rather than with vagueness—is not *Papachristou*, as is generally supposed, but the 1837 case of *New York v. Miln*, which upheld a state *immigration* statute requiring captains to post bond for the human cargo they unloaded onto the shores of New York City.[2] *Miln* addressed vagrancy laws only indirectly, as one manifestation of the state's power to police its dominion. Yet, perhaps better than any other case, *Miln* places vagrancy within a larger system of police, and of people police in particular, directed toward the elimination of threats to the state from within and without. *Miln* thus also exposes the connection between the control of internal human threats, through vagrancy, and those external to the family of the state, through immigration control.

While the *Miln* Court found it "difficult to define . . . a subject so diversified and multifarious" as the scope of the state's power to police, it did specify its objects, "the persons and things within her territorial limits." The Court also offered various illustrations of the power, including the right to punish those "obnoxious to the law"[3] and "to guard, by anticipation, against the commission of an offence against its laws."[4]

The challenged statute provided another illustration. It aimed to prevent human contamination of the body politic, much like the vagrancy statute upheld by the Maine Supreme Court in *In re Nott* three years before:

We think it as competent and as necessary for a state to provide precautionary measures against the moral pestilence of paupers, vagabonds, and possibly convicts; as it is to guard against the physical pestilence, which may arise from unsound and infectious articles imported, or from a ship, the crew of which may be labouring under an infectious disease.[5]

The Court thus wholeheartedly adopted the position advanced by counsel for the city, that "the law in question is altogether a police regulation: as much so as laws prohibiting entrance into a walled city after dark; laws prohibiting masters from bringing convicts into the state; or the laws prohibiting free negroes from being introduced among slaves."[6] Much as the " 'lord of the territory may, whenever he thinks proper, forbid its being entered,' "[7] so the state now had the right to regulate the influx of "paupers and gunpowder."[8] In fact, the state was obligated to "prevent her citizens from being oppressed by the support of multitudes of poor persons, who come from foreign countries without possessing the means of supporting themselves." Thus "[t]here can be no mode in which the power to regulate internal police could be more appropriately exercised. New York, from her particular situation, is, perhaps more than any other city in the Union, exposed to the evil of thousands of foreign emigrants."[9]

Police, in other words, has an internal and an external aspect, as we know at least since Locke.[10] The policer must protect the police against all threats, no matter where they come from or what they look like. This connection between internal and external police was crucial to the decision in *Miln*. The statute was upheld because, although it was directed at outsiders, it nonetheless was designed to protect the police of insiders. Under the competing view, the statute would have been conceptualized as affecting the relations among nations, i.e., international law. In that case it would have fallen within the power of the United States to regulate international commerce. Instead, the Court emphasized the state's interest in protecting its police against the external threat posed by immigrants. The statute governed the relation between the state and potential threats to its police, rather than the relation among coequal states.

Immigration regulations thus appear as but one—outward looking—aspect of the police authority of the state. Immigration control was in its infancy when *Miln* was decided. That's a good thing for our purposes, because it forced the Court to find a conceptual place for them, rather than dealing with immigration as *sui generis*. And that place was the police power.

By the end of the nineteenth century, immigration regulations had begun to come into their own, institutionally, through the creation of the Immigration and Naturalization Service, and legally, through the passage of federal immigration acts. And yet, even in the 1890s, the system of immigration regulation had not quite settled in. Once again, novelty raised basic questions of conceptualization that disappear with the routinization of an administrative practice. And once more, the concept of police proved a useful tool of classification as well as insulation from principled scrutiny.

Take, for example, the 1892 case of *United States v. Hing Quong Chow*, out of the Eastern District of Louisiana. In this case the judge found himself confronted with an indictment under a new federal immigration statute. That statute provided that "any Chinese person, or person of Chinese descent, arrested under the provisions of this act or the acts hereby extended, shall be adjudged to be unlawfully within the United States, unless such person shall establish by affirmative proof, to the satisfaction of such justice, judge, or commissioner, his lawful right to remain in the United States." Furthermore, "any such Chinese person, or person of Chinese descent, convicted and adjudged to be not lawfully entitled to be or remain in the United States, shall be imprisoned at hard labor for a period not exceeding one year, and thereafter removed from the United States. . . . "

The judge quashed the indictment on the ground that the statute upon which it was based did not define a crime. Instead, it was a police measure designed to extinguish the threat Chinese immigrants posed to the public police:

> That statute, as it seems to me, deals with the coming in of Chinese as a police matter, and is the re-enacting and continuing of what might be termed a "quarantine against Chinese." They are treated as would be infected merchandise, and the imprisonment is not a punishment for a crime, but a means of keeping a damaging individual safely till he can be sent away. In a summary manner, and as a political matter, this coming in is to be prevented. The matter is dealt with as political, and not criminal.[11]

Classifying the statute as a police measure, however, proved no easy matter. For the statute had certain tell tale characteristics of a criminal law. It was, in Freund's words, "technically a crime":

> The words used are those which are ordinarily found in criminal statutes; but the intent of congress is, as it seems to me, unmistakable. What is termed "being convicted and adjudged" means "found," "decided" by the commissioner, representing not the criminal law, but the political department of the government.[12]

Any doubts about the "political" rather than the legal nature of the statute were removed by a consideration of the process set out for its application. A process this inconsistent with the acknowledged principles of procedural criminal law simply could not have been meant as a criminal process at all:

By section 4 it is this finding [of being unlawfully in the U.S.] which is to be followed by the consequence which, it is urged, authorizes a sentence under a criminal law. I cannot believe this was the intent of congress. A reversal of the presumption of conduct or presence being lawful might be introduced into procedures which were political in character, and assimilated to those relating to quarantine; but it seems to me well-nigh impossible that congress should have intended that in proceedings in their nature criminal there should be the presumption of guilt, and that the accused should be found guilty unless he proves himself to be innocent. The whole proceeding of keeping out of the country a class of persons deemed by the sovereign to be injurious to the state, to be effective of its object, must be summary in its methods, and political in its character. It could have no place in the criminal law, with its forms and rights and delays.[13]

And not even the sanction imposed on those who violated the statute, one year's imprisonment, a sanction ordinarily associated with criminal punishment, could turn this police measure into a criminal statute:

After the unlawful presence of the alien is determined, he must be sent back to his country by the treasury department at Washington. To prevent an unreasonable and possibly oppressive detention it must be within one year. Meanwhile he must keep from entering the community of the people of the United States, and therefore he is to be imprisoned. To prevent expense to the government, and as a sanitary matter, he is to be made to work. This, it seems to me, is the meaning of the clause relied upon to authorize trial and punishment for a crime.[14]

To summarize, the immigration statute looked and felt like a criminal statute, and imposed what looked and felt like punishment. But, it deviated from principles of substantive and procedural criminal law in certain fundamental respects. It criminalized a mere status, (that of *being* in the United States and nothing more), and required no *mens rea* of any kind. Procedurally, it established a summary process that "could have no place in the criminal law, with its forms and rights and delays." Instead of discarding the statute as unconstitutional, however, the court simply reclassified it. Despite considerable evidence to the contrary, the court declared the statute to be a police measure, and therefore beyond the realm of law, and the principles that bogged it down. The statute was patently unconstitutional on its face; *therefore* it must be a police measure, which by definition is constitutional. Once again, the police label insulated state action from principled scrutiny.

All of this is familiar from the vagrancy cases. Vagrancy statutes too punished a status, and applied to a "class of persons," rather than a type of conduct. They too were analogized to sanitary measures and public health initiatives, like quarantines. They too called for summary proceedings. And they too were saved from scrutiny by reclassification as police measures. Immigration police was simply the outward analogue to internal police control of vagrants and other "dangerous classes." Immigration police was an aspect of what Locke called the "federative" power, and vagrancy police of what he termed the "executive" power.[15] The "political" power in *Hing Quong Chow* is the federative and the executive power combined.

Still, there is one noteworthy difference. The statute in *Hing Quong Chow* was a *federal* statute; the vagrancy statutes and the *Miln* statute all were state statutes. This is significant because while everyone agreed that each state had the power to police, the federal government was to have none. The *Hing Quong Chow* case thus illustrates, I think, two things. First, it shows how the police concept can immunize state acts inconsistent with basic principles of substantive and procedural criminal law. So eager was the federal judge in *Hing Quong Chow* to invoke the concept for this purpose that he neglected another cardinal rule of police power jurisprudence in our federal system of government, a rule to which we will now turn, namely that police is the states', and only the states'.

Second, the opinion suggests that this cardinal rule was a rule of rhetoric, but not a statement of fact. In fact, the federal government enjoyed wide ranging police powers, of which the power to police immigrants as threats to the public police was but one example. In rhetoric, however, the denial of police power to the federal government allowed the states to maintain at least the veneer of sovereignty.

Miln, on its face, wasn't about vagrancy laws. It was about the distinction between state and federal power. It captured the breadth of police, external and internal, personal and apersonal while it illustrated the role of the police concept in American jurisprudence as the boundary of state power vis-à-vis the power of the national government. The classification of a state action as an exercise of its police power not only served to insulate it from constitutional scrutiny—or to justify ex post a finding of constitutionality—when the relationship between the individual and the state was at stake. In the broader context of the relation between the state and the nation, such a classification also drew the line between state and federal power. The label "police" thus served to insulate the state both downward, against individuals, and upward, against the nation.

Miln started as an attempt by the mayor of New York City to recover a debt incurred under an 1824 state statute, "An act concerning passengers in vessels coming to the port of New York." The statute required captains of foreign ships to post bond, of $300 or less, for each passenger to cover any expenses the port city, New York, might incur in poor relief, so as to "to indemnify and save harmless the mayor, &c., of the city of New York, and the overseers of the poor of the city from all expenses of the maintenance of such person, or of the child or children of such person, born after such importation."[16] Failure to post the bond was punishable by a fine of $500 per person.

The constitutional issue in the case was whether the statute regulated external commerce. As a regulation of commerce the statute would have been unconstitutional because the power to regulate interstate, and international, commerce was limited to the federal government. The Court, however, upheld the statute as "a mere regulation of internal police," rather than of commerce. And the power to police was limited to the states, as it was not among the powers explicitly transferred to the national government in the national constitution.

Therefore, the question of police was, yet again, a question of classification. Once the law in question was classified as a police measure, its constitutionality was settled. This classification exercise was undertaken in case after case, even after it had become clear that the federal government enjoyed a considerable police power of its own. But if, as the Court and commentators stressed again and again, the power to police was incident to the power to govern, so that a government without a police power was no government at all, then surely the federal government too had to have such a power.

What's more, differentiating between a power to police and a power to regulate commerce proved to be difficult. Commerce, after all, was but one aspect of the police. Certainly, a state could regulate internal commerce, i.e., commerce within its territory, under its police power. The police of the state might very well require the policing of monopolies or of trade in materials hazardous to the public health, or of public morals. Similarly, if the federal government could regulate commerce, what goal would it pursue if not the police of the nation? What's the police power if not the power to regulate with an eye toward the police of the political community?

No matter how difficult, keeping police and commerce separate was crucial, if the sovereignty of the states were to survive in the federal system. Or so it was thought. It made little sense to shield the state's power to police against federal incursion if the federal power to regulate commerce amounted to much, or even some, of the same thing. And so the distinction remained a central feature of the federalist compromise.

Acknowledging the existence of a federal police power, by that or any other name, would mark the states as objects of police, as members of a macro household under the authority of a macro householder: the federal government. At the same time, looking inward, the states maintain their own householder status by retaining the police power over their dominion. The federal power to regulate *interstate* commerce limits the United States to arbitrating relations among equals, instead of acting as the superior subject of police administering objects within its territory.

To say that *Miln* was about the distinction between commerce and police thus is to say that *Miln* was about federalism, and the same is true of many police power cases since then, and before then.[17] The most recent example is the case of *United States v. Lopez*, where the Supreme Court struck down a federal criminal gun possession statute on the ground that it constituted an exercise of the police power, rather than of the power to regulate commerce.[18] This opinion triggered an uproar of criticism because it deviated from the Court's practice, over the previous decades, to classify federal legislation as an exercise of the *commerce* power, and therefore to uphold its constitutionality. Note, however, that both the Court and its critics assume, first, that there is no federal police power, second, that the classification of a federal governmental act as an exercise of the commerce power is tantamount to its constitutionality, and, third, that the same act undertaken by a state as an exercise of its *police* power would be constitutional as well.

More generally, the question of the scope and origin of the power to police tends to be obscured by the question of its proper locus. The police power is discussed in the context of the struggle between the respective power of national and local governments. Rather than investigating the limitations upon the power to police generally speaking, i.e., as a matter of political theory, courts and scholars alike debate what limitations, if any, the constitution places on that power, or more precisely what limitations the *federal* constitution places on the *state's* power to police.

The origin and therefore the scope of the underlying power of the state is largely beyond scrutiny, judicial and scholarly. If the federal constitution, as interpreted by the federal Supreme Court, places no limitations on the state's police power, then that power is unlimited. Similarly, if the federal constitution, as interpreted by the federal Supreme Court, does not grant the federal government the power to police, then that government has no power to police.

At the very least, this focus on federalism, and on the federal Supreme Court in particular, results in a failure to investigate the substantive principles governing the exercises of the police power, regardless of where that power might be located. The leading American case on the judicial power to make common law crimes illustrates the point. This case, *United States v.*

Hudson & Goodwin,[19] did not in fact address the question of the constitution-ality of judicial criminal lawmaking. There was no need to reach the sub-stantive issue, because it was enough to decide that, even if other—state—courts enjoyed the power, the federal courts did not. The decision makes sense, particularly if we recall the connection between the police power and common law crimes. As we've seen, the power to define common law crimes as needed amounted to a judicial police power, i.e., the power to protect the police of the political community even in the absence of legislative provi-sions.[20] But the United States was said to have no such power. Surely, one could not deny the police power to the federal legislature and then grant it to the federal courts.

The substantive question of the constitutionality of judicial criminal law-making has never been addressed by the Supreme Court, nor by any other American court. In some American states the practice of judicial criminal lawmaking persisted for centuries. Where it no longer exists, the change was brought about by statutory reform, rather than by a judicial finding of un-constitutionality. Perhaps it would have been expecting too much from the courts to deprive themselves of a power on constitutional grounds. And yet the practice of judicial criminal lawmaking may implicate several constitu-tional issues, including some that brought about the downfall of legislative police measures such as vagrancy, including problems of retroactivity and vagueness. Recall, for instance, Ms. Keller's punishment for "indecent dis-position of a dead body," a crime that didn't exist at the time she committed it and that is ill-defined if not malaprop—and thus managed to be both retroactive and vague at the same time.[21]

To say that the Supreme Court made frequent use of the police power to mark the distinction between state and federal government, with police power being roughly synonymous with state power, is not to say that it never considered the police power in a different context. We've already seen that the police power made for a useful point of contrast to the power of eminent domain, and in this role could justify state interference with property rights without just compensation. Moreover, the concept of police came in handy when the need was felt, in the nineteenth century, to justify apparently in-congruous police measures like vagrancy. Here we've already left the Supreme Court behind, however, and entered the realm of the state courts. The Supreme Court, after all, didn't directly consider the constitutionality of vagrancy laws until the 1970s, and then without reference to the police power.

In each of these contexts the concept of police, and the state power which carried its name, fulfilled roughly the same, rhetorical, function: It insulated state action from principled, and constitutional, scrutiny. This function emerged clearly enough, once the jurisprudential discourse about the police power had been stripped of its layers of technical obfuscation. As the non-jurisprude authors of the entry on "police power" in the Encyclopedia of the Social Sciences put it in 1933:

> Police power is an idiom of apologetics which belongs to the vocabulary of constitutional law. In American government the validity of any regulatory statute may, in "a genuine case in controversy," be tested by judicial review. If the act is sustained, the police power is usually invoked as the sanction.[22]

The police power still serves to shield state action from principled scrutiny to this day. One difference is that courts, and the Supreme Court in particular, today pay—even—less attention to the question of the source of state power than at a time when certain manifestations of state governance were first challenged, and therefore called for an investigation into origins. Takings jurisprudence provides the most obvious illustration of the continuing insulating effect of the police concept. As we saw, this branch of constitutional law still is concerned with the classification of state acts as exercises of the police power. And if they are, then they remain outside the realm of justice, and of just compensation in particular.

We've also mentioned the Court's renewed interest in the distinction between (state) police power and (federal) commerce power when reviewing federal statutes passed ostensibly to regulate commerce, rather than to police. Here the classification as police has the opposite result—it condemns, rather than insulates. But it's important to keep in mind the other, state, side of the coin. The classification of federal statutes as police measures is as fatal as the classification of state statutes as police measures is protective.

Police Offenses and Public Welfare Offenses

It turns out, however, that the Court found a way to employ the police concept in upholding *federal* statutes as well. For this purpose, however, the concept had to be renamed—after all, the federal government officially had no general police power whatsoever. And so police offenses appeared in federal constitutional jurisprudence as "public welfare" offenses, where public welfare is synonymous with police, and fulfills precisely the same, insulating, function. Whereas the police concept was used in the vagrancy cases to neutralize the *actus reus* principle in substantive criminal law, and virtually the entire panoply of procedural principles, its main function here was to carve out an exception to the other great principle of Anglo-American criminal law, *mens rea*. It's in this context that these cases still play a role in American jurisprudence, as the constitutional endorsement of "strict liability" offenses, rather than as the general constitutional immunization of police power offenses. But the insulation against *mens rea* scrutiny was only one illustration of the comprehensive protection against principled constraints that the classification as a police measure brought about.[23]

The transition from police to public welfare was gradual, and took place over several decades. It began in 1910, with the Supreme Court's review of a state statute, in *Shevlin-Carpenter Co. v. Minnesota*.[24] A Minnesota law specified civil and criminal sanctions for, among other things, the "casual and involuntary" cutting of timber on state lands without a permit. It declared this "trespass" to be a felony, punishable by a fine of up to $1,000. The defendant complained that this was a blatant violation of the *mens rea* requirement. But the Court was not impressed. In fact, there was nothing left for it to decide, it explained. The state court already had disposed of the issue, by identifying the statute as a police measure:

> The supreme court of the state . . . decided that the legislation was in effect an exercise of the police power, and cited a number of cases to sustain the proposition that public policy may require that in the prohibition or punishment of particular acts it may be provided that he who shall do them shall do them at his peril, and will not be heard to plead in defense good faith or ignorance. Those cases are set forth in the opinion of the court, and some of them reviewed.
>
> We will not repeat them. It was recognized that such legislation may, in particular instances, be harsh, but we can only say again what we have so often said, that this court cannot set aside legislation because it is harsh.[25]

The immunizing power of the police power was so great, in 1910, that even the defendant exempted "certain instances within the police power" from the *mens rea* requirement.[26] The problem with the statute was not that it violated the *mens rea* requirement, the defendant argued, but that it wasn't an exercise of the police power. Even under the defendant's logic, therefore, once the police label was attached, the constitutionality of the statute followed *a fortiori*.

It's interesting, but without consequence for the future development of jurisprudence in this area, that it was the Supreme Court itself, rather than the defendant, which hinted at the constitutional irrelevance of the distinction between police measures and other state acts. So the Court remarked that "[i]f, as contended, intent is an essential element of crime, or, more restrictively, if intent is essential to the legality of penalties, it must be so, *no matter under what power of the state they are prescribed*."[27] For, while it "is true that the police power of a state is the least limitable of its powers," nonetheless "even it may not transcend the prohibition of the Constitution of the United States."[28] One of the reasons why these intimations of the limits of the police power had no visible effect on the future development of the jurisprudence of public welfare offenses might have been that the Court, immediately after making them, proceeded to uphold the challenged statute on the ground that it was, contrary to the defendant's contention, an exercise of the police power after all, like other similar regulations before it.

Twelve years later, when the Court took up another challenge to a strict liability police offense, in *United States v. Balint*,[29] it disposed of the issue by declaring that it had been settled by *Shevlin-Carpenter*.[30] And it once again pointed to the established practice of doing away with *mens rea* in the pursuit of the public police:

> Many instances of this are to be found in regulatory measures in the exercise of what is called the police power where the emphasis of the statute is evidently upon achievement of some social betterment rather than the punishment of the crimes as in cases of mala in se.[31]

There would be nothing noteworthy about *Balint* had it not considered a challenge to a federal, rather than a state, statute. The problem was, of course, that the federal government doesn't possess a police power. The Court's attempt to insulate the statute by labeling it as a police measure therefore came at the price of violating one of the cherished principles of federalism, a principle that would doom the federal statute in *Lopez*, to cite one recent example.

The next case in the familiar series of police offense opinions, *United States v. Dotterweich*, simply extended the chain of precedent begun with *Shevlin*. As *Balint* had invoked *Shevlin*, so *Dotterweich* now cited *Balint*:[32]

> The prosecution to which Dotterweich was subjected is based on a now familiar type of legislation whereby penalties serve as effective means of regulation. Such legislation dispenses with the conventional requirement for criminal conduct—awareness of some wrongdoing. In the interest of the larger good it puts the burden of acting at hazard upon a person otherwise innocent but standing in responsible relation to a public danger. United States v. Balint, 258 U.S. 250, 42 S.Ct. 301, 66 L.Ed. 604.[33]

Dotterweich once again was about a federal statute. And intentionally or not, but perhaps wisely, Justice Frankfurter's majority opinion does not mention the police power. The citation to *Balint*, and the characterization of "the familiar type of legislation" that employs "penalties . . . as effective means of regulation" is clear enough. This case is about a police offense.

But *Dotterweich* moves beyond *Balint* in another way. *Balint*, and *Shevlin*, had been content to declare the *mens rea* requirement inapplicable to police offenses. *Dotterweich* went a step further. As many commentators have pointed out since then, Frankfurter's opinion approves not only strict liability for police offenses, but vicarious liability as well. That is, Dotterweich was not only convicted without proof of intent, knowledge, recklessness, or negligence. He also was punished for an act he did not personally commit, namely the "introduction or delivery for introduction into interstate commerce of any adulterated or misbranded drug." Combining strict and vicarious liability meant, as the dissent put it, that "[g]uilt is imputed to the respondent solely on the basis of his authority and responsibility as president and general manager of the corporation."[34]

The last, and most carefully argued, opinion in this line of police offense cases is *Morissette v. United States*.[35] Decided nine years after *Dotterweich*, *Morissette* is the only case to affirm a *mens rea* requirement.[36] But *Morissette* left the previous decisions undisturbed. It adopted their general rule, that criminal statutes were not subject to a *mens rea* requirement as long as they were exercises of the police power. The only difference was that the statute in *Morissette* was no mere police measure. Instead, the Court decided, it was simply a modern version of an old common law crime, larceny, which as all common law crimes, required a showing of *mens rea*.[37]

Morissette, unlike its predecessors, made some effort to capture the nature of police offenses, so that it could explain why the statute before it didn't qualify as one. The Court began by identifying the "antecedents and origins" of police offenses, which it located in the nineteenth century:

> The industrial revolution multiplied the number of workmen exposed to injury from increasingly powerful and complex mechanisms, driven by freshly discovered sources of energy, requiring higher precautions by employers. Traffic of velocities, volumes and varieties unheard of came to subject the wayfarer to intolerable casualty risks if owners and drivers were not to observe new cares and uniformities of conduct. Congestion of cities and crowding of quarters called for health and welfare regulations undreamed of in simpler times. Wide distribution of goods became an instrument of wide distribution of harm when those who dispersed food, drink, drugs, and even securities, did not comply with reasonable standards of quality, integrity, disclosure and care. Such dangers have engendered increasingly numerous and detailed regulations which heighten the

duties of those in control of particular industries, trades, properties or activities that affect public health, safety or welfare.[38]

In fact, as we've seen, the roots of the police power go much deeper. Still, while the Court didn't quite get around to exposing the "antecedents and origins" of police offenses in general, it did provide a sensible explanation for the "antecedents and origins" of the *increase* in police offenses beginning in the nineteenth century. Designed to prevent anticipated dangers, one would expect police measures to increase as dangers increase, and new police measures to respond to the creation of new dangers. After all, from the very beginning, the ability to respond quickly to novel threats was always a hallmark of police authority, unhampered by the constraints of law.

The Court then went on to introduce the notion of "public welfare offenses," and attempted to distinguish them from traditional, common law, crimes on the basis of their "nature and peculiar quality"[39]:

[L]awmakers, whether wisely or not, have sought to make such regulations more effective by invoking criminal sanctions to be applied by the familiar technique of criminal prosecutions and convictions. This has confronted the courts with a multitude of prosecutions, based on statutes or administrative regulations, for what have been aptly called "public welfare offenses." These cases do not fit neatly into any of such accepted classifications of common-law offenses, such as those against the state, the person, property, or public morals. Many of these offenses are not in the nature of positive aggressions or invasions, with which the common law so often dealt, but are in the nature of neglect where the law requires care, or inaction where it imposes a duty. Many violations of such regulations result in no direct or immediate injury to person or property but merely create the danger or probability of it which the law seeks to minimize. While such offenses do not threaten the security of the state in the manner of treason, they may be regarded as offenses against its authority, for their occurrence impairs the efficiency of controls deemed essential to the social order as presently constituted.[40]

Here the Court borrowed heavily from a 1933 article by Francis Sayre, which coined the term "public welfare offenses,"[41] and traced the history of these offenses in much the same way as the Court would do some twenty years later. That "public welfare offenses" is but a convenient synonym for "police offenses" is plain enough—convenient because it avoids the recognition of a federal police power (*Morissette* too was about a federal statute). They have the same object: threats. They are measured by the same standard: efficiency. They take the same form: regulations. And they protect the same cluster of interests: public welfare (or "social betterment") and social order, and the authority of the state necessary to maintain them.

Morissette is useful because it places the concept of police, or public welfare, offenses into a broader context. As *Morissette* makes clear, the phenomenon of strict liability is not limited to white collar crime, or corporate criminality. And the reason why the statute in *Morissette* was subject to the *mens rea* requirement—constitutional or not—was not that "conversion" isn't a corporate crime, and Morissette not a white collar criminal, but because theft isn't a police crime. The exemption from the *mens rea* requirement—as from principled constraints generally speaking—instead is a feature of police offenses generally speaking. And the reach of police offenses is as broad as that of the police power. Police offenses, after all, simply are police measures that employ criminal sanctions, rather than, say, imposing licensing schemes.[42]

Whatever critical bite *Morissette* might have depends on where the line between police offenses and other offenses is drawn, assuming it can be drawn at all. For *Morissette* does nothing to challenge the traditional assumption that exercises of the police power are beyond constitutional scrutiny. If one subscribes to the view that all criminal offenses are police offenses since all criminal law represents an exercise of the police power, then criminal law in its entirety is subject to no principled constraints, including the venerable *mens rea* requirement. Obviously *Morissette* implies a more limited view of police offenses, since it identifies conversion as a non-police offense. While it tries to give an account of the origin and the nature of police offenses, however, the opinion fails to explain where non-police offenses come from and what power of the state they manifest. In a move familiar from much common law opinion writing, *Morissette* instead assumes that non-police offenses are *just there*, the product of a historical chain of precedents whose origin is unfathomable. But why wouldn't conversion, say, count as a police offense? Isn't conversion a crime precisely because it protects the public welfare, just like recognized police offenses such as drug crimes and traffic violations? What's the difference between conversion and the distribution of cocaine other than that it's an *older* police offense?

Above all, the line of public welfare offense cases from *Shevlin* to *Morissette* provides another illustration of the apologetic function of the police concept. More recently the police power has done much of its work of inoculating state action against principled constraints below the surface of doctrinal rhetoric. Police classification exercises have become rare, with the notable exception of takings jurisprudence. In cases like *Miln* or *Balint*, the Court at least had to make some effort to explain why a particular statute counted as a police measure. Once the classification had been accomplished, the result fell easily into place—constitutional in the case of a state statute, unconstitutional if the statute was a federal one. But at least the classification had to be made.

In general, when today's Supreme Court refers to the police power, it tends do so almost as an afterthought. No effort is made to explain why a particular statute falls under the police power. Often enough, no effort is made to explain why a particular statute arises under *any* power of the state. The question of origin is simply not addressed. It's not considered significant. So we can read, in a recent Supreme Court opinion addressing a First Amendment challenge against a city ordinance prohibiting nude dancing, that the city's "efforts to protect public health and safety are clearly within the city's police powers."[43] Nothing follows from this proposition, which apparently is included as a point of information to the interested reader. No argument is presented in its support.

And yet, it's no surprise that the Court ends up upholding the statute in this case, *City of Erie v. Pap's A.M.* Although the Court doesn't make this clear, the ordinance in question, which defines the "Summary Offense" of "Public Indecency," is a classic police measure. The inquiry into its constitutionality is over before it has begun. For, at the very outset of the opinion, the Court quotes extensively from the preamble to the challenged ordinance:

> the Council of the City of Erie has, at various times over more than a century, expressed its findings that certain lewd, immoral activities carried on in public places for profit are highly detrimental to the public health, safety and welfare, and lead to the debasement of both women and men, promote violence, public intoxication, prostitution and other serious criminal activity.

Now this analysis of the threat to the public police emanating from nude dancing could have stemmed from one of the judicial "guardians of public morals" we encountered earlier on. The one difference is that the moral police, i.e., the moral well-being of the public, isn't mentioned among the aspects of the public welfare under threat, though presumably the "lewd" and "immoral" nature of the activities to be eliminated is not without significance to their dangerousness. At any rate, the absence of moral police doesn't condemn the ordinance. Instead, it merely forces the Court to uphold the ordinance as an effort to prevent not the immoral activities for their own sake, but rather for the sake of their "secondary effects" on other aspects of the public police, in particular the "public health, safety and welfare." Nude dancing, in other words, may be proscribed because it indirectly poses a threat to certain aspects of the public police. Either way, as a direct moral police measure or an indirect health, safety and welfare measure, the ordinance is precisely the type of anticipatory state action that serves to stifle the fountains of evil.

PART III

Police, Law, Criminal Law

7

The Forgotten Power and
the Problem of Legitimation

Today references to the police power in Supreme Court jurisprudence have become sporadic. Tracking the Court, the scholarly literature too has paid little attention to the concept. Only in the takings literature does the concept appear regularly, again echoing the Court's practice. There is little recognition of the fact, however, that the police concept has any significance beyond the question of whether state interference with property amounts to a taking or qualifies as a "mere" police regulation. The recent uproar over the Court's rediscovery of the distinction between the police power and the power to regulate commerce, in *Lopez*, illustrated not only that the power to regulate commerce had become a phrase of constitutional apologetics, but also that the power to regulate police had suffered the same fate.

The last treatise on the police power was Ernst Freund's. Published in 1904, it never appeared in a second edition. After that, the police power largely ceased to exist as a subject of scholarly inquiry.[1] Freund himself turned to studies of "American Legislation,"[2] "Legislative Regulation,"[3] and, most interestingly, "Administrative Power over Persons and Property."[4] The title of the last mentioned treatise nicely captures much of the essence of the police power, without mentioning it, and in this way is symptomatic of the continued, but hidden, role of the police power in modern American legal discourse. We've seen that police from the very start was about problems of administration, from the master's management of his household to the police science taught at training academies for the administrators manning the expanding networks of the emerging European bureaucracies. And police al-

157

ways also meant power, the power to take whatever actions were necessary to preserve the welfare of the household-community, by any means necessary, including physical force. And finally, police always distinguished itself by reaching any threats to that welfare, no matter who or what it might be, including persons and property alike. Police always was people and thing police.

Freund's was the last attempt at a comprehensive and systematic account of the police power. It was comprehensive in that it aimed to present an overview of the power in its full breadth, covering persons as well as property, human as well as inanimate nuisances. It was systematic because Freund treated the "idea of police" as a fundamental mode of governance, and sought to "assign to it its place among governmental powers."[5] His primary interest was not constitutional law, or the defense or critique of state action from a constitutional perspective. His first concern was analysis, to gain a better appreciation of governance in general, and of police in particular. Once mapped and understood, the exercise of these powers could then be challenged, under constitutional or other principles. But the critique presupposed the analysis.

This attempt to find a place for police in governance generally speaking implied a distinction between police and governance. Freund distinguished between three "[g]reat objects of government":

- the maintenance of national existence;
- the maintenance of right, or justice;
- and the public welfare.[6]

These three objectives of government corresponded to two modes of government, justice and police. The second goal defined the realm of law, or justice. The first and the third goal defined the realm of police, or policy, corresponding roughly to its external and internal aspects, respectively. In this way, they were generally analogous to Locke's federative and executive powers.

As we've seen, this broad distinction between police and law, the two modes of state governance, is not sufficiently nuanced. For example, it fails to capture the different types of interference associated with police and law (prevention and remedy), the different objects of that interference (threats and persons), the different styles of government (informality and formality, flexibility and definiteness), the different types of scrutiny applied (effectiveness and justice), and—perhaps most important—the different relationships between the subject and the object of government that characterize police and law as modes of governance (hierarchy and equality). The full extent of the distinction between police and law, in all of its aspects, emerges only after an appreciation of its historical roots. It's impossible to understand the nature of the police power, and to appreciate the challenges it faces, particularly in a modern state, by taking an ahistorical view.

The idea of police is as old as human governance. In fact, it's older than the idea of law, or right. The idea of right is based on the recognition of the equality of all persons as persons, rather than, say, as householders. And the one quality that all persons share as such is the capacity for self-government, or autonomy.

Without recalling the origin of the police power in the authority of the householder, the *patria potestas* of Roman law, the *grið* or *mund* of Anglo-Saxon law, or *munduburdium* of Frankish law, the nature and scope of this power is all too easily forgotten. And this is precisely what has happened in modern American law. The police power, as a jurisprudential concept, has been relegated to specific doctrinal corners, where it persists detached from the broader political context to which it belongs. There is not a police power of the takings clause, and another police power of the commerce clause. There is only one police power, the power of the state to govern the persons and things within its dominion as a householder would his household.

There lies considerable danger in failing to appreciate the nature and scope of the power to police. A power obscured cannot be checked. It doesn't help, of course, if the existence of a state power is acknowledged only so that its exercise can be insulated from constitutional scrutiny, as is the case in takings jurisprudence. But retaining the concept of police only in the context of reviewing challenges to the regulation of property and to the expansion of federal power not only blocks the view to the police power as a whole. It also ignores precisely those manifestations of the police power that are most in need of scrutiny, and of justification, if possible—namely the exercise of the police power against persons, or people police.

The regulation of property is an instance of thing police. An inanimate object is policed to maximize the public welfare. Thing police affects persons only indirectly, insofar as the thing policed is someone's property, i.e., insofar as a person owns or at least possesses it. The police of things that belong to no particular person, such as "public lands," or rivers or forests or mountains or wild animals, doesn't affect the rights of any particular person. For that reason, it doesn't require a justification for the interference with personal rights. It simply doesn't touch upon the realm of law, or justice. The forest police has its own rules, even its own science, forestry, but it is not subject to any moral constraints, provided that one doesn't view flora and fauna as bearers of rights.[7]

Insofar as thing police is directed at things possessed or owned by persons, however, it is subject to constraints of justice. And the removal of these constraints, in the name of the police power, requires a justification. This justification often has been replaced with an exercise in taxonomy, in which every justifiable interference with property is labeled a police regulation. Nonetheless, the need for a justification has been felt, however vaguely.

Now, in the case of people police the need for justification is even greater. Here the relation between the police act and the person is no longer indirect, because an inanimate object of police happens to be owned or possessed by a person. Instead the object of police is the individual person. Whether vagrancy laws affect persons, and therefore rights, is not a matter of happenstance. As people police measures, vagrancy laws are designed to reach persons directly, so as to eliminate them as threats to the public police.

The distinction between thing and people police may be difficult to maintain in some cases. For example, a police measure ostensibly directed at a thing-threat to the public police may in fact aim to eliminate a person-threat. This is the modus operandi of possession offenses, i.e., offenses that criminalize the possession of a thing considered a threat to the public police. It turns out, however, that the possession of the thing tends to be criminalized if the person possessing it represents a public threat. For instance, gun possession by felons is prohibited not because guns are dangerous, but because felons are.[8]

The basic reason why people police raises questions of legitimacy that thing police does not, is plain enough. Policing people runs the risk of treating them as things, in two senses. First, the distinction between people and things becomes irrelevant from the perspective of governance as police, which seeks to maximize the welfare of the community by eliminating threats to that welfare. As threats, people and things are indistinguishable. Second, by regarding persons as threats one abstracts from their capacity for self-government, or autonomy. That capacity includes both the capacity for self-*control*, i.e., the ability to engage in voluntary action according to rules, and the capacity for self-*government*, strictly speaking, i.e., the ability to assume the moral point of view and act according to moral principles. People, like things or animals, may be dangerous. But only people can choose not to put that dangerousness into action.

This tension between governing people through police and through law is of fairly recently vintage. It didn't arise until what J. B. Schneewind has termed "the invention of autonomy"[9] in enlightenment political and moral philosophy, and particularly in the work of Rousseau and Kant. Only at that time was autonomy identified as a characteristic of personhood, rather than as an attribute of status, and of householder status in particular. Until then, the idea of policing people wasn't problematic. It was taken as a given that certain people lacked the capacity for autonomy and, for that reason, required policing by someone who possessed not only the capacity for autonomy, but actual autonomy, the householder.

While there were other features that distinguished paupers from animals and trees, the capacity for autonomy wasn't among them. The discovery, or "invention," of these distinguishing features certainly marked a preliminary step along the way to the recognition of personhood and its attending capacity for autonomy, but it did nothing to challenge the legitimacy of policing people. These distinctions between people and things did not erase the distinctions between people and people, some of whom were autonomous and others weren't, and couldn't be. Take, for example, the discovery by the medieval Christian Church that slaves had souls.[10] This discovery helped distinguish slaves from inanimate members of the household, and had certain consequences for purposes of religious practice, including that "the slave has a soul to be saved, that he can be sinned against and can sin, that his marriage is a sacrament."[11] But it didn't affect the slave's status as an object of police governance. The householder's task of "employing" the slave as a resource for household management, including through the use of disciplinary measures whenever necessary, remained the same.

Now the invention of autonomy may make critiquing the legitimacy of people police possible, as a matter of theory. As a matter of fact, however, this critical apparatus will never be put to use if there is nothing to be critiqued, i.e., if it turns out that there is no such thing as people police. And it's precisely the fundamental fact of the existence of people police that becomes obscured if one, like the Supreme Court and its commentators, holds a cramped view of police that has no room for the policing of people and instead focuses on the question of when a police regulation of property becomes a taking and, even more remote, on the question of whether a particular federal statute qualifies as an exercise of the police power.

The current failure to recognize, or at least to acknowledge, the existence of police measures directed at human threats is illustrated by the Supreme Court's recent disposition of an attack on a people police measure par excellence, the Kansas sexual predator law, in *Kansas v. Hendricks*.[12] One could hardly imagine a more obvious example of human policing, i.e., the elimination of potential human threats to the public police, than the practice of indefinitely detaining persons convicted of sex offenses who have been deemed to be "sexually violent predators." And yet the term police power doesn't appear anywhere in the Court's analysis in that case. Nonetheless, the police power permeates the Court's opinion, if not in word, than certainly in spirit. The statute, it turns out, is upheld because it is a police measure. It is designed to eliminate human threats in the form of "sexual violent predators" who (that?) are characterized by a "mental abnormality" in the form of a "congenital or acquired condition affecting the emotional or volitional capacity which predisposes the person to commit sexually violent offenses in a degree constituting such person a menace to the health and safety of others." Rather than punish these "menaces," the statute merely provides for his or her (or its?) diagnosis and "long-term care and treatment," meaning indefinite incarceration, possibly for the rest of the predator's life.

The Court thus characterizes predator laws in very much the same way as courts and commentators portrayed vagrancy laws in the nineteenth century. And that characterization as a police measure, rather than as a punishment law, has very much the same effect. It insulates the statute from principled, and particularly constitutional, critique. Because the predator statute is not a criminal law, but rather "of a kind with . . . civil commitment statutes," due process places negligible constraints on the legislature's design of an efficient commitment process, and the constitutional prohibition of double jeopardy and ex post facto legislation don't apply at all. Although this argument wasn't raised in *Hendricks*, the police label also would have removed the predator law from the scope of the Eighth Amendment's prohibition of cruel and unusual punishments, as it did in several lower court cases, and the prohibition against vague criminal statutes.[13]

Much like the traditional vagrancy laws, the predator laws too must be seen in the context of a comprehensive system for the "police control" of a "dangerous class."[14] Sexual predators are but a subset of the wider class of sex offenders, and their indefinite incarceration but the most intrusive police measures taken against that class. Recall that in the case of vagrants, the police system began with sureties for keeping the peace or for good behavior which any justice of the peace could demand from all "that be not of good fame." If these police measures proved ineffective, the vagrancy laws then inflicted sanctions tailored to the degree of dangerousness associated with a particular person. By the eighteenth century, vagrants were placed into one of three categories: "idle and disorderly persons" faced one month in prison, "rogues and vagabonds" whipping in addition to six months' imprisonment, and, eventually, "incorrigible rogues" whipping and up to two years in prison.[15]

Similarly, many states place sex offenders in various categories of dangerousness, with corresponding police measures whose intrusiveness is proportional to the degree of dangerousness, ranging from registration with the police authorities to "community" notification.[16] Others are less sophisticated. They impose registration and notification requirements on all "sex offenders," without regard to their level of dangerousness.[17] And the most dangerous—and the least human—of them all, the *predators*, are subjected to the most intrusive form of police control, commitment, and in fact indefinite commitment.

Now to find courts appreciating the police nature of these sex offender laws one must leave the Supreme Court behind, and look at the lower courts. There one finds the issue framed explicitly in police power terms:

> Plaintiffs characterize the Registration Act as a law which punishes sex offenders for their past conduct. Defendants characterize it as a proper exercise of the state's police power which does not punish past offenses, but regulates present conduct.[18]

The Supreme Court instead focuses on another distinction, that between "civil" and "criminal." The labeling exercise is very much the same. If a state statute is marked as civil it is beyond the reach of serious constitutional scrutiny. If it's labeled as criminal, it must pass muster under the constitutional provisions just mentioned. In this context, it's particularly telling that civil measures are exempt from the principle of "legality"—i.e., of lawness—in its various aspects, some of which are constitutionalized, others aren't. These include the principles of prospectivity (the prohibition of retroactivity), specificity (the prohibition of vagueness), lenity (strict construction), and legislativity (the prohibition of judicial lawmaking).

It is misleading, however, to focus on the distinction between civil and criminal. The distinction between nonpunitive and punitive, which is often mistaken for the same thing, is far less so. The reason why the legality principle, for example, doesn't apply to state actions labeled "civil" is not that they are civil, rather than criminal, but that they are police measures, rather than rules of law, or right. They deal with matters of policy, rather than of legality. To the extent that the legality principle is a principle of justice, it doesn't apply to police measures, which by definition fall outside the realm of justice. This could not be said of civil matters. Civil law, as law, is governed also by principles of justice. Tort law and contract law, for instance, are manifestations of the idea of law, or right, insofar as they address interactions between autonomous persons, and resolve conflicts among them.

Civil police, however, as police is not governed by the principles of right, including the manifestations of the legality principle. What matters is the classification as a police measure, in other words, not the classification as civil or criminal. The distinction between nonpunitive and punitive is more helpful because it better tracks that between police and law. As we've seen time and time again, police seeks to prevent, rather than to punish. Police is the power to prevent the need for law, whether that law be the "common" law of nuisance or the "statutory" law of homicide. For this reason, the distinction between "remedial" and "punitive" state action is also inappropriate. This distinction has been used in many cases to insulate state actions labeled as remedial from constitutional scrutiny. But remedy and punishment are simply two concepts within the realm of law, or right. The remedy of past harm is no more a police matter than is the punishment for past harm.

Police and Punishment

It may be that the distinction between police and punishment has disappeared from Supreme Court jurisprudence because the Court no longer sees a difference between the two. Recall that under an expansive view of police, the power to punish was but one aspect of the power to police. In that case, the power to define crimes, to apply them, and to enforce them flowed from the state's obligation to protect the public police from threats internal and external. The Supreme Court has never had occasion to consider this matter squarely. Nonetheless, it's not hard to find evidence suggesting that at least some Justices regard punishment as a police matter.

For instance, Justice Thomas in his majority opinion in the recent case of *United States v. Morrison*, declares flat out that "we can think of no better example of the police power, which the Founders denied the National Government and reposed in the States, than the suppression of violent crime and vindication of its victims."[19] Note, however, that Thomas here may well be confusing police power with state sovereignty. Given the context of the particular case, a successful post-*Lopez* attack on a federal statute exposed by the Court as another (impermissible) police regulation camouflaged as a (permissible) commerce regulation, the emphasis certainly lay on the connection between criminal law and the *state* police power, rather than the state *police* power.

That some Supreme Court Justices today would regard all punishment, even in cases of traditional crime, as a police matter isn't preposterous. After all, this idea has deep roots in American legal and political thought.

The elimination of threats to the public police already lay at the very heart of Locke's theory of the essence of political power, surrendered by the individual to the state (personified by the magistrate):

> so that the end and measure of this power, when in every man's hands, in the state of Nature, being the preservation of all of his society—that is, all mankind in general—it can have no other end or measure, when in the hands of the magistrate, but to preserve the members of that society in their lives, liberties, and possessions, and so cannot be an absolute, arbitrary power over their lives and fortunes, which are as much as possible to be preserved; but *a power to make laws, and annex such penalties to them as may tend to the preservation of the whole, by cutting off those parts, and those only,*

which are so corrupt that they threaten the sound and healthy, without which no severity is lawful.[20]

Closer to home, Massachusetts Attorney General Rufus Choate, in one of the great early police power cases before Chief Justice Shaw, used the execution of a person convicted of murder to illustrate the distinction between the police power and power of eminent domain. The power of eminent domain stood to the police power in the realm of things as the power of punishment stood to the police power in the realm of persons, Choate argued, successfully, in *Fisher v. McGirr*.[21] Murderers are eliminated as human nuisances just as wharfs (or, in this case, "a quantity of brandy and other spirituous liquors, with the barrels, demijohns, jugs and bottles") are destroyed as inanimate ones. The suggestion that the seizure and destruction of threats to the public police is a taking for public use without just compensation was patently absurd, for

> it might as well be said that the life of a murderer is taken for public uses. That is not the object for which property is taken under this law; it is wasted, or sacrificed, or destroyed, as unfit to be part of the mass of property protected by the constitution. There is no taking for public uses, but a putting away of it, as a nuisance, out of the land.[22]

We've already noted Tiedeman's view of the criminal law as a species of police, and Justice Taney's remark, in the *License Cases*, that the police power encompassed "law[s] to punish offenses."[23] Similar, and similarly off-hand, remarks about the connection between the power to punish and the power to police have appeared in opinions since then. For instance, in a post–World War I opinion affirming the criminal syndicalism conviction of a member of The Industrial Workers of the World, the Washington Supreme Court opined that "[t]he legislature, in defining and providing for the punishment of crime, is exercising only one phase of the broad police power of the state."[24] More recently, an Illinois appellate court declared that "[u]nder the State's police power, the legislature has the discretion to prescribe penalties for defined offenses."[25] And the Ohio Supreme Court said much the same thing a few years later.[26]

Perhaps the best way of putting the considered state of judicial opinion regarding the origin of the power to punish in general, as opposed to the power to punish police offenses in particular, is to say that, whenever a court finds it necessary or prudent to comment on the origin of the power to punish, chances are that it traces the power to punish back to the power to police.

The problem is, however, that these occasions are few and far between, and when they do arise, little if anything turns on the position the court ends up taking. There simply is no interest in the origin of the power to punish. It is just there, not unlike the power to police. Presumably the fact of the state's power to punish is too obvious for words, not unlike the fact of the state's power to police. And so the question of its origins is simply irrelevant. Like the police power, it is in Chief Justice Shaw's words in *Alger*, within "the nature of well ordered civil society."[27] And since the power to punish is so much *like* the police power, we may as well attribute the former to the latter. The police after all isn't just the means to an end, public welfare or the well-being of the household. It's the end itself.

The Minnesota Supreme Court nicely captured the straightforward, but rarely articulated, connection between the power to punish and the fundamental power to police, in a 1918 opinion affirming a conviction for the topical crime of "interfering with and discouraging the enlistment of men in the military or naval forces of the United States or of Minnesota":

> The state has control of its internal affairs, and in the exercise of its police power may prescribe rules of conduct for its citizens, and may forbid whatever is inimical to the public interests, or contrary to the public policy of the state.[28]

Given that general pronouncements about the origins of the power to punish, and to proscribe under threat of punishment, are hard to come by, it's no surprise that elaborations of the theory of the state and of the criminal law underlying them aren't any easier to find. For these, still more fundamental, matters one must turn to the commentators. Tiedeman and Freund we've already discussed. One held that all criminal law was an exercise of the police power, and the other that only some "technically criminal" statutes, the police offenses in the narrow sense, were. But then both proceeded to discuss only police offenses in the narrow sense and paid no attention to the criminal law.[29]

Writers on police thus had little to say about criminal law. But writers on criminal law had a lot to say about police, although not in so many words. In fact, the idea that criminal law was nothing but an exercise of the police power lay at the very core of progressive penology, a theory of criminal law that first appeared in America at the turn of the twentieth century and that still underlies much of American thinking about criminal law to this day. These reformers, Roscoe Pound chief among them, were anxious to modernize American criminal law, by stripping it of its anachronistic moral elements which had become frozen into a byzantine construct of common law principles, substantive and procedural.

In their view, traditional criminal law was unduly obsessed with individual rights, in two senses. First, references to violations of the king's peace and so on notwithstanding, criminal law never quite managed to shed its origins in interpersonal conflict, with one person interfering with the rights of another. But the whole point of criminal law, and its point of distinction from tort law, was that it didn't address interferences with the rights of individuals. Instead, what made the criminal law criminal was its focus on, and only on, *public* interests. (This much the Minnesota court recognized.)

But not only the individual rights of the victim were of no interest to the criminal law. The individual rights of the offender likewise had been much exaggerated. It was time to put the protection of individual rights, manifested in the myriad of principles and protections that had accumulated throughout the history of substantive and procedural criminal law, into the proper, broader, context. And that context was the primacy of public interests over individual rights. Certainly, individual rights needed to be protected to the maximum extent possible, but that extent was defined by the primary mission of criminal law, namely the promotion of public welfare in all its aspects, i.e., police. It was high time, in the words of Roscoe Pound, to move beyond the "extreme tenderness toward accused persons"[30] and embrace the police of the community as the goal of criminal law.

There's no better formulation of this view of punishment as police than one finds in Francis Sayre's influential 1933 article on public welfare offenses, which we've already mentioned. Sayre located the evolution of public welfare offenses within a larger movement toward acknowledging the primacy of public welfare over individual rights, or what he called "the trend of the day away from nineteenth century individualism toward a new sense of the importance of collective interests."[31] This "shift of emphasis from the protection of individual interests which marked nineteenth century criminal administration to the protection of public and social interests"[32] manifested itself, among other things, in the abandonment of strict guilt requirements, including *mens rea*:

> During the nineteenth century it was the individual interest which held the stage; the criminal law machinery was overburdened with innumerable checks to prevent possible injustice to individual defendants. The scales were weighted heavily in his favor, and, as we have found to our sorrow, the public welfare often suffered. In the twentieth century came reaction. We are thinking today more of the protection of social and public interest; and coincident with the swinging of the pendulum in the field of legal administration in this direction modern criminologists are teaching the objective underlying correctional treatment should change from the barren aim of punishing human beings to the fruitful one of protecting social interests. As a direct result of this new emphasis upon public and social, as contrasted with individual, interests, courts have naturally tended to con-

centrate more upon the injurious conduct of the defendant than upon the problem of his individual guilt.[33]

But the prioritization of public welfare, or police, over the protection and vindication of the individual rights of offenders and victims alike, was but one aspect of the new model of criminal administration. So important was the protection of the public welfare that a police oriented system of criminal administration could not afford to await the actual infliction of harm to the police. It instead shifted its emphasis from the punishment for past injury to the prevention of potential threats. This point was emphasized, once again, by Pound, who explained, in his introduction to Sayre's criminal law casebook that progressive criminal law sought not "punishment" but "interference to prevent disobedience,"[34] disobedience to the state's commands issued under its authority to maintain public order. In sum,

> criminal law . . . should be reserved for the direct and immediate maintaining of the general security and the general morals against well recognized types of anti-social individuals and of anti-social conduct. More and more we must rely upon preventive justice as the most effective agency of social control.[35]

Pound thus captured another characteristic of a police criminal law, besides its goal of protecting the public police through prevention, namely its hierarchical structure which contrasts the superior authority of the subject of police with the inferior otherness of its object, the state with the anti-social individual, whose dangerous disobedience must be prevented through social control. All aspects of the punishment system, including its moral connotations, were enlisted in the pursuit of discipline: "[t]he moral obloquy and the social disgrace incident to criminal conviction are whips [!] which lend effective power to the administration of criminal law."[36]

Although Pound speaks of preventive *justice*, this mode of governance is measured in terms of its "effectiveness" as an "agency of social control," rather than as one constrained by principles of justice that govern conflicts and other relations among equal persons. The anti-social individual requires the "appointed penal treatment" at the earliest possible moment. Only then will the "development of preventive justice" prove "as epoch-making for the science of law as the development of preventive medicine has been for medical science."[37]

Criminal law, as Pound recognized, was not unique in its pursuit of public police, or "social interests," in Pound's terminology. Among the various types of law employed by the state, it was merely the one most single-mindedly concerned with protecting social interests as such. It had absolutely no interest in individual interests. "Criminal law has for its province the securing of social interests regarded directly as such, that is, disassociated from any immediate individual interests with which they may be identified."[38] And these social interests were simply another term for the, now very familiar, aspects of public police: "The general security, the security of social institutions, the general morals, the conservation of social resources, the general progress, and the individual life."[39]

Police, in other words, is a fundamental mode of governance. In fact, in Pound's view, it appeared as the *only* mode of governance. Even justice was interpreted in terms of effectiveness. And even an essential individual right, the right to life, becomes a police interest. At any rate, the point is, once again, that police stands not merely in contrast to punishment, and police offenses to "real crimes," but that it is a basic power of government, and mentality of governance, that manifests itself in various ways, including the control of human threats to the police of the community, or "social interests."

One effect of equating government with police is the insulation of government in its entirety from constraints of justice, and constitutional scrutiny. More narrowly, the identification of governing through criminal law with police regulation exempts criminal law from demands of moral legitimacy. This is the tenor of Pound's and Sayre's descriptions of the new model of criminal administration. Modern criminal administration was to be a complex system of social control, where potential threats are diagnosed and treated according to their level and type of dangerousness. Principles of justice would only interfere with the proper operation of this sophisticated "machinery of detection, conviction, and penal treatment."[40] That's why the time had come to put in place summary proceedings without non-expert jurors burdened with arcane rules of evidence that complicated the diagnostic process, if it didn't make diagnosis impossible altogether. Substantive principles of criminal law, like *actus reus*, *mens rea*, or guilt, similarly were expendable as irrelevant and anachronistic hangovers from a bygone era of criminal law as a system of justice, rather than of police.

Sayre, however, attempted to limit the scope of police, and therefore its insulating effect. Focusing on the *mens rea* requirement, he tried to exempt only one type of crime from principled constraint, rather than exempting the entirety of criminal law. Strict liability—i.e., exemption from the *mens rea* requirement—was to be available only to Sayre's newly labeled class of public welfare offenses. "[T]rue crimes," by contrast, were to remain subject to the "orthodox requirement of mens rea."[41]

This attempt, however, was naïve at best, if not hypocritical. Once Sayre had accepted the general equation of the power to police and the power to punish, that is, once he had endorsed the broad view of the connection between police and punishment, he could not then turn around and embrace the narrow view of the connection, insisting that only some offenses should be placed beyond the realm of law. He couldn't have his cake and eat it too.

Sayre, after all, began his inquiry into strict liability by describing nothing less than a fundamental paradigm shift in criminal law. The modern conception of criminality," he diagnosed, "seems to be shifting from a basis of individual guilt to one of social danger."[42] Like Pound, and the progressive penologists in general, Sayre noticed, and advocated, a fundamental reconceptualization of criminal law in its entirety. The abandonment of *mens rea* in what he called public welfare offenses was but one, minor, symptom of a much larger development. Even within the limited realm of public welfare offenses, *mens rea* wasn't the only principle to fall. As we've seen in our discussion of the *Shevlin-Dotterweich* line of cases, public welfare offenses paid no more attention to other principles like *actus reus* (by criminalizing omissions) and the personalness of guilt (by imposing vicarious liability).[43]

And yet Sayre insisted that the abandonment of *mens rea* be limited to a subset of crimes, his public welfare offenses, or "police offenses of a merely regulatory nature."[44] The line separating these from the rest of criminal law was vague and thin, and must have seemed so to Sayre himself. He differentiated true crimes from public welfare offenses on two grounds, "the character of the offense" and, most importantly, the "possible penalty." The first distinction was vague, and really no distinction at all, but a sliding scale. All criminal laws, Sayre explained, "serve the double purpose of singling out wrongdoers for the purpose of punishment or correction and of regulating the social order."[45] True crimes and police offenses differ merely insofar as "often the importance of one far outweighs the other." In other words, police offenses differed from true crimes insofar as they were "police offenses of a merely regulatory nature," which didn't say much of anything.

The second distinction was more important. A true crime was punishable by imprisonment (or, presumably, death), a police offense by some lesser penalty.[46] This second distinction was clear enough, but faced a problem. It didn't work. As we know from Blackstone, there always had been police offenses that were punishable by severe penalties, including imprisonment, whipping, "ducking" (for the common scold), even death. Sayre himself acknowledged bigamy and adultery, along with statutory rape, were "often cited among the cases of" public welfare offenses.[47] But he then excluded them from "the general class of police regulations being considered within this paper,"[48] because each of them has been punished severely, and therefore didn't match his definition of a public welfare offense.

In the end, Sayre's definition of police offenses thus comes down to a prescription: police offenses are offenses that are punishable by something less than imprisonment. But not even this prescription has anything to do with police offenses, at least not directly. For its basis is another prescription, that offenses punishable by imprisonment require proof of *mens rea*. If we search for the source of this norm in turn, we find this: "To subject persons entirely free from moral blameworthiness to the possibility of prison sentences is revolting to the community sense of justice: and no law which violates this fundamental instinct can long endure."[49] There is no discussion of what a community sense of justice is in general, what it is in this particular instance, what community Sayre has in mind, or why suddenly considerations of justice should come into play, after the paradigm shift from just punishment to effective social control.

At any rate, "the community sense of justice," without more, doesn't erect much of a fence around public welfare offense to prevent the spread of police thinking to other areas of criminal law. Having proclaimed the transformation of criminal law into criminal administration, Sayre fails to put the police genie back into bottle. He appears to have been aware of this problem:

> the modern rapid growth of a large body of offenses punishable without proof of a guilty intent is marked with real danger. Courts are familiarized with the pathway to easy convictions by relaxing the orthodox requirement of a *mens rea*. The danger is that in the case of true crimes where the penalty is severe and the need for ordinary criminal law safeguards is strong, courts following the false analogy of the public welfare offenses may now and again similarly relax the *mens rea* requirement, particularly in the case of unpopular crimes, as the easiest way to secure desired convictions.[50]

Having just pinned the distinction between public welfare offenses and true crimes on "the community sense of justice," Sayre realizes that these very communal attitudes toward persons convicted of particular offenses will result in the collapse of the distinction, and therefore the extension of strict liability to crimes that would no longer qualify as police offenses, at least according to his definition, on account of their severe punishment. He even provides an illustration of this phenomenon: He attributes the Supreme Court's decision in *United State v. Balint*, which we've already encountered, to "extreme popular disapproval of the sale of narcotics.[51] The felony statute upheld in *Balint*, and upheld *as a police offense*, provided for punishment of up to five years' imprisonment.[52]

Much of what Sayre saw as a "real danger" became reality. Police as a mode, or mentality, of governance spread across the entirety of criminal law. Criminal law became a system of people police. The distinction between police offenses proper and true crimes became as irrelevant as those between the power to police and the power to punish, and between police and law. All of criminal law, including and especially the traditional criminal law, became recognized not merely as one, but as the paradigmatic, illustration of the police power: "we can think of no better example of the police power, which the Founders denied the National Government and reposed in the States, than the suppression of violent crime and vindication of its victims."[53]

Pound's "interference to prevent disobedience" became the central modus operandi of the criminal law as people police. (Since I have described this model of police criminal law in some detail elsewhere, I will confine myself to a few illustrations.)[54] So-called "inchoate" offenses, like attempt and conspiracy, played a central role in this police system. Since the point was to stifle the fountains of evil, inchoate offenses were far preferable as a target of prevention than completed offenses.[55]

The use of inchoate inchoate offenses, such as possession, moved the point of preventive interference farther away from the actual infliction of harm to protected interests. Possession of an object, such as a quantity of drugs, a gun, or "instruments of crime," indicated the possibility of its use. Its use in turn indicated the possibility of its use to inflict harm. Possession, in this sense, was an attempt to commit an attempt to commit a crime, or, in other words, an inchoate inchoate offense. It enabled early intervention, even before the doctrinal line between mere "preparation" and punishable "attempt" had been crossed.

Preventing inchoate offenses was one thing. Eliminating inchoate offenders was even more effective. Inchoate offenses, after all, revealed an abnormal dangerousness in the inchoate offender that required police attention. And that attention came in the form of penal treatment and discipline, applied in correctional institutions by correctional officers. Certain individuals, however, displayed such a high degree of dangerousness that incapacitive treatment was called for. That incapacitation came in the form of imprisonment, up to and including life imprisonment without the possibility of parole, and capital punishment.

This "interference to prevent disobedience" in the form of penal treatment was not inconsistent with the welfare of its object. Curing the abnormally dangerous eliminated not only a danger to the public police, but also an abnormality in the individual offender. In some cases, however, a cure was not forthcoming. In that event, the protection of the public police naturally took precedence. The threat to the public police posed by the incurable, the incorrigible, was eliminated not by cure, but by elimination of the person carrying it by nature.

At bottom, however, penal treatment remained a police measure. It sought to anticipate, prevent, and eliminate threats to public, rather than individual, interests. Neither the individual offender nor the individual victim were of independent interest. As an illustration of the role of public interests, consider the rise of federal criminal law. This expansion was crucial to the establishment of a comprehensive police criminal law. And federal criminal law, by its very nature, concerned itself with public interests. As we've already noted, the federal government possessed no police power, at least not on paper. Instead, it was authorized to regulate interstate commerce.[56] The vast bulk of federal criminal law was built on this narrow plank. This means that federal criminal law was dedicated to the protection of a single, public, interest: interstate commerce. The paradigmatic federal crime was "interference with interstate commerce." Every specific offense had to be traced back to this federal *ur*crime.

Take the foundation of federal drug criminal law, for example. The creation and expansion of federal drug criminal law was one of the most significant developments of the past century, and contributed greatly to the new system of police criminal law. According go the Congressional findings and declarations accompanying the federal statutes containing the bulk of federal criminal law, the "illegal importation, manufacture, distribution, and possession and improper use of controlled substances have a substantial and detrimental effect on the health and general welfare of the American people."[57]

In other words, drug traffic threatens the police of the American public. Since the federal government has no direct police power, however, the protection of the public interest could not by itself justify federal action. That justification had to stem from the federal commerce power. The drug traffic had to interfere with interstate commerce. And that it did, substantially and directly:

(3) A major portion of the traffic in controlled substances flows through interstate and foreign commerce. Incidents of the traffic which are not an integral part of the interstate or foreign flow, such as manufacture, local distribution, and possession, nonetheless have a substantial and direct effect upon interstate commerce because—

(A) after manufacture, many controlled substances are transported in interstate commerce,

(B) controlled substances distributed locally usually have been transported in interstate commerce immediately before their distribution, and

(C) controlled substances possessed commonly flow through interstate commerce immediately prior to such possession.

(4) Local distribution and possession of controlled substances contribute to swelling the interstate traffic in such substances.

In sum, federal drug criminal law, with its penalties of up to life imprisonment without the possibility of parole, constituted an attempt to protect one public interest (the police of the American people, in particular its health) by protecting another (interstate commerce). Literally millions of people have been arrested, prosecuted, and punished, often severely, in the name of regulating commerce among the states. Even those who didn't directly interfere with interstate commerce, say by shipping drugs across state lines, but possessed or distributed them locally, were swept within the power to regulate interstate commerce. Their activities, after all, "contribute[d] to swelling the interstate traffic in such substances."

Now federal drug criminal law was unusual in that it rolled two public interests into one. That is, the actual interest to be protected (the health of the American people) was as much a public interest as the interest the legislation was said to be protecting (interstate commerce). But, thanks to the commerce clause, *every* federal crime became a public interest offense.

There are federal crimes that appear to straightforwardly protect individual interests. These statutes make no mention of a "substantial and direct effect upon interstate commerce." And yet they are police offenses nonetheless.[58] For these crimes serve to maintain the police among communities within the dominion of the United States, in particular the military,[59] Indian reservations,[60] and territories and insular possessions, over which the United States holds quasi-patriarchal power.[61]

The all-out effort to protect public interests resulted not only in an expansion of the scope of penal interference to reach threats of threats of harm, or inchoate inchoacies. It also broadened the objects of criminal police. The point was to eliminate any and all threats to the public police. Traditional distinctions between proper and improper objects of punishment came under pressure, and often gave way. The "shifting from a basis of individual guilt to one of social danger"[62] meant that the incapacity, or diminished capacity, for guilt on grounds such as infancy or insanity became irrelevant. So juveniles who posed a threat were subjected to penal treatment and the insanity defense was abandoned, or cut back.[63]

Strict liability spread, as Sayre feared, to very serious offenses. Life imprisonment without the possibility of parole became an acceptable penalty for simple possession of drugs.[64] But inanimate threats too were eliminated. The seizure, forfeiture, and destruction of "guilty" objects, tainted by their association with dangerous persons, became an integral part of the comprehensive policing effort. Among the objects of police criminal law, one therefore finds not only persons, like sexual predators, but also Various Items of Personal Property,[65] United States Currency in the Amount of One Hundred Forty-Five Thousand, One Hundred Thirty-Nine Dollars,[66] One Lot

Emerald Cut Stones,[67] One Assortment of 89 Firearms,[68] and One 1958 Plymouth Sedan.[69]

Traditionally, exercises of the police power required some sort of exigency. And so did the construction of police criminal law. When President Nixon declared a war on crime in the late 1960s, he in fact declared a state of emergency that continues to this day. Extraordinary threats to the public police required extraordinary protective measures. The war on crime, however, merely accelerated and intensified the transformation of criminal law into criminal police. As our discussion of Sayre and Pound made clear, this process had begun much earlier. And the exigency existed long before the declaration of a state of emergency. As we know from police power jurisprudence, any threat to the welfare of the community constituted an exigency, justifying whatever preventive measures the state deemed appropriate.

The policer's discretion to determine whether an exigency existed or not was, as we've seen, symptomatic of the police power's flexibility in general. As the householder was free to determine how to protect his household, as long as he acted in good faith, so the state is free to determine when and how to bring its police power to bear on its objects. The police power thus is generally free of external constraints of principle. And the conceptualization of criminal law as a police regime therefore implies a similar aprincipled status. Sayre advocated a partial exemption of criminal law from principled scrutiny, by distinguishing between police offenses and other crimes, and retaining principled scrutiny for the latter. To the extent that this distinction collapses and crimes become police offenses, principles of criminal law become mottos without a legal referent, anachronistic, baseless and pointless.

The policing of criminal law thus explains the various manifestations of a policy of "interference to prevent disobedience" while it accounts for the failure to place that policy within principled limits in general, and the Supreme Court's failure to subject police criminal law to serious constitutional scrutiny. As our look at the history of policing has shown, it is a mistake to think of the police power as confined to the legislature and the executive. English and American courts for centuries have played a significant policing role. With the elimination of the power to create police offenses under the mantel of common law misdemeanors, courts have had to surrender much of their original policing function. But they can still participate in the policing efforts, if now primarily by giving the acknowledged holders of the police power a free hand to take the necessary protective action without undue interference from principles of justice.

Today there are no meaningful constitutional limits on the state's exercise of its police power through the criminal law. The state is free to determine what constitutes a public threat requiring elimination and how to eliminate

it.[70] The principles of *actus reus*, *mens rea*, and personal guilt have no constitutional significance—with the exception of punishment for suffering from
a disease, other than abnormal dangerousness.[71] No constitutional obstacles
stand in the way of abandoning the principle that those who cannot be
blamed, cannot be punished, as manifested in the defenses of insanity and infancy.[72] Once identified, threats to the public police can be dealt with as the
state sees fit. The Supreme Court has refused to place significant constraints
on the state's choice of penal treatment, including the elimination of threats
through preventive detention, before and after trial.[73]

   This is not to deny that the Supreme Court's opinions on substantive
criminal law cannot be read to nod in the direction of this principle or that.
The point instead is that in general the Court has done its best to let the
state-householder have its way. There are exceptions to this rule, which we'll
get to in a moment. But the rule remains clear.

   In contrast to substantive criminal law, the law of criminal procedure has
received considerable attention from the Supreme Court. The federal constitution contains several explicit procedural guarantees, and the Court has
interpreted them broadly. Despite the retrenchment of the post–Warren
Court decades, the criminal process today remains subject to fairly elaborate
constitutional constraints.[74]

   But this focus on procedure is familiar as well. Recall that nineteenth-
century courts could find no fault with police offenses like vagrancy as a matter of substantive criminal law. Despite violating the fundamental principles
of Anglo-American criminal law, *actus reus* and *mens rea*, vagrancy laws were
upheld as a matter of course. Instead courts focused on the process by which
these laws were applied.[75]

   Similarly, when Chief Justice Shaw was confronted with a thing police
statute, which affected persons indirectly as owners of the thing, he found no
substantive fault with the statute, but went so far as to strike it down on procedural grounds. The dangerous thing to be defused was liquor, rather than
a vagrant. An 1852 Massachusetts statute declared the possession of liquor
unlawful and provided for its seizure and confiscation or destruction. Shaw
made it clear that he had "no doubt that it is competent for the legislature to
declare the possession of certain articles of property, either absolutely, or
when held in particular places, and under particular circumstances, to be unlawful, because they would be injurious, dangerous or noxious; and by due
process of law, by proceeding *in rem*, to provide both for the abatement of
the nuisance and the punishment of the offender, by the seizure and
confiscation of the property, by the removal, sale, or destruction of the noxious articles."[76] The problem with the statute was that it ran afoul of a list of
procedural requirements not unlike that drawn up in the vagrancy cases:

"This statute declares that a subject may be deprived of his property under the forms of law, without meeting the witnesses face to face, without being fully heard in his defence, in an unusual mode, not by the judgment of his peers, or the law of the land."[77]

The habit of subjecting the process of applying a criminal statute to a far more intensive constitutional scrutiny than the statute itself persists to this day. The Supreme Court's death penalty jurisprudence provides one, if particularly dramatic, example. Despite serious misgivings and some extensive handwringing, reminiscent of the uneasiness about vagrancy laws one senses in cases like *Phillips* and *Forbes*, the Court could find no fault with the punishment of death, as a matter of substantive criminal law. In fact, the Court has made it clear that "capital punishment" for the purpose of eliminating a human threat to the public, i.e., as people police, is not unconstitutional.[78]

Instead the Court imposed elaborate constitutional constraints on the process for applying the death penalty. It has created a separate sentencing trial in capital cases, with the professed goal of rendering the process of application less arbitrary. Regardless of whether this goal has been met, we can be sure that the Court's imposition of stringent, and complex, procedural requirements on death penalty cases has had two other effects. First, it has made death penalty cases very expensive and time consuming. And second, it has made them prone to error, thus opening up a myriad of opportunities for direct and collateral appellate review. One way of looking at the Court's capital jurisprudence, therefore, is to view it as a backhanded attempt to throw a wrench into the death penalty system, and thereby to express substantive uneasiness with capital punishment in procedural terms.[79]

The most extreme way of trying to address substantive problems by procedural means is to strike the criminal statute down altogether, rather than complicating its mode of application. Recall that the Court didn't strike down vagrancy laws on substantive grounds. The problem with vagrancy was not that it punished status (thus violating the *actus reus* principle), nor that it required no proof of intent (thus violating the *mens rea* principle). Jacksonville's vagrancy ordinance was struck down in *Papachristou* because it was vague. A vague criminal statute, however, provides insufficient notice to potential vagrants and, for our purposes most significant, insufficient guidance to those charged with its application: judges, prosecutors, and police officers. The Court spent some time belaboring the first—notice—rationale, emphasizing that it was difficult to appreciate the ordinance's scope given that it appears to reach patently innocent conduct, like "nightwalking," since "sleepless people often walk at night, perhaps hopeful that sleep-inducing relaxation will result."[80] This problem, however, might be solved by defining "nightwalking" more narrowly so that wandering insomniacs wouldn't fall within its scope. At any rate, the second—administration—rationale appears to have been the preferred one. Among the petitioners in *Papachristou* were two interracial couples (two black men and two white women, one of whom was Ms. Papachristou) who were arrested while driving down "the main thoroughfare in Jacksonville" on their way to a nightclub. "The arresting officers denied that the racial mixture in the car played any part in the decision to make the arrest,"[81] according to the Court.

One, perhaps the main, problem with the Jacksonville vagrancy ordinance therefore lay in the possibility, or perhaps probability, of its arbitrary application. Unlike in the case of capital punishment, however, the Court addressed this problem not by prescribing a cumbersome process—as did the courts in *Phillips* and *Forbes*—but by striking down the statute itself, presumably on the ground that its nonarbitrary application was so unlikely, or at least so difficult as not to be worth the trouble.

Now striking down a statute because of the likelihood of its arbitrary application and striking it down because the statute itself violates principles of substantive law leads to the same result. Nonetheless, if the procedural rationale is employed merely to justify a decision based on substantive considerations, a straightforward exploration of the substantive shortcomings of a statute would be preferable. At any rate, the outright invalidation of a statute on procedural grounds is rare enough. In the ordinary case, the review of processes of administration shields a substantively questionable statute from the scrutiny it deserves. At best, the invocation of procedural principles may make the statute less effective in a police system designed for maximum effectiveness. (This, arguably, has been the effect of the Court's procedural death penalty jurisprudence.) At worst, the focus on process creates the impression that any substantive defect can be cured by procedural means. Anything goes as long as it follows the proper procedure.

There is another difficulty with using procedure to curb the impact of substantively problematic statutes. As long as they are on the books, they can be applied. And the application process is, in the end, difficult to control. Even if it were possible in theory to fix substance with process, there remains the danger that the procedural prerequisites will be ignored in practice. (This compliance problem obviously does not arise when the statute itself is invalidated, for then there's nothing left to apply.)

Take the practice of plea bargaining, for example. Trials take time and effort on the part of all process participants, including the judge, the prosecutor, and the defense attorney. Insisting that trials adhere to certain procedural principles only adds to the required time and effort. As a result, the process participants make every effort to avoid the cumbersome procedure. They instead prefer another, more efficient, process. That process is called plea bargaining and is employed in the overwhelming majority of criminal cases in this country.[82] The plea bargaining process is governed by very few, if any, principles, with the blessing of the Supreme Court which has turned a blind constitutional eye. In contrast to its refusal to scrutinize the standard criminal process, the Court continues to place considerable constitutional constraints on the criminal trial before a jury.

There is always a certain otherworldliness to judicial discussions of procedural principles. The very need for extensive treatments of these process rights is evidence of their habitual violation. So *Phillips* and *Forbes* strongly suggest that the summary vagrancy process was quick and dirty, with little attention paid to formal niceties. In fact, *Forbes* complains of some of the very same procedural irregularities that *Phillips* had noted years before, and sought to remedy once and for all. The reality of administration simply is too complex, with too many rules to be followed by too many officials at too many levels, to expect anything resembling perfect compliance with whatever procedural rules a court might insist on. For that reason alone it is preferable to constrain the state's power to punish at the definitional phase, rather than at the applicatory phase, assuming of course a genuine interest in subjecting this power to meaningful scrutiny in light of fundamental principles of legitimacy.

This commitment to constrain criminal law, and the power to punish, has been lacking. Its absence makes sense if it is seen as based upon a conception of criminal law as a form of social control, and of the power to punish as a manifestation of the power to police. Threats don't have rights, and they don't get punished; they get policed.

8

The Law of Police: Internal and External Constraints

The police power is by its nature free from principled constraint. Policing is an art, even a science. But it is not a matter of moral legitimacy. Moral questions are inappropriate because morality, in the modern sense, governs interactions among persons. Morality is a quality of personhood, and rights are personal. Police, however, doesn't deal with persons, but with resources and threats. An object of police governance is either a resource for the welfare of the community or a threat to that welfare. The job of the policer is to classify everyone and everything properly, and to treat each object according to its classification.

If all government were police, moral principles of legitimacy or individual rights would have no place. And yet government cannot be all police, and principles of legitimacy and individual rights remain relevant, as police affects persons, whose significance always exceeds their potential effect on the public police. Inanimate objects as well as animals, plants, and other "natural resources" can be wholly captured as police objects, to be used, controlled, or eliminated. But persons cannot.

In theory, the concept of law places significant constraints on the pursuit of police, and of police directed at persons in particular. Legality draws the legitimacy of police into question, because the treatment of persons as threats represents an exercise of what Bentham termed the power of "contrectation," by which persons are controlled as human threats through punishment for disobedience, and thereby "assimilated to things."[1] People police is, on the face of it, inconsistent with the equality of all persons as endowed with the capacity for self-government, or autonomy. It maintains the distinction between governor and governed and denies the capacity of persons to act contrary to their police classification as threats to the public welfare (or "menaces to the community"). Persons are always more than objects of police. And therein lies the legitimacy challenge of police.

When turned against persons, the police power, rather than *immunizing* state action from principled scrutiny, renders that state action presumptively illegitimate. People police requires more, not less, scrutiny than people punishment. And yet current jurisprudence is right to ignore the traditional principles of Anglo-American criminal law. To invoke *actus reus* and *mens rea* today is to invoke a tradition without a foundation. As common law principles, the principles of Anglo-American criminal law have gone the way of the common law. As statutes replaced common crimes, common law principles simply became irrelevant. When criminal statutes appeared that played fast and loose with *actus reus* and *mens rea*, justified by the state's authority to maintain the police of the community, English courts could do nothing but insist that these principles continued to control the prosecution of common law crimes.[2] What's more remarkable, however, is that their American colleagues, and successors, did no more, even though they were equipped with the power to scrutinize the constitutionality of exercises of state power, including the power to police.

The reason for the toothlessness of these common law principles of criminal law in the face of the power to police lay in their groundlessness. While it was easy enough to think of the criminal law as an exercise of the police power, with its characteristic flexibility and moral alegitimacy, an alternative view of the criminal law, complete with principles of justice to ground and constrain it, never quite developed. As a result, whatever principles of criminal law there were could easily be ignored, compromised, and restricted to some other area of criminal law than the one under consideration.

To withstand the pressure of the police governmentality, principles of American statutory criminal law would have to be grounded not in English common law precedent but in an alternative view of the criminal law as a system of law, or right, structuring relationships and conflicts among persons, rather than controlling threats to the household. For principles of justice to stick, they must first be shown to have relevance. And they have relevance only to matters of right among equal persons, i.e., as matters of law, rather than of police.

A full exploration and derivation of this alternative view of criminal law as *law* is beyond the scope of this book. The remaining pages instead will be devoted to exploring what such an account of criminal law, set against the tension between police and law, might look like. In doing so, I will draw on, and reemphasize, selected aspects of the genealogy of the police power laid out so far. I will conclude, in the final chapter, by applying the general distinction between the governmentalities of law and police to the most famous, and controversial, of the American police power cases, *Lochner v. New York*.

Good Police: Prudence and Fitness

It's clear that the police power has no place in a theory of legitimacy if one continues to use police as "an idiom of apologetics." But we shouldn't be so quick to judge police by its rhetorical use. For, despite the refrain of indefinability or unlimitability, the power to police has always been subject to constraints, at least in theory. To say that police is alegitimate, in other words, is not to say that it is illegitimate, nor is it to say that it is entirely without limits.

To give police its due, it may be useful to distinguish internal from external limitations on the power to police, i.e., between limitations that are inherent in the concept of police itself and those that aren't. I'll begin by considering the internal limitations, and two in particular, prudence and fitness. These turn out to be more significant than one might think, in light of the long-standing association between police power and unlimited authority.

In the end, however, the internal constraints of police—as the policer's self-police—are no substitute for the external demands of equality and autonomy. Even a well-policed police state remains alegitimate. The legitimacy of any police state instead will turn on its compliance with external constraints, and in particular the one principle of political legitimacy: autonomy. The best-ordered society, and the most "expedient" system of criminal police, will be illegitimate if it presumes a qualitative distinction between governor and governed, and thus fails to respect each of its constituents as capable of self-government.

Internally, there is good police and bad police, police that achieves its end, and police that doesn't. Expediency isn't a moral standard, but it's a standard nonetheless. And certainly a macro householder should strive to be a good householder, or economist. He should, in other words, heed the advice of his police scientists and utilize the resources within his household in the most efficient way possible.

Within the realm of police the householder is subject to guidelines of prudence, not to principles of right, in the terms of Smith's distinction between the two aspects of jurisprudence.[3] The assembly of these rules of prudential princely conduct occupied the minds of political thinkers for millennia, and generated guidebooks of governance as diverse as Marcus Aurelius's *Meditations*,[4] Machiavelli's *The Prince*,[5] and, in colonial America, slaveowners' "plantation manuals and rule-books, . . . enforced with whipping and other punishments, including death."[6] The need for good government did survive the enlightenment, but it can no longer legitimate itself—if it ever did, or set out to do so.[7]

Now in some cases policing may be so bad, and the connection between means and end (police) so unfathomably remote, that one might suspect that the policer is bad, or at least incompetent, himself. Inexpediency thus would amount to evidence of unfitness. Unfitness, however, arguably is qualitatively different from run-of-the mill incompetence, and thus generates the second internal constraint on the power to police.

In colonial Virginia, "[t]he power of masters to whip their slaves was in practice almost unlimited."[8] "*Almost* unlimited" because the master, in his management of the slave as of any other resource within his household, was presumed to act for the well-being of his household, the plantation. This limitation on the master's police power derived not from the slave's status as a person endowed with rights. Instead it sprang from the nature of the police authority itself. And the enforcement of these limits upon the micro householder's authority in turn constituted an exercise of the police power of the macro householder, the state sovereign, in this case the English king. From the king's perspective, the master enjoyed authority over his household only by delegation of the king's supreme police authority over every member of his royal household, which included slave and master alike.[9]

Policers thus could prove themselves unfit to police, and better suited to being policed themselves. Evidence of this unfitness came in two basic forms. First, the policer could prove himself incapable of discharging his duty to maximize the welfare of the household through behavior evincing "bad faith." Second, even a policer acting in good faith could lose police authority if he proved simply incapable of preserving his household. This failure might then justify the state's assumption of householding authority in loco parentis.[10]

For our purposes more relevant—since we're concerned primarily with the criminal law—is the first limitation on the householder's disciplinary authority. In the context of the family, for example, the father's right to discipline members of his household was specifically limited to measures undertaken in "good faith" and "prompted by true paternal love." "[P]arental control and custody," in short, was justified "on the theory of the child's good, rather than the parent's."[11] By contrast, punishment out of "malice" was not permissible, for it was motivated not by concern for the welfare of its object, or of the family as a whole. Self-gratifying cruelty was impermissible:

> A husband is responsible for the acts of his wife, and he is required to govern his household, and for this purpose the law permits him to use towards

his wife such a degree of force as is necessary to control an unruly temper and make her behave herself; and unless some permanent injury be inflicted, or there be excess of violence, or such a degree of cruelty as shows that it is inflicted to gratify his own bad passions, the law will not invade the domestic forum or go behind the curtain.[12]

Similar rules applied to the use of correctional measures in quasi-households. So a military officer was entitled to enforce obedience, even by whipping, unless it turned out his "heart is wrong,"[13] which is just another way of saying that he acted out of malice.[14]

Restrictions on the means of correction reflected restrictions on its end. The use of measures "so great and excessive to put life and limb in peril, or where permanent injury to the person was inflicted" provided evidence of that "malicious and wrongful spirit" which marked the policer as unfit for his supervisory post.[15] In the context of discipline on board of a ship, as enforced by the captain against his crew, "clear and unequivocal marks of passion on the part of the captain," punishment "manifestly excessive and disproportionate to the fault," and, for our purposes most interesting, the use of "unusual or unlawful instruments," likewise revealed that the disciplinary measure wasn't in fact disciplinary at all, but motivated by the policer's self-regarding interest in gratifying an evil impulse.[16]

In this light, the constitutional prohibition of "cruel and unusual" punishment can be seen as an *internal* limitation upon the state's power to police, inherent within the power itself. Cruel and unusual punishment is prohibited because it reveals an improper, self-regarding, motive.[17] And indeed the Eighth Amendment's cruel and unusual punishments clause has been interpreted to prohibit correctional measures inflicted out of "malice or sadism."[18] This standard is applied to actions to enforce prison discipline, such as solitary confinement, as opposed to actions taken, or not taken, in the course of the everyday business of enforcing judicially imposed sentences. In the case of prison disciplinary measures, good faith on the part of the warden, or other correctional officers, is presumed. That is, whatever action is taken is presumed to have been motivated by a concern for the welfare of its object, or at least the prison community as a whole. A correction officer who punishes with "malice or sadism," however, has proved himself unfit for police authority.[19]

By contrast, a less permissive standard, "deliberate indifference," is applied to actions taken in the course of executing punishments prescribed by the legislature and applied by the judiciary.[20] Here the correctional officer is not acting as a micro householder intent on maintaining order within his household, but merely giving effect to a judgment of law. He is an instrument of the law rather than a keeper of the police. It therefore makes sense that his authority in this function be more carefully circumscribed. In executing a legal sentence, the prison guard confronts the inmate not as a policer faces the policed within the hierarchy of a household. The inmate in this context appears as an object of law, i.e., as a person, and therefore on equal footing with those who are charged with ensuring that the legal judgment is carried out.[21]

And yet, even in this legal context, the prison inmate remains in the custody and charge of the warden, much as every "inmate" of a Teutonic household was under the power of the householder.[22] Prison officials not only prevent the inmates from escaping, but are also responsible for their well-being. The prison makes its inmates entirely helpless, and places them at the mercy of their keepers. To show "deliberate indifference" toward inmates thus constitutes a violation of the warden's duty of care, as a failure to provide the necessary conditions for the execution of legal punishment against persons. Unlike in the case of prison discipline, however, the point here is not to maintain order in the prison household, but to make a particular mode of legal punishment, imprisonment, possible.

If, based on these attempts to limit police internally, one were to develop constraints on the state's police power in general, presumably based on the cruel and unusual punishments clause or its state equivalents, one might end up with something that looks a lot like Francis Sayre's well-known "definition" of police offenses. In his much-cited 1933 article on "public welfare offenses," which we've already encountered in a different context, Sayre defined police offenses mainly in terms of their potential punishment: police offenses could not trigger imprisonment; otherwise, they would no longer be police offenses.[23] Reading this definition instead as a normative standard, one might say that any punishment beyond a certain severity indicates that the punisher is not motivated by concern for the welfare of the punished. "Disproportionate" punishment would establish a presumption that the punisher was driven by malice, rather than by concerns for the police of his household.

In doctrinal fact, the internal limits on police discipline often are expressed in terms of proportionality. So an "excess of violence" and correction that is "manifestly excessive and disproportionate to the fault" is said to exceed the bounds of police. More generally the cruel and unusual punishments clause is thought to prohibit disproportionate, or grossly disproportionate, punishments.[24]

But what sorts of internal limits would criminal police impose upon itself? If we follow Sayre on this point as well, punishment as *police* would preclude the use of imprisonment.[25] In 1962, the Model Penal Code made a similar attempt to limit police offenses, as a rule, to a new type of "non-criminal" offenses, punishable by "a fine, or fine and forfeiture or other civil penalty."[26] Two decades later, that's also where Congress drew the line when it instructed the federal sentencing commission to do away with sentences of imprisonment imposed for the purpose of rehabilitation.[27] That imprisonment is rarely, if ever, to the benefit of the imprisoned is a sad reality of American criminal justice.[28]

And yet one could hardly say that the choice of imprisonment as a sanction necessarily reflects the sort of self-regarding malice (or cruelty) that would disqualify it as a police measure. Custody, or "restraint," has had a long tradition as a household sanction.[29] But there is nothing in the concept, or history, of imprisonment that would prevents its use as a *legal* sanction.

Imprisonment instead appears as a deeply ambiguous sanction that has straddled the distinction between police measure directed against public threats (through rehabilitation or incapacitation) and criminal punishment of persons convicted of crime. Depending on its purpose and its use, imprisonment thus may be a legal remedy as well as a police tool. And even as a police tool, it may well, but certainly need not, reflect malice on the part of the policer. The notion of police itself thus cannot generate from within itself a general rule against imprisonment as a sanction, which is not to say of course that imprisonment may not be so disproportionate as to give rise to a presumption of malice in a particular case. But that's true of every sanction.

By contrast, another traditional police sanction, corporal punishment, and whipping in particular, may well fall short of standards internal to the police realm. Today, whipping probably would evince the sort of self-regarding motivation, or cruelty, which disqualifies anyone inflicting it from a position of police authority.[30] This is a development of the past one hundred years or so.[31] Until well into the nineteenth century, there was no inconsistency between whipping and the sort of public spirit thought to be a prerequisite for police authority. At that time, various levels and types of corporal punishment were distinguished, some of which fell below the line of acceptable police motivation. But whipping in general was not considered unfit for a householder.

One of the general limitations on the use of corporal punishment was the prohibition, familiar from old English Law, of chastisement so harsh that it cost its object life or limb.[32] A version of this standard survived, as we saw, in the American law of domestic violence, which prohibited correction "so great and excessive to put life and limb in peril."[33] The same applied to disciplinary measures that inflicted permanent injury. Although excess, or disproportionality, wasn't enough by itself, the effects of the punishment provided evidence of disproportionality, which in turn suggested a self-regarding, and therefore unhouseholderlike, motivation.

But the application of these limitations to the state, as the macro householder, isn't obvious. For even in medieval English law, the prohibition against taking life or limb applied only to the micro householder—the lord or the bishop—not to the macro householder—the king. So the entire system of amercement was based on the view that by committing certain gross violations of the king-householder's peace, or *mund*, the offender placed life and limb at the king's mercy. It was up to the king to decide whether to take life, or limb, or simply money.[34]

Consider in particular the case of capital punishment, i.e., of taking life, rather than merely limb. No claim can be made that killing serves a corrective purpose. Taking life is never rehabilitative. It cannot be justified as beneficial to its object. Its police justification therefore must rest on its incapacitative effect—some human threats are so dangerous and so *incurably* dangerous that the public police requires their permanent elimination.

This means that, *from within the realm of police*, capital punishment is not impermissible as a general matter. Like imprisonment, it may betray a malignant heart, but it need not. Given the severity of the sanction, however, it is more likely to fall outside the scope of proper policing than other sanctions, because it is more likely to appear out of proportion to the threat it seeks to eliminate. A prudent householder certainly would consider destroying a household resource only upon clear evidence that it cannot, and could not, be put to use for the benefit of the household, or at least that the effort required to generate a positive contribution to the community's police would far outweigh the extent of the potential negative contribution. Rather than being impermissible, capital punishment is on the contrary presumptively justified, "'since it cannot be presumed that prepensed malice . . . should induce any man to destroy his owne estate.'"[35]

Whether a correctional measure is disproportionate, from the standpoint of police, depends on whether it appears generally appropriate to the type and degree of the threat to the public police. A lengthy whipping in response to a smirk, interpreted as an expression of disobedience, may well be entirely out of proportion, and therefore indicative of some motivation other than maintaining household welfare by maintaining household order by maintaining household authority. Whether the police measure was indeed disproportionate, however, will be difficult to decide after the fact, because much will turn on the particular circumstances of the case. A skillful householder, based on his experience in the field, will be able to gauge the nature of a particular threat to his authority, even one that may appear insignificant to the untrained eye. For that reason, judgments of proportionality are left generally to the person doing the policing.[36]

The important point, now, is not that it is difficult to assess the proper proportion between threat and response, and then to second-guess that on-the-spot determination. It's instead that this proportion, or lack thereof, has no significance in and of itself. It is of merely evidentiary interest, as a possible indication of malice, and therefore of unfitness to police. It reflects no right on the part of the sanction's object, the policed; at best it reflects on the fitness, or unfitness, of its subject, the policer. It's not a matter of right, or justice, but of good government.

Right Police: Legitimacy

The notion of police proportionality between threat and threat control contrasts sharply with another type of proportionality, that between fault and punishment. Discipline that is "manifestly excessive and disproportionate *to the fault*" may evince malice.[37] By drawing on the notion of fault, however, this standard already has moved beyond the realm of police. For fault (or culpability or blame) is alien to the considerations of threat elimination characteristic of police. That's why police offenses can, in Sayre's view, do without fault requirements, *mens rea* in particular. Threats aren't at fault, nor are they guilty, properly speaking. That's also why they're eliminated, or abated, rather than punished.

A similar reach beyond the scope of police also underlies talk about the "inhuman treatment"[38] of the policed. For, strictly speaking, the humanness of a threat to the police is irrelevant. A householder who handles the human resources within his household exactly as he does his other resources, including animals and inanimate objects, may be a bad householder, but he's not evil.[39] His treatment of the human resource is not "inhuman," and therefore illegitimate, but merely unwise, or imprudent.

Police policing itself cannot take account of the fact that punishment is a human institution, something done by humans to humans for something done by humans to humans. As such punishment is subject to basic principles of moral legitimacy, insofar as humans, as persons, are the bearers of moral rights. The constraints upon state action that arise from this fact cannot be fully captured by internal limits police places upon itself. The point is not to police police, but to legalize it, i.e., to bring it into compliance with the basic principles of law, which reflect the basic principles of morality in the realm of the state, or politics.

Police presumes not only the difference between governor and governed, but also their inequality, in particular the inferiority of the governed vis-à-vis the governor. As a result, police is free of the requirement of consent.[40] The consent of the policed is irrelevant precisely because they are the policed. They are resources to be employed, and often enough threats to be eliminated, in the public interest. Their consent adds nothing to the legitimacy of the police actions against them—though their consultation may render that action more effective. Acceptance, if not consent, or even prior notice, may be prudent as a matter of wise police, as such measures may improve compliance, because obedience is more likely, and because it's easier to obey orders after they have been given, rather than before.[41]

From the perspective of law, and of right, constraints upon state power, including the power to police, ultimately derive from the rights of its objects as persons. This shift in perspective generates different constraints and different interpretations of, and foundations for, familiar limiting principles. So, for instance, the constitutional prohibition against cruel and unusual punishments does not specify an evidentiary mechanism for the determination of the motivation underlying a particular exercise of the power to police, as it did from the perspective of police. Instead, it manifests the principle of the equal dignity of all persons, or in the words of Justice Stevens: "the ethical tradition that accords respect to the dignity and intrinsic worth of every individual."[42]

Once it is read as safeguarding "the dignity of man,"[43] the cruel and unusual punishments clause develops a much sharper critical bite, opening up new ways of subjecting exercises of state power to critical analysis. Consider, for instance, Justice Brennan's constitutional critique of capital punishment based on reading the clause as embodying a principle of right, rather than a rule of police:

> The true significance of these punishments is that they treat members of the human race as nonhumans, as objects to be toyed with and discarded. They are thus inconsistent with the fundamental premise of the Clause that even the vilest criminal remains a human being possessed of common human dignity.[44]

Brennan here articulates the legitimacy problem faced by people police as such, from the perspective of law, or right: its treatment of persons as nonpersons, and in particular as resources for the public welfare at best, and as threats to that welfare at worst. From the perspective of law, the legitimacy of punishment in general, and its particular manifestations, turns not on its consistency with a prudential ideal of the punisher, but on its consistency with a moral ideal of the punished. So capital punishment, Brennan argues, is illegitimate because it treats its object as something other than, and less than, a person. Whipping similarly would be illegitimate, not because it evinces the punisher's malice, but because it "degrades" the punished, or rather treats him as an object of householder discipline, rather than as a person.[45]

9

Lochner's Law and Substantive Due Process

Police, in other words, conflicts with personhood. To set up this conflict, however, is one thing, to give it meaning is another. Talk of human dignity doesn't make for a meaningful standard by which state action can be measured, unless we get a better sense of what human dignity is, and what personhood implies.

Without a clear understanding of what personhood requires, it can become as oppressively vague a category of governance as police has been. Just as the invocation of an undefined and unlimited concept of police can insulate state action from scrutiny, so can the invocation of a similarly malleable concept of personhood. And depending on who wields the concept, the oppression by means of the one may be preferable to oppression by means of the other. But oppression it nonetheless remains.

I think that's one of the lessons from the best known attempt to subject the legislature's police power to judicial scrutiny, in *Lochner v. New York*.[1] In *Lochner*, a majority of the U.S. Supreme Court used an undefined concept of personhood to interfere with the legislature's exercise of an undefined police power. This was objectionable because, all other things being equal, the legislature trumps the courts (or at least the Supreme Court) because its members are elected, and therefore presumptively more legitimate, given that legitimacy in a democratic republic derives from the self-government of its constituents.

Thanks to Justice Holmes's dissent, this is how *Lochner* has come to be interpreted.[2] But there is another side to *Lochner*. When one shifts focus from the undefined concept of personhood invoked by the Justices to the undefined concept of police invoked by the New York legislature, *Lochner* emerges as a case that stands for the proposition that the state's police power is not unlimited. *Lochner* in this light illustrates the need to work out not only an understanding of the nature of police—which I've tried to do—but also an understanding of its legitimate limits. There is no doubt that the *Lochner* court failed to do either, though it did a better job on the former task than on the latter.[3] In the end, its attempt to limit a manifestation of state power was itself little better, and in fact in many ways worse, than that manifestation itself.

To appreciate *Lochner's* significance as a police power case, it's useful to contrast it with other cases in which the Court has struck down police measures, but for different reasons, and without challenging the basic assumption that police power is unlimited and unlimitable, and therefore a trump of constitutionality. Take *United States v. Lopez* for example.[4] There the Court didn't review an exercise of the police power. It instead revealed that a statute ostensibly passed under the federal power to regulate commerce was in fact a police regulation. And that classification by itself was enough to condemn the statute. For when it comes to federal statutes, the label of police power is tantamount to unconstitutionality. *Any* federal police measure is unconstitutional, no matter how reasonable, because the federal government has no police power. But *Lopez* did not question the unlimitability of *state* police power. If the statute in *Lopez* had been a state statute, it would have been upheld.

In *Lochner* the Court reviewed a state statute. This means that the opposite rules apply: classification as a police regulation guarantees constitutionality, rather than unconstitutionality. For it's the states that have the power to regulate police, and the federal government that has the power to regulate commerce. But in *Lochner*, there wasn't even a suggestion that the state law impinged on the federal government's right to regulate commerce, as there had been in *Miln* and many other cases like it. And yet the New York statute prohibiting bakery owners from "requiring or permitting" their employees to work more than ten hours a day was struck down. (As a repeat offender under the statute, Joseph Lochner had been convicted of a misdemeanor, sentenced to a $50 fine, and "to stand committed until paid, not to exceed fifty days in the Oneida County jail."[5])

There is one reading of *Lochner* that leaves the general insulating effect of the police power intact. As the Court stresses again and again, the problem with the law was that it was merely camouflaged as a police measure—just as the *Lopez* statute had been disguised as a commerce regulation. In fact it wasn't a police law but a labor law: "It seems to us that the real object and purpose were simply to regulate the hours of labor between the master and his employes (all being men, *sui juris*), in a private business, not dangerous in any degree to morals or in any real and substantial degree, to the health of the employes."[6] Once stripped of its police cover and revealed as "a labor law, pure and simple," it didn't have a leg to stand on, as a classic example of class legislation.[7] The New York legislature, in other words, had taken sides, and improperly weighted the scales in favor of one class, labor, over another, business. In this light, the *Lochner* opinion does resemble that in *Lopez*. In *Lopez* a pretended exercise of the commerce power was exposed as an actual exercise of the *police* power, which was as clearly unconstitutional—since the federal government has no such power—as was the New York's meddling in labor affairs, at least in the opinion of the *Lochner* Court.

This is a weakness of the *Lochner* opinion, and it's a weakness it shares with *Lopez*. The identification of the challenged statute as a "labor law" didn't settle the constitutional question anymore than did the classification of the gun possession statute as a police measure in *Lopez*. The categorical rule that the state is prohibited from passing statutes regulating the relationship between employers and workers is no more tenable than the categorical rule that the federal government is prohibited from passing statutes regulating the police of the American political community. It's in the very failure to see the need for a further, more differentiated, inquiry following their respective abstract classification exercises that the true colors of the *Lochner* and *Lopez* courts shine through. The categorical illegitimacy of labor regulation is obvious only to those who see no need for state intervention to protect the minimal interests of workers in their inferior position vis-à-vis their employers, and who seize on apparently categorical rules to avoid having to make that view explicit. Today, the presumed categorical illegitimacy of federal police measures fulfills much the same function for those Supreme Court Justices who seek to limit the power of the federal government vis-à-vis the states.

This is only one, and a rather tendentious, way of reading *Lochner*. For *Lochner* in fact goes beyond *Lopez*: it not only uncovers the real nature of the challenged statute, but it also scrutinizes the statute as the police regulation it held itself out to be. In *Lochner*, the classification as an exercise of the police power doesn't end the constitutional inquiry, even if that classification is in fact incorrect, given what the majority saw as "the real object and purpose" of the law. (Given the counterfactual assumption underlying this scrutiny, however, it qualifies only as dictum.) The Court announces that "there is a limit to the valid exercise of the police power by the State,"[8] and then proceeds to determine whether that limit had been exceeded.

The limits of the police power, however, turned out to be no more specific than its definition. According to the *Lochner* Court, the decisive question was whether the state action in question is "a fair, reasonable and appropriate ex-

ercise of the police power of the State" rather than "an unreasonable, unnecessary and arbitrary interference with the right of the individual to his
personal liberty or to enter into those contracts in relation to labor which
may seem to him appropriate or necessary for the support of himself and his
family."[9] Now, although an "exact description and limitation of [the police
power] have not been attempted by the courts," it was clear enough that the
power protected "the safety, health, morals and general welfare of [the] public."[10] The New York statute did protect safety and health. But, it protected
the safety and health of bakers, rather than of the public in general.[11] (The
argument that healthier bakers bake healthier bread the Court dismissed as
farfetched.)

For that reason the statute did not further an end encompassed by the
power to police, *public* police in its various aspects, including safety and
health, nor was it set up for that purpose. Instead, as we saw, the Court decided that the statute was designed to assist bakers in labor negotiations with
their employers. This was bad enough. It didn't help that it did so by interfering with the bakers' liberty of contract, thus harming them and helping
them at the same time, and certainly harming them for their own good. The
Court ended up denying the bakers state assistance in a contractual relationship in the name of protecting their liberty of contract.[12] After *Lochner*, the
bakers were free to harm themselves again.

The *Lochner* decision has been roundly dismissed as an instance of treach-
erous judicial usurpation of the legislative prerogative by surreptitiously
smuggling the Justices' conservative anti-labor laissez-faire views into constitutional doctrine under the cover of the vague oxymoron that later came
to be known as substantive due process, or rather " 'substantive' due
process."[13] This judicial coup d'état stood in the way of progressive social
legislation, and eventually the New Deal, until the reactionary robed legislators manqués finally were put, or rather put themselves, in their places in
the late 1930s.[14]

This story is too familiar to be worth recounting here. And in the political context of the early twentieth century, it's not hard to see why *Lochner*
might have attracted the ire of progressives and modernists struggling to implement their social reform agenda. It's hard to deny the reactionary bias underlying the decision. The outcome was anything but preordained, and
whenever the Court was confronted with a choice for or against the legislation, it chose the latter path. It had upheld a maximum hours law just seven
years before, in the case of miners. But instead of simply applying this decision to bakers, as Harlan's dissent would have done, the majority instead decided to distinguish this case, *Holden v. Hardy*, on the ground the miners
worked more dangerously than did bakers.[15]

In *Holden* the Court also had shown considerable sensitivity to the imbalance of power between employers and employees and acknowledged the possibility that state interference might be appropriate to place the two sides on a more equal footing, so that employees might be protected from agreeing to labor terms exposing them—rather than "the public"—to health and safety hazards. In *Lochner* that sensitivity was nowhere to be seen. Instead, once the majority decided that the bakers' law amounted to a labor regulation, rather than a police regulation, the law was doomed, or so it seems.

The Court's protection of the bakers' freedom to enter into labor contracts with insufficient protection for their health and safety is ironic at best, and hypocritical at worst. In the end, then, the Court's use of the due process clause as a limitation on the state's police power was just as insincere, arbitrary, and oppressive as the state's use of the police power it pretended to curb.

Hostility toward *Lochner* is understandable, among American reformers of the time. Still, *Lochner* probably wasn't quite as bad as its critics, first and foremost among them Holmes, made it out to be.[16] The distrust of partial legislation designed to benefit only a subset of the public was nothing new, nor was it anything inherently reactionary. The basic idea was simple: the state should not use its police power, i.e., the power to maximize the welfare of the public as a whole, to maximize the welfare of the few, by granting monopoly rights, by setting up professional licensing schemes, and so on. And the notion of freedom of contract in the labor context was not entirely cynical either. Autonomy was seen by many nineteenth-century liberals as the core value of the modern, post-slavery, labor relationship.[17] Here the idea was that the new worker was free to choose whatever trade he chose to pursue, wherever he chose, and with (and, presumably, for) whomever he chose. The power of this idea emerges clearly when it is contrasted with the constraints on occupation and residence not only under slavery, but under traditional master-servant regimes as well. As an idea, or perhaps an ideal, freedom of labor contract thus made perfect sense. To what extent it had manifested itself in actual labor relations is another matter, of course.[18]

For our purposes most important, *Lochner* was a case that subjected the state's exercise of its police power to serious scrutiny. The point here is not that the statute at issue in *Lochner* was in fact struck down as an invalid exercise of the police power, though this fact is certainly noteworthy. The point isn't even that the *Lochner* Court did a particularly good job in scrutinizing the police regulation in question, for it clearly did not. Perhaps the majority was too eager to reach a result it considered politically appropriate to engage in careful reasoning. So the standard it employed is unclear, even sloppy, and its application neither careful nor compelling, all signs of an ex post facto rationalization.

But careless formulation and arbitrary application do not render the basic inquiry illegitimate. *Lochner* did what courts, and the public, should do in the American view of law and government: It subjected state action to principled scrutiny. More specifically, it scrutinized the state's exercise of its police power, a power that traditionally had been defined by its undefinability, and therefore had emerged as something of a carte blanche of governance, justifying anything and everything.

Lochner thus must be seen in the broad, at times all-encompassing, context of the police power. *Lochner* merely scrutinized the exercise of a particular aspect of the police power in a specific context. While the particular form and execution of that scrutiny might have been objectionable, surely the larger enterprise of exploring the limits of state police power is not.

The general contours of *Lochner's* analysis had been established for some time. What was unusual about *Lochner* was not so much its mode of analysis, but its attitude and its result. *Holden* had applied much the same standard to Utah's miner law. But it exuded deference toward legislative pronouncements. And it reached the opposite result. Where *Lochner* could not see an emergency that would justify the state invoking its police power, *Holden* found one in the unusually hazardous working conditions underground and, more important, was happy to leave the determination of its existence to the legislature, quoting extensively from Chief Justice Shaw's opinion in *Alger*. Where *Lochner* saw no connection between the welfare of bakers and the public welfare, the proper object of the public police power, *Holden* saw no need to investigate that connection, apart from remarking fairly cryptically, if admirably, that "[t]he whole is no greater than the sum of all the parts, and when the individual health, safety and welfare are sacrificed or neglected, the State must suffer."[19]

That same police power analysis generated a different result both before *Lochner*, and after it. Only three years later, the Court *upheld* a maximum hours law for female laundry workers, in *Muller v. Oregon*.[20] Here the Court apparently presumed the existence of an emergency, taking the Oregon legislature by its word that "as the female employés in the various establishments are not protected from overwork, an emergency is hereby declared to exist."[21] It was "woman's physical structure, and the functions she performs in consequence thereof, [that] justify special legislation restricting or qualifying the conditions under which she should be permitted to toil."[22] And those "functions" also established the necessary connection between women's welfare and that of the public, or rather "the race," in general:

her physical structure and a proper discharge of her maternal functions—
having in view not merely her own health, but the well-being of the race—
justify legislation to protect her from the greed as well as the passion of
man.[23]

As a result, "[t]he limitations which this statute places upon her contractual
powers, upon her right to agree with her employer as to the time she shall
labor, are not imposed solely for her benefit, but also largely for the benefit
of all."[24]

The results in *Holden* and *Muller* demonstrate that the analysis of state exercises of the police power used in *Lochner* did not preordain the unconstitutionality of the sort of economic and social regulation so dear to progressives of the time. Contemporary critics of *Lochner* didn't like the result. They
had no problem with the analysis of police power.[25] Nor did they object to
the rationale in *Muller* which, from today's standpoint, surely is no less offensive—and considerably more patriarchal—that the rationale in *Lochner*.

Progressive critics of *Lochner*, like Holmes, didn't object to the Court's reviewing exercises of the police power as exercises of the police power, as long
as it was understood that police power was a justificatory label. The Court's
mistake in *Lochner* was to misunderstand the point of the police power, and—
unlike Holmes—to treat it as more than a rationalizing device. The *Lochner*
Court thus took itself at its word, putting teeth into the generally meaning-
less proviso, mouthed religiously in every police power case, that the police
power, though limitless, was "of course" not without limits.

In the end, however, the vilification of *Lochner* resulted in the vanishing of
the entire enterprise of scrutinizing the state's police power from the face of
American constitutional law. And with it disappeared the broader view
of state power, and the inquiry into the source and nature of that power. But
the police power, as a general mode of governance, encompassed more than
maximum hours legislation, and other "social legislation." As I have stressed
again and again, under this power, the state impinged not only on economic
and social rights, as in *Lochner*, but upon life and liberty as well. With the
abandonment of police power scrutiny, an entire mode of governance
dropped out of constitutional law, and therefore out of the most important
medium of principled scrutiny in American legal and political discourse.

The narrow issue in *Lochner* was the propriety of a particular piece of social legislation. The broad issue was the legitimacy of state police power, and
the need to justify exercises of that power in every instance, and in reference
to specific criteria subject to meaningful scrutiny, not only by the courts, and
not only under the constitution, but by the political community at large and
on the basis of whatever principles of legitimacy that define it.

It's important not to confuse the particular exercise of the police power at issue in *Lochner* with the police power itself. To recognize the consequences of rejecting any meaningful judicial review of police power legislation it's useful to recall the scope and variety of measures generated in the name of this power. We've already seen that police power measures included all manner of vagrancy laws designed to control the dangerous classes, as well as strict liability criminal statutes that imposed vicarious omissions liability. (*Shevlin-Carpenter* was decided five years after *Lochner*, *Balint* seventeen years later, all at the height of Lochnerism.[26]) But the police power also was invoked to justify the Louisiana segregation statute upheld in *Plessy v. Ferguson*,[27] the criminal prohibition of interracial marriage (until 1967),[28] the forced sterilization of "defectives,"[29] and the criminalization of homosexual sex,[30] along with a host of other threats to the moral police of the public.

When the entirety of criminal law is said to spring from the police power, equating Lochnerism with toothful judicial review of police power legislation amounts to insulating the entirety of criminal law from such review. And when, under the most expansive reading, police is taken as synonymous with government, then any state action is similarly immunized.

It's also important not to confuse principled scrutiny with judicial review, another common error, and one that is characteristic of American legal and political thought. Since American constitutional law discourse tracks the work of the United States Supreme Court, it's easy to mistake the Supreme Court's constitutional jurisprudence for constitutional law—and furthermore to mistake constitutional law for the theory of political legitimacy. It's one thing to express concern about the intrusiveness of judicial review of the constitutionality of legislative enactments. For, given that self-government, or autonomy, is the fundamental principle of legitimacy in a democratic republic, the legislature does enjoy greater presumptive legitimacy than do the courts, and particularly the unelected United States Supreme Court. But it's quite another to abandon all scrutiny of state action simply because the *Supreme Court's* scrutiny is perceived as too intrusive. Commentary providing a critical analysis of the police power within the context of state power generally has disappeared partly because the police power has disappeared as a concept of Supreme Court jurisprudence. But neither the legitimacy of state action, nor its constitutionality, is a matter exclusively, or even primarily, for the Supreme Court. It's a matter for all state officials, including the legislative and the executive, and for all lay persons.[31] State power will not be checked effectively, and legitimated through public scrutiny, unless the modes of governance are exposed for all to see.

Those who abandoned *Lochner* in the 1930s still understood that the end of *Lochner* meant neither the end of the police power as a mode of governance nor the need for scrutinizing its exercise. So even decidedly post-*Lochner* cases like *Nebbia v. New York*[32] and *West Coast Hotel v. Parrish*[33] were police power cases. In *Nebbia* the Court upheld a milk price control statute as an exercise of the police power. As in *Lochner* it insisted that there be an emergency justifying the exercise of the police power and that the state action was designed to protect the police of all, rather than the welfare of some. But this time, both requirements were met. The emergency was provided by the Great Depression.[34] And the regulation of milk prices was a matter of public police because milk was "a commodity needed by the public":

> If the law-making body within its sphere of government concludes that the conditions or practices in an industry make unrestricted competition an inadequate safeguard of the consumer's interests, produce waste harmful to the public, threaten ultimately to cut off the supply of a commodity needed by the public, or portend the destruction of the industry itself, appropriate statutes passed in an honest effort to correct the threatened consequences may not be set aside because the regulation adopted fixes prices reasonably deemed by the legislature to be fair to those engaged in the industry and to the consuming public.[35]

The difference between *Nebbia* lies not in the analysis, but in the attitude, and of course in the result. The attitude is deferential, once again. As in many police cases before *Lochner*, the Court signaled its willingness to uphold the challenged legislation by quoting from some of the now-classic definitions of the police power as indefinable. These included Chief Justice Taney's declaration, in the *License Cases*, that the "police powers" were "nothing more or less than the powers of government inherent in every sovereignty to the extent of its dominions." But the opinion also featured a lengthy quote from the opinion in *New York v. Miln*, where the Court used a sweeping definition of police to justify the control of passengers on foreign ships as, you may recall, a "precautionary measure against the moral pestilence of paupers, vagabonds, and possibly convicts" analogous to "the physical pestilence, which may arise from unsound and infectious articles imported, or from a ship, the crew of which may be labouring under an infectious disease."[36]

The opinion in *West Coast Hotel* doesn't concern itself much with the question of emergency, deferring to the legislature on this matter, as Shaw had done almost a century before. *West Coast Hotel* was about a women's labor regulation and, on the issue of the public interest to be protected by the police measure, the Court followed *Muller* (decided shortly after *Lochner*) in highlighting women's "maternal functions," including "preserv[ing] the strength and vigor of the race."[37] It did, however, unearth another connection between protecting the health of workers and the public police. Sick or injured workers would become public charges, so it made sense to prevent harm to their health and safety at the workplace, rather than remedying it later on:

> There is an additional and compelling consideration which recent economic experience has brought into a strong light. The exploitation of a class of workers who are in an unequal position with respect to bargaining power and are thus relatively defenceless against the denial of a living wage is not only detrimental to their health and well being but casts a direct burden for their support upon the community. What these workers lose in wages the taxpayers are called upon to pay.[38]

This argument wasn't novel. It had been used by the *Miln* Court exactly one hundred years earlier, in 1837, to justify the New York law that required captains of foreign ships to give security that their passengers will not become public charges. This law, the Court explained at the time, served "to prevent [New York's] citizens from being oppressed by the support of multitudes of poor persons, who come from foreign countries without possessing the means of supporting themselves."[39]

The cases, then, that are generally recognized as putting an end to *Lochner* were police power cases. They began by identifying the mode of governance that was said to authorize the state action in question, the power to police. They then considered whether the police power in fact justified that action. This meant testing its end as well as its means toward that end. The end of any supposed exercise of the police power must be the police, i.e., the order of the relevant political community—a state. This public police had various aspects, including safety, health, and morals. In an emergency, the state was authorized to use its coercive power, including even the power to punish, to protect the public police. Therefore, assuming some aspect of the public police was the object of the legislation, the means employed in connection with that end both had to be necessary and had to actually have some chance of success. The use of an unnecessary measure unrelated to the end of police suggested that the legislature in fact didn't face an emergency after all, nor did it act with the police in mind.

The contours of this police power test were clear enough. The test was perhaps best captured in *Lawton v. Steele*, decided some ten years before *Lochner*:[40]

> To justify the State in thus interposing its authority in behalf of the public, it must appear, first, that the interests of the public generally, as distin-

guished from those of a particular class, require such interference; and, second, that the means are reasonably necessary for the accomplishment of the purpose, and not unduly oppressive upon individuals.[41]

Like *Lochner*, *Lawton* dealt with a typical police power measure. Unlike *Lochner*, *Lawton* also was a typical police power case: The challenged statute passed constitutional muster. Much like the law in *Miln*, the police regulation in *Lawton* sought to anticipate and eliminate potential threats to the public police. Only this time the threat was inanimate, fishing nets rather than immigrants. A New York law declared any net whereby fish "may be taken" in violation of laws for the protection of fish a public nuisance that "may be abated and summarily destroyed by any person, and it shall be the duty of each and every [state fish] protector . . . to seize, remove, and forthwith destroy the same."

The "preservation of game and fish," it turned out, was a matter of public police. And the means employed by the statute to achieve this end was a classic instance of policing through stifling the fountains of evil: "The legislature . . . undoubtedly possessed the power not only to prohibit fishing by nets in these waters, but to make it a criminal offence, and to take such measures as were reasonable and necessary to prevent such offences in the future. It certainly could not do this more effectually than by destroying the means of the offence."[42]

As to the summary nature of the process of eliminating the threat to the public police, that too was typical of police measures against human and nonhuman threats, or nuisances, and therefore beyond reproach:

> There is not a State in the Union which has not a constitutional provision entitling persons charged with crime to a trial by jury, and yet from time immemorial the practice has been to try persons charged with petty offences before a police magistrate, who not only passes upon the question of guilt, but metes out the proper punishment. This has never been treated as an infraction of the Constitution, though technically a person may in this way be deprived of his liberty without the intervention of a jury. So the summary abatement of nuisances without judicial process or proceeding was well known to the common law long prior to the adoption of the Constitution, and it has never been supposed that the constitutional provision in question in this case was intended to interfere with the established principles in that regard.[43]

Although police power analysis thus preceded *Lochner* and survived its official demise, the two eventually became inextricably linked. As *Lochner* went so went the police power. There is an obvious explanation for this derivative demise. Between the 1930s and 1960s, *Lochner* became universally demonized as an illustration of judicial overreaching in the dreaded name of "substantive due process." As the rejection of *Lochner* emerged as the foundational consensus of American constitutional law, anything associated with this case became tainted.

The demise of police power could already be seen in Holmes's *Lochner* dissent. This dissent, which was to become the orthodox reading of *Lochner*, not only revealed the majority Justices as forcing their reactionary laissez faire views onto the constitution, and therefore on the people of New York, and through so patently asubstantive a concept as "due process." The entire enterprise of identifying the police power as the mode of governance at issue, and then proceeding to explore its limits struck Holmes as absurd. Recall that to him the "police power" by itself meant nothing. It served the rhetorical purpose of rationalizing judicial affirmation of the legislature's power to do what it deemed best for the welfare of the state. In other words, it made no sense to identify the police power as the relevant governmental power for the simple reason that *all* governmental power was police power. And it made no more sense to explore in case after case just where the limits of that power were to be drawn. For the power to police was in fact unlimited. To identify a state action as an exercise of the police power was to affirm its constitutionality. That was all there was to it.

Once the police power was shown to be empty, no self-respecting constitutional jurisprude, on or off the Court, could be expected to engage in its careful analysis. It was relegated to occasional appearances to perform its ex post rationalization function, and even there the Court preferred to invoke derivate labels, such as "civil," "preventive," or "public welfare," instead. It's ironic that the police power was to exert its most enduring influence in takings law, only after Holmes himself had endorsed its (entirely rhetorical) use, at the height of the *Lochner* era, in 1922.[44] *Lochner's* concept of "'substantive' due process" was abandoned as an empty rhetorical shell, a mere cover for judicial arrogance. Its concept of a substantive police power subject to meaningful constraints was likewise dropped.

Since police power and substantive due process were joined at the hip, their fate became inextricably linked. So talk of the police power disappeared along with talk of substantive due process. Or, more precisely, since *Lochner* says nothing about substantive due process, and little about due process in general, its police power scrutiny with bite was polemically redubbed substantive due process, and then tossed out altogether. Substantive due process and police power became taboo. In the 1960s and 70s, the revival of substantive due process scrutiny of police power measures to protect various aspects of the public police that culminated in *Roe v. Wade* did without either mentioning substantive due process or the fact that every single one of the statutes reviewed—and struck down—was a clear cut example of a police measure—and a criminal one at that.[45] The Court was too anxious to distance itself from *Lochner* and everything *Lochner*.[46]

As a result, the basic question at the bottom of these "privacy" cases, namely the state's authority to use coercion—*penal* coercion—to protect the moral police of the public, i.e., the moral health of the political community, was never framed, never mind addressed. This authority was simply, and implicitly, assumed by the Court. The problem with the criminal prohibition of using and distributing contraceptives (dealt with in *Eisenstadt* or *Griswold*) thus was *not* that it was none of the state's business to employ penal sanctions to protect the moral police. This problem emerges only if one takes a broader view, and locates the particular exercise of state power within the general array of state powers, and thereby recurs to the basic question of the foundation of state power and its limits. This the Court did not do.

Roe was a harder case than *Eisenstadt* or *Griswold* because it considered the constitutionality of a state action that arguably drew on more than the state's power to police. Unlike the contraceptive statutes, the abortion statute was designed not merely to protect the public police (public health, public morals), but also sought to discharge that other fundamental state function, to do justice.[47] The struggle in *Roe* can be seen as a struggle to define it as a police power case or as a criminal law case. As a police power case, the legislature's authority was suspect. At least since Sayre, the use of severe punishment for any policing purposes was questionable. It didn't help that in this case the state employed the criminal law to protect the most controversial aspect of the public police, morality. Viewed in the context of the Court's previous criminal moral police cases, *Griswold* and *Eisenstadt*, *Roe* was an easy case.

The trouble with *Roe* was that it could also be viewed as a criminal law case. Abortion statutes, after all, were also justified as protecting not some public police interest, but the most personal interest of all, the right to life. In this light, the state action in *Roe* appeared not as a particularly harsh police measure, but as a traditional criminal statute, more akin to the prohibition of homicide than to the prohibition of immoral sex.[48] In the context of right, rather than police, *Roe* was about protecting the personal right to life of the fetus without unduly interfering with the personal right to autonomy of the mother. There was nothing facially suspect about either concern, for both fell squarely within the state's justice power, i.e., the authority—and the duty—to protect the right of its constituents.

These conflicting views of *Roe* didn't emerge in the Justices' opinions because the Court had long ago abandoned its inquiry into the sources and nature of state power. The distinction between police and justice, or right, as the two central functions of government, and between police power and justice power, had disappeared from view. And so *Roe* and its predecessors came to be thought of as something completely new, having to do with novel notions like "penumbras"[49] of enumerated rights and "the right to privacy," rather than as a continuation of the struggle to define and limit state power, and the power to police in particular.

Lochner and State Criminal Law

The link between substantive due process and police power proved inextricable not only in disappearance, but in reappearance as well. While the Supreme Court continues to be wary of substantive due process, state courts now treat it as a viable concept of constitutional law. And with the rediscovery of substantive due process in state constitutional law has come the rediscovery of the police power. Several state courts now do precisely what the U.S. Supreme Court would never think of doing; they explicitly investigate "substantive due process" limitations on exercises of the "police power." So complete has been the rejection of these concepts by the U.S. Supreme Court that they are perfectly suited for recent attempts by state courts to stake out an independent constitutional jurisprudence. It's no accident that the new state police power cases tend to reach contrary results, striking down exercises of the police power upheld by the federal high court.[50]

Consider, for example, the analysis of criminal sodomy statutes in the U.S. Supreme Court and in various state supreme courts. In 1986, the federal high court famously upheld a Georgia statute that declared "sodomy" a felony punishable by "not less than one nor more than 20 years."[51] "Police power" or "substantive due process" do not appear in Justice White's majority opinion in that case, nor in any of the other opinions. The majority opinion does not identify the governmental power that would authorize the state to criminalize sodomy, apart from the passing remark that "[t]he law," and presumably also the statute in question, "is constantly based on notions of morality." That fact has normative significance because, "if all laws representing essentially moral choices are to be invalidated under the Due Process Clause, the courts will be very busy indeed."[52] There is also a grudging acknowledgment that "despite the language of the Due Process Clauses of the Fifth and Fourteenth Amendments, which appears to focus only on the processes by which life, liberty, or property is taken, the cases are legion in which those Clauses have been interpreted to have substantive content,"[53] followed, however, by the requisite warning about the potential illegitimacy of this practice, which once recognized led to the post-*Lochner* "repudiation of much of the substantive gloss that the Court had placed on the Due Process Clauses of the Fifth and Fourteenth Amendments."[54]

Starting in the early 1980s, state courts also began considering constitutional challenges to similar sodomy statutes. Unlike *Hardwick*, these cases as a rule identified the source of the state's authority to pass the statute in question, the power to police, and then went on to see if the statute could be justified as a legitimate exercise of that power, within the limits placed upon it. One of the first, and the most carefully argued, of these cases is the Pennsylvania case of *Commonwealth v. Bonadio*.[55] Its police power scrutiny of the state's Voluntary Deviate Sexual Intercourse Statute is worth quoting at length:

> The Commonwealth's position is that the statute in question is a valid exercise of the police power pursuant the authority of states to regulate public health, safety, welfare, and morals. Yet, the police power is not unlimited, as was stated by the United States Supreme Court in *Lawton v. Steele*, 152 U.S. 133, 137, 14 S.Ct. 499, 501, 38 L.Ed. 385 (1894). . . . The threshold question in determining whether the statute in question is a valid exercise of the police power is to decide whether it benefits the public generally. The state clearly has a proper role to perform in protecting the public from inadvertent offensive displays of sexual behavior, in preventing people from being forced against their will to submit to sexual contact, in protecting minors from being sexually used by adults, and in eliminating cruelty to animals. To assure these protections, a broad range of criminal statutes constitute valid police power exercises, including proscriptions of indecent exposure, open lewdness, rape, *involuntary* deviate sexual intercourse, indecent assault, statutory rape, corruption of minors, and cruelty to animals. The statute in question serves none of the foregoing purposes and it is nugatory to suggest that it promotes a state interest in the institution of marriage. The Voluntary Deviate Sexual Intercourse Statute has only one possible purpose: to regulate the private conduct of consenting adults. Such a purpose, we believe, exceeds the valid bounds of the police power while infringing the right to equal protection of the laws guaranteed by the Constitution of the United States and of this Commonwealth.
>
> With respect to regulation of morals, the police power should properly be exercised to protect each individual's right to be free from interference in defining and pursuing his own morality but not to enforce a majority morality on persons whose conduct *does not harm others*. . . . Enactment of the Voluntary Deviate Sexual Intercourse Statute, despite the fact that it provides punishment for what many believe to be abhorrent crimes against

nature and perceived sins against God, is not properly in the realm of the temporal police power.[56]

The most recent, and the most dramatic, illustration of the new state police power jurisprudence came after *Hardwick*. In 1998, the Georgia Supreme Court in *Powell v. State* struck down the very same sodomy statute the U.S. Supreme Court had upheld twelve years before. Once again, the state argued that the sodomy proscription fell within its police power, defined as "the governing authority's ability to legislate for the protection of the citizens' lives, health, and property, and to preserve good order and public morals."[57] And once again, the court held that the statute failed the *Lawton* test, in language reminiscent of *Bonadio*:

> [T]he legislation must serve a public purpose and the means adopted to achieve the purpose must be reasonably necessary for the accomplishment of the purpose and not unduly oppressive upon the persons regulated. In recent years, legislative bodies in Georgia have exercised the "police power" to combat the negative effects of the combination of alcohol and nude dancing; to limit land usage through zoning restrictions; to regulate the health professions; and to impose reasonable regulations on the establishment and operation of cemeteries. That the legislative body has determined that it is properly exercising its police powers "is not final or conclusive, but is subject to the supervision of the courts." Lawton v. Steele, 152 U.S. 133, 137 (14 S. Ct. 499, 38 L. Ed. 385) (1894). Thus, the suggestion that OCGA § 16–6–2 is a valid exercise of the police power requires us to consider whether it benefits the public generally without unduly oppressing the individual. Since . . . the only possible purpose for the statute is to regulate the private conduct of consenting adults, the public gains no benefit, and the individual is unduly oppressed by the invasion of the right to privacy. Consequently, we must conclude that the legislation exceeds the permissible bounds of the police power.[58]

Both opinions illustrate the virtues of police power analysis, along with its weaknesses. They focus the inquiry on the public nature of the interest to be protected, for after all the power to police is to ensure the police of the entire political community considered as a household, rather than of a particular segment thereof. Police means public welfare, nothing less, and nothing more. (It must be shown, in the terms of the *Lawton* test, that the police measure was designed to protect "the interests of the public generally, as distinguished from those of a particular class.") On this point, the courts didn't openly challenge the state's power to protect the public's *moral* police. The problem instead was that though *someone's* moral well-being was being pre-served, it wasn't the *public's* moral police, but rather that of a group within the public.

The *Lawton* police power analysis also highlights the requirement of a par-ticular need, even a necessity, for the particular state action in question. The courts didn't dwell on this aspect of the analysis, though it is an important question particularly in the case of criminal statutes. Even if the state is in general authorized to regulate a given threat to the public police, the ques-tion still remains whether it was necessary to employ the criminal law, rather than a less intrusive measure, such as a licensing scheme. (The protection of the public police must "require such interference" and the means must be "reasonably necessary for the accomplishment of the purpose.") This ques-tion has received insufficient attention in American constitutional law, which in general confines itself to considering the legitimacy of state interference in general, rather than in the particular form of the criminal law.[59] (Recall that even a commentator like Sayre, who did not approach the subject from the constitutional perspective, distinguished not between criminal and non-criminal police measures, but between criminal police measures of various levels of punishability.[60])

Finally, *Bonadio* and *Powell* identify the potential conflicts between the pro-tection of public police and the rights of persons, in this case "the right of pri-vacy." (The measure must be "not unduly oppressive upon individuals.") The *Bonadio* court went so far as to hold that every person has the right to be free from state interference provided that her conduct doesn't harm another per-son. In support of its holding, the court revealed that "[t]he concepts underly-ing our view of the police power in the case before us were once summarized . . . by the great philosopher, John Stuart Mill, in his eminent and apposite work, ON LIBERTY (1859)," and then proceeded to quote at length from Mill's famous discussion of the so-called harm principle (that "the only purpose for which power can be rightfully exercised over any member of a civilised com-munity, against his will, is to prevent harm to others").[61] "This philosophy," the court went on to conclude, "as applied to the issue of regulation of sexual morality presently before the Court, or employed to delimit the police power generally, properly circumscribes state power over the individual."[62]

The sodomy cases are among the more dramatic, but they are by no means the only, illustrations of a new police power jurisprudence in the state courts. As another example, consider the constitutional scrutiny of sex offender reg-istration, notification, and indefinite commitment statutes. Here too one finds state courts striking down statutes under a police power analysis, and the federal high court upholding them without making reference to the gov-ernmental power that authorizes their creation and use in the first place. The

Supreme Court case upholding the Kansas sexual predator statute, for instance, doesn't mention the police power, and it cites what it calls "'substantive' due process" only to dismiss it as inapposite. The reason why "'substantive' due process" appears in the Court's opinion at all is that the Kansas Supreme Court had explicitly subjected the statute to a substantive due process scrutiny, and found it wanting.[63]

And there are other, more mundane, cases as well. So Florida courts have struck down a number of criminal statutes under a general police power test first enunciated in the 1963 case of *Delmonico v. State*, which invalidated a criminal statute prohibiting the possessing of spearfishing equipment.[64] Like the U.S. Supreme Court had done some decades earlier in *Lawton*, upholding a criminal ban on the possession of fishing nets, the Florida Supreme Court too acknowledged the usefulness of possession prohibition as a preliminary policing tool.[65] Unlike the U.S. Supreme Court, however, the Florida court stressed that this usefulness alone didn't establish the constitutionality of the police measure in question:

> In order to meet constitutional limitations on police regulation, this prohibition, i.e. against possession of objects having a common and widespread lawful use, must under our previous decisions be reasonably "required as incidental to the accomplishment of the primary purpose of the Act." There is little doubt that the penalty against possession of such equipment will simplify the problem of enforcing the primary prohibition against spearfishing in the area covered by the statute. Expediency, however, is not the test, and we conclude that convenience of enforcement does not warrant the broad restriction imposed by [the statute].[66]

Since then, the Florida courts have refined their police power scrutiny. The leading case now is *State v. Saiez*,[67] which explains that the "state 'police power' . . . derives from the state's sovereign right to enact laws for the protection of its citizens."[68] Though difficult to pin down, this power nonetheless is "not boundless and is confined to those acts which may be reasonably construed as expedient for protection of the public health, safety, welfare, or morals." The courts' task is to ensure a proper "balance . . . between substantive due process and the police power of the state."[69] Under this test, Florida courts have invalidated criminal statutes prohibiting "the possession of the machinery designed to reproduce instruments purporting to be credit cards,"[70] "the wearing of any mask or covering 'whereby any portion of the face is so hidden, concealed, or covered as to conceal the identity of the wearer,' "[71] "the possession of a lawfully dispensed controlled substance in any container other than that in which the substance was originally delivered,"[72] as well as a sentencing provision in the "Criminal Street Gang Prevention Act of 1996" which enhanced the sentence for anyone declared to be "a member of a criminal street gang."[73] A similar jurisprudence has emerged in other states.[74]

These state cases tend not to invoke the authority of *Lochner*, for obvious reasons. They instead rely either on state police power jurisprudence, extending back to the great state police power cases of the nineteenth century (e.g., *Alger*), or on pre-*Lochner* federal jurisprudence (e.g., *Lawton*). *Lochner* does, however, make an occasional appearance in dissenting opinions, where its specter is ominously raised. So one judge on the New York Court of Appeals chided his brethren for striking down the state criminal sodomy statute on the basis of what he referred to as "the discredited doctrine of 'substantive due process,' "[75] or the "*Lochner* doctrine," for short, which "was ultimately rejected by the Supreme Court, in part because it had placed the court in the position of a 'superlegislature' enabling it to use the 'vague contours' of the due process clause as a vehicle for striking down State legislation which it found to be inconsistent with its own contemporary views of natural law."[76]

One reason state police power jurisprudence can do without *Lochner* is that it has no more relevance to a state court's resolution of a state constitutional issue than does any other federal constitutional law opinion of the federal high court. But there is another reason. For *Lochner* is ordinarily characterized as a case involving economic, or social, rights, invalidating a piece of "social legislation" dealing with matters of "political economy." So *Lochner's* demise can be limited to cases involving state regulation of political economy that threatens to impinge on the same type of rights.[77]

At first glance, this appears as a plausible attempt to retain police power analysis without retaining *Lochner*. What is political economy, after all, if not an important aspect of—if not a synonym for—"police"? As Blackstone explained, the same patriarchal power of the king-householder underlay the panoply of criminal police offenses, ranging from nuisance to the common scold, and his regulation of "public marts . . . as may be most convenient for the neighborhood."[78] And Blackstone certainly wasn't alone in recognizing the connection between political economy and police. So did Beccaria and Rousseau, Smith and Jefferson.[79]

There are at least two problems with this approach to *Lochner*, however. To begin with, the attempt to limit *Lochner* to "economic rights" or "social rights," "political economy," or "social legislation," is only as meaningful as these concepts are themselves.[80] Unfortunately, clear definitions of economic or social rights, or for that matter of political economy or social legislation, are hard to come by. The one thing that seems clear enough about economic and social rights is that they are somehow inferior to some other type of right, even including the right to privacy. That other type of right, however, in turn is defined in terms of its superiority to economic and social rights, which doesn't help matters. Moreover, the relative status of the two types of right is determined by the state's discretion in interfering with them for the sake of the public police. So economic (and social rights) are rights that receive less protection against state interference than other rights, which are termed, simply, "noneconomic."[81]

To restrict *Lochner*, and therefore the impact of its demise, to the regulation of the political economy thus may amount to no restriction at all. More might be said on this topic, but for our purposes another implication of framing *Lochner* as a case about "social legislation" is particularly significant. To read the *Lochner* statute as a measure of socioeconomic regulation is to divert attention from personal rights in more ways than one. *Lochner*, after all, interfered not only with the "economic right" of bakery employees to enter into labor contracts of their choice. True, the *Lochner* majority focused on this right, and so did its critics. But the statute affected not only bakery employees, but also bakery owners, and in particular Joseph Lochner. It affected the liberty of contract of both parties to the contract. But what's more important, it had a far more severe impact on another bundle of Lochner's rights, namely the right to property and the right to freedom of movement, in fact the very essence of Lochner's liberty as a person.

The statute in *Lochner* was a criminal statute. This means that it affected the lives of all New York bakery owners—and not their employees—by declaring certain behavior on their part unlawful, and criminal (a misdemeanor), and then threatening its commission with sanctions, including criminal punishment, ranging from a fine to imprisonment. And, in Lochner's case, the state didn't stop at the threat. It charged, prosecuted, convicted, and then sentenced him to a $50 fine, and "to stand committed until paid, not to exceed fifty days in the Oneida County jail."[82]

Lochner thus was threatened with, and had imposed upon him, a criminal punishment that constituted a clear interference with his right to liberty and property, or, put another way, a deprivation of liberty and property. *Lochner* wasn't just about the economic rights of bakers, nor was it just about the economic rights of bakery owners. It was also about the very "noneconomic" rights of all bakery owners, and of Lochner in particular.

An undifferentiated demonization of *Lochner* and everything Lochnerian may end up throwing out the baby with the bath water. The excision of *Lochner* has resulted in the abandonment of all principled review of exercises of state police power, even in cases that have nothing to do with the very social legislation that progressive critics of *Lochner* wanted to shield from judicial scrutiny, or that—like *Lochner* itself—are not only about this type of benevolent regulation of the "political economy." As *Lochner* illustrates, the immunization of state actions that could be—however vaguely—characterized as social legislation from judicial scrutiny automatically inoculates *any* type of state action thus characterized, including a type of state action that, everyone would agree, implicates higher order "noneconomic" rights of liberty and property: the criminal law.

Conclusion

Toward a Critical Analysis of Police and Punishment

The history of American law and government can profitably be seen as a continuing attempt to resolve, and to submerge, the inherent tension between police and law, between public welfare and individual rights, and between heteronomy and autonomy. A better understanding of the patriarchal origins, and nature, of police cannot harmonize patriarchy and democracy, or politics and economics. It can, however, help us see more clearly the nature of the challenge faced by a system of government that seeks not only efficiency, but legitimacy as well.

The project of critically analyzing the power to police is a crucial part of the general project of critically analyzing state power.[1] In fact, the two inquiries are identical under the broadest interpretation of the police power as coextensive with the power to govern. The more expansive the view of the police power, the more important the scrutiny of its origin and limitations becomes—unless of course one follows Holmes and takes the police power to be defined precisely by its immunity from scrutiny.

The basic question is whether police within the limits of law is possible. How can persons capable of autonomy be policed without denying their personhood? How can objects of police remain legal subjects? What role can an essentially hierarchical autocratic ahuman mode of governance play in a country where not the householder, but the law is king? How can an essentially heteronomous mode of governance comply with the basic principle of legal legitimacy, autonomy?

While police power scrutiny, and with it any attempt openly to grapple with these fundamental questions of American government, has largely disappeared from Supreme Court jurisprudence over the past century, it survives in some pockets of state constitutional jurisprudence. State courts, in general, have been more confident in their handling of the police power, and even of substantive due process, than has the federal high court, presumably because state courts reviewing state statutes feel more secure in their legitimacy, rightly or wrongly, and are unhampered by federalism concerns. And there have been calls in the academic literature for a retention, or development, of some sort of meaningful review of state actions implicating "noneconomic" rights, i.e., the sort of rights *not*—or at least apparently not—implicated by *Lochner*, and in particular of state actions employing the criminal law. In general, these pleas for judicial action speak in terms of substantive due process, and less frequently of the police power as well. As a rule, they follow the trend of American legal discourse and react to, and are directed at, the jurisprudence of the United States Supreme Court, even though the police power has always been, and will always remain, primarily a state court issue. For that reason, these two developments—in the state courts and in the academic literature—have yet to reinforce each other as much as they might.[2]

State police power jurisprudence recognizes the tension between police and law, and takes some important steps toward its resolution. If nothing else, it helps expose the tension between police and law as such, and therefore makes it at least possible to confront it. Admittedly, the cases could go farther in their analysis of the nature of police power. But the importance of recognizing the need to identify the state power in question, of beginning to appreciate the origins and scope of this power, and of placing a particular exercise of that power within the context of other exercises should not be underestimated.

But beyond analysis, critique is needed. Here too, the state cases have taken important initial steps. And here too, the tools of critique require considerable refinement. Reading the state police power cases, one often gets the impression of judges groping for a theory, for a principle upon which they can rest their critical analysis of the police power. Lengthy quotations from the works of eminent philosophers, as in *Bonadio*, cannot take the place of legal analysis, no matter how luminous the philosopher—and illuminating the quotation—might be.

Perhaps Mill's "harm principle," an abstract principle of political philosophy, implies certain limitations on the state's authority to employ the law in general, and the criminal law in particular.[3] If so, these limitations must be spelled out. And once spelled out, we need an explanation of why they should matter given that, at least on its face, no constitution, state or federal, enacts Mill's political philosophy any more than it does, "Mr. Herbert Spencer's Social Statics," as Holmes pointed out in his *Lochner* dissent.[4]

The "right of privacy," though more frequently invoked than Mill's principle, rests on similarly shaky ground. The privacy right has the advantage of being presented as a principle of law, rather than of political philosophy. But within the realm of legal rights, it occupies an uneasy position, suspended between the penumbrae of other rights and the oxymoronic notion of substantive due process. The right of privacy is most closely associated with the notion of substantive due process. Given the purely polemical origin of this category, it's of limited usefulness in an affirmative theory, or in a constitutional standard. The mere invocation of substantive due process all too often condemns a judicial opinion to criticism, if not reversal or even derision.

The association of police power jurisprudence with substantive due process bears another danger. Defining the limits on police power in terms of substantive due process may be taken to imply that no other limits exist. That is not the case, however. As we've seen, the Eighth Amendment's prohibition against cruel and unusual punishments (and its state analogues) can also be interpreted as placing legal limits on the police power, by insisting that persons be treated as such even in punishment. Other constitutional principles can likewise be read as spelling out particular aspects of the general right of autonomy enjoyed by all persons.[5] These principles likely will include various *procedural* guarantees as well, such as the right to a jury of one's peers, along with the various rights of participation (and non-participation) throughout the criminal process.[6]

The police power should be appreciated in its comprehensiveness as a mode of governance, rather than as a particular variety of governmental regulation. And so its limitations should be viewed not as a set of independent constraints. In fact, they shouldn't be seen as limitations alone. For personal autonomy isn't just a limiting principle. It's also the core of another basic mode of governance, the power to do justice, or the power of right or law. As Ernst Freund, the last great American student of the police power, recognized, "[t]he maintenance of right and the redress of wrong"[7] is a governmental obligation distinct from the "promotion of public welfare,"[8] just as "the power to define and punish crimes," which manifests itself in the criminal law, is a governmental power distinct from the power to police.[9] The maintenance of autonomy, after all, not only prohibits the state from interfering with it in the exercise of some power called the police power. It also obligates the state to take affirmative steps to protect the autonomy of its constituents, in their dealings with the state (as in a criminal trial) and against interference by other persons (as in a crime). In fact, from the perspective of criminal law, the protection of the person against the power of the state comes into play only as the state discharges its prior obligation, enforcing the autonomy of one person (the "victim") in the face of an attack upon it by another person (the "offender"). In the criminal process, the tables are turned and the potential aggressor is transformed into the potential victim of (state) aggression.[10]

In general, the state police power cases go deeper than Supreme Court cases, which generally pay no attention to the question of the origin and nature of the state power said to justify a particular state action. But they don't go deep enough. They still take for granted more than they should, given their enterprise of critical analysis. For instance, they all too often fail to scrutinize the general scope of the police power, as opposed to its use in a specific case. So courts still recite, unthinkingly, the long established list of interests protected by the police power. That list includes, significantly, the moral well-being of the political community, the moral police. Even cases that strike down criminal morals offenses, like criminal sodomy statutes, reaffirm the state's general power to safeguard the moral police. The problem with sodomy statutes, however, is that the state protection of the public's moral health can justify no state action of any kind, or at least no state action in the form of a criminal statute.

Similarly, all too many state courts and commentators uncritically assume that the police power is the origin of all criminal law. Those among them who nonetheless insist on scrutinizing the state police power thus view their task as distinguishing between permissible and impermissible exercises of the police power in the form of criminal legislation. Combining the notion of substantive due process with that of the criminal law as police power, they conclude that the "concern here is with substantive due process as a constitutional limitation on the boundaries of the police power."[11] As a result, they don't recognize the fundamental tension between police, and criminal law, as law. Their inquiry already assumes that police within the limits of law is possible.

What's missing, in the end, is an account of law, or right, as such, based on the basic legal right of autonomy. Of course such an account would have to fit into a broader account of state power, and therefore of political legitimacy. And here it may well turn out that the *political* harm principle implies a *legal* principle, once harm is understood in a particular sense, namely as interference with autonomy. Thus legally reinterpreted, the harm principle might play a role in the review of state action, and of state police power action in particular. Similarly, the right of privacy can be seen as capturing one aspect of the more fundamental right of autonomy, namely the right of autonomy vis-à-vis the state as opposed to other persons. A general account of right also would do without a distinction of convenience like that between "economic" and "noneconomic" rights. That's not to say that all rights are created equal. The status of each right, however, would derive from its proximity to the basic right of autonomy. The right to physical integrity, for example, would deserve greater protection than would the right to enter into contracts of one's choice, not because the former is noneconomic and the latter economic, but because the former is crucial to the maintenance of autonomous personhood, and the other isn't, or at least it needn't be (which isn't to say that it can't be, as the case of slavery illustrates).

From the standpoint of law, and of the autonomy it protects, *Lochner* for instance can be criticized on the ground that the maximum hours statute was designed to *enhance*, rather than to restrain, the autonomy of bakery employees. The New York legislature, one might argue, passed the statute precisely because the relationship between bakery owners and bakery employees was not one among equal autonomous persons. Instead, the bakers were, like the miners in *Holden v. Hardy* before them, forced into accepting labor conditions, and contracts establishing these conditions, by their inferior bargaining position. While they were generally capable of self-government, and therefore of entering into contracts of any kind, that abstract capacity for autonomy could not be exercised, given the superior power of their contractual partner.

That's not to say, however, that the enhancement of the bakers' contractual autonomy could justify the interference with the autonomy of the bakery owners through the threat and use of *criminal punishment*. Surely, the state had at its disposal less intrusive means to achieve its autonomy enhancing end, perhaps by establishing a presumption, rebuttable or irrebuttable, that certain contracts were so unfavorable to one of the parties, in particular the bakery employees, as to be considered null and void on the ground that they did not reflect the autonomy of both parties. Contracts of this kind could include not only those providing for working hours beyond a certain maximum, but also providing for inadequate pay, a hazardous work environment, insufficient vacation time, inadequate job security, and so on.

In this reading, *Lochner* wasn't a police power case at all, but a justice power case. The New York statute sought not to, indirectly, protect the public police by protecting bakery employees. Instead it protected the status of bakery employees as autonomous persons under law, by allowing them to manifest their capacity for autonomy in their contractual relationship with their employers, rather than falling prey to the employers' superior power, thus becoming a victim of heteronomy, rather than an agent of autonomy, an object of police, rather than a subject of law.

Put another way, *Lochner* turns out to be a case about what is generally considered to be a particular, and particularly problematic, manifestation of the police power: the criminal law. And surely if the misdemeanor in Joseph Lochner's case deserves careful scrutiny, then so does the far more intrusive rest of the law of crime and punishment.

Ironically, a critical analysis of American criminal law, ostensibly derived from the police power of the state, could draw on the work of the thinker and doer who is as closely associated with the idea of an American police power as anyone else: Thomas Jefferson. Here it's worth remembering that when Jefferson, in 1779, set up the chair in "law and police" at the College of William & Mary, he created not only the first American professorship in police, but also the first professorship in law.[12]

As author of the Declaration of Independence and as Governor of Virginia, Jefferson saw the connection between government in general and punishment in particular more clearly than anyone at the time, or perhaps since. In the Declaration of Independence, he set out the theory of legitimacy of the new American state, based on the equality of "all men" endowed with "unalienable rights" to "life, liberty and the pursuit of happiness." And it was "to secure these rights, [that] governments are instituted among men, deriving their just powers from the consent of the governed."

Two years later, in the preamble to his "Bill for Proportioning Crimes and Punishments,"[13] now-Governor Jefferson set himself the task of applying these principles to the power of punishment, through which the state infringes the unalienable rights it exists to protect, in order to protect them:

> Whereas it frequently happens that wicked and dissolute men, resigning themselves to the dominion of inordinate passions, commit violations on the lives, liberties, and property of others, and the secure enjoyment of these having principally induced men to enter into society, government would be defective in its principal purpose, were it not to restrain such criminal acts by inflicting due punishments on those who perpetrate them; but it appears at the same time equally deducible from the purposes of society, that a member thereof, committing an inferior injury, does not wholly forfeit the protection of his fellow citizens, but after suffering a punishment in proportion to his offence, is entitled to their protection from all greater pain.[14]

In the end, the substance of Jefferson's draft didn't quite live up to its preamble. Instead of delivering the "deduc[tion] from the purposes of society" he promised, Jefferson was largely content to invoke the authority of common law, and even Anglo-Saxon, statutes and commentators.[15] We learn, for instance, that "the laws of Æthelstan and Canute," a set of Anglo-Saxon dooms from the tenth and eleventh centuries, punished counterfeiters with cutting off the hand "that he the foul [crime] with wrought," and then displaying it "upon the mint-smithery."[16]

To subject the police power, and the law of crime and punishment which it is said to justify, to critical analysis thus means nothing more, and nothing less, than finishing Jefferson's project. When Jefferson returned to Virginia from the Inaugural Congress, he felt that "our whole code must be reviewed, adapted to our republican form of government, and, now that we had no negatives of Councils, Governors & Kings to restrain us from doing right, that it should be corrected, in all it's [sic] parts, with a single eye to reason, & the good of those for whose government it was framed."[17] What was true of the Virginia code in 1776 still holds for much of American law, and for American criminal law in particular, insofar as its patriarchal origins in the power to police have precluded principled scrutiny to this day.

Notes

Introduction

1. License Cases, 46 U.S. 504, 583 (1847).
2. Slaughter-House Cases, 83 U.S. 36, 49 (1873).
3. "Constitutional Law," 16A Am. Jur. 2d § 317.
4. Slaughter-House Cases, 83 U.S. 36, 49–50 (1873).
5. In fact, the federal government has long exercised a general police power despite the limitation of that power to the states in theory. See already Ernst Freund, *The Police Power: Public Policy and Constitutional Rights* 63 (1904) ("impossible to deny that the federal government exercises a considerable police power of its own").
6. See, e.g., Foucha v. Louisiana, 504 U.S. 71, 80 (1992) (state's right to punish "pursuant to its police power"); Wayne R. LaFave and Austin W. Scott, Jr., *Substantive Criminal Law* § 2.10 (2d ed. 1986) (states' and federal government's right to punish under police power's "considerable authority"); see already Clarence E. Laylin and Alonzo H. Tuttle, "Due Process and Punishment," 20 *Mich. L. Rev.* 614, 622 (1922) ("creation of crimes is an exercise of the police power—the state's right of self-defense"); Sutton v. New Jersey, 244 U.S. 258 (1917) (restraint and punishment of crime).
7. See Christopher L. Tomlins, *Law, Labor, and Ideology in the Early American Republic* 57 (1993).
8. 1 *The Records of the Federal Convention of 1787*, at 157 (Max Farrand ed., rev. ed. 1966) (cited in William J. Novak, *The People's Welfare: Law and Regulation in Nineteenth-Century America* 11 [1996]).
9. Thomas Jefferson, Notes on the State of Virginia, query xv (1781); Thomas Jefferson, A Bill for Amending the Constitution of the College of William and Mary, and Substituting More Certain Revenues for Its Support (1779). According to the appendix to Jefferson's bill to amend the college's constitution, this chair was to cover both "municipal" and "oeconomical" law. Municipal law, or law in the narrow sense, included "common law, equity, law merchant, law maritime, and law ecclesiastical." "Oeconomical law," or police, encompassed "politics" and "commerce."
10. Robert A. Ferguson, *Law and Letters in American Culture* 11 (1984).
11. 4 William Blackstone, *Commentaries on the Laws of England* 162 (1769).

12. See Ernst Freund, *The Police Power: Public Policy and Constitutional Rights* 2 and n.2 (1904).

13. Among the more recent judicial invocations of Blackstone's police definition is a staple of first-year criminal law courses, Commonwealth v. Keller, 35 D. & C.2d 615 (Pa. Ct. Com. Pleas 1964) (convicting mother who had hidden away two newborns in boxes of "indecent disposition of a dead body," a newly created common law misdemeanor).

14. Thomas M. Cooley, *A Treatise on the Constitutional Limitations Which Rest Upon the Legislative Power of the States of the American Union* 704 n.1 (6th ed. 1890); Christopher G. Tiedeman, *A Treatise on the Limitations of Police Power in the United States Considered From Both a Civil and Criminal Standpoint* 2 (1886); Ernst Freund, *The Police Power: Public Policy and Constitutional Rights* 2 (1904).

15. In Rousseau's words, "[t]he word Economy, or Œconomy, is derived from *oikos, a house,* and *nomos, law,* and meant originally only the wise and legitimate government of the house for the common good of the whole family. The meaning of the term was then extended to the government of that great family, the State." Jean Jacques Rousseau, *Discourse on Political Economy* (1755).

16. By patriarchy I mean, quite literally, government of the family, as household, by its head (ordinarily the father), as householder, and, more loosely, the power associated with this form of government. Carole Pateman's classic account of patriarchy in political theory focuses on the patriarchal power of the household head, as husband, over one particular member of the household, his wife. Carole Pateman, *The Sexual Contract* (1988). She argues persuasively that traditional histories, and systems, of political theory have not appreciated the central significance of this intrafamilial relationship—defined by what she calls the "sexual contract"—and instead have paid exclusive attention to the interfamilial relationships among (male) household heads. This book broadens Pateman's focus to consider household governance more generally, while also insisting on the insufficiency of any attempt to construct a history or theory of government that disregards—and dismisses as irrelevant—"private" as opposed to "public" governance, or "police" as opposed to "law." It thereby joins a growing body of work dedicated to uncovering—and rediscovering—modes of governance that have been ignored, if not suppressed, by traditional legal and political histories. See, e.g., Mariana Valverde, "Police Science, British Style: Pub Licensing and Knowledges of Urban Disorder," 32 *Economy & Society* 234 (2003); Mariana Valverde, *Law's Dream of a Common Knowledge* (2003); Mark Neocleous, *The Fabrication of Social Order: A Critical Theory of Police Power* (2000); William J. Novak, *The People's Welfare: Law and Regulation in Nineteenth-Century America* (1996).

17. On the notion of governmentalities, and technologies of governance, see Michel Foucault, "Governmentality," in *The Foucault Effect: Studies in Governmentality* 87, 102 (Graham Burchell, Colin Gordon, and Peter Miller eds. 1991). For more on Foucault on police in particular, see infra ch. 3.

18. See *Lectures on Justice, Police, Revenue and Arms delivered in the University of Glasgow By Adam Smith Reported by a Student in 1763* (Edwin Cannan ed. 1896).

19. The inherent connection between police science and the police state of absolute continental monarchies exposes a deep tension between police and democratic governance, and between police and law, that has not been sufficiently noted by recent work on early American notions of police. See, e.g., Christopher L. Tomlins, *Law, Labor, and Ideology in the Early American Republic* (1993); William J. Novak, *The People's Welfare: Law and Regulation in Nineteenth-Century America* (1996). The operative distinction between police and law was not that between a substantive political community—or "commonwealth"—and an abstract system of rules, nor that between local and central government, between self-government and other-government, or between progressivism and conservatism.

The political community of police might have been a family, but it was a family governed by a *paterfamilias* with indefinite power over the household resources at his disposal. The historical tension between police and law is not to be confused with the current tension between communitarianism and liberalism.

There was also nothing inherently local about the notion of police. Policing occurred at all levels of government, from small municipalities to the national government. The fiction that police power was limited to the states—rather than the federal government—played a crucial role in the federalist compromise, but it was nonetheless a fiction.

The distinction between autonomy and heteronomy does indeed map onto that between police and law. But it was police that was associated with heteronomy and law with autonomy, rather than the other way around.

Finally, the fact that progressives turned to the police power to implement their social reform agenda at the turn of the twentieth century doesn't make the police power inherently progressive. At around the same time, the police power was invoked to justify racial segregation, Plessy v. Ferguson, 163 U.S. 537, 545 (1896), and the forced sterilization of "defectives," Buck v. Bell, 143 Va. 310, 318–19 (1925), aff'd, 274 U.S. 200 (1922).

In general, I think it's a mistake to read the history of American police power backward, through the lens of the traditional reading of the Supreme Court's "*Lochner* Era," which portrays the Court as interfering with popular will—as manifested in progressive social legislation—in the name of abstract principles (in particular liberty of contract). For a more detailed discussion of *Lochner*, see ch. 9.

20. Gordon S. Wood, *The Creation of the American Republic, 1776–1787*, at 432 (2d ed. 1998).

21. Benjamin Franklin to Charles Carroll, May 25, 1789, in 10 *The Writings of Benjamin Franklin* 7 (Albert Henry Smyth ed. 1907) (quoted in Gordon S. Wood, *The Creation of the American Republic, 1776–1787*, at 432 [2d ed. 1998]).

22. License Cases, 46 U.S. 504, 583 (1847).

23. William J. Novak, "Common Regulation: Legal Origins of State Power in America," 45 *Hastings L.J.* 1061, 1076 (1994).

24. 198 U.S. 45 (1905).

25. Walton H. Hamilton and Carlton C. Rodee, "Police Power," in 12 *Encyclopedia of the Social Sciences* 190 (1933) (quoted in William J. Novak, "Common Regulation: Legal Origins of State Power in America," 45 *Hastings L.J.* 1061, 1082 n.58 [1994]).

26. See, e.g., Powell v. State, 270 Ga. 327 (1998) (striking down state sodomy statute upheld in Bowers v. Hardwick, 478 U.S. 186 [1986]). Only recently did the U.S. Supreme Court invalidate a sodomy statute, without, however, framing its decision as a review of an exercise of the power to police. See Lawrence v. Texas, 539 U.S. 558 (2003).

27. 4 William Blackstone, *Commentaries on the Laws of England* 127 (1769).

1. Police as *Patria Potestas*

1. Thomas Paine, *Common Sense* (1776).

2. Thomas Jefferson, A Bill for Amending the Constitution of the College of William and Mary, and Substituting More Certain Revenues for Its Support (1779). On the relationship between law and police, with a particular focus on German criminal law, see the excellent essay by Wolfgang Naucke, "Vom Vordringen des Polizeigedankens im Recht, d.i.: vom Ende der Metaphysik im Recht," in *Recht, Gericht, Genossenschaft und Policey: Studien zu Grundbegriffen der germanistischen Rechtshistorie* 177 (Gerhard Dilcher & Bernhard Diestelkamp eds. 1986). The roots of German criminal law in the discipline of unfree servants are explored in the classic essay by Gustav Radbruch, "Der Ursprung des Strafrechts aus dem Stande der Unfreien," in *Elegantiae Juris Criminalis: Vierzehn Studien zur Geschichte des Strafrechts* (2d ed. 1950).

3. Hannah Arendt, *The Human Condition* 26–27 (1958). In *The Human Condition*, Arendt presents a suggestive account of the distinction between economics and politics in classical Athens, and the gradual erosion of that distinction since then. See id. ch. 2. The trajectory of the concept of economics parallels that of the concept of police, from the micro household of the family to the macro household of the state, and from *Wirtschaft* to *Volkswirtschaft*. See, e.g., Otto Brunner, "Das 'ganze Haus' und die alteuropäische 'Ökonomik'," in *Neue Wege der Sozialgeschichte* 33 (1956). More precisely, the concept of police enters political discourse exactly at the moment when the concept of economics is expanded, or transferred, to the management of the state, and thereby masks the paradox underlying the novel notion of governing citizens

as household members, by transforming the state into a macro household. That paradox lies much closer to the surface of the conceptual monstrosity of "political economy." Arendt, supra at 29. For a brilliant and broad sweeping recent study of the genealogy of household governance, see William James Booth, *Households: On the Moral Architecture of the Economy* (1993).

4. On the connection between political autonomy and democracy, see Cornelius Castoriadis, "The Greek *Polis* and the Creation of Democracy," in *The Castoriadis Reader* 267 (David Ames Curtis trans. & ed. 1997).

5. Contra Joel Feinberg, "Autonomy, Sovereignty, and Privacy: Moral Ideals in the Constitution?," 58 *Notre Dame L. Rev.* 445 (1983) (autonomy as individual sovereignty).

6. See Hannah Arendt, *Between Past and Future: Six Exercises in Political Thought* 117 (1961); see also Carole Pateman, *The Sexual Contract* 178–79 (1988) ("men's self-consciousness is not purely the consciousness of free civil equals (the story of the social contract)—it is also the consciousness of patriarchal masters (the story of the sexual contract)").

7. See Hannah Arendt, *The Human Condition* 30–31 (1958).

8. On the connection between suffrage and householdership through much of the nineteenth century in the United States, see Robert J. Steinfeld, "Property and Suffrage in the Early American Republic," 41 *Stan. L. Rev.* 335 (1989).

9. Including, of course, real property.

10. See Plato, *The Republic* bk. V, 463; Plato, *Statesman* 259b-c. Plato tended to emphasize the connections, Aristotle the distinctions.

11. Aristotle, *Politics* bk. I, iii. What's more, Aristotle saw the household as the original political association, "the original seed of the *polis*," which is why his *Politics* begins with a discussion of household governance. Curtis N. Johnson, *Aristotle's Theory of the State* 62 (1990); see also William J. Booth, "Politics and the Household: A Commentary on Aristotle's *Politics* Book One," 2 *History of Political Thought* 203, 216–20 (1981). Associations, in turn, were characterized by "the distinction between ruling and ruled elements." Id. at 217.

12. Aristotle, *Politics* bk. 1, iv.

13. Aristotle, *Nicomachean Ethics* bk. V, vi; see also Hannah Arendt, *The Human Condition* 34 (1958) ("the ancient household head, while he might exert a milder or harsher rule, knew neither of laws nor justice outside the political realm"); but see Fred D. Miller, *Nature, Justice, and Rights in Aristotle's* Politics 84–85 (1995); Judith A. Swanson, *The Public and the Private in Aristotle's Political Philosophy* 27–30 (1992).

14. Aristotle, *Politics* bk. I, iv.

15. Id. at xii.

16. David Herlihy, *Medieval Households* 2 (1985).

17. According to M.I. Finley, the "*paterfamilias* was not the biological father but the authority over the household, an authority that the Roman law divided into three elements. . . . , *potestas* or power over his children (including adoptees), his children's children and his slaves, *manus* or power over his wife and his sons' wives, and *dominium* or power over his possessions." M. I. Finley, *The Ancient Economy* 19 (1973). Finley stresses the practical irrelevance of these intrafamilial distinctions in the face of paternal power: "the head manages and controls both the personnel and the property of the group, without distinction as to economic or personal or social behaviour, distinction which could be drawn as an abstract intellectual exercise but no in actual practice." Id.

18. 1 James Leigh Strachan-Davidson, *Problems of the Roman Criminal Law* 38 (1912) (citing Henry Maine, *Ancient Law* 126 and 369 ff. [1861]). On intertribal relations as the origins of international law, see also Gustav Radbruch, "Der Ursprung des Strafrechts aus dem Stande der Unfreien," in *Elegantiae Juris Criminalis: Vierzehn Studien zur Geschichte des Strafrechts* (2d ed. 1950).

19. See infra. ch 3.

20. Aristotle, *Politics* bk. I, xiii. On the significance of the persistent assumption that women, unlike male children, lack the capacity for citizenship (or *political* personhood), see Carole Pateman, *The Sexual Contract* 94–96 (1988). One variant of this claim is the similarly persistent view—espoused by Rousseau, Freud, Piaget, and Kohlberg—that women, unlike men, are in-

capable of developing an abstract "sense of justice," as opposed to a feeling of attachment to one's fellow community members. See Carole Pateman, "'The Disorder of Women': Women, Love, and the Sense of Justice," in *The Disorder of Women: Democracy, Feminism, and Political Theory* 17 (1989); see also Carol Gilligan, *In a Different Voice: Psychological Theory and Women's Development* (1982).

21. Aristotle, *Politics* bk. I, xiii.

22. David Herlihy, *Medieval Households* 2 (1985). Written "before the middle of the fourth century B.C.," the *Oikonomikos* was "a work of practical advice to the gentleman landowner about the sound management of an estate, its slaves, household, and land." Scott Meikle, *Aristotle's Economic Thought* 5 (1995) (citing M. I. Finley, *The Ancient Economy* 17–20 [1973]).

23. William J. Booth, "Politics and the Household: A Commentary on Aristotle's *Politics* Book One," 2 *History of Political Thought* 203, 213 (1981) (property as "sum of instruments," animate and inanimate alike).

24. David Herlihy, *Medieval Households* 2–3 (1985).

25. Id. at 48.

26. M. I. Finley, *The Ancient Economy* 17 (1973) ("The word 'economics', Greek in origin, is compounded from *oikos*, a household, and the semantically complex root, *nem-*, here in its sense of 'regulate, administer, organize'."); see also Jean Jacques Rousseau, *A Discourse on Political Economy* (1755).

27. Jefferson to Pendleton, Aug. 13, 1776, in 1 *Jefferson Papers* 492 (Julian P. Boyd ed. 1950) (quoted in Gordon S. Wood, *The Creation of the American Republic, 1776–1787*, at 122 [2d ed. 1998]). It's no accident that Jefferson's draft criminal code for Virginia relied heavily on Anglo-Saxon dooms. See Kathryn Preyer, "Crime, the Criminal Law and Reform in Post-Revolutionary Virginia," 1 *Law & Hist. Rev.* 53 (1983).

28. See, e.g., Rudolf His, *Deutsches Strafrecht bis zur Karolina* 16–21 (1928).

29. Heinrich Brunner, "Ueber absichtslose Missethat im altdeutschen Strafrechte," in *Forschungen zur Geschichte des deutschen und französischen Rechtes* 487, 507 (1894).

30. 1 Frederick Pollock and Frederic William Maitland, *The History of English Law Before the Time of Edward I* 419 (2d ed. 1898).

31. Id.

32. Heinrich Brunner, "Ueber absichtslose Missethat im altdeutschen Strafrechte," in *Forschungen zur Geschichte des deutschen und französischen Rechtes* 487, 522 (1894). Paul Hyams has analogized the status of medieval villeins to that of dogs today. Paul R. Hyams, *King, Lords and Peasants in Medieval England: The Common Law of Villeinage in the Twelfth and Thirteenth Centuries* 125–26 (1968). As Hyams points out, both were (almost) without protection against maltreatment by their master *and* incapable of enforcing whatever protection they did enjoy, and for the same reason: they lacked standing as objects of legal rights. The analogy is apt for another reason, however. Villeins and dogs both were similarly situated *as members of the master's household*, as resources to be employed. The only difference between then and now is that the villein's merely instrumental status has changed, and in fact disappeared, but the dog's hasn't.

33. On the prevalence of plea bargaining, see Markus Dirk Dubber, "American Plea Bargains, German Lay Judges, and the Crisis of Criminal Procedure," 49 *Stan. L. Rev.* 547 (1997).

34. Julius Goebel, "King's Law and Local Custom in Seventeenth Century England," 31 *Colum. L. Rev.* 416 (1931).

35. David Herlihy, *Medieval Households* 48 (1985); see also Paul R. Hyams, *King, Lords and Peasants in Medieval England: The Common Law of Villeinage in the Twelfth and Thirteenth Centuries* 96 (1968) (pointing out that Bracton equated the lord's authority over the villein "with the Roman law *potestas*, which a master had over his slave, a *paterfamilias* over his family"). The old notion of *mund* survives in a few German words, such as "Vormund" (guardian) and "mündig" (of age or responsible, as in "strafmündig" (criminally responsible).

36. Oliver Wendell Holmes, "Agency," 4 *Harv. L. Rev.* 345 (1891).

37. 2 Frederick Pollock and Frederic William Maitland, *The History of English Law Before the Time of Edward I* 530 (2d ed. 1898).

38. 1 Frederick Pollock and Frederic William Maitland, *The History of English Law Before the*

Time of Edward I 485 (2d ed. 1898); see also Henry Maine, *The Ancient Law* 93–94 (1972) (1861) ("I do not know how the operation and nature of the ancient Patria Potestas can be brought so vividly before the mind as by reflecting on the prerogatives attached to the husband by the pure English Common Law, and by recalling the rigorous consistency with which the view of a complete legal subjection on the part of the wife is carried by it.").

39. Internal insubordination should be distinguished from disputes among equal status members of the household, which did not—or not necessarily—threaten the *mund*. See Rudolf His, *Deutsches Strafrecht bis zur Karolina* 40 (1928).

40. Anglo-American criminal law, of course, has retained the amorphous offense of "breach of the peace." German criminal law retains several offenses explicitly defined as breaches of various peaces, *Hausfriedensbruch* (breach of the peace of the house), § 123 StGB, *Landfriedensbruch* (breach of the peace of the country), § 125 StGB, and *Störung des öffentlichen Friedens* (disturbance of the public peace), § 126 StGB. Cf. Walter Kargl, "Rechtsgüter und Tatobjekte der Strafbestimmung gegen Hausfriedensbruch," 54 *Juristenzeitung* 930 (1999). The traditional Anglo-American crime of burglary incorporates elements of the German crime of breach of the house peace. The analogy is even closer for the similarly deep-rooted crime of "breaking and entering."

41. 1 Frederick Pollock & Frederic William Maitland, *The History of English Law Before the Time of Edward I* 454 (2d ed. 1898). Julius Goebel vociferously attacked what the saw as "the 'peace' of the nineteenth-century romantics," advocating a more mundane view of the king's peace as "a scheme of special protection." Julius Goebel, Jr., *Felony and Misdemeanor* 428–29, 439 (1937). Goebel may well have a point, as talk of peace royal and imperial occasionally slips into mysticism, or at least metaphysics, but whether he does or not makes little difference to our discussion.

42. Paul Vinogradoff, "Foundations of Society," 2 *Cambridge Medieval History* 630, 638 (1913).

43. Burchard of Worms: Lex Familie Wormatiensis, Charter of Immunity for the Church of Worms, July 29, 1014, in *Quellen zur deutschen Verfassungs-, Wirtschafts- und Sozialgeschichte*, doc. 22 (Lorenz Weinrich ed. 1977).

44. For an interesting discussion of canon criminal law as "the practice of the church in disciplining its own army of clergy," see Harold J. Berman, *Law and Revolution: The Formation of the Western Legal Tradition* 185–92 (1983).

45. The Rule of St. Augustine, ch. vi, § 3.

46. Id. ch. vii.

47. 2 Frederick Pollock and Frederic William Maitland, *The History of English Law Before the Time of Edward I* 433 (2d ed. 1898); see also Paul R. Hyams, *King, Lords and Peasants in Medieval England: The Common Law of Villeinage in the Twelfth and Thirteenth Centuries* 126 (1968) ("civil death") (citing Bracton, *De Legibus et Consuetudinibus Angliae* [H.N. ed. 1569, f. 421b.]).

48. To say that "in the criminal law of the feudal epoch there is hardly any distinction between free men and villeins" is of course to say not only that villeins weren't treated worse than free men, but also that free men were treated no better than villeins. See, e.g., Paul R. Hyams, *King, Lords and Peasants in Medieval England: The Common Law of Villeinage in the Twelfth and Thirteenth Centuries* 132 (1968) (quoting Vinogradoff). Against the lord, his men are equal.

49. 2 Frederick Pollock and Frederic William Maitland, *The History of English Law Before the Time of Edward I* 438 (2d ed. 1898).

50. Id. at 441. Presumably the "benefit of clergy" helped entice bishops to surrender their household members to outside lay courts, i.e., to the authority of another householder, ordinarily the king. Conversely this partial immunity of clerks in civilian courts reflected their membership in another household, the church, and therefore another disciplinary authority. See generally Leona C. Gabel, *Benefit of Clergy in England in the Later Middle Ages* (1928); see also George W. Dalzell, *Benefit of Clergy in America and Related Matters* (1955).

51. 2 Frederick Pollock and Frederic William Maitland, *The History of English Law Before the Time of Edward I* 444 (2d ed. 1898).

52. Eberhard Schmidt, *Einführung in die Geschichte der deutschen Strafrechtspflege* 29 (3d ed. 1963). For an interesting exploration of the genealogy of the idea of sanctuary, see Karl Shoe-

maker, "Medieval Sanctuary Law: Changing Conceptions of Law, Crime and Punishment" (Ph.D. diss. Berkeley 2001).

53. See, e.g., Heinrich Brunner, "Abspaltungen der Friedlosigkeit," in *Forschungen zur Geschichte des deutschen und französischen Rechtes* 444, 453 (1894).

54. Id. at 459.

55. Id.

56. See, e.g., Model Penal Code § 221.1.

57. 1 Frederick Pollock and Frederic William Maitland, *The History of English Law Before the Time of Edward I* 576 (2d ed. 1898).

58. Id. at 577; cf. "Laws of Æthelstan," c. 1, in 4 *The Library of Original Sources* 232 (Oliver J. Thatcher ed., 1907) ("that no thief be spared, who may be taken 'hand-haebende' "). A pale remnant of this awesome householder power can still be seen in American criminal law. The use of deadly force against burglars caught red-handed is often discussed, and justified, in terms of the householder's right to defend his household. So when Herbert Wechsler, the drafter of the American Law Institute's influential Model Penal Code, decided to curb that power in the Code, he was told by the membership of the Institute that "basic sentiments of the community" and "popular sentiment" recognized the right of every "householder" to defend himself and "the members of his household" against a burglar. Note, "The Use of Deadly Force in the Protection of Property Under the Model Penal Code," 59 *Colum. L. Rev.* 1212, 1223, 1224, 1223 n.56, 1216 (1959); see also Restatement Torts (Second) § 77 cmt. l. For an introduction to the Model Penal Code, see Markus D. Dubber, *Criminal Law: Model Penal Code* (2002).

59. 1 Frederick Pollock and Frederic William Maitland, *The History of English Law Before the Time of Edward I* 576 (2d ed. 1898). As every householder had his peace, so he had his jurisdiction "'under his roof-gutter' (unter der Dachtraufe) and within the hedge." Paul Vinogradoff, "Foundations of Society," 2 *Cambridge Medieval History* 630, 651 (1913). "Personal authority over domestic servants and slaves," Vinogradoff continues, "took, among other things, the shape of criminal and police jurisdiction (Dienstrecht)." Id. On the notion of the lord's "disciplinary jurisdiction" over his tenants, see S.F.C. Milsom, *The Legal Framework of English Feudalism* (1976); R. H. Hilton, "Peasant Movements in England Before 1381," in 2 *Essays in Economics History* 73, 77 (E.M. Carus-Wilson ed. 1962) ("manorial discipline").

60. See, e.g., Heinrich Brunner, "Abspaltungen der Friedlosigkeit," in *Forschungen zur Geschichte des deutschen und französischen Rechtes* 444 (1894).

61. See id. at 458; Rudolf His, *Deutsches Strafrecht bis zur Karolina* 51 (1928).

62. 1 Frederick Pollock and Frederic William Maitland, *The History of English Law Before the Time of Edward I* 31 (2d ed. 1898).

63. Id. at 461.

64. See, e.g., Bruce R. O'Brien, "From *Morðor* to *Murdrum*: The Preconquest Origin and Norman Revival of the Murder Fine," 71 *Speculum* 321, 348 (1996).

65. 1 Frederick Pollock and Frederic William Maitland, *The History of English Law Before the Time of Edward I* 45 (2d ed. 1898).

66. Id. Royal justices were not shy about giving ever expanding interpretations of the king's peace, to the point where "it was sometimes said that anything done against the king's command was done against his peace." S.F.C. Milsom, *Historical Foundations of the Common Law* 427 (2d ed. 1981).

67. 1 Frederick Pollock and Frederic William Maitland, *The History of English Law Before the Time of Edward I* 45 (2d ed. 1898).

68. Id. at 513.

69. "Household," Guide to Medieval Terms, http://orb.rhodes.edu/Medieval_Terms.html (J.J. Arkenberg ed.) [Apr. 8, 2001].

70. On the significance of manorial governance, rather than royal governance through the common law of the royal courts, for early American settlers, see Julius Goebel, "King's Law and Local Custom in Seventeenth Century England," 31 *Colum. L. Rev.* 416 (1931).

71. Laws of William, c. 1 & 2. Throughout I use fealty in the loose sense of "a general obligation of . . . faithful obedience (*fidelitas*) which is owed by all subjects of the lord without dis-

tinction of rank." Paul Vinogradoff, "Feudalism," 3 *Cambridge Medieval History* 458, 461 (1924). That's not to say that it might not have been possible to distinguish two types of fealty, the fealty derived from "the oath of fealty, which accompanied the homage ceremony" and the fealty "of the base and non-privileged population," which owed fealty even without an oath. Id. at 468; cf. R.H. Hilton, "Peasant Movements in England Before 1381," in 2 *Essays in Economic History* 73, 74 (E.M. Carus-Wilson ed. 1962) (whatever reciprocity between lord and serf—service for protection—there might have been originally had dissipated by the twelfth century). The point is that, one way or another, everyone within a lord's household ended up owing the lord fealty. In this light, William's fealty oath extends the duty of fealty, thereby reducing the once free to a subservient status formerly reserved for slaves and serfs.

72. See Frederic William Maitland, "Domesday Book," in *Domesday and Beyond: Three Essays in the Early History of England* 1, 172 (1966) (1897).

73. Id. at 34.

74. Michel Foucault, "Governmentality," in *The Foucault Effect: Studies in Governmentality* 87, 102 (Graham Burchell, Colin Gordon, & Peter Miller eds. 1991).

75. John Locke, *Second Treatise of Government* § 147 (1690).

76. Id. § 151.

77. 1 William Blackstone, *Commentaries on the Laws of England* 354–55 (Of the Rights of Persons) (1765).

78. Paul Vinogradoff, "Foundations of Society," 2 *Cambridge Medieval History* 630, 642 (1913); see also Paul Vinogradoff, "Feudalism," 3 *Cambridge Medieval History* 458, 459 (1924) (tenant's *homagium* and lord's *investitura* as "acts constituting the feudal contract"); Keechang Kim, *Aliens in Medieval Law: The Origins of Modern Citizenship* 128 (2000) ("bond of mutual confidence" between lord and tenant).

79. The Laws of Alfred, Gudrun, and Edward the Elder, Of Oaths, c. 1.

80. It didn't help matters that villeins, in general, had no one to complain to about mistreatment by their lord except the lord himself. See generally Paul R. Hyams, *King, Lords and Peasants in Medieval England: The Common Law of Villeinage in the Twelfth and Thirteenth Centuries* (1968); S.F.C. Milsom, *The Legal Framework of English Feudalism* 11 (1976). The two exceptions to this rule, injury to life or limb and sedition, are discussed below.

81. 1 Frederick Pollock and Frederic William Maitland, *The History of English Law Before the Time of Edward I* 300 (2d ed. 1898). This practice could still be found in colonial America. According to a—fairly typical—1740 South Carolina law, killing a slave was subject to a £700 fine. Michael Stephen Hindus, *Prison and Plantation: Crime, Justice, and Authority in Massachusetts and South Carolina, 1767–1878*, at 132 (1980). By contrast, a slave's murder of his master was petit treason and as such subject to the harshest of punishments, qualified execution.

82. 1 Frederick Pollock and Frederic William Maitland, *The History of English Law Before the Time of Edward I* 303 (2d ed. 1898). For a similar use of *morð* or *morðor* in Old English "to label the crime of betrayal of one's lord and the punishment for such treason," see Bruce O'Brien, *God's Peace and King's Peace: The Laws of Edward the Confessor* 79 (1999); Bruce R. O'Brien, "From *Morðor* to *Murdrum*: The Preconquest Origin and Norman Revival of the Murder Fine," 71 *Speculum* 321 (1996). O'Brien argues that murder, contrary to received wisdom, did not originally refer to secret killings, but a noncompensable killing or a species of treason. Id. at 343. Of course, the first use of *morð* and *morðor* may collapse into the second; murder may have been noncompensable precisely because it amounted to betraying one's lord, the *ur*crime. And to say that a crime is noncompensable isn't to say that it could not be compensated, but merely that it wasn't compensable as a matter of course. Having placed himself in the lord's *misericordia*, the murderer-traitor would suffer whatever punishment his lord deemed appropriate.

83. 3, 7; 46, 3; 53, 4; 88, 14, in 1 *Die Gesetze der Angelsachsen* (Felix Liebermann ed. 1903).

84. 1 Frederick Pollock and Frederic William Maitland, *The History of English Law Before the Time of Edward I* 303–04 (2d ed. 1898).

85. Id. at 304.

86. Id. at 45.

87. Id. at 48.

88. See, e.g., Heinrich Brunner, "Abspaltungen der Friedlosigkeit," in *Forschungen zur Geschichte des deutschen und französischen Rechtes* 444, 465 (1894).

89. Heinrich Brunner, "Ueber absichtslose Missethat im altdeutschen Strafrechte," in *Forschungen zur Geschichte des deutschen und französischen Rechtes* 487, 495 (1894) (citing Statute of Gloucester, 6 Edw. 1); see also Bruce R. O'Brien, "From *Morðor* to *Murdrum*: The Preconquest Origin and Norman Revival of the Murder Fine," 71 *Speculum* 321, 356 (1996) ("When Edmund's code ordained that for those who violate the king's *mund* . . . 'it shall be for the king to decide whether his life shall be preserved' . . . the author meant the king to appear as a truly powerful monarch.").

90. Laws of William, c. 10.

91. 2 Frederick Pollock and Frederic William Maitland, *The History of English Law Before the Time of Edward I* 451 (2d ed. 1898); Rudolf His, *Deutsches Strafrecht bis zur Karolina* 17 (1928) (castration and whipping).

92. See, e.g., Heinrich Brunner, "Abspaltungen der Friedlosigkeit," in *Forschungen zur Geschichte des deutschen und französischen Rechtes* 444, 465 (1894).

93. 2 Frederick Pollock and Frederic William Maitland, *The History of English Law Before the Time of Edward I* 513 (2d ed. 1898).

94. Id. at 451.

95. Id. at 452–53.

96. Aristotle, *Politics* bk. I, iv.

97. 1 Joel Prentiss Bishop, *New Commentaries on the Criminal Law Upon a New System of Legal Exposition* 224 (8th ed. 1892) (quoting Coke in Beverley's Case, 4 Co. 123 b, 124 b).

98. 25 Edw. 3 stat. 5 c. 2.

99. U.S. Constitution art. 3, § 3.

100. Id. art. 1, § 8.

101. Id. art. 3, § 3.

102. 4 William Blackstone, *Commentaries on the Laws of England* 35 (1769).

103. 1 Joel Prentiss Bishop, *New Commentaries on the Criminal Law Upon a New System of Legal Exposition* 224 (8th ed. 1892).

104. Johannes Martin Ritter, *Verrat und Untreue an Volk, Reich und Staat* 121 (1942) (quoting Car. Guilhelm. Gaertner, *Institutiones iuris criminalis (iam auctae curante Christian. Henric. Breuning)* 9 [1765]) ("casus autem feloniarum omnes certa lege nec definiti sunt nec definiri possunt").

105. 2 Frederick Pollock and Frederic William Maitland, *The History of English Law Before the Time of Edward I* 500 (2d ed. 1898).

106. 1 Frederick Pollock and Frederic William Maitland, *The History of English Law Before the Time of Edward I* 351 (2d ed. 1898).

107. 2 Frederick Pollock and Frederic William Maitland, *The History of English Law Before the Time of Edward I* 504 n.2 (2d ed. 1898).

108. Id. at 503–04 (imagining death of lord); see also id. at 508 n.4 (plot to kill vs. plot to imprison, depose, or coerce king).

109. 4 William Blackstone, *Commentaries on the Laws of England* 75 (1769).

110. 9 Geo. 4, c. 31, § 2.

111. See, e.g., An Act Concerning Murder, 2 Laws of New York 1785–1788, ch. 22, at 391 (1787).

112. N.Y. Penal Code § 182 (1881).

113. 1 Frederick Pollock and Frederic William Maitland, *The History of English Law Before the Time of Edward I* 48–49 (2d ed. 1898).

114. 2 Frederick Pollock and Frederic William Maitland, *The History of English Law Before the Time of Edward I* 511 (2d ed. 1898).

115. Id. at 501 & n.1.

116. 4 William Blackstone, *Commentaries on the Laws of England* 92 (1769).

117. Michel Foucault, *Discipline and Punish: The Birth of the Prison* 3 (Alan Sheridan trans. 1979).

118. By limiting treason to "levying war against [the United States], or in adhering to their

enemies, giving them aid and comfort," the American Founding Fathers hoped to cleanse them-selves of the taint of traitordom. In particular, Americans were intent on drawing a clear dis-tinction between real treason and *constructive* treason, and then distancing themselves from the latter. The doctrine of "constructive" treason had been developed to cover acts of disobedience against royal officials, rather than against the king himself. James Fitzjames Stephen, *History of the Criminal Law of England* 303–04 (1883); see also 1 Mathew Hale, *The History of the Pleas of the Crown* 59 (treason an act "against the person or government of the King," where "person" also included state officials). As we've seen, the original Treason Act drew no such distinction.

Americans of the revolutionary generation had become intimately familiar with the doctrine of constructive treason as they railed continuously against the oppression they suffered at the hands of officials the king had seen fit to appoint to the colonies. Frequently, attacks on the cor-ruption and incompetence of these officials emphasized that they were not directed against the king himself—and thus did not constitute "real" treason.

The revolutionaries' commitment to a circumscribed notion of treason, however, was sorely tested both during and after the revolution, when they encountered conduct they themselves might consider traitorous. Consider, for instance, the following New York resolution from 1776, imposing outlawry on anyone who refused to take an oath of allegiance: "Whereas by a Reso-lution of the Convention of this State, passed the 27th of December, 1776, all the male Inhabi-tants of the County of Westchester, from the Age of sixteen Years and upwards, without Dis-crimination, were required to take an Oath of Allegiance to the State, within a certain limited Time, or *be put out of the Protection of the State, and treated as open Enemies.*" Laws of New York, Third Session, Chap. LIX: An Act for relieving certain Persons in the County of Westchester, against the Penalty contained in a Resolution of Convention, passed the 27th of December, 1776, requiring the inhabitants of the said Count to take an Oath of Allegiance (Mar. 13, 1780) (em-phasis added). Though not technically a treason statute, the Sedition Act of 1798, 1 Stat. 596, is testimony to just how tempting it is to stamp out challenges to established political power once that power has been achieved following a successful revolution.

119. Arthur P. Scott, *Criminal Law in Colonial Virginia* 161–62 (1930).

120. Jonathan A. Bush, "Free to Enslave: The Foundations of Colonial American Slave Law," 5 *Yale J. L. & Humanities* 417, 456–57 (1993).

121. Cf. Mark D. Cahn, "Punishment, Discretion, and the Codification of Prescribed Penal-ties in Colonial Massachusetts," 33 *Am. J. Legal Hist.* 107, 135 (1989) (in 1648 Laws and Liberties, capital offenses include "cursing or smiting parents" and "rebelling against one's father").

122. Raphael Semmes, *Crime and Punishment in Early Maryland* 93 (1938).

123. Id. at 94.

124. Arthur P. Scott, *Criminal Law in Colonial Virginia* 195 (1930).

125. Id.

126. Id. at 196.

127. Raphael Semmes, *Crime and Punishment in Early Maryland* 120 (1938).

128. 1 Frederick Pollock and Frederic William Maitland, *The History of English Law Before the Time of Edward I* 415 (2d ed. 1898).

129. Carole Pateman notes that, in England, husbands could use home confinement to police their obstreperous wives until the late nineteenth century. Carole Pateman, *The Sexual Contract* 116, 123 (1988).

130. 1 Frederick Pollock and Frederic William Maitland, *The History of English Law Before the Time of Edward I* 444 (2d ed. 1898).

131. Arthur P. Scott, *Criminal Law in Colonial Virginia* 299 (1930).

132. Beirne Stedman, "Right of Husband to Chastise Wife," 3 *Virginia Law Register [N.S.]* 241, 243 (1917).

133. Model Penal Code § 3.08(1)(b).

134. 1 James Leigh Strachan-Davidson, *Problems of the Roman Criminal Law* 171 n.1 (1912) (cit-ing Modestinus, *Digest*, XLIX. 16. 3).

135. Max Radin, "Enemies of Society," 27 *J. Crim. L.* 308, 333–34 (1936).

136. Garcia v. Territory, 1 N.M. 415, 418 (1869).

137. United States v. Bevans, Fed. Cas. No. 14,589 (U.S. Cir. Ct. D. Mass. 1816) (Story, J., Circuit Justice).

138. For a similar expression of astonishment, in another criminal case, see Story's opinion in United States v. Cornell, 25 F. Cas. 650, 657–58 (Cir. Ct. R.I. 1820).

139. Act of Congress of 23 of April, 1800, c. 33 (2 Stat. 45).

140. Joel Prentiss Bishop, *New Commentaries on the Criminal Law* 532 (8th ed. 1892).

141. 1 Frederick Pollock and Frederic William Maitland, *The History of English Law Before the Time of Edward I* 49 (2d ed. 1898); 2 Frederick Pollock and Frederic William Maitland, *The History of English Law Before the Time of Edward I* 517 (2d ed. 1898).

142. See Ruffin v. Commonwealth, 62 Va. 790, 796 (1871) (felons as slaves of the state). The view of imprisonment as enslavement was widely held, and not only in the United States. See Cesare Beccaria, *Of Crimes and Punishments* § 16 (imprisonment as enslavement), § 30 (enslavement as punishment for theft); Immanuel Kant, *Rechtslehre* A199/B229 (same), A193–194/B222–224 (punishment as enslavement), B163 (same).

143. According to Michael Hindus's stimulating discussion of prison discipline in nineteenth century Massachusetts, prison authorities, and reformers, were not shy about mixing household metaphors. Michael Stephen Hindus, *Prison and Plantation: Crime, Justice, and Authority in Massachusetts and South Carolina, 1767–1878*, at 166 (1980) (prisoners as machines); id. (prisoners subject to "the most perfect military order"); 168 (prisoners as children).

144. See generally Simeon E. Baldwin, "Whipping and Castration as Punishments for Crime," 8 *Yale L.J.* 371 (1899).

145. Raphael Semmes, *Crime and Punishment in Early Maryland* 37 (1938).

146. In Massachusetts, for example, discretionary whipping was not abandoned until 1858, and then only because a prison warden exercised his discretion *not* to whip. Michael Stephen Hindus, *Prison and Plantation: Crime, Justice, and Authority in Massachusetts and South Carolina, 1767–1878*, at 171–73 (1980).

147. Christopher G. Tiedeman, *A Treatise on the Limitations of Police Power in the United States Considered From Both a Civil and Criminal Standpoint* 624 (1886); see also id. at 97 ("for serious cases of insubordination, corporal punishment is very often inflicted, even in those States in which the whipping-post has been abolished").

148. Cf. Jackson v. Bishop, 404 F. 2d 571 (8th Cir. 1968) (in 1968 [!], reviewing prison disciplinary measures in Arkansas, including "such devices as the crank telephone or teeter board" and "whipping to the bare skin of prisoners").

149. This is quite literally what happened in antebellum South Carolina, where "[o]wners of difficult slaves could send them to the workhouse to have a specific punishment applied," with the "master of the workhouse function[ing] as the paid agent of the slavemaster. . . . " Michael Stephen Hindus, *Prison and Plantation: Crime, Justice, and Authority in Massachusetts and South Carolina, 1767–1878*, at 147 (1980).

150. As Charles Sydnor explained some time ago, while Southern gentlemen challenged each other to duels, "[t]o punish an insulting inferior, one used not a pistol or sword but a cane or a horsewhip." Charles S. Sydnor, "The Southerner and the Laws," 6 *J. Southern Hist.* 3, 17 (1940). Perhaps the most famous illustration of the demeaning connotation of corporal punishment is the Brooks-Sumner affair of 1856, when Senator Preston Brooks of South Carolina took it upon himself to cane Senator Charles Sumner of Massachusetts on the Senate floor. According to Sydnor, Brooks gave considerable thought to the question of "whether he should use horsewhip, cowhide, or cane, all of which were weapons of dishonor." Id. at 21–22.

151. Herber v. State, 7 Tex. 69 (1851). This case concerned the question whether a statutory amendment in 1849 changing the penalty from thirty-nine lashes to imprisonment for one to six years amounted to a mitigation and therefore should be applied retroactively. The trial judge held it didn't; the supreme court disagreed.

152. Howard Garfinkel, "Conditions of Successful Degradation Ceremonies," 61 *Am. J. Sociology* 420, 421 (1956).

153. 1 James Leigh Strachan-Davidson, *Problems of the Roman Criminal Law* 170 (1912).

154. Id. at 171.

155. Raphael Semmes, *Crime and Punishment in Early Maryland* 38, 39 (1938).

156. Arthur P. Scott, *Criminal Law in Colonial Virginia* 293–94 (1930).

157. The Laws of Alfred, Guthrum, and Edward the Elder, c. 13 ("How a twelve-hynde man shall be paid for").

158. Id. Of Oaths, c. 13 ("Of the Mercian oath").

159. 1 Frederick Pollock and Frederic William Maitland, *The History of English Law Before the Time of Edward I* 460 (2d ed. 1898) (citing Select Pleas of the Crown, p. 3) (villein).

160. 2 Frederick Pollock and Frederic William Maitland, *The History of English Law Before the Time of Edward I* 548 (2d ed. 1898).

161. See Gustav Radbruch, "Der Ursprung des Strafrechts aus dem Stande der Unfreien," in *Elegantiae Juris Criminalis: Vierzehn Studien zur Geschichte des Strafrechts* (2d ed. 1950). To say that all members of the macro household were now eligible for afflictive punishment, however, does not mean that all status distinctions among sanctions disappeared. As a matter of fact, if not always of law, higher status members of the macro household—and micro householders in particular—generally remained beyond the scope of afflictive punishment in general and corporal punishment in particular.

162. Pollock and Maitland have been taken to task, repeatedly, for failing to appreciate that the old system of *bót* and *wíte* wasn't all that different from the new practice of amercements, and for thinking, mistakenly, that whatever significant transition did occur—if not from *bót* and *wíte* to amercement, then *within* the old *wergild* system itself—actually took place before, rather than after, the Conquest. See, e.g., Patrick Wormald, "Maitland and Anglo-Saxon Law: Beyond Domesday Book," in *The History of English Law: Centenary Essays on "Pollock and Maitland"* (Proceedings of the British Academy No. 89) 1, 14 (John Hudson ed. 1996); John Hudson, "Maitland and Anglo-Norman Law," in id., 21, 44–45; Henry Summerson, "Maitland and the Criminal Law in the Age of *Bracton*," in id., 115, 117.

163. Frederic William Maitland, "Domesday Book," in *Domesday and Beyond: Three Essays in the Early History of England* 1, 33 (1966) (1897).

164. Id. at 99. "The Anglo-Saxon *ceorl*, from being the typical free householder sank into the position of a churl sitting on land burdened with rent (*gafol*). The Frankish *villanus*, which ought to designate a member of the township, came to be regarded as a man of vile, low origin and condition." Paul Vinogradoff, "Foundations of Society," 2 *Cambridge Medieval History* 630, 652 (1913).

165. Id. at 151.

166. Frederic William Maitland, "England before the Conquest," in *Domesday and Beyond: Three Essays in the Early History of England* 220, 321 (1966) (1897).

167. Frederic William Maitland, "Domesday Book," in id. 1, 34; see also 1 Frederick Pollock and Frederic William Maitland, *The History of English Law Before the Time of Edward I* 421–22 (2d ed. 1898) (taxation).

168. 1 Frederick Pollock and Frederic William Maitland, *The History of English Law Before the Time of Edward I* 419 (2d ed. 1898); 2 Frederick Pollock and Frederic William Maitland, *The History of English Law Before the Time of Edward I* 529 (2d ed. 1898).

169. See J. B. Schneewind, *The Invention of Autonomy: A History of Modern Moral Philosophy* (1998).

170. See Paul Vinogradoff, "Feudalism," 3 *Cambridge Medieval History* 458, 470 (1924) ("[T]he circle of tenants constituting the peers' court was a most complete expression of the principle of equality as between allied sovereigns."); Frederick Pollock, "The King's Peace in the Middle Ages," 13 *Harv. L. Rev.* 177, 187 (1900) ("transformation of the jury . . . from a special commission of inquiry into a regular and necessary tribunal, and from a piece of superior administrative machinery into a popular and representative institution").

171. 1 James Leigh Strachan-Davidson, *Problems of the Roman Criminal Law* 170 (1912).

172. 2 Frederick Pollock and Frederic William Maitland, *The History of English Law Before the Time of Edward I* 465 (2d ed. 1898).

173. Christopher G. Tiedeman, *A Treatise on the Limitations of Police Power in the United States Considered From Both a Civil and Criminal Standpoint* 23 (1886); see generally Rudolf His, *Deutsches Strafrecht bis zur Karolina* 4–5 (1928).

174. 2 Frederick Pollock and Frederic William Maitland, *The History of English Law Before the Time of Edward I* 467 n.3, 497 (2d ed. 1898).

175. Rudolf His, *Deutsches Strafrecht bis zur Karolina* 5 (1928). There may be a more straightforward explanation for treating larceny as harshly as treason: because both were felonia, a direct violation of the obligation of fealty. See Patrick Wormald, "Maitland and Anglo-Saxon Law: Beyond Domesday Book," in *The History of English Law: Centenary Essays on "Pollock and Maitland"* (Proceedings of the British Academy No. 89) 1, 15 (John Hudson ed. 1996) ("the 'oath and pledge' taken by twelve-year-olds extended fidelity to disavowal of theft").

176. 2 Frederick Pollock and Frederic William Maitland, *The History of English Law Before the Time of Edward I* 493 (2d ed. 1898).

177. See Garcia v. Territory, 1 N.M. 415 (1869).

178. See the old doctrine of homicide "avec guet-apens" in French criminal law. Code Pénal art. 296 ("meurtre commis avec préméditation ou guet-apens").

179. This leveling results in a sort of equality, "the equality of household members before the despotic power of the household head." Hannah Arendt, *The Human Condition* 39 (1958). One might think of this equality as equal inferiority, *police* equality, as opposed to *legal* equality, as it retains the fundamental distinction between ruler and ruled which law denies.

180. 1 James Leigh Strachan-Davidson, *Problems of the Roman Criminal Law* 172 (1912).

181. Joel Prentiss Bishop, *New Commentaries on the Criminal Law* 534–38 (8th ed. 1892).

182. Id. at 531.

183. Id. at 532.

184. 1 Frederick Pollock and Frederic William Maitland, *The History of English Law Before the Time of Edward I* 415–16, 437 (2d ed. 1898); Paul R. Hyams, *King, Lords and Peasants in Medieval England: The Common Law of Villeinage in the Twelfth and Thirteenth Centuries* 127 (1968). The other exception to the general rule that villeins had no access to royal courts to seek a remedy against harm suffered at the hands of their lord makes the same point. No matter how rightless they might be in other respects vis-à-vis their lord, villeins always could make it before a royal court by accusing their lord of sedition, or serious disloyalty against their common macro householder, the king. Paul R. Hyams, *King, Lords and Peasants in Medieval England: The Common Law of Villeinage in the Twelfth and Thirteenth Centuries* 135–36 (1968).

185. Beirne Stedman, "Right of Husband to Chastise Wife," 3 *Virginia Law Register [N.S.]* 241, 245 (1917) (quoting State v. Mabrey, 64 N.C. 592, 593 [1870]).

186. United States v. Clark, 31 F. 710 (U.S. Cir. Ct. E.D. Mich. 1887) (emphasis added).

187. Hudson v. McMillian, 503 U.S. 1 (1992).

188. This limitation on prison disciplinary measures is to be distinguished from that placed upon the conduct of prison officials in furtherance of their duty to inflict the judicially prescribed punishment. There the threshold is "deliberate indifference." Estelle v. Gamble, 429 U.S. 97 (1976).

189. Foote v. State, 59 Md. 264 (1883).

190. Paul R. Hyams, *King, Lords and Peasants in Medieval England: The Common Law of Villeinage in the Twelfth and Thirteenth Centuries* 128 (1968).

191. Id. at 135–36.

192. For a medieval analogue, see id. at 127–28, 151 (villeins as royal subjects). The implications of extending royal protection to slaves—and villeins—for the inferior status of masters was as clear to English lords in the twelfth century as it was to Virginia plantation owners in the eighteenth. Southern plantation owners, in fact, often thought of themselves as manor lords, and as such "[n]ot only . . . assume[d] control over their households and slaves, they resented and opposed the intrusion into their own affairs." Michael Stephen Hindus, *Prison and Plantation: Crime, Justice, and Authority in Massachusetts and South Carolina, 1767–1878*, at 9 (1980) (South Carolina low country).

193. Arthur P. Scott, *Criminal Law in Colonial Virginia* 202 (1930).

194. See generally Naomi D. Hurnard, *The King's Pardon for Homicide Before A.D. 1307* (1969); see also Thomas A. Green, "Societal Concepts of Criminal Liability in Mediaeval England," 47 *Speculum* 669 (1972).

195. See J. H. Baker, *An Introduction to English Legal History* 601 (3d ed. 1990) (excusable homicide "'contempt' to the king for depriving him of a subject").

196. Cf. The Queen v. Dudley and Stephens, 14 Q.B.D. 273 (1884) (court convicts defendants on the ground that necessity is no defense to murder, as a matter of law, precipitating their royal pardon, as a matter of mercy).

197. Cf. Harold J. Berman, *Law and Revolution: The Formation of the Western Legal Tradition* 191 (1983) (*contemptus* in canon law). Consider, in this context, the case of John de Warenne, who in 1270 severely wounded Alan de la Zouche in Westminster. As J. M. Kaye points out, "the real enormity of Warenne's offence was not so much the wounding of Alan, for which an amercement would ordinarily have sufficed, as the contempt to the king shown by the violation of the peace of his hall." It's the "deliberate, intentional insult to the king," according to Kaye, that calls for disciplinary action, not the "wounding *ex malitia praecogitata*." J.M. Kaye, "The Early History of Murder and Manslaughter," 83 *Law Q. Rev.* 365, 374 (1967).

198. Id. at 201, 203.

199. Id. at 199.

200. Id. at 200.

201. Joel Prentiss Bishop, *New Commentaries on the Criminal Law* 530–31 (8th ed. 1892).

202. That rule is subject to famous exceptions, chief among them Lochner v. New York, 198 U.S. 45 (1905), which was thought so exceptional it ushered in its very own "era" of Supreme Court jurisprudence, which lasted thirty years.

203. On the importance of self-police in American slave government, see Ariela L. Gross, "'Like Master, Like Man': Construing Whiteness in the Commercial Law of Slavery, 1800–1861," 18 *Cardozo L. Rev.* 263, 275–82 (1996) ("statesmanship").

204. John Locke, *Second Treatise of Government* § 151 (1690) (emphasis added).

205. Preamble, Constitution of Pennsylvania (September 28, 1776).

206. John Locke, *Second Treatise of Government* § 235 (1690).

207. Id. § 200.

208. James I, *The True Law of Free Monarchy, or the reciprocall and mutuall duty betwixt a free King and His naturall Subjects* 4–5 (1642) (1st ed. 1598).

209. See Frederick Pollock, "Locke's Theory of the State," 2 *Proceedings of the British Academy* 237–49 (1904).

210. For an interesting discussion of patriarchal elements in Hobbes's political theory, see Carole Pateman, *The Sexual Contract* 46–50 (1988).

211. John Locke, *Second Treatise of Government* § 147 (1690).

2. Blackstone's Police

1. Jean Jacques Rousseau, *Discourse on Political Economy* (1755).

2. Id.

3. Id.

4. 1 William Blackstone, *Commentaries on the Laws of England* 264 (1765).

5. 4 William Blackstone, *Commentaries on the Laws of England* 162 (1769).

6. Id. at 127.

7. Id. at 162.

8. See Ernst Freund, *The Police Power: Public Policy and Constitutional Rights* 2 & n.2 (1904).

9. 1 William Blackstone, *Commentaries on the Laws of England* 354 (1765).

10. On the patriarchal tradition in Western political thought, see generally Gordon J. Schochet, *Patriarchalism in Political Thought: The Authoritarian Family and Political Speculation and Attitudes Especially in Seventeenth-Century England* (1975); Carole Pateman, *The Sexual Contract* (1988) (with particular emphasis on men's patriarchal right over women).

11. See Jean Jacques Rousseau, *A Discourse on Political Economy* (1755).

12. Cf. 2. Reichspolizeiordnung of June 30, 1548 (quoted in Georg-Christoph von Unruh, "Polizei, Polizeiwissenschaft und Kameralistik," in 1 *Deutsche Verwaltungsgeschichte (Vom Spät-*

mittelalter bis zum Ende des Reiches) 388, 393–94 [Kurt G. A. Jeserich, Hans Pohl and Georg-Christoph von Unruh eds. 1983] (imperial ordinance instructing householders to ensure that their servants and children refrain from blasphemy and drunkenness).

13. 23 Edw. 3, New Statute, c. 1 (1349), 25 Edw. 3, Stat. 1, c. 1 (1350).

14. 27 Hen. 8, c. 25 (1536).

15. 39 Eliz c. 17; 4 William Blackstone, *Commentaries on the Laws of England* 165 (1769).

16. 1 & 2 Ph. & M. c. 4 & 5 Eliz. c. 20; 4 William Blackstone, *Commentaries on the Laws of England* 165, 166 (1769).

17. Arthur P. Scott, *Criminal Law in Colonial Virginia* 273–74 (1930).

18. Laws of Æthelstan (924–939 A.D.), c. 2, in 4 *The Library of Original Sources* 232 (Oliver J. Thatcher ed. 1907).

19. Quoted in Robert J. Steinfeld, *The Invention of Free Labor: The Employment Relation in English and American Law and Culture, 1350–1870*, at 58 (1991).

20. Id.

21. On warning out, see Ruth Wallis Herndon, *Unwelcome Americans Living on the Margin in Early New England* (2001); Josiah Henry Benton, *Warning Out in New England* (1911); see also Marilyn Baseler, *"Asylum for Mankind": America, 1607–1800* (1998). Transients were not warned out if they were servants and "responsible to a master." Douglas Lamar Jones, "The Strolling Poor: Transiency in Eighteenth-Century Massachusetts," 8 *J. Social Hist.* 28, 43, 48 (1975).

22. 4 William Blackstone, *Commentaries on the Laws of England* 170 (1769).

23. Id. at 249.

24. Id. at 250.

25. On the use of peace bonds in colonial Pennsylvania, see Kathryn Preyer, "Penal Measures in the American Colonies: An Overview," 26 *Am. J. Legal Hist.* 326, 337 (1982); see also David H. Flaherty, "Crime and Social Control in Provincial Massachusetts," 24 *Historical Journal* 339, 351 (1981) (imposition of "bonds for good behaviour" in colonial Massachusetts, including upon acquitted persons).

26. 4 William Blackstone, *Commentaries on the Laws of England* 253 (1769).

27. 1 William Blackstone, *Commentaries on the Laws of England* 269 (1765).

28. 2 Frederick Pollock and Frederic William Maitland, *The History of English Law Before the Time of Edward I* 501 n.1 (counterfeiting punished as treason by drawing and hanging), 504–05 (forgery punished as treason) (2d ed. 1898).

29. 4 William Blackstone, *Commentaries on the Laws of England* 163 (1769).

30. The association between stranger and enemy remains strong. Modern sociology has added little to Abraham Lincoln's observation that "[f]rom the first appearance of man upon the earth, down to very recent times, the words *"stranger"* and *"enemy"* were *quite* or *almost,* synonymous." Address before the Wisconsin State Agricultural Society, Milwaukee, Wisconsin, Sept. 30, 1859.

31. 4 William Blackstone, *Commentaries on the Laws of England* 170 (1769).

32. For an excellent recent study of sumptuary laws, see Alan Hunt, *Governance of the Consuming Passions: A History of Sumptuary Law* (1996).

33. 4 William Blackstone, *Commentaries on the Laws of England* 171–74 (1769).

34. 22 Hen. VII. c. 9 (1541–42).

35. Cf. the offense of "criminal impersonation" in modern American criminal law. See, e.g., N.Y. Penal Law §§ 190.25 ("[p]retends to be a public servant, or wears or displays without authority any uniform, badge, insignia or facsimile thereof by which such public servant is lawfully distinguished").

36. 4 William Blackstone, *Commentaries on the Laws of England* 174 (1769).

37. Id.

38. 1 William Blackstone, *Commentaries on the Laws of England* 410 (1765).

39. Id. at 416 (correction of apprentices and servants), 433 (wife), 440 (child).

40. Some members of the micro household, children, are potential future householders and will leave the original micro household to form their own. Paternal discipline of children thus benefits both the micro, and the macro, household in the short run, insofar as every member of

the micro household is also a member of the royal *über*family. In the long run, and this is a matter of great interest to the macro householder, properly disciplined children will become competent householders, and therefore competent administrators within the macro household of the king, long after they have left their father's micro household behind. See Aristotle, *Politics* bk. I, xiii.

41. See, e.g., Robert A. Ferguson, *Law and Letters in American Culture* 11 (1984).

42. Ernst Freund, *The Police Power: Public Policy and Constitutional Rights* 2 & n.2 (1904).

43. Thomas M. Cooley, *A Treatise on the Constitutional Limitations Which Rest Upon the Legislative Power of the States of the American Union* 704 n.1 (6th ed. 1890); Christopher G. Tiedeman, *A Treatise on the Limitations of Police Power in the United States Considered From Both a Civil and Criminal Standpoint* 2 (1886); Ernst Freund, *The Police Power: Public Policy and Constitutional Rights* 2 (1904).

44. Eells v. People, 5 Ill. 498 (1843).

45. Commonwealth v. McHale, 97 Pa. 397, 408 (1881).

46. See also Adam Smith, *Lectures on Jurisprudence* 486 (R.L. Meed et al. eds. 1978); Jeremy Bentham, "An Introduction to the Principles of Morals and Legislation," ch. XVI, in 1 *The Works of Jeremy Bentham* 102 n.† (John Bowring ed. 1962) (1789).

47. Jonathan A. Bush, "Free to Enslave: The Foundations of Colonial American Slave Law," 5 *Yale J. L. & Humanities* 417, 462 (1993).

48. David Thomas Konig, "'Dale's Laws' and the Non-Common Law Origins of Criminal Justice in Virginia," 26 *Am. J. Legal Hist.* 354–375 (1982); see generally Jonathan A. Bush, "Free to Enslave: The Foundations of Colonial American Slave Law," 5 *Yale J. L. & Humanities* 417, 460 (1993).

49. Raphael Semmes, *Crime and Punishment in Early Maryland* 1–4 (1938); Arthur P. Scott, *Criminal Law in Colonial Virginia* 164 (1930).

50. Herbert William Keith Fitzroy, "The Punishment of Crime in Provincial Pennsylvania," *Pa. Mag. Hist. & Biography* 242 (July 1936).

51. Robert J. Steinfeld, *The Invention of Free Labor: The Employment Relation in English and American Law and Culture, 1350–1870*, at 57 (1991). On church discipline in colonial Massachusetts, see Emil Oberholzer, *Delinquent Saints: Disciplinary Action in the Early Congregational Churches of Massachusetts* (1956).

52. Robert J. Steinfeld, *The Invention of Free Labor: The Employment Relation in English and American Law and Culture, 1350–1870*, at 57 (1991).

53. Id. at 58.

54. See J.B. Schneewind, *The Invention of Autonomy: A History of Modern Moral Philosophy* 251, 509 (1998).

55. Julius Goebel, "King's Law and Local Custom in Seventeenth Century England," 31 *Colum. L. Rev.* 416 (1931).

56. Jonathan A. Bush, "Free to Enslave: The Foundations of Colonial American Slave Law," 5 *Yale J. L. & Humanities* 417 (1993).

57. Id. at 426.

58. Id. at 433. Note, once more, the inclusion of omission and status offenses, also familiar from Blackstone's compendium of police offenses.

59. Id. at 434.

60. Cf. Arthur P. Scott, *Criminal Law in Colonial Virginia* 303 (1930) (discussing 1680 Virginia statute providing that "for lifting a hand in opposition to any Christian a negro was to receive thirty lashes").

3. Continental Police Science

1. Queen Anne, 13 Dec. 1714.

2. "Police," n., *Oxford English Dictionary*, at 1069, 1069, col. 2 (definition 3.).

3. See *Lectures on Justice, Police, Revenue and Arms delivered in the University of Glasgow By*

Adam Smith Reported by a Student in 1763 (Edwin Cannan ed. 1896); see generally Adam Smith, *Lectures on Jurisprudence* (R.L. Meed, D.D. Raphael, and P.G. Stein eds. 1978). On Smith, see also Mark Neocleous, *The Fabrication of Social Order: A Critical Theory of Police Power* ch. 2 (2000); Mariana Valverde, *Law's Dream of a Common Knowledge* ch. 6 (2003).

4. Introduction, Adam Smith, *Lectures on Jurisprudence* 1, 3 (R.L. Meed, D.D. Raphael, and P.G. Stein eds. 1978) (quoting Dugald Stewart, Account of the Life and Writings of Adam Smith, LL.D.).

5. Adam Smith, *Juris Prudence or Notes from the Lectures on Justice, Police, Revenue, and Arms delivered in the University of Glasgow by Adam Smith Professor of Moral Philosophy, in Lectures on Jurisprudence* 396, 398 (R.L. Meed, D.D. Raphael, and P.G. Stein eds. 1978).

6. Id.

7. A fellow Scot, who later made his career in London, personified the comprehensiveness of police: Patrick Colquhoun (1745–1820). Colquhoun was a police scientist of continental ambition. Most relevant for our purposes, he called for the establishment of a national police system ("A treatise on the police of the metropolis" [1795]). He also wrote, among many other things, a treatise on river police ("A treatise on the commerce and police of the river Thames"[1798]), education police ("A new and appropriate system of education for the labouring people; . . . containing an exposition of the nature and importance of the design, as it respects the general interest of the community: with *details, explanatory of the particular economy of the institution,* and the methods prescribed for the purpose of securing and preserving a greater degree of moral rectitude, as a means of *preventing criminal offences by habits of temperance, industry, subordination, and loyalty, among that useful class of the community,* comprising the labouring people of England" [1806]) (emphasis added), as well as treatises on the police of the micro household ("Useful suggestions favourable to the comfort of the labouring people, and of *decent housekeepers* explaining how a small income may be made to go far in a family, so as to occasion a considerable saving in the article of bread" (1795) (emphasis added) and, eventually, the macro household, a sort of *Wealth of Nations* for the British Empire ("A treatise on the wealth, power, and resources of the British Empire" [1814]). Not surprisingly, Colquhoun's works on police science were quickly translated into French and German. See, e.g., *Traité sur la police de Londres* (L. Collin trans. 1807); *P. Colquhoun's Polizey von London* (J.W. Volkmann trans. 1802). On Colquhoun, see also Mark Neocleous, *The Fabrication of Social Order: A Critical Theory of Police Power* ch. 3 (2000); Mariana Valverde, *Law's Dream of a Common Knowledge* ch. 6 (2003).

8. In fact, there are perhaps only two features of police that could claim something like widespread agreement. One is that it's indefinable. The other is that it's French. See, e.g., Jeremy Bentham, "An Introduction to the Principles of Morals and Legislation" ch. XVI, in 1 *The Works of Jeremy Bentham* 102 n.† (John Bowring ed. 1962) (1789); L.A. Warnkönig, *Französische Staatsgeschichte* 309, 365, 474 (1846) (quoted in Georg-Christoph von Unruh, "Polizei, Polizeiwissenschaft und Kameralistik," in 1 *Deutsche Verwaltungsgeschichte (Vom Spätmittelalter bis zum Ende des Reiches)* 388, 390 n.3 [Kurt G.A. Jeserich, Hans Pohl and Georg-Christoph von Unruh eds. 1983]); see also Mark Neocleous, *The Fabrication of Social Order: A Critical Theory of Police Power* 9–11 (2000).

9. "Police," n., *Oxford English Dictionary,* at 1069, 1069, col. 2 (definition 3.).

10. Report of 1762–3, Adam Smith, *Lectures on Jurisprudence* 1, 331 (R.L. Meed, D.D. Raphael, and P.G. Stein eds. 1978) (original spelling retained). Smith also specifically refers to de la Mare's famous and weighty treatise on police. Id. at 332 (citing Nicolas de la Mare, *Traité de la Police* [1705–38]).

11. This was the title of Smith's lectures, according to student notes. See Adam Smith, *Juris Prudence or Notes from the Lectures on Justice, Police, Revenue, and Arms delivered in the University of Glasgow by Adam Smith Professor of Moral Philosophy, in Lectures on Jurisprudence* (R.L. Meed, D.D. Raphael, and P.G. Stein eds. 1978). The significance of this title isn't clear, of course, and it's probably best not to place to much weight on it. Cf. *J. Inst.* 1.1.1 (classic definition of iuris prudentia); 2 Bracton, *De Legibus* 25.

12. "Police," n., *Oxford English Dictionary,* at 1069, 1069, col. 2 (definition 3.).

13. Id.

14. 1 William Blackstone, *Commentaries on the Laws of England* 264 (1765).

15. 4 William Blackstone, *Commentaries on the Laws of England* 162 (1769). At around the same time, John Erskine, the Professor of Municipal Law at the University of Edinburgh, wrote in his *Institute of the Law of Scotland*, that "[o]ffences against the laws enacted for the police or good government of a country are truly crimes against the state." John Erskine, *An Institute of the Law of Scotland* 1095 (Alexander MacAllen ed., Edinburgh 1838) (1773); see "Police," n., *Oxford English Dictionary*, at 1069, 1069, col. 2 (definition 3.). Erskine died in 1768, and the first edition of the *Institute* was published posthumously in 1773. John Erskine, *An Institute of the Law of Scotland* v–vi (Alexander MacAllen ed., Edinburgh 1838) (1773). His reference to "police or good government" appears at the outset of a short section on "Offences against the Laws of Police.— Forestallers and Regraters," and is almost exclusively devoted to a brief discussion of "forestalling" and "regrating" merchandise, and corn in particular, a crime of considerable "enormity" due to "its mischievous consequences to the commonwealth." John Erskine, *An Institute of the Law of Scotland* 1095 (Alexander MacAllen ed. 1838) (1768). This section is followed by similarly short sections on the "Punishment of Sturdy Beggars and Vagabonds" and "Smaller Offences.—Breaking Inclosures, Destroying Timber, Killing Game, Salmon, &c.," after which Erskine turns his attention to "Murder." His treatment of offenses against the police completes his discussion of "Crimes against the State," which in turns follow that of "Crimes against God." Id. at 1085. Perhaps most interesting is Erskine's differentiation among crimes against the state: "some are levelled immediately against the supreme power, and strike at the constitution itself, while others merely discover such a contempt and disregard to the law as may contribute to baffle its authority, or slacken the reins of government." Presumably police offenses would fall in the last category. Id. at 1086.

16. 1 William Blackstone, *Commentaries on the Laws of England* 355 (1765).

17. L.A. Warnkönig, *Französische Staatsgeschichte* 309, 365, 474 (1846) (quoted in Georg-Christoph von Unruh, "Polizei, Polizeiwissenschaft und Kameralistik," in 1 *Deutsche Verwaltungsgeschichte (Vom Spätmittelalter bis zum Ende des Reiches)* 388, 390 n.3 [Kurt G.A. Jeserich, Hans Pohl and Georg-Christoph von Unruh eds. 1983]).

18. So when Christoph Martin Wieland went to Weimar in 1772 to serve as tutor for the 15-year-old crown prince Carl August of Saxony, he instructed him in, among other things, state economy and police science. Drefa-Projektgruppe, Geschichte Mitteldeutschland, Christoph Martin Wieland, http://www.mdr.de/geschichte/archiv/personen/c-m-wieland.htm [Apr. 8, 2001].

19. See, e.g., 4 William Blackstone, *Commentaries on the Laws of England* 3 (1769); Thomas Jefferson, A Bill for Proportioning Crimes and Punishments §§ iv, xii, xiii, xiv (1778); Thomas Jefferson, *Autobiography* (1821); James Wilson, Executive Department, Lectures on Law, in 2 *The Works of James Wilson* 442–44 (Robert Green McCloskey ed. 1967) (1791); Benjamin Rush, *An Enquiry into the Effects of Public Punishments Upon Criminals and Upon Society* (1787); see generally Bernard Baylin, *The Ideological Origins of the American Revolution* 27 (2d ed. 1992).

20. Cesare Beccaria Bonesana, *Elementi di economia pubblica* 23 (1804) (quoted and translated in Pasquale Pasquino, "Theatrum Politicum: The Genealogy of Capital—Police and the State of Prosperity," in *The Foucault Effect: Studies in Governmentality* 105, 109 [Graham Burchell, Colin Gordon, and Peter Miller eds. 1991]). On Beccaria's influence, see Christopher L. Tomlins, *Law, Labor, and Ideology in the Early American Republic* 43 n.23 (1993).

21. Cesare Beccaria, *A Discourse on Public Economy and Commerce* (1804).

22. See supra. ch. 2.

23. On Vattel's influence, see William J. Novak, *The People's Welfare: Law and Regulation in Nineteenth-Century America* 29, 263 n.46 (1996).

24. See, e.g., License Cases, 46 U.S. 504, 618, 628 (1847) (Woodbury, J., concurring) (citing Vattel, B. 1, ch. 19, §§ 219, 231).

25. Emmerich de Vattel, *The Law of Nations or, Principles of the Law of Nature, applied to the Conduct and Affairs of Nations and Sovereigns* § 172, at 82 (Joseph Chitty trans., ed. 1852).

26. Id. § 174, at 83.

27. Id.

28. Thomas M. Cooley, *A Treatise on the Constitutional Limitations Which Rest Upon the Legislative Power of the States of the American Union* 704 n.1 (6th ed. 1890).

29. Jeremy Bentham, "An Introduction to the Principles of Morals and Legislation" ch. XVI, in 1 *The Works of Jeremy Bentham* 101 (John Bowring ed. 1962) (1789).

30. Id. at 102.

31. Jeremy Bentham, *The Theory of Legislation* 242 (C.K. Ogden ed. 1931).

32. See, e.g., Albert Cremer, "L'administration dans les encyclopédies et dictionnaires français du 17e et du 18e siècle," in *Formation und Transformation des Verwaltungswissens in Frankreich und Deutschland (18./19. Jh.)*, 1 *Jahrbuch für Europäische Verwaltungsgeschichte* 1, 1 (1989) (quoting Louis XIV's 1667 order to separate "la Justice contentieuse & distributive" from police "qui consiste à assurer le repos du Public & des Particuliers, à purger la Ville de ce qui peut causer les desordres, à procurer l'abondance, & à faire vivre chacun selon sa condition & son devoir").

33. Jeremy Bentham, "An Introduction to the Principles of Morals and Legislation" ch. XVI, in 1 *The Works of Jeremy Bentham* 102 n.† (John Bowring ed. 1962) (1789).

34. Id.

35. See Jeremy Bentham, "Anarchical Fallacies, Being an Examination of the Declaration of Rights Issued During the French Revolution" (1791), in 2 *The Works of Jeremy Bentham* 501 (John Bowring ed. 1843).

36. Jeremy Bentham, *The Theory of Legislation* 271 (C.K. Ogden ed. 1931) (emphasis in the original). Note the disease metaphor, which appears frequently in writings on police in general, and on police as criminal law in particular. See, e.g., Alexander Hamilton, "Federalist" No. 28, at 146, 146 ("seditions and insurrections" as "maladies as inseparable from the body politic as tumors and eruptions from the natural body"); Tomas J. Philipson and Richard A. Posner, "The Economic Epidemiology of Crime," 39 *J. Law & Econ.* 405 (1996).

37. Jeremy Bentham, *The Theory of Legislation* 270 (C.K. Ogden ed. 1931).

38. Georg-Christoph von Unruh, "Polizei, Polizeiwissenschaft und Kameralistik," in 1 *Deutsche Verwaltungsgeschichte (Vom Spätmittelalter bis zum Ende des Reiches)* 388, 390 (Kurt G.A. Jeserich, Hans Pohl and Georg-Christoph von Unruh eds. 1983).

39. Franz-Ludwig Knemeyer, "Polizei," in 4 *Geschichtliche Grundbegriffe: Historisches Lexikon zur politisch-sozialen Sprache in Deutschland* 875, 878 (Otto Brunner, Werner Conze, and Reinhart Koselleck eds. 1978).

40. James Goldschmidt, *Das Verwaltungsstrafrecht* 70 (1902) (citing Reichsregimentsordnung of 1495 § 40).

41. 1. Reichspolizeiordnung of Nov. 19, 1530 (quoted in Georg-Christoph von Unruh, "Polizei, Polizeiwissenschaft und Kameralistik," in 1 *Deutsche Verwaltungsgeschichte [Vom Spätmittelalter bis zum Ende des Reiches]* 388, 393 [Kurt G.A. Jeserich, Hans Pohl and Georg-Christoph von Unruh eds. 1983]).

42. 2. Reichspolizeiordnung of June 30, 1548 (quoted in Georg-Christoph von Unruh, "Polizei, Polizeiwissenschaft und Kameralistik," in 1 *Deutsche Verwaltungsgeschichte (Vom Spätmittelalter bis zum Ende des Reiches)* 388, 393 [Kurt G.A. Jeserich, Hans Pohl and Georg-Christoph von Unruh eds. 1983]).

43. 2. Reichspolizeiordnung of June 30, 1548 (quoted in Georg-Christoph von Unruh, "Polizei, Polizeiwissenschaft und Kameralistik," in 1 *Deutsche Verwaltungsgeschichte (Vom Spätmittelalter bis zum Ende des Reiches)* 388, 394 [Kurt G.A. Jeserich, Hans Pohl and Georg-Christoph von Unruh eds. 1983]).

44. Georg-Christoph von Unruh, "Polizei, Polizeiwissenschaft und Kameralistik," in 1 *Deutsche Verwaltungsgeschichte (Vom Spätmittelalter bis zum Ende des Reiches)* 388, 411 [Kurt G.A. Jeserich, Hans Pohl and Georg-Christoph von Unruh eds. 1983]); see also Michel Foucault, "Governmentality," in *The Foucault Effect: Studies in Governmentality* 87, 102 (Graham Burchell, Colin Gordon, and Peter Miller eds. 1991).

45. Justus Christoph Dithmar, *Einleitung in die oeconomische Policei- und Cameral-Wissenschaften* 4, 1, § 4 (1745); see also 1 Johann Christian Majer, *Teutsches weltliches Staatsrecht* 102 (1775) (cited in Franz-Ludwig Knemeyer, "Polizei," in *Geschichtliche Grundbegriffe: His-*

torisches Lexikon zur politisch-sozialen Sprache in Deutschland 875, 885 [Otto Brunner, Werner Conze, and Reinhart Koselleck eds. 1978]).

46. Guillaume de La Perrière, *Miroir politique* (1576) (quoted in Michel Foucault, "Governmentality," in *The Foucault Effect: Studies in Governmentality* 87, 89 [Graham Burchell, Colin Gordon, and Peter Miller eds. 1991]).

47. Michel Foucault, "Governmentality," in *The Foucault Effect: Studies in Governmentality* 87, 95 (Graham Burchell, Colin Gordon, and Peter Miller eds. 1991). The ahuman nature of the objects of police can also be seen in a peculiar American usage of the term that appeared in the nineteenth century and continues today. In the American military, to police means "to make or keep clean or orderly." "Police," v., *Oxford English Dictionary*, at 1070, 1070, col. 1 (definition 2.b.). The result of this policing is the police of the camp. And the soldiers assigned to perform the police task are called, police. "Police," n., *The American Heritage Dictionary of the English Language: Fourth Edition* (2000) (definitions 3.a. and b.). The task of the military police thus, all in all, is to "preserve civil order and attend to sanitary arrangements." "Police," n., *Webster's Revised Unabridged Dictionary* (1913) (definition 4.). Thanks to Robert Steinfeld for bringing this usage to my attention.

48. On the irrelevance of persuasion in household governance, see Hannah Arendt, *The Human Condition* 26–27 (1958).

49. Jablonski, *Lexikon*, vol. 2, at 824 (2d ed. 1748) (cited in Franz-Ludwig Knemeyer, "Polizei," in *Geschichtliche Grundbegriffe: Historisches Lexikon zur politisch-sozialen Sprache in Deutschland* 875, 882 [Otto Brunner, Werner Conze, and Reinhart Koselleck eds. 1978]); see also Johann Heinrich Ludwig Bergius, "Cammersachen," in 2 *Policey- und Cameral-Magazin* 65 (1768) (cited in Franz-Ludwig Knemeyer, "Polizei," in *Geschichtliche Grundbegriffe: Historisches Lexikon zur politisch-sozialen Sprache in Deutschland* 875, 885 [Otto Brunner, Werner Conze, and Reinhart Koselleck eds. 1978]).

50. Verordnung wegen verbesserter Einrichtung der Provinzial-Polizei und Finanzbehörden of Dec. 26, 1808, § 3 (cited in Franz-Ludwig Knemeyer, "Polizei," in *Geschichtliche Grundbegriffe: Historisches Lexikon zur politisch-sozialen Sprache in Deutschland* 875, 888 [Otto Brunner, Werner Conze, and Reinhart Koselleck eds. 1978]).

51. Michel Foucault, "Governmentality," in *The Foucault Effect: Studies in Governmentality* 87, 92 (Graham Burchell, Colin Gordon, and Peter Miller eds. 1991).

52. Id.

53. Georg-Christoph von Unruh, "Polizei, Polizeiwissenschaft und Kameralistik," in 1 *Deutsche Verwaltungsgeschichte (Vom Spätmittelalter bis zum Ende des Reiches)* 388, 421 (Kurt G.A. Jeserich, Hans Pohl and Georg-Christoph von Unruh eds. 1983).

54. See, e.g., Josias Ludwig Gosche, *Philosophische Aphorismen über Staatswirtschaft* 22 (1789) (cited in Franz-Ludwig Knemeyer, "Polizei," in *Geschichtliche Grundbegriffe: Historisches Lexikon zur politisch-sozialen Sprache in Deutschland* 875, 886 (Otto Brunner, Werner Conze, and Reinhart Koselleck eds. 1978).

55. Georg-Christoph von Unruh, "Polizei, Polizeiwissenschaft und Kameralistik," in 1 *Deutsche Verwaltungsgeschichte (Vom Spätmittelalter bis zum Ende des Reiches)* 388, 407–09 (Kurt G.A. Jeserich, Hans Pohl and Georg-Christoph von Unruh eds. [1983]).

56. Franz-Ludwig Knemeyer, "Polizei," in *Geschichtliche Grundbegriffe: Historisches Lexikon zur politisch-sozialen Sprache in Deutschland* 875, 897 (Otto Brunner, Werner Conze, and Reinhart Koselleck eds. 1978).

57. Id. at 883–84.

58. Jeremy Bentham, *The Theory of Legislation* 270 (C.K. Ogden ed. 1931).

59. Verordnung wegen verbesserter Einrichtung der Provinzial-Polizei und Finanzbehörden of Dec. 26, 1808, § 3 (cited in Franz-Ludwig Knemeyer, "Polizei," in *Geschichtliche Grundbegriffe: Historisches Lexikon zur politisch-sozialen Sprache in Deutschland* 875, 888 [Otto Brunner, Werner Conze, and Reinhart Koselleck eds. 1978]).

60. Id. § 50 (cited in Franz-Ludwig Knemeyer, "Polizei," in *Geschichtliche Grundbegriffe: Historisches Lexikon zur politisch-sozialen Sprache in Deutschland* 875, 891 [Otto Brunner, Werner Conze, and Reinhart Koselleck eds. 1978]).

61. Id. § 3 (cited in Franz-Ludwig Knemeyer, "Polizei," in *Geschichtliche Grundbegriffe: Historisches Lexikon zur politisch-sozialen Sprache in Deutschland* 875, 888 [Otto Brunner, Werner Conze, and Reinhart Koselleck eds. 1978]).

62. Id.

63. [Heinrich] Rosin, "Polizeiliche Strafverfügungen," in 2 *Wörterbuch des Deutschen Verwaltungsrechts* 266 (Karl von Stengel ed. 1890).

64. Paul Johann Anselm Feuerbach, "Über die Polizeistrafgesetzgebung überhaupt und den zweiten Teil eines 'Entwurfs des Strafgesetzbuchs, München 1822,'" in *Paul Johann Anselm Ritter von Feuerbachs Leben und Wirken* 590, 594, 597–99, 608–16 (Ludwig Feuerbach ed., 2d ed. 1852).

65. See, e.g., [Heinrich] Rosin, "Polizeistrafrecht," in 2 *Wörterbuch des Deutschen Verwaltungsrechts* 273, 275 (Karl von Stengel ed. 1890); cf. Christian Reinhold Köstlin, *Neue Revision der Grundbegriffe des Kriminalrechts* 28 (1845); Christian Reinhold Köstlin, *System des deutschen Strafrechts, I. Abteilung* (1855).

66. For a critical, and highly influential, discussion of Feuerbach's views, see Johann Michael Franz Birnbaum, "Ueber das Erforderniß einer Rechtsverletzung zum Begriffe des Verbrechens, mit besonderer Rücksicht auf den Begriff der Ehrenkränkung," *Archiv des Criminalrechts (Neue Folge)* 149 (1834). Birnbaum is credited with establishing that the purpose of criminal law is the protection of *Rechtsgüter* (legal goods), one of the central tenets of German criminal law. Framed as a critique of Feuerbach, who sought to limit criminal law to the protection of personal rights, Birnbaum's article mounts a sustained defense of police criminal law. The point of replacing rights with legal goods, or interests, was to make room for what in American criminal law came to be known as police offenses, i.e., offenses against various aspects of the public police, including the moral, and religious, police. See, e.g., id. at 160–62. Birnbaum made clear that, in the modern criminal law of police, the paradigmatic victim of criminal offenses was the state, whose interests the criminal law sought to protect. Id. at 161.

67. Paul Johann Anselm Feuerbach, "Über die Polizeistrafgesetzgebung überhaupt und den zweiten Teil eines 'Entwurfs des Strafgesetzbuchs, München 1822,'" in *Paul Johann Anselm Ritter von Feuerbachs Leben und Wirken* 590, 599 (Ludwig Feuerbach ed., 2d ed. 1852).

68. See, e.g., 1 Karl Binding, *Die Normen und ihre Übertretung* 409 (4th ed. 1922).

4. Policing the New Republic

1. 4 William Blackstone, *Commentaries on the Laws of England* 162 (1769).

2. Jean Jacques Rousseau, *Discourse on Political Economy* (1755).

3. On patriarchal elements of the modern "welfare state," see Carole Pateman, "The Patriarchal Welfare State," in *The Disorder of Women: Democracy, Feminism, and Political Theory* 179 (1989); see also *"Sicherheit" und "Wohlfahrt": Polizei, Gesellschaft und Herrschaft im 19. und 20. Jahrhundert* (Alf Lüdtke ed. 1992); Ralph Jessen, "Polizei, Wohlfahrt und die Anfänge des modernen Sozialstaats in Preußen während des Kaiserreichs," 20 *Geschichte und Gesellschaft* 157 (1994).

4. 4 William Blackstone, *Commentaries on the Laws of England* 127, 162 (1769).

5. Cf. Carole Pateman, *The Sexual Contract* 3, 32 and ch. 4 (1988) ("fraternal patriarchy"); see also Carole Pateman, "The Fraternal Social Contract," in *The Disorder of Women: Democracy, Feminism, and Political Theory* 33 (1989). Interestingly, as Pateman also points out, even the post hoc theorization of American government in John Rawls's work is formulated in terms of "heads of families," who in the public realm—most abstractly, the original position—make representative choices on behalf of their households. Carole Pateman, *The Sexual Contract* 43 (1988); see also id. at 45 (discussing Keith Tribe's work). In this light, the process of political legitimation appears as a continuous (re)particularization of autonomy, from the king to the states to the head of household, but no farther. Even in modern liberalist political theory, then, the unit of deliberation is still not the person, or the individual, but remains the householder.

6. See William J. Novak, "Common Regulation: Legal Origins of State Power in America," 45 *Hastings L.J.* 1061, 1077–78 (1994) (discussing 1830s reforms in Michigan and Massachusetts).

7. See generally Robert J. Steinfeld, "Property and Suffrage in the Early American Republic," 41 *Stan. L. Rev.* 335 (1989).

8. 1 William Blackstone, *Commentaries on the Laws of England* 171 (1765).

9. See Robert J. Steinfeld, "Property and Suffrage in the Early American Republic," 41 *Stan. L. Rev.* 335 (1989).

10. 27 Vt. 140 (1854).

11. Id. at 156.

12. Thomas Paine, *Common Sense* (1776).

13. Ernst Freund, *The Police Power: Public Policy and Constitutional Rights* 63 (1904); see also William J. Novak, "The Legal Origins of the Modern American State," in *Looking Back at Law's Century* 249, 269–70 (Austin Sarat, Bryant Garth, and Robert A. Kagan eds. 2002).

14. Alexander Hamilton, "Federalist" No. 15, at 73, 78; Alexander Hamilton, "Federalist" No. 21, at 106.

15. Alexander Hamilton, "Federalist" No. 16, at 81, 85.

16. Alexander Hamilton, "Federalist" No. 1, at 1, 3.

17. Alexander Hamilton, "Federalist" No. 28, at 146, 146.

18. Ernst Freund, *The Police Power: Public Policy and Constitutional Rights* 64 (1904); cf. 25 C.F.R. pt. 11 ("Law and Order on Indian Reservations") (extensive police regulation issued by the Bureau of Indian Affairs, part of the U.S. Department. of the Interior); Felix S. Cohen, *Handbook of Federal Indian Law* x, 91–93 (1948) (1941).

19. See 21 U.S.C. § 801(3). See also 21 U.S.C. § 801(2) ("substantial and detrimental effect on the health and general welfare of the American people," an open—but widely ignored—reference to the police functions of federal drug criminal law).

20. 514 U.S. 549 (1995).

21. Id. at 567.

22. Benjamin Rush to Prichard Price, June 2, 1787, in 1 *Letters of Benjamin Rush* 418–19 (L.H. Butterfield ed. 1951) (quoted in Gordon S. Wood, *The Creation of the American Republic, 1776–1787*, at 466 [2d ed. 1998]).

23. Benjamin Franklin to Charles Carroll, May 25, 1789, in 10 *The Writings of Benjamin Franklin* 7 (Albert Henry Smyth ed. 1907) (quoted in Gordon S. Wood, *The Creation of the American Republic, 1776–1787*, at 432 [2d ed. 1998]).

24. Gordon S. Wood, *The Creation of the American Republic, 1776–1787*, at 432 (2d ed. 1998).

25. Id. at 477.

26. William J. Novak, "Common Regulation: Legal Origins of State Power in America," 45 *Hastings L.J.* 1061, 1076 (1994).

27. Mariana Valverde regards "the metonymic technique of 'the list'" as typical of governance through police and identifies three central features: "(1) the heterogeneity of governance objects; (2) the simultaneous institution of very broad categories ('public nuisance,' for example) that create swamps of discretion; and (3) the dearth of theoretical justification for selecting these particular objects." Mariana Valverde, *Law's Dream of a Common Knowledge* 157–63 (2003).

28. William J. Novak, *The People's Welfare: Law & Regulation in Nineteenth-Century America* 11 (1996).

29. Ernst Freund, *The Police Power: Public Policy and Constitutional Rights* 2 and n.2 (1904).

30. Thomas Jefferson, A Bill for the More General Diffusion of Knowledge (1779).

31. Thomas Jefferson, *Autobiography* (1821).

32. Georg-Christoph von Unruh, "Polizei, Polizeiwissenschaft und Kameralistik," in 1 *Deutsche Verwaltungsgeschichte (Vom Spätmittelalter bis zum Ende des Reiches)* 388, 451 (Kurt G.A. Jeserich, Hans Pohl and Georg-Christoph von Unruh eds. 1983); see also David F. Lindenfeld, "The Decline of Polizeiwissenschaft: Continuity and Change in the Study of Administration in German Universities during the 19th Century," in *Formation und Transformation des Verwaltungswissens in Frankreich und Deutschland (18./19. Jh.)*, 1 *Jahrbuch für Europäische Verwaltungsgeschichte* 141 (1989). On the particular significance of police science at Göttingen, see Heinz Mohnhaupt, "Vorstufen der Wissenschaften von 'Verwaltung' und 'Verwaltungsrecht' an der Universität Göttingen (1750–1830)," in id. at 73–103; Michel Foucault, "The Political Technol-

ogy of Individuals," in *Technologies of the Self: A Seminar with Michel Foucault* 145, 158 (Luther H. Martin, Huck Gutman, and Patrick H. Hutton eds. 1988). Among the more prominent police scientists on the Göttingen faculty was Friedrich Christoph Dahlmann (1785–1860), one of the Göttingen Seven.

33. Georg-Christoph von Unruh, "Polizei, Polizeiwissenschaft und Kameralistik," in 1 *Deutsche Verwaltungsgeschichte (Vom Spätmittelalter bis zum Ende des Reiches)* 388, 451 (Kurt G.A. Jeserich, Hans Pohl and Georg-Christoph von Unruh eds. 1983).

34. Id.; see generally A.W. Small, *The Cameralists* (1909).

35. Thomas Jefferson, A Bill for Amending the Constitution of the College of William and Mary, and Substituting More Certain Revenues for Its Support, appendix (1779). Jefferson's reforms of William and Mary are discussed in some detail in Herbert Baxter Adams, "The College of William and Mary," 1 *Contributions to American Educational History* no. 1 (U.S. Board of Education, 1887). Writing in 1887, Adams laid particular stress on the parallels between Jefferson's reforms and continental police academies, and in fact advocated the creation of an American civil service academy dedicated to the study of police, or "scientific politics and good administration." Id. at 79. Adams was particularly taken with the *École Libre des Sciences Politiques* in Paris and the Prussian Statistical Bureau in Berlin, "a training school for university graduates of the highest ability in the art of administration, and in the conduct of statistical and other economic inquiries that are of interest and importance to the Government." Id. at 80. Note that by Adams's time, "police"—in Jefferson's chair of "law and police"—already required an explanatory footnote: "This was much the same as the modern science of administration, which is just beginning anew to creep into our university courses in America. What the German would call *Polizeiwissenschaft*, and what the Greeks termed πολιτεία, was taught for nearly a century at the college of William and Mary under the head of *"police."* That name would probably suggest nothing but constabulary associations to most college faculties in these modern days." Id. at 39 n.1.

36. On George Washington's plan for "a national school of politics and administration," see Herbert Baxter Adams, "The College of William and Mary," 1 *Contributions to American Educational History* no. 1, at 43–47 (U.S. Board of Education 1887). In his will, Washington called for the "establishment of a UNIVERSITY in a central part of the United States, to which the youths of fortune and talents from all parts thereof may be sent for the completion of their education, in all the branches of *polite* literature, in arts and sciences, *in acquiring knowledge in the principles of politics and good government.*" Id. at 43 (emphases added).

37. Thomas Jefferson, A Bill for the More General Diffusion of Knowledge (1779).

38. Id.

39. James I, *The True Law of Free Monarchy, or the reciprocall and mutuall duty betwixt a free King and His naturall Subjects* 4–5 (1642) (1st ed. Edinburgh 1598); see also John Locke, *Second Treatise of Government* § 170 (1690).

40. Veit Ludwig von Seckendorff, *Teutscher Fürstenstaat* (1656) (cited in Franz-Ludwig Knemeyer, "Polizei," in *Geschichtliche Grundbegriffe: Historisches Lexikon zur politisch-sozialen Sprache in Deutschland* 875, 885 [Otto Brunner, Werner Conze, and Reinhart Koselleck eds. 1978]).

41. Georg-Christoph von Unruh, "Polizei, Polizeiwissenschaft und Kameralistik," in 1 *Deutsche Verwaltungsgeschichte (Vom Spätmittelalter bis zum Ende des Reiches)* 388, 407 (Kurt G.A. Jeserich, Hans Pohl and Georg-Christoph von Unruh eds. 1983).

42. Verordnung wegen verbesserter Einrichtung der Provinzial-Polizei und Finanzbehörden of Dec. 26, 1808, § 3 (cited in Franz-Ludwig Knemeyer, Polizei, in *Geschichtliche Grundbegriffe: Historisches Lexikon zur politisch-sozialen Sprache in Deutschland* 875, 888 [Otto Brunner, Werner Conze, and Reinhart Koselleck eds. 1978]).

43. Compare the emphasis in Blackstone's oft-quoted police definition on "propriety" and "good manners." 4 William Blackstone, *Commentaries on the Laws of England* 162 (1769).

44. Thomas M. Cooley, *A Treatise on the Constitutional Limitations Which Rest Upon the Legislative Power of the States of the American Union* (6th ed. 1890) (emphasis added); Christopher G. Tiedeman, *A Treatise on the Limitations of Police Power in the United States Considered From Both a Civil and Criminal Standpoint* (1886) (emphasis added).

45. Ernst Freund, *The Police Power: Public Policy and Constitutional Rights* (1904).

46. Already by the mid-nineteenth century, a leading German scholar of police science (and administrative law), Lorenz von Stein, despaired that the subject of police was too vast to handle for any single person. See David F. Lindenfeld, "The Decline of Polizeiwissenschaft: Continuity and Change in the Study of Administration in German Universities during the 19th Century," in *Formation und Transformation des Verwaltungswissens in Frankreich und Deutschland (18./19. Jh.)*, 1 *Jahrbuch für Eurpäische Verwaltungsgeschichte* 141–59, 150 (1989).

47. Ernst Freund, *Standards of American Legislation* 66 (2d ed. 1965) (1st ed. 1917) (nuisance law "the common law of the police power, striking at all gross violations of health, safety, order, and morals").

48. 4 William Blackstone, *Commentaries on the Laws of England* 167 (1769).

49. N.Y. Penal Law of 1909, § 1530.

50. Cf. Christopher G. Tiedeman, *A Treatise on the Limitations of Police Power in the United States Considered From Both a Civil and Criminal Standpoint* 440 (1886).

51. Ernst Freund, *The Police Power: Public Policy and Constitutional Rights* 554 (1904).

52. See supra. ch. 2

53. 4 William Blackstone, *Commentaries on the Laws of England* 169 (1769).

54. Arthur P. Scott, *Criminal Law in Colonial Virginia* 179 (1930).

55. United States v. Royall, 27 F. Cas. 906 (Cir. Ct. D.C. 1829); see also Commonwealth v. Mohn, 52 Pa. 243 (1866).

56. Com. v. DeGrange, 97 Pa. Super. 181, 186 (1929) (noting, however, that the original "engine of correction," the ducking-stool, had since been replaced by "fine and imprisonment at the discretion of the court").

57. 4 William Blackstone, *Commentaries on the Laws of England* 169 (1769).

58. The term "misdemeanor" has attracted considerably less etymological attention than has its frequent companion, "felony." Like felony, however, misdemeanor carries strong connotations of disobedience and hierarchy. To demean oneself, after all, means to render oneself mean, to degrade oneself, or perhaps to reveal oneself as mean. As late as the sixteenth century, misdemeanor was used as synonymous with petit felony. See *Oxford English Dictionary*, "misdemeanour," no. 2 ("the which mysse demeanure of this woman, that she had innaturally slayne hir lorde and husbonde") (1516). As evidence of baseness (or self-debasement), misdemeanor from early on was associated with removal from positions of authority. Id. ("His . . . misdemeaner shall cause the officer . . . to loose his office.") (1579).

59. Commonwealth v. Sharpless, 2 Serg. and Rawle 91 (Pa. 1815).

60. R. v. Sedley, 1 Siderfin 168, 1 Keble 620 (1664). See generally R. M. Jackson, "Common Law Misdemeanors," 6 *Cambridge L.J.* 13 (1938).

61. R. v. Read, Fort. 98 (1708).

62. R. v. Curl, 3 Str. 788 (1727).

63. R. v. Crunden, 2 Camp. 89 (1809).

64. Commonwealth v. Sharpless, 2 Serg. and Rawle 91 (Pa. 1815) (emphasis added).

65. Lincoln v. Smith, 27 Vt. 328, 337–38 (1855).

66. Commonwealth v. Sharpless, 2 Serg. and Rawle 91 (Pa. 1815).

67. See, e.g., New York v. Miln, 36 U.S. 102 (1837) ("moral pestilence"); License Cases, 46 U.S. 504 (1847) (alcohol's effect on morals of the people); Ernst Freund, *The Police Power: Public Policy and Constitutional Rights* iii (1904).

68. On the policing—and licensing—of liquor in Britain, see Mariana Valverde, *Law's Dream of a Common Knowledge* ch. 6 (2003). Valverde notes that early-twentieth-century British policymakers were eager to distance themselves from their American counterparts, and stressed that they—like Blackstone before them—were motivated not by "a policy of Temperance Reform" but by considerations of "national efficiency," given that "drink, as a primary and as a secondary factor, was one of the main causes of inefficiency." Id. at 156 (quoting Henry Carter, *The Control of the Drink Trade: A Contribution to National Efficiency* ix, 5 [1918]).

69. Respublica v. Teischer, 1 U.S. 335, 338 (Pa. 1788).

70. Id. at 337.

71. Commonwealth v. Wing, 26 Mass. 1 (1829).

72. State v. Buckman, 8 N.H. 203 (1836).

73. Commonwealth v. McHale, 97 Pa. 397 (1881).

74. Id. at 409–10.

75. Id. at 410.

76. Pennsylvania Crimes Code § 107(B); Commonwealth v. Gaal, 63 D. and C.2d 507 (Pa. Ct. Com. Pleas 1973).

77. Commonwealth v. Keller, 35 D. and C.2d 615 (Pa. Ct. Com. Pleas 1964).

78. R. v. Lynn, 2 T. R. 733 (1788).

79. R. v. Price, 12 Q. B. D. 247, 255 (1884).

80. Cf. R.M. Jackson, "Common Law Misdemeanors," 6 *Cambridge L.J.* 13, 18 (1938) (public mischief, a common law misdemeanor created by English courts in 1933, "is any conduct that happens to be sufficiently distasteful to the judges").

81. N.Y. Penal Law of 1909, § 43 (emphasis added); cf. R. v. Wellard, 14 Q. B. D. 63, 67 (1894) ("whatever openly outrages decency and is injurious to public morals is a misdemeanor at common law").

82. State v. Bradbury, 136 Me. 347 (1939).

83. N.Y. Penal Law of 1909, § 1530.

84. Id. § 43 (emphasis added).

85. Spalding v. Preston, 21 Vt. 9, 13 (1848).

86. Commonwealth v. Alger, 61 Mass. 53 (1851).

87. An act to preserve the harbor of Boston, and to prevent encroachments therein of Apr. 19, 1837, St. 1837, c. 229, 7 Special Laws, 808.

88. See, e.g., Thomas M. Cooley, *A Treatise on the Constitutional Limitations Which Rest Upon the Legislative Power of the States of the American Union* 705 (6th ed. 1890).

89. Commonwealth v. Alger, 61 Mass. 53, 82 (1851).

90. Id. at 85.

91. Id. at 90.

92. Id.

93. Ernst Freund, *The Police Power: Public Policy and Constitutional Rights* 6 n.7 (1904) (quoting Chief Baron Fleming's argument in Bates' Case [1606]).

94. Id. at 6.

95. Rex v. Hampden, 3 Howell, State Trials 825, 1194 (1637) (Hutton, J.); id. at 860 (St. John for defendant) (quoted in Julius Goebel, Jr., "Constitutional History and Constitutional Law," 38 *Colum. L. Rev.* 555, 573 n.50 [1938]).

96. Constitution of Massachusetts art. iv (emphasis added).

97. See, e.g., James Wilson's attempt to find room for the royal pardoning power in the new American republic. (He ends up assigning it to the U.S. President.) James Wilson, Executive Department, Lectures on Law, in 2 *The Works of James Wilson* 442–44 (Robert Green McCloskey ed. 1967) (1791); see also Alexander Hamilton, "Federalist" No. 69, 383, 386 ("prerogative of pardoning"), No. 74, 415, 415–16 (presidential pardoning power).

98. Fontain v. Ravenel, 58 U.S. 369, 384 (1854) (citing Wheeler v. Smith, 50 U.S. 55 [1850]).

99. Commonwealth v. Alger, 61 Mass. 53, 84–85 (1851).

100. Although reported as an 1851 case, *Alger* wasn't decided until 1853. *Thorpe* was reported as an 1854 case, but wasn't published until the next year.

101. For an elaboration of this theme, see Christopher L. Tomlins, *Law, Labor, and Ideology in the Early American Republic* (1993) and William J. Novak, *The People's Welfare: Law & Regulation in Nineteenth-Century America* 1996).

102. Ernst Freund, *The Police Power: Public Policy and Constitutional Rights* 6 n.7 (1904) (quoting Chief Baron Fleming's argument in Bates' Case [1606]).

103. Institutes I.I.3 (emphasis added).

104. J. B. Schneewind, *The Invention of Autonomy: A History of Modern Moral Philosophy* 248 (1998).

105. Immanuel Kant, *Rechtslehre* AB 43 (1797).

106. Id. at A172–73/B202–03.
107. N.Y. Penal Law § 1530 (1909).
108. 11 Metc. 55 (1846).
109. Leonard W. Levy, *The Law of the Commonwealth and Chief Justice Shaw* 247 (1957) (quoting 11 Metc. 55, 57 [1846]).
110. The notion of necessity, and of emergency, has always been central to police as a mode of paternal governance: "Natural community in the household . . . was born of necessity, and necessity ruled over all activities performed in it. The realm of the *polis*, by contrast, was the sphere of freedom. . . . What all Greek philosophers, no matter how opposed to *polis* life, took for granted is that freedom is exclusively located in the political realm, that necessity is primarily a prepolitical phenomenon, characteristic of private householder organization, and that *force and violence are justified in this sphere because they are the only means to master necessity*—for instance, by ruling over slaves—and to become free." (Hannah Arendt, *The Human Condition* 30–31 1958).
111. 21 Vt. 9 (1848).
112. See, e.g., Thomas M. Cooley, *A Treatise on the Constitutional Limitations Which Rest Upon the Legislative Power of the States of the American Union* 705 (6th ed. 1890) (quoting *Alger*).
113. Lawton v. Steele, 152 U.S. 133, 144 (1894) (Fuller, C.J., dissenting).
114. Spalding v. Preston, 21 Vt. 9, 12–13 (1848).
115. Id. at 14.
116. 61 Mass. 53, 104 (1851).
117. Lawton v. Steele, 152 U.S. 133, 144 (1894) (Fuller, C.J., dissenting); see generally William J. Novak, "Common Regulation: Legal Origins of State Power in America," 45 *Hastings L.J.* 1061, 1091–92 (1994).
118. Thomas M. Cooley, *A Treatise on the Constitutional Limitations* 594–95 (1868).
119. For the classic discussion of this case, and others like it, see The Queen v. Dudley and Stephens, 14 Q.B.D. 273 (1884).
120. On the nineteenth-century fire cases, see William J. Novak, *The People's Welfare: Law and Regulation in Nineteenth-Century America* 66–79 (1996).
121. See, e.g., Christopher G. Tiedeman, *A Treatise on the Limitations of Police Power in the United States Considered From Both a Civil and Criminal Standpoint* 13 (1886): "It is the province of the law-making power to determine when the exigency exists for calling into exercise the police power of the State." (quoting Lake v. Rose Hill Cemetery, 70 Ill. 192 [1873]).
122. 61 Mass. 53, 96 (1851).
123. 46 U.S. 504, 592 (1847).

5. Definition by Exclusion

1. Jeremy Bentham, "An Introduction to the Principles of Morals and Legislation," ch. XVI, in 1 *The Works of Jeremy Bentham* 102 n.† (John Bowring ed. 1962) (1789).
2. Ernst Freund, *The Police Power: Public Policy and Constitutional Rights* iii (1904).
3. Id. at 2.
4. "Constitutional Law," 16A Am. Jur. 2d § 315 (1999) (citing McInerney v. Ervin, 46 So. 2d 458 (Fla. 1950); Hunter v. Green, 142 Fla. 104 (1940); Bruck v. State ex rel. Money, 228 Ind. 189 (1950); Brewer v. Valk, 204 N.C. 186 (1933); State ex rel. Cleveringa v. Klein, 63 N.D. 514 (1933) (emphasis added).
5. New York v. Miln, 36 U.S. 102 (1837).
6. 2 Frederick Pollock and Frederic William Maitland, *The History of English Law Before the Time of Edward* I 472 (2d ed. 1898).
7. See Ernst Freund, *The Police Power: Public Policy and Constitutional Rights* 26 (1904).
8. See, e.g., Nebbia v. New York, 291 U.S. 502, 523 (1934) (citing License Cases, 5 How. 504, 583 [1847]); see also New York v. Miln, 36 U.S. 102, 141 (1837) (police power of state covers "the persons and things within her territorial limits, and therefore within her jurisdiction"); Barker

v. Palmer, 217 N.C. 519, 8 S.E.2d 610 (1940) ("the power to protect the public health and the public safety, to preserve good order and the public morals, to protect the lives and property of citizens, and to govern men and things by any legislation appropriate to that end").

9. 260 U.S. 393 (1922).

10. On Holmes's appreciation of the rhetorical, inoculating, significance of "police power," see Robert Brauneis, "'The Foundation of Our "Regulatory Takings" Jurisprudence': The Myth and Meaning of Justice Holmes's Opinion in *Pennsylvania Coal Co. v. Mahon*," 106 *Yale L.J.* 613, 622–23 & n.40 (1996).

11. 260 U.S. 393, 417 (1922) (Brandeis, J., dissenting).

12. Id. at 418.

13. Lochner v. New York, 198 U.S. 45, 75 (1905) (Holmes, J., dissenting). For more on *Lochner*, see infra ch. 9.

14. 61 Mass. 53 (1851).

15. 21 Vt. 9 (1848).

16. Id. at 14.

17. License Cases, 46 U.S. 504, 589 (1847) (emphasis added).

18. See Markus Dirk Dubber, *Victims in the War on Crime: The Use and Abuse of Victims' Rights* pt. 1 (2002).

19. Christopher G. Tiedeman, *A Treatise on the Limitations of Police Power in the United States Considered From Both a Civil and Criminal Standpoint* 483 (1886).

20. See also Charles Loring Brace, *The Dangerous Classes of New York, and Twenty Years' Work Among Them* 28–29 (1872) ("great masses of destitute, miserable, and criminal persons"); Erik H. Monkkonen, *The Dangerous Class: Crime and Poverty in Columbus, Ohio, 1860–1885* (1975); see also Richard F. Wetzell, *Inventing the Criminal: A History of German Criminology, 1880–1945* (2000) (study of dangerous classes in early European criminology).

21. Christopher G. Tiedeman, *A Treatise on the Limitations of Police Power in the United States Considered From Both a Civil and Criminal Standpoint* 70, 102 (1886).

22. Id. at 113.

23. Id. at 105, 114. The state, in other words, enjoyed precisely the same discretionary power over those who had offended against its commands as did the medieval king. The offender had placed himself within the mercy of the macro householder, who (or which) could exercise it as he (or it) saw fit.

24. Id. at 70.

25. Id. at 114.

26. License Cases, 46 U.S. 504, 583 (1847) (emphasis added); see also State v. Noyes, 47 Me. 189, 211 (1859) (identifying *salus populi suprema lex*, "the great principle on which the statutes for the security of the people is based," as "the foundation of criminal law, in all governments of civilized countries, and other laws conducive to safety and consequent happiness of the people").

27. Roscoe Pound, "Introduction," in Francis Bowes Sayre, *A Selection of Cases on Criminal Law* xxix, xxxii (1927). On Pound's views on criminal law, see Thomas A. Green, "Freedom and Criminal Responsibility in the Age of Pound: An Essay on Criminal Justice," 93 *Mich. L. Rev.* 1915 (1995); Markus Dirk Dubber, *Victims in the War on Crime: The Use and Abuse of Victims' Rights* 27–28, 124–28, 144–45 (2002).

28. Roscoe Pound, "Introduction," in Francis Bowes Sayre, *A Selection of Cases on Criminal Law* xxix, xxxv (1927).

29. Id. at xxxiii.

30. Id.; see also Gustav Radbruch, "Der Ursprung des Strafrechts aus dem Stande der Unfreien," in *Elegantiae Juris Criminalis: Vierzehn Studien zur Geschichte des Strafrechts* 1 (1950); cf. *Theodor Mommsen, Römisches Strafrecht* 16–17 (1899) (origin of Roman criminal law in patria potestas); but see 1 James Leigh Strachan-Davidson, *Problems of the Roman Criminal Law* 28 (1912).

31. Roscoe Pound, "Introduction," in Francis Bowes Sayre, *A Selection of Cases on Criminal Law* xxix, xxxvii (1927).

32. Id. at xxxvi.

33. Id. at xxxvii.

34. An exception here is Nicola Lacey, *State Punishment: Political Principles and Community Values* (1988).

35. Commenting on the shared subject matter of (late) police science and (early) administrative law in nineteenth-century Germany, David Lindenfeld points to "the division of the objects of [police] activities into physical, spiritual, and economic life," where "[t]he physical included population, health, and care of the poor and needy; the spiritual included education and religion; the economic included agriculture, forestry, mining, manufacturing . . . , and commerce." David F. Lindenfeld, "The Decline of Polizeiwissenschaft: Continuity and Change in the Study of Administration in German Universities during the 19th Century," in *Formation und Transformation des Verwaltungswissens in Frankreich und Deutschland (18./19. Jh.),* 1 *Jahrbuch für Europäische Verwaltungsgeschichte* 141–59, 155 (1989).

36. State v. Noyes, 47 Me. 189, 211 (1859).

37. See most recently Lawrence v. Texas, 539 U.S. 558 (2003).

38. See, e.g., Com. v. Bonadio, 490 Pa. 91 (1980); Powell v. State, 270 Ga. 327 (1998).

39. Christopher G. Tiedeman, *A Treatise on the Limitations of Police Power in the United States Considered From Both a Civil and Criminal Standpoint* 150 (1886); Ernst Freund, *The Police Power: Public Policy and Constitutional Rights* 2 (1904) ("decisions of the courts").

40. Cf. Holden v. Hardy, 169 U.S. 366, 372–73 (1898) (Jeremiah M. Wilson, counsel for plaintiff) ("A general criminal law is to punish something wrong in itself, without regard to the time, place or manner of doing it, and of course such a law, whether enacted by original or delegated authority, is not a police regulation.").

41. Ernst Freund, *The Police Power: Public Policy and Constitutional Rights* 1–2 (1904).

42. Id. at 4.

43. Id. at 5–6.

44. Id. at 21 n.29 (quoting Montesquieu, *Spirit of Laws* bk. xxvi, § 24 [1748]). This passage appears in a section entitled, straightforwardly, "*That the regulations of the police are of a different class from other civil laws,*" which begins as follows: "There are criminals whom the magistrate punishes [punit], there are others whom he reproves [corrige]. The former are subject to the power of the law, the latter to his authority."

45. Id. at 24. Freund, more appropriately but also more revealingly, might have quoted the famous, and much earlier, missive by Louis XIV of 1667, which declared that "the functions of justice and police are often incompatible," and therefore separated "la Justice contentieuse & distributive" from police "qui consiste à assurer le repos du Public & des Particuliers, à purger la Ville de ce qui peut causer les desordres, à procurer l'abondance, & à faire vivre chacun selon sa condition & son devoir." Albert Cremer, "L'administration dans les encyclopédies et dictionnaires français du 17e et du 18e siècle," in *Formation und Transformation des Verwaltungswissens in Frankreich und Deutschland (18./19. Jh.),* 1 *Jahrbuch für Europäische Verwaltungsgeschichte* 1, 1 (1989).

46. Ernst Freund, *The Police Power: Public Policy and Constitutional Rights* 20 (1904).

47. Id. at 21–22.

48. Id. at 21.

49. Christopher G. Tiedeman, *A Treatise on the Limitations of Police Power in the United States Considered From Both a Civil and Criminal Standpoint* 114 (1886).

50. Ernst Freund, *The Police Power: Public Policy and Constitutional Rights* 23 (1904).

51. Christopher G. Tiedeman, *A Treatise on the Limitations of Police Power in the United States Considered From Both a Civil and Criminal Standpoint* 116–17 (1886) (quoted in Chicago vs. Morales, 527 U.S. 41, 104 n.4 (1999) [Thoman, J., dissenting].

52. State v. Hogan, 63 Oh. St. 202, 211 (1900).

53. Id. at 211 (emphasis added).

54. In re Nott, 11 Me. 208, 208 (1834).

55. Id.

56. Id. at 211.

57. Id. at 211, 212.

58. People v. Phillips, 1 Edmund's Select Cases 386, 389 (1847).

59. Id. at 388–89.

60. See, e.g., Christopher G. Tiedeman, *A Treatise on the Limitations of Police Power in the United States Considered From Both a Civil and Criminal Standpoint* 121–22 (1886).

61. See People v. Phillips, 1 Edmund's Select Cases 386, 390, 392 (1847).

62. In re Forbes, 11 Abb. Pr. 52 (N.Y. Sup. Ct. 1860).

63. Ernst Freund, *The Police Power: Public Policy and Constitutional Rights* 100 (1904).

64. In re Forbes, 11 Abb. Pr. 52 (N.Y. Sup. Ct. 1860).

65. People v. Phillips, 1 Edmund's Select Cases 386, 390, 392 (1847).

66. In re Forbes, 11 Abb. Pr. 52 (N.Y. Sup. Ct. 1860).

67. Id.

68. See supra ch. 1.

69. Morgan v. Nolte, 37 Ohio St. 23, 25 (1881).

70. Id.

71. Id. at 26.

72. Ernst Freund, *The Police Power: Public Policy and Constitutional Rights* 99 (1904).

73. Papachristou v. Jacksonville, 405 U.S. 156 (1972).

6. Police Power and Commerce Power

1. 405 U.S. 156 (1972); see also Chicago v. Morales, 527 U.S. 41, 104 n.4, 107 (1999) (Thomas, J., dissenting) (quoting Tiedeman and Freund).

2. 36 U.S. 102 (1837).

3. Id. at 140.

4. Id. at 139.

5. Id. at 142–43; see In re Nott, 11 Me. 208 (1834).

6. 36 U.S. at 112 (counsel for plaintiff).

7. Id. at 132 (quoting Vattel).

8. Id. at 130 (counsel for plaintiff).

9. Id. at 141.

10. See supra. ch. 1.

11. United States v. Hing Quong Chow, 53 F. 233, 234 (E.D. La. 1892).

12. Id. at 234.

13. Id.

14. Id. at 234–35.

15. John Locke, *Second Treatise of Government* § 147 (1690).

16. New York v. Miln, 36 U.S. 102 (1837). These policies were nothing new, as Marilyn Baseler points out: "In Massachusetts, statutes were passed, beginning in 1701, to prevent the landing of the 'poor, vicious and infirm,' laws that required the master of each vessel to post a bond that towns receiving any 'lame, impotent, or infirm persons, incapable of maintaining themselves . . . would not be charged with their support.' In the absence of this security, the captain was to return such passengers to their port of embarkation." Marilyn Baseler, *"Asylum For Mankind": America, 1607–1800*, at 71–72 (1998).

17. See, e.g., Gibbons v. Ogden, 22 U.S. 1 (1824).

18. United States v. Lopez, 514 U.S. 549, 567 (1995).

19. 11 U.S. 32 (1812).

20. See supra ch. 4.

21. See id.

22. Walton H. Hamilton and Carlton C. Rodee, "Police Power," in 12 *Encyclopedia of the Social Sciences* 190 (1933) (quoted in William J. Novak, "Common Regulation: Legal Origins of State Power in America," 45 *Hastings L.J.* 1061, 1082 n.58 [1994]).

23. It's easy to forget that police does away with more than *mens rea*. See, e.g., Francis Bowes Sayre, "Public Welfare Offenses," 33 *Colum. L. Rev.* 55 (1933).

24. 218 U.S. 57 (1910).

25. Id. at 70.

26. Id. at 69. Note that this decision acknowledging, without questioning, the aconstitutionality of police regulation came five years *after Lochner v. New York*, the opinion which is generally credited with launching three decades of intrusive police power scrutiny. See infra ch. 9.

27. Id. at 70 (emphasis added).

28. Id. at 69–70.

29. 258 U.S. 250 (1922).

30. Id. at 252.

31. Id.

32. 320 U.S. 277 (1943).

33. Id. at 280–81.

34. 320 U.S. 277, 285, 286 (1943) (Murphy, J., dissenting).

35. 342 U.S. 246 (1952).

36. Technically, the issue was one of statutory interpretation, as it was in all of the previous federal police offense cases. The Court interpreted the statute in question as requiring proof of *mens rea*. Whether the statute, if not susceptible to this interpretation, would have been struck down as unconstitutional, is another question.

37. Once again, it's not clear whether the Congress could constitutionally have abandoned the *mens rea* requirement. As with the act requirement, it appears that the *mens rea* requirement also applied only to common law crimes, and not to statutory ones.

38. Id. at 253–54.

39. Id. at 259.

40. Id. at 255–56.

41. Francis Bowes Sayre, "Public Welfare Offenses," 33 *Colum. L. Rev.* 55 (1933).

42. On the usefulness and operation of licensing in modern governmentality in general, and at the intersection of law and police in particular, see Mariana Valverde, *Law's Dream of a Common Knowledge* ch. 6 (2003).

43. City of Erie v. Pap's A.M., 529 U.S. 277, 296 (2000); see also Robinson v. California, 370 U.S. 660, 664 (1962) ("'There can be no question of the authority of the state in the exercise of its police power to regulate the administration, sale, prescription and use of dangerous and habit-forming drugs.'" (quoting Whipple v. Martinson, 256 U.S. 41, 45 [1921]); Com. v. Koczwara, 397 Pa. 575, 581 (1959) ("'There is perhaps no other area of permissible state action within which the exercise of the police power of a state is more plenary than in the regulation and control of the use and sale of alcoholic beverages.'") (quoting In re Tahiti Bar, 395 Pa. 355, 360 [1959]).

7. The Forgotten Power and the Problem of Legitimation

1. Very much the same thing had begun to happen in Germany some decades earlier, as administrative law replaced police science in university curricula. At Göttingen, generally recognized as a center of police science, the first lecture on administrative law was offered in 1876. Heinz Mohnhaupt, "Vorstufen der Wissenschaften von 'Verwaltung' und 'Verwaltungsrecht' an der Universität Göttingen (1750–1830)," in *Formation und Transformation des Verwaltungswissens in Frankreich und Deutschland (18./19. Jh.)*, 1 *Jahrbuch für Europäische Verwaltungsgeschichte* 73, 73 (1989). It's important to recognize this development as a shift in focus, not in substance. As David Lindenfeld explains, "[i]t was easy to transfer [police] categories to administrative law, which simply involved treating them from a different perspective, namely the legal limits within which administrative officials must operate." David F. Lindenfeld, "The Decline of Polizeiwissenschaft: Continuity and Change in the Study of Administration in German Universities during the 19th Century," in id. at 141, 155 (citing Michael Stolleis, "Verwaltungslehre und Verwaltungsrechtswissenschaft 1866–1914," in 2 *Deutsche Verwaltungsgeschichte (Vom Reichsdeputations-*

hauptschluß bis zur Auflösung des Deutschen Bundes) 56, 88 [Kurt G.A. Jeserich, Hans Pohl and Georg-Christoph von Unruh eds. 1983]).

2. Ernst Freund, *Standards of American Legislation* (2d ed. 1965) (1917).

3. Ernst Freund, *Legislative Regulation: A Study of the Ways and Means of Written Law* (1932).

4. Ernst Freund, *Administrative Powers over Persons and Property: A Comparative Survey* (1928).

5. Ernst Freund, *The Police Power: Public Policy and Constitutional Rights* iii (1904).

6. Id. at 3.

7. This is no longer a foregone conclusion. See, e.g., Tom Regan, *The Case for Animal Rights* (1983). Note that Christopher Tiedeman, the nineteenth-century American police commentator, thought that animals "must be recognized as subjects of legal rights," so that animal protection laws weren't police offenses "against public morality," but criminal violations of the rights of the animals themselves. "And why should they not be so recognized?," Tiedeman inquired: "Is it not self-conceit for man to claim that he alone, of all God's creatures, is the possessor of inalienable rights?" Christopher G. Tiedeman, *A Treatise on the Limitations of Police Power in the United States Considered From Both a Civil and Criminal Standpoint* 513 (1886).

8. For a detailed exploration of this point, see Markus Dirk Dubber, "Policing Possession: The War on Crime and the End of Criminal Law," 91 *J. Crim. L. & Criminology* 829 (2002); Markus Dirk Dubber, *Victims in the War on Crime: The Use and Abuse of Victims' Rights* pt. I (2002).

9. J. B. Schneewind, *The Invention of Autonomy: A History of Modern Moral Philosophy* (1998).

10. Frederic William Maitland, "England before the Conquest," in *Domesday and Beyond: Three Essays in the Early History of England* 220, 325 (1966) (1897); see also Paul Vinogradoff, "Feudalism," 3 *Cambridge Medieval History* 458, 479 (1924) (villeins). Interestingly, Vinogradoff lists the right to be punished among the consequences of the attribution of a soul and a will. Id. ("He was set in the stocks and hanged for crimes."). On the significance of the right to be punished as an aspect of autonomy, see Markus Dirk Dubber, "The Right to Be Punished: Autonomy and Its Demise in Modern Penal Thought," 16 *Law & Hist. Rev.* 113 (1998).

11. Frederic William Maitland, "England before the Conquest," in *Domesday and Beyond: Three Essays in the Early History of England* 220, 325 (1966) (1897).

12. 521 U.S. 346 (1997).

13. Rowe v. Burton, 884 F. Supp. 1372, 1380 (D. Alaska 1994) (citing cases).

14. Christopher G. Tiedeman, *A Treatise on the Limitations of Police Power in the United States Considered From Both a Civil and Criminal Standpoint* (1886)

15. See supra. ch. 2.

16. Wayne A. Logan, "A Study in 'Actuarial Justice': Sex Offender Classification Practice and Procedure," 3 *Buff. Crim. L. Rev.* 593 (2000).

17. See Rowe v. Burton, 884 F. Supp. 1372 (D. Alaska 1994) (discussing Alaska law).

18. Id. at 1377; see also State v. Williams, 1999 Ohio App. LEXIS 217, at *8-*9 (Ct. App. Ohio 1999), rev'd, 88 Ohio St. 3d 513 (2000) ("Megan's Law is clearly an exercise of the state's police powers.").

19. 529 U.S. 598, 618–19 (2000); see also United States v. Hickman, 179 F.3d 230, 238 (5th Cir. 1999) (punishment of robbery exercise of police power).

20. John Locke, *Second Treatise of Government* § 171 (1690) (emphasis added).

21. Fisher v. McGirr, 67 Mass. 1 (1854).

22. Id.

23. 46 U.S. 504, 583 (1847).

24. State v. Hennessy, 114 Wash. 351, 365–66 (1921).

25. People v. Rasmussen, 233 Ill. App. 3d 352, 363 (1992).

26. State v. Thompkins, 75 Ohio St. 3d 558, 560 (1996).

27. Commonwealth v. Alger, 61 Mass. 53, 84–85 (1851).

28. State v. Holm, 139 Minn. 267, 275 (1918).

29. See supra. ch. 5.

30. Roscoe Pound, "Introduction," in Francis Bowes Sayre, *A Selection of Cases on Criminal Law* xxix, xxxiv (1927).

31. Francis Bowes Sayre, "Public Welfare Offenses," 33 *Colum. L. Rev.* 55, 67 (1933).

32. Id.

33. Id. at 68.

34. Roscoe Pound, "Introduction," in Francis Bowes Sayre, *A Selection of Cases on Criminal Law* xxix, xxxv (1927).

35. Id. at xxxvi.

36. Francis Bowes Sayre, "Public Welfare Offenses," 33 *Colum. L. Rev.* 55, 79 (1933).

37. Roscoe Pound, "Introduction," in Francis Bowes Sayre, *A Selection of Cases on Criminal Law* xxix, xxxvii (1927).

38. Id. at xxxii.

39. Id. at xxx.

40. Id. at xxxvii.

41. Francis Bowes Sayre, "Public Welfare Offenses," 33 *Colum. L. Rev.* 55, 79 (1933).

42. Id. at 55.

43. See supra. ch. 6.

44. Id. at 72.

45. Id.

46. Id.

47. Id. at 75.

48. Id. at 65 n.33; see also id. at 75.

49. Id. at 72.

50. Id. at 79.

51. Id. at 80.

52. See Herbert L. Packer, "Mens Rea and the Supreme Court," 1962 *Sup. Ct. Rev.* 107, 114.

53. 529 U.S. 598, 618–19 (2000); see also United States v. Hickman, 179 F.3d 230, 238 (5th Cir. 1999) (punishment of robbery exercise of police power).

54. Markus Dirk Dubber, "Policing Possession: The War on Crime and the End of Criminal Law," 91 J. *Crim. L. & Criminology* 829 (2002); Markus Dirk Dubber, *Victims in the War on Crime: The Use and Abuse of Victims' Rights* pt. I (2002).

55. And so, at a time when English criminal law lacked a general doctrine of attempt, courts turned to status offenses familiar from Blackstone's list of police offenses to punish those whose criminal plans had not come to fruition, for one reason or another. See J. M. Kaye, "The Early History of Murder and Manslaughter," 83 *Law Q. Rev.* 365, 382 (1967) ("*communis perturbator pacis, vagabundus de nocte,* or the like").

56. U.S. Const. art. I, § 8.

57. 21 U.S.C § 801(2).

58. See Wayne R. LaFave & Austin W. Scott, Jr., *Criminal Law* § 2.8 (2d ed. 1986).

59. See 10 U.S.C. ch. 47 (Uniform Code of Military Justice).

60. See 18 U.S.C. §§ 1151–1153.

61. See 18 U.S.C. ch. 48.

62. Francis Bowes Sayre, "Public Welfare Offenses," 33 *Colum. L. Rev.* 55, 55 (1933).

63. See Markus Dirk Dubber, "Penal Panopticon: The Idea of a Modern Model Penal Code," 4 *Buff. Crim. L. Rev.* 53 (2000).

64. See Harmelin v. Michigan, 501 U.S. 957 (1991).

65. Various Items of Personal Property v. United States, 282 U.S. 577 (1931).

66. United States v. United States Currency in the Amount of One Hundred Forty-Five Thousand, One Hundred Thirty-Nine Dollars, 18 F.3d 73 (2d Cir.), cert. denied sub nom. Etim v. United States, 513 U.S. 815 (1994).

67. One Lot Emerald Cut Stones v. United States, 409 U.S. 232 (1972) (per curiam).

68. United States v. One Assortment of 89 Firearms, 465 U.S. 354 (1984).

69. One 1958 Plymouth Sedan v. Pennsylvania, 380 U.S. 693 (1965).

70. See already Henry M. Hart, Jr., "The Aims of the Criminal Law," 23 *Law & Contemp.*

Probs. 401, 431 (1958) ("What sense does it make to insist upon procedural safeguards in criminal prosecutions if anything whatever can be made a crime in the first place?").

71. See Robinson v. California, 370 U.S. 660, 667 (1962) ("Even one day in prison would be a cruel and unusual punishment for the 'crime' of having a common cold.")

72. See "State v. Herrera: The Utah Supreme Court Rules in Favor of Utah's Controversial Insanity Defense Statute," 22 *J. Contemp. L.* 221 (1996); "Due Process—Insanity Defense—Idaho Supreme Court Upholds Abolition of Insanity Defense Against State and Federal Constitutional Challenges," 104 *Harv. L. Rev.* 1132 (1991). But see Finger v. State, 27 P.3d 66 (Nev. 2001).

73. United States v. Salerno, 481 U.S. 739 (1988) (before trial); United States v. Edwards, 430 A.2d 1321, 1343 (D.C. 1981), cert. denied, 455 U.S. 1022 (1982) (same); Kansas v. Hendricks, 521 U.S. 346 (1997) (after trial).

74. See Markus Dirk Dubber, "Toward a Constitutional Law of Crime and Punishment," 55 *Hastings L.J. 509* (2004); William J. Stuntz, "Substance, Process, and the Civil-Criminal Line," 7 *J. Contemp. Legal Issues* 1 (1996).

75. People v. Phillips, 1 Edmund's Select Cases 386, 397–98 (1847) (quoting Geter v. Commissioners for Tobacco Inspection, 1 Bay 354, 357 [S.C. Ct. Common Pleas & General Sessions of the Peace 1794]).

76. Fisher v. McGirr, 67 Mass. 1, 27 (1854).

77. Id. at 39.

78. See Penry v. Lynaugh, 492 U.S. 302 (1989).

79. See Markus Dirk Dubber, "The Pain of Punishment," 44 *Buff. L. Rev.* 545 (1996).

80. Papachristou v. Jacksonville, 405 U.S. 156, 163 (1972).

81. Id. at 159.

82. See Markus Dirk Dubber, "American Plea Bargains, German Lay Judges, and the Crisis of Criminal Procedure," 49 *Stan. L. Rev.* 547 (1997).

8. The Law of Police: Internal and External Constraints

1. H.L.A. Hart, "Sovereignty and Legally Limited Government," in *Essays on Bentham: Studies in Jurisprudence and Political Theory* 220, 220 (1982) (citing Jeremy Bentham, "Of Laws in General," in *The Collected Works of Jeremy Bentham* [H.L.A. Hart ed. 1968]).

2. See, e.g., the response by eighteenth-century English courts to criminal possession statutes. They upheld convictions pursuant to these statutes, all the while declaring that possession remained a noncrime under the common law because it lacked an actus reus. See, e.g., Regina v. Dugdale, 1 El. & Bl. 435 (1853).

3. See supra ch. 3.

4. Marcus Aurelius, *The Meditations* (George Long trans. 1991) (167 A.D.)

5. Niccolo Machiavelli, *The Prince* (W. K. Marriott ed. 1908) (1515).

6. See Jonathan A. Bush, "Free to Enslave: The Foundations of Colonial American Slave Law," 5 *Yale J. L. & Humanities* 417, 426 (1993).

7. Government as police may well be subject to certain ethical, as opposed to moral, constraints. See, e.g., Max Weber, "Politics as a Vocation," in *Max Weber: Essays in Sociology* 77 (H. H. Gerth & C. Wright Mills trans. & eds. 1946) (ethic of responsibility).

8. Arthur P. Scott, *Criminal Law in Colonial Virginia* 299 (1930).

9. This limitation upon the power of one householder thus presumes the superior power of another. This limitation therefore is itself an exercise of the power to police.

10. See supra. ch. 5.

11. Joel Prentiss Bishop, *New Commentaries on the Criminal Law* 531 (8th ed. 1892); see generally Beirne Stedman, "Right of Husband to Chastise Wife," 3 *Va. L. Register [N.S.]* 241, 244 (1917).

12. State v. Black, 60 N.C. 262 (1864).

13. United States v. Clark, 31 F. 710 (E.D. Mich. 1887).

14. Id.; see also Com. v. Eckert, 2 Browne 249 (Ct. of Quarter Sessions Pa. 1812) (malice evidence of "a depraved or wicked heart").

15. State v. Mabrey, 64 N.C. 592, 593 (1870).

16. Joel Prentiss Bishop, *New Commentaries on the Criminal Law* 532 (8th ed. 1892) (quoting Butler v. McLellan, 1 Ware 219, 320).

17. For a similar interpretation of the constitutional prohibition against ex post facto laws, see Calder v. Bull, 3 U.S. 386, 389 (1798) (ex post facto lawmaking "stimulated by ambition, or personal resentment, and vindictive *malice*").

18. Hudson v. McMillian, 503 U.S. 1 (1992).

19. The malice test still can be seen reflected, more or less clearly, in other attempts to circumscribe the disciplinary power of householders and quasi-householders in various contexts. See, e.g., White v. Frank, 855 F.2d 956 (2d Cir. 1988) (tort of "malicious prosecution"); Wayne R. LaFave, Jerold H. Israel, & Nancy J. King, *Criminal Procedure* § 13.5 (1999) (due process defense of "vindictive prosecution"); Ingraham v. Wright, 430 U.S. 651, 677 (1977) (malicious corporal punishment inflicted by teachers upon students).

20. Estelle v. Gamble, 429 U.S. 97 (1976).

21. On the—not always interpersonal—relationship between prison guards and inmates in the United States and Europe, see James Q. Whitman, *Harsh Justice: Criminal Punishment and the Widening Divide Between America and Europe* (2003).

22. Paul Vinogradoff, "Foundations of Society (Origins of Feudalism)," 2 *Cambridge Medieval History* 630 (1913).

23. Francis Bowes Sayre, "Public Welfare Offenses," 33 *Colum. L. Rev.* 55 (1933).

24. Whether this proportionality requirement has any bite is another question. See most recently Ewing v. California, 538 U.S. 11 (2003).

25. This wasn't Sayre's point at all, of course. He wasn't interested in imprisonment in general; he was interested in police offenses. And police offenses were less objectionable if they weren't punished with imprisonment.

26. Model Penal Code § 1.04(5).

27. 28 U.S.C. § 994(k).

28. See, e.g., Robert Blecker, "Haven or Hell? Inside Lorton Central Prison: Experiences of Punishment Justified," 42 *Stan. L. Rev.* 1149 (1990).

29. 1 Frederick Pollock and Frederic William Maitland, *The History of English Law Before the Time of Edward I* 415, 444 (2d ed. 1898). Whipping was the preferred disciplinary measure, because the imprisoned servant couldn't work.

30. See Jackson v. Bishop, 404 F. 2d 571, 580 (8th Cir. 1968) (Blackmun, J.) (disciplinary whipping of prisoners "degrading to the punisher and to the punished alike"). But see Ingraham v. Wright, 430 U.S. 651, 684 n.1 (1977) (White, J., dissenting) (noting that the Supreme Court has never found corporal discipline of prisoners violative of the Eighth Amendment).

31. See State v. Cannon, 55 Del. 587 (1963) (whipping doesn't violate "cruel punishments" clause of Del. constitution).

32. 1 Frederick Pollock and Frederic William Maitland, *The History of English Law Before the Time of Edward I* 415 (serfs), 437 (church clerks) (2d ed. 1898).

33. State v. Mabrey, 64 N.C. 592, 593 (1870).

34. See, e.g., Heinrich Brunner, "Abspaltungen der Friedlosigkeit," in *Forschungen zur Geschichte des deutschen und französischen Rechtes* 444, 465 (1894).

35. Arthur P. Scott, *Criminal Law in Colonial Virginia* 199 (1930).

36. Compare the reluctance of courts to second-guess prison officials' exercise of their disciplinary power to maintain order among their inmates.

37. See supra. p. 184.

38. Ariela L. Gross, "'Like Master, Like Man': Construing Whiteness in the Commercial Law of Slavery, 1800–1861," 18 *Cardozo L. Rev.* 263, 282 (1996) (1866 Louisiana prosecution of master for "harsh, cruel & inhuman treatment towards his slaves").

39. On the need for differentiating management of different household resources, see already Aristotle, *Politics* bk. I, sec. XIII.

40. Cf. Holt Civic Club v. Tuscaloosa, 439 U.S. 60 (1978) (status as object of "police jurisdiction" does not imply right to vote).

41. Cf. Lon L. Fuller, *The Morality of Law* 207–17 (rev. ed. 1969) (rule of law principles as prudential guidelines of "managerial direction").

42. Hudson v. Palmer, 468 U.S. 517 (1984) (Stevens, J., dissenting) (quoting United States ex rel. Miller v. Twomey, 479 F.2d 701, 712 [7th Cir. 1973]).

43. Trop v. Dulles, 356 U.S. 86, 100 (1958).

44. Furman v. Georgia, 408 U.S. 238, 272–73 (1972) (Brennan, J., concurring).

45. This idea is made explicit in analogous norms of international human rights law. See, e.g., Convention Against Torture and Other Cruel, Inhuman or Degrading Treatment or Punishment (1984).

9. *Lochner's* Law and Substantive Due Process

1. 198 U.S. 45 (1905).

2. There is now a considerable body of literature challenging this long-orthodox reading of *Lochner*. See generally Charles W. McCurdy, " 'The Liberty of Contract' Regime in American Law," in *Freedom of Contract and the State* (Harry Scheiber ed., 1997); Barry Cushman, "Rethinking The New Deal Court," 80 *Va. L. Rev.* 201 (1994); Richard D. Friedman, "Switching Time and Other Thought Experiments: The Hughes Court and Constitutional Transformation," 142 *U. Pa. L. Rev.* 1891 (1994); Howard Gillman, *The Constitution Besieged* (1993); Barry Cushman, "A Stream of Legal Consciousness: The Current of Commerce Doctrine from Swift to Jones & Laughlin," 61 *Fordham L. Rev.* 105 (1992); Barry Cushman, "Doctrinal Synergies and Liberal Dilemmas: The Case of the Yellow-Dog Contract," 1992 *Sup. Ct. Rev.* 235; Michael Les Benedict, "Laissez Faire and Liberty: A Re-evaluation of the Meaning and Origins of Laissez-Faire Constitutionalism," 3 *Law & Hist. Rev.* 293 (1985); Charles W. McGurdy, "The Roots of 'Liberty of Contract' Reconsidered," 1984 *Y.B. Sup. Ct. Hist. Soc.* 20 (1984); Charles W. McGurdy, "Justice Field and the Jurisprudence of Government-Business Relations," 61 *J. Am. Hist.* 970 (1975); Harry Scheiber, "Government and the Economy: Studies in the 'Commonwealth' Policy in Nineteenth-Century America," 3 *J. Interdisc. Hist.* 135, 137 (1972). For an interesting discussion of the contemporary (in)significance and eventual impact of that dissent, see G.. Edward White, "Holmes and American Jurisprudence: Revisiting Substantive Due Process and Holmes's *Lochner* Dissent," 62 *Brooklyn L. Rev.* 87 (1997).

3. See 198 U.S. 45, 62 (1905) (state, in this exercise of its police power, assumed "the position of a supervisor, or *paterfamilias*").

4. 514 U.S. 549 (1995).

5. Id.

6. 198 U.S. 45, 64 (1905).

7. Id. at 57.

8. Id. at 56.

9. Id.

10. Id. at 53.

11. Actually, the argument wasn't quite this simple. The Court also had to argue its way around the fact that it had upheld a similar hours law regarding miners only seven years earlier, in *Holden v. Hardy*, 169 U.S. 366 (1898). It distinguished *Holden* on the ground that miners, unlike bakers, worked under conditions that were so extraordinarily hazardous as to warrant state interference.

12. This was of course Lochner's argument, not the state's, nor the bakers'. As Justice Brown had pointed out in *Holden*, this "argument would certainly come with better grace and greater cogency from the employees." Holden v. Hardy, 169 U.S. 366, 397 (1898).

13. See, e.g., Kansas v. Hendricks, 117 S. Ct. 2072 (1997).

14. In 1937, to be precise. See West Coast Hotel Co. v. Parrish, 300 U.S. 379 (1937).

15. 169 U.S. 366 (1898).

16. See sources cited supra note 2.

17. See John Fabian Witt, "Toward a New History of American Accident Law: Classical Tort Law and the Cooperative First Party Insurance Movement," 114 *Harv. L. Rev.* 690, 723 (2001).

18. See generally Robert J. Steinfeld, *Coercion, Contract, and Free Labor in the Nineteenth Century* 13 & n.26 (2001).

19. 169 U.S. 366, 397 (1898).

20. 208 U.S. 412 (1908).

21. Id. at 416 (H. B. Adams & Louis D. Brandeis, for defendant).

22. Id. at 420.

23. Id. at 422.

24. Id.

25. See, e.g., Ernst Freund, "Limitation of Hours of Labor and the Federal Supreme Court," 17 *Green Bag* 411, 417 (1905).

26. See supra. ch.6.

27. 163 U.S. 537, 544 (1896) ("Laws permitting, and even requiring, the separation [of the races] in places where they are liable to be brought into contact do not necessarily imply the inferiority of either race to the other, and have been generally, if not universally, recognized as within the competency of the state legislatures in the exercise of their police power.").

28. Plessy v. Ferguson, 163 U.S. 537, 545 (1896) (citing State v. Gibson, 36 Ind. 389 [1871]); Loving v. Virginia, 388 U.S. 1 (1967).

29. Buck v. Bell, 274 U.S. 200 (1922). While the police power rationale of Justice Holmes's opinion for the Supreme Court remained implicit, though clear enough in tone, the Virginia Supreme Court did not mince words: "The act is not a penal statute. The purpose of the legislature was not to punish but to protect the class of socially inadequate citizens named therein from themselves, and to promote the welfare of society by mitigating race degeneracy and raising the average standard of intelligence of the people of the state. . . . *The right to enact such laws rests in the police power, . . . and the exercise of that power the Virginia Constitution provides shall never be abridged.*" (Buck v. Bell, 143 Va. 310, 318–19 (1925) [emphasis added])

30. Powell v. State, 270 Ga. 327 (1998).

31. Cf. James B. Thayer, "The Origin and Scope of the American Doctrine of Constitutional Law," 7 *Harv. L. Rev.* 129, 155–56 n.1 (1893).

32. 291 U.S. 502 (1934).

33. 300 U.S. 379 (1937).

34. 291 U.S. 502, 510–11 (1934) (argument by Henry S. Manley, counsel for New York) ("That the period 1930–1933 has brought this Nation and every part of it some unprecedented problems is of course known to the Supreme Court of the United States.").

35. 291 U.S. 502, 538 (1934)

36. New York v. Miln, 36 U.S. 102, 142–43 (1837).

37. 300 U.S. 379, 394 (1937).

38. Id. at 399.

39. 36 U.S. 102, 141 (1837). For yet earlier examples of this policy, see Marilyn Baseler, *"Asylum For Mankind": America, 1607–1800*, at 71–72 (1998).

40. 152 U.S. 133 (1894).

41. Id. at 137.

42. Id. at 139.

43. Id. at 141–42 (citations omitted).

44. Pennsylvania Coal Co. v. Mahon, 260 U.S. 393 (1922).

45. Recently, the Court has become a little less reluctant to speak of substantive due process. Currently, substantive due process isn't quite taboo, but remains undesirable. Cf. Washington v. Glucksberg, 521 U.S. 702, 720–21 (1997) (rejecting substantive due process argument); Kansas v. Hendricks, 521 U.S. 346, 356 (1997) (same); see also Chicago v. Morales, 527 U.S. 41, 64 n.35 (1999) (refusing to address substantive due process claim).

46. See, e.g., Griswold v. Connecticut, 381 U.S. 479, 481–82 (1965) (criminal case; no mention of police power); see also Eisenstadt v. Baird, 405 U.S. 438 (1972) (criminal case; ostensible

purpose of statute protection of public health and morals; police power, however, mentioned only in Burger dissent); Roe v. Wade, 410 U.S. 113 (1973) (criminal case; state "interests in safeguarding health, in maintaining medical standards, and in protecting potential life"; no mention of police power).

47. On the distinction between police and right, see Ernst Freund, *The Police Power: Public Policy and Constitutional Rights* 6–7 (1904).

48. Even after *Roe*, many criminal codes continue to deal with abortion in the context of offenses against the person. See, e.g., N.Y. Penal Law art. 125.

49. Griswold v. Connecticut, 381 U.S. 479 (1965).

50. See generally, Raymond Ku, "Swingers: Morality Legislation and the Limits of State Police Power," 12 *St. Thomas L. Rev.* 1 (1999); Glenn H. Reynolds and David B. Kopel, "The Evolving Police Power: Some Observations for a New Century," 27 *Hastings Const. L.Q.* 511 (2000).

51. Bowers v. Hardwick, 478 U.S. 186 (1986).

52. Id. at 196.

53. Id. at 191.

54. Id. at 195. In 2003, the Supreme Court overturned *Hardwick* in an opinion that, however, also makes no mention of the police power. Lawrence v. Texas, 539 U.S. 558 (2003). *Lawrence* nonetheless is significant insofar as it refocused the constitutional inquiry onto the right to autonomy, even if it did not explicitly explore the conflict between autonomy and police as the presumed foundation of criminal law. See Markus Dirk Dubber, "Toward a Constitutional Law of Crime and Punishment," 55 *Hastings L.J.* 509 (2004).

55. 490 Pa. 91 (1980); see also People v. Onofre, 51 N.Y.2d 476 (1980).

56. 490 Pa. 91, 95–96 (1980) (citations omitted).

57. Powell v. State, 270 Ga. 327, 334 (1998) (citations omitted).

58. Id.

59. Cf. Markus Dirk Dubber, "Toward a Constitutional Law of Crime and Punishment," 55 *Hastings L.J.* 509 (2004); William J. Stuntz, "Substance, Process, and the Civil-Criminal Line," 7 *J. Contemp. Legal Issues* 1 (1996).

60. See supra. ch. 7.

61. 490 Pa. 91, 96–98 (1980). For a recent, considerably more ambitious, attempt to develop a constitutional concept of crime on the basis of the harm principle, see Claire Finkelstein, "Positivism and the Notion of an Offense," 88 *Calif. L. Rev.* 335 (2000). The most extensive account of the constraints placed upon criminal law by the harm principle, as a matter of principle rather than of constitutional law, is of course Joel Feinberg, *The Moral Limits of the Criminal Law* (4 vols. 1984–88). The point here is not to endorse the harm principle as a limitation upon police power, but to illustrate the general project of subjecting the police power to principled scrutiny. See generally Note, "Limiting the State's Police Power: Judicial Reaction to John Stuart Mill," 37 *U. Chi. L. Rev.* 605 (1969–70).

62. 490 Pa. at 98.

63. In re Hendricks, 259 Kan. 246 (1996); see also Young v. Weston, 898 F. Supp. 744 (W.D. Wash. 1995); cf. Rowe v. Burton, 884 F. Supp. 1372, 1377 (D. Alaska 1994) (Megan's Law); Ohio v. Williams, 1999 Ohio App. LEXIS 217 (Ct. App. Ohio 1999) (same).

64. 155 So. 2d 368 (Fla. 1963).

65. On possession offenses as prototypical police measures, see generally Markus Dirk Dubber, "Policing Possession: The War on Crime and the End of Criminal Law," 91 *J. Crim. L. & Criminology* 829 (2002); Markus Dirk Dubber, *Victims in the War on Crime: The Use and Abuse of Victims' Rights* pt. I (2002); see also Markus Dirk Dubber, "The Possession Paradigm: The Special Part and the Police Model of the Criminal Process," in *Defining Crimes* (R.A. Duff & Stuart Green eds., forthcoming 2005).

66. 155 So. 2d. at 370.

67. 489 So. 2d 1125 (Fla. 1986).

68. Id. at 1127.

69. Id. at 1129.

70. State v. Saiez, 489 So. 2d 1125 (Fla. 1986); see also Foster v. State, 286 So. 2d 549, 551 (Fla.

1973) ("it would be an unconstitutional act—in excess of the State's police power—to criminalize the simple possession of a screwdriver").

71. Robinson v. State, 393 So. 2d 1076 (Fla. 1980).

72. State v. Walker, 444 So. 2d 1137 (Fla. Dist. Ct. App.), affirmed and lower court opinion adopted, 461 So. 2d 108 (Fla. 1984).

73. State v. O.C., 748 So. 2d 945 (1999).

74. See, e.g., People v. Wright, 194 Ill. 2d 1 (2000) (possession of vehicle title without complete assignment) and cases cited there. In fact, it may be misleading to speak of a reappearance of police power, and substantive due process, in state constitutional criminal law cases, since this analysis never quite disappeared. See generally Wayne R. LaFave and Austin W. Scott, Jr., *Criminal Law* § 2.12(b) & (c) (2d ed. 1986); Monrad G. Paulsen, "The Persistence of Substantive Due Process in the States," 34 *Minn. L. Rev.* 91 (1950).

75. People v. Onofre, 51 N.Y.2d 476, 494, 501 (1980) (Gabrielli, J., dissenting).

76. Id. at 502.

77. See Raymond Ku, "Swingers: Morality Legislation and the Limits of State Police Power," 12 *St. Thomas L. Rev.* 1, 30–31 (1999).

78. 1 William Blackstone, *Commentaries on the Laws of England* 162, 264 (1765).

79. See supra. ch. 3.

80. Louis Henkin, "Economic Rights Under the United States Constitution," 32 *Colum. J. Transnat'l L.* 97 (1994).

81. See, e.g., William E. Nelson, *The Fourteenth Amendment: From Political Principle to Judicial Doctrine* 200 (1988).

82. Lochner v. New York, 198 U.S. 45 (1905).

Conclusion

1. On legal historiography as a form of critical analysis of law, see Markus Dirk Dubber, "Historical Analysis of Law," 16 *Law & Hist. Rev.* 159 (1998).

2. But see now Neil Coleman McCabe, "State Constitutions and Substantive Criminal Law," 71 *Temple L. Rev.* 521 (1998); Raymond Ku, "Swingers: Morality Legislation and the Limits of State Police Power," 12 St. *Thomas L. Rev.* 1 (1999); Glenn H. Reynolds and David B. Kopel, "The Evolving Police Power: Some Observations for a New Century," 27 *Hastings Const. L.Q.* 511 (2000).

3. Commonwealth v. Bonadio, 490 Pa. 91 (1980); see also People v. Onofre, 51 N.Y.2d 476 (1980).

4. 198 U.S. 45, 74, 75 (1905) (Holmes, J., dissenting).

5. See generally Markus Dirk Dubber, "Toward a Constitutional Law of Crime and Punishment," 55 *Hastings L.J.* 509 (2004); cf. Claire Finkelstein, "Positivism and the Notion of an Offense," 88 *Calif. L. Rev.* 335 (2000) ("basic right to liberty").

6. Cf. Markus Dirk Dubber, "The Criminal Trial and the Legitimation of Punishment," in *The Trial on Trial: Truth and Due Process* (R.A. Duff et al. eds. forthcoming 2004).

7. Ernst Freund, *The Police Power: Public Policy and Constitutional Rights* 4 (1904).

8. Id. at 6.

9. Id. at 1–2.

10. See generally Markus Dirk Dubber, *Victims in the War on Crime: The Use and Abuse of Victims' Rights* (2002).

11. Wayne R. LaFave and Austin W. Scott, Jr., *Criminal Law* 148 (2d ed. 1986); see also id. § 2.9.

12. Thomas Jefferson, Notes on the State of Virginia, query xv (1781).

13. Id.

14. Thomas Jefferson, A Bill for Proportioning Crimes and Punishments § 1 (1778). See gen-

erally Kathryn Preyer, "Crime, the Criminal Law and Reform in Post-Revolutionary Virginia," 1 *Law & Hist. Rev.* 53 (1983).

15. On the American revolutionaries' affection for their Anglo-Saxon forefathers, see Gordon S. Wood, *The Creation of the American Republic, 1776–1787*, at 122 (2d ed. 1998) (quoting Jefferson to Pendleton, Aug. 13, 1776, in 1 *Jefferson Papers* 492 [Julian P. Boyd ed. 1950]).

16. Æthelstan was King of England from 924 to 939, Canute from 1016 to 1035. Cf. *Laws of Æthelstan (924–939 A.D.)*, c. 14, in 4 *The Library of Original Sources* 234 (Oliver J. Thatcher ed. 1907).

17. Thomas Jefferson, *Autobiography* (1821). Once again, the implementation of this plan left much to be desired—and done. The deliberations of the four-person law reform committee, including Jefferson, apparently took up all of one day in January of 1777. "As the law of Descents, & the criminal law fell of course within my portion," Jefferson reports, "I wished the commee to settle the leading principles of these, as a guide for me in framing them. . . . On the subject of the Criminal law, all were agreed that the punishment of death should be abolished, except for treason and murder; and that, for other felonies should be substituted hard labor in the public works, and in some cases, the Lex talionis." "These points," Jefferson continues, "being settled, we repaired to our respective homes for the preparation of the work." Id.

Index